ALL GLORY TO ŚRĪ GURU AND GAURĀṄGA

ŚRĪMAD BHĀGAVATAM

of

KṚṢṆA-DVAIPĀYANA VYĀSA

कलेर्दोषनिधे राजन्नस्ति ह्येको महान् गुणः ।
कीर्तनादेव कृष्णस्य मुक्तसंगः परं व्रजेत् ॥५१॥

kaler doṣa-nidhe rājann
asti hy eko mahān guṇaḥ
kīrtanād eva kṛṣṇasya
mukta-saṅgaḥ paraṁ vrajet
(*Śrīmad Bhāgavatam* 12.3.51)

Books by His Divine Grace
A. C. Bhaktivedanta Swami Prabhupāda:

Bhagavad-gītā As It Is
Śrīmad-Bhāgavatam (1st to 10th Cantos)
Śrī Caitanya-Caritāmṛta (9 vols.)
Kṛṣṇa, The Supreme Personality of Godhead
Teachings of Lord Caitanya
The Nectar of Devotion
The Nectar of Instruction
Śrī Īśopaniṣad
Light of the Bhāgavata
Easy Journey to Other Planets
The Science of Self-Realization
Kṛṣṇa Consciousness: The Topmost Yoga System
Perfect Questions, Perfect Answers
Teachings of Lord Kapila, the Son of Devahuti
Transcendental Teachings of Prahlāda Mahārāja
Teachings of Queen Kuntī
Kṛṣṇa, the Reservoir of Pleasure
The Path of Perfection
Life Comes from Life
Message of Godhead
The Perfection of Yoga
Beyond Birth and Death
On the Way to Kṛṣṇa
Rāja-vidyā: The King of Knowledge
Elevation to Kṛṣṇa Consciousness
Kṛṣṇa Consciousness: The Matchless Gift
Selected Verses from the Vedic Scriptures
Back to Godhead magazine (founder)

ŚRĪMAD BHĀGAVATAM

Twelfth Canto

"The Age of Deterioration"

With the Original Sanskrit Text,
Its Roman Transliteration, Synonyms,
Translation and Elaborate Purports

by disciples of

His Divine Grace
A. C. Bhaktivedanta Swami Prabhupāda
Founder-*Ācārya* of the International Society for Krishna Consciousness

THE BHAKTIVEDANTA BOOK TRUST

Readers interested in the subject matter of this book are invited by The Bhaktivedanta Book Trust to correspond with its secretary at the following address:

The Bhaktivedanta Book Trust
Hare Krishna Land,
Juhu, Mumbai 400 049, India.

Website / E-mail :
www.indiabbt.com
admin@indiabbt.com

Śrīmad Bhāgavatam Twelfth Canto (English)

First printing in India : 2,000 copies
Second to Seventeenth printings : 52,500 copies
Eighteenth printing, November 2018 : 7,000 copies

ISBN : 978-93-84564-18-6 (v.18)
ISBN : 978-93-84564-00-1 (18-volume set)

Published and Printed by
The Bhaktivedanta Book Trust.

SJ1K

Table of Contents

CHAPTER EIGHT

Mārkaṇḍeya's Prayers to Nara-Nārāyaṇa Ṛṣi   205

CHAPTER NINE

Mārkaṇḍeya Ṛṣi Sees the Illusory Potency of the Lord   237

CHAPTER THIRTEEN

The Glories of Śrīmad-Bhāgavatam   361

Appendixes   379

Preface

nama oṁ viṣṇu-pādāya kṛṣṇa-preṣṭhāya bhū-tale
śrīmate bhaktivedānta-svāmin iti nāmine

I offer my most respectful obeisances at the lotus feet of His Divine Grace A. C. Bhaktivedanta Swami Prabhupāda, who is very dear to Lord Kṛṣṇa on this earth, having taken shelter at His lotus feet.

namas te sārasvate deve gaura-vāṇī-pracāriṇe
nirviśeṣa-śūnyavādi-pāścātya-deśa-tāriṇe

I offer my most respectful obeisances unto the lotus feet of His Divine Grace A. C. Bhaktivedanta Swami Prabhupāda, who is the disciple of Śrīla Bhaktisiddhānta Sarasvati Ṭhākura and who is powerfully distributing the message of Caitanya Mahāprabhu and thus saving the fallen Western countries from impersonalism and voidism.

Śrīmad-Bhāgavatam, with authorized translation and elaborate purports in the English language, is the great work of His Divine Grace Oṁ Viṣṇupāda Paramahaṁsa Parivrājakācārya Aṣṭottara-śata Śrī Śrīmad A. C. Bhaktivedanta Swami Prabhupāda, our beloved spiritual master. Our present publication is a humble attempt by his servants to complete his most cherished work of *Śrīmad-Bhāgavatam.* Just as one may worship the holy Ganges River by offering Ganges water unto the Ganges, similarly, in our attempt to serve our spiritual master, we are offering to him that which he has given to us.

Śrīla Prabhupāda came to America in 1965, at a critical moment in the history of America and the world in general. The story of Śrīla Prabhupāda's arrival and his specific impact on world civilization, and especially Western civilization, has been brilliantly documented by Satsvarūpa dāsa Goswami. From Satsvarūpa Goswami's authorized biography of Śrīla Prabhupāda, called *Śrīla Prabhupāda-līlāmṛta,* the reader can fully understand Śrīla Prabhupāda's purpose, desire and mission in presenting *Śrīmad-Bhāgavatam.* Further, in Śrīla Prabhupāda's own preface to the *Bhāgavatam* (reprinted as the foreword in this volume), he clearly states that this transcendental literature will provoke a cultural revolution in the world, and that is now underway. I do not wish to be redundant by repeating what Śrīla Prabhupāda has so eloquently stated in his preface, or that which has been so abundantly documented by Satsvarūpa Goswami in his authorized biography.

It is necessary to mention, however, that *Śrīmad-Bhāgavatam* is a completely transcendental, liberated sound vibration coming from the spiritual world. And, being absolute, it is not different from the Absolute Truth Himself, Lord Śrī Kṛṣṇa. By understanding *Śrīmad-Bhāgavatam,* consisting of twelve cantos, the reader acquires perfect knowledge, by which he or she may live peacefully and progressively on the earth, attending to all material necessities and simultaneously achieving supreme spiritual liberation. As we have worked to prepare this and other volumes of *Śrīmad-Bhāgavatam,* our intention has always been to faithfully serve the lotus feet of our spiritual master, carefully trying to translate and comment exactly as he would have, thus preserving the unity and spiritual potency of this edition of *Śrīmad-Bhāgavatam.* In other words, by our strictly following the disciplic succession, called in Sanskrit *guru-paramparā,* this edition of the *Bhāgavatam* will continue to be throughout its volumes a liberated work, free from material contamination and capable of elevating the reader to the kingdom of God.

Our method has been to faithfully follow the commentaries of previous *ācāryas* and exercise a careful selectivity of material based on the example and mood of Śrīla Prabhupāda. One may write transcendental literature only by the mercy of the Supreme Personality of Godhead, Śrī Kṛṣṇa, and the authorized, liberated spiritual masters coming in disciplic succession. Thus we humbly fall at the lotus feet of the previous *ācāryas,* offering special gratitude to the great commentators on the *Bhāgavatam,* namely Śrīla Śrīdhara Svāmī, Śrīla Jīva Gosvāmī, Śrīla Viśvanātha Cakravartī Ṭhākura and Śrīla Bhaktisiddhānta Sarasvatī Gosvāmī, the spiritual master of Śrīla Prabhupāda. We also offer our obeisances at the lotus feet of Śrīla Vīrarāghavācārya, Śrīla Vijayadhvaja Ṭhākura and Śrīla Vaṁśīdhara Ṭhākura, whose commentaries have also helped in this work. Additionally, we offer our humble obeisances at the lotus feet of the great *ācārya* Śrīla Madhva, who has made innumerable learned comments on *Śrīmad-Bhāgavatam.* We further offer our humble obeisances at the lotus feet of the Supreme Personality of Godhead, Śrī Kṛṣṇa Caitanya Mahāprabhu, and to all of His eternally liberated followers, headed by Śrīla Nityānanda Prabhu, Advaita Prabhu, Gadādhara Prabhu, Śrīvāsa Ṭhākura and the six Gosvāmīs, namely Śrīla Rūpa Gosvāmī, Śrīla Sanātana Gosvāmī, Śrīla Raghunātha dāsa Gosvāmī, Śrīla Raghunātha Bhaṭṭa Gosvāmī, Śrīla Jīva Gosvāmī and Śrīla Gopāla Bhaṭṭa Gosvāmī. Finally we offer our most respectful obeisances at the lotus feet of the Absolute Truth, Śrī Śrī Rādhā and

Kṛṣṇa, and humbly beg for Their mercy so that this great work of *Śrīmad-Bhāgavatam* can be quickly finished. *Śrīmad-Bhāgavatam* is undoubtedly the most important book in the universe, and the sincere readers of *Śrīmad-Bhāgavatam* will undoubtedly achieve the highest perfection of life, Kṛṣṇa consciousness.

In conclusion, I again remind the reader that *Śrīmad-Bhāgavatam* is the great work of His Divine Grace A. C. Bhaktivedanta Swami Prabhupāda, and that the present volume is the humble attempt of his devoted servants.

Hare Kṛṣṇa

Hridayananda dāsa Goswami

Foreword

We must know the present need of human society. And what is that need? Human society is no longer bounded by geographical limits to particular countries or communities. Human society is broader than in the Middle Ages, and the world tendency is toward one state or one human society. The ideals of spiritual communism, according to *Śrīmad-Bhāgavatam,* are based more or less on the oneness of the entire human society, nay, of the entire energy of living beings. The need is felt by great thinkers to make this a successful ideology. *Śrīmad-Bhāgavatam* will fill this need in human society. It begins, therefore, with an aphorism of Vedānta philosophy, *janmādy asya yataḥ,* to establish the ideal of a common cause.

Human society, at the present moment, is not in the darkness of oblivion. It has made rapid progress in the fields of material comforts, education and economic development throughout the entire world. But there is a pinprick somewhere in the social body at large, and therefore there are large-scale quarrels, even over less important issues. There is need of a clue as to how humanity can become one in peace, friendship and prosperity with a common cause. *Śrīmad-Bhāgavatam* will fill this need, for it is a cultural presentation for the respiritualization of the entire human society.

Śrīmad-Bhāgavatam should be introduced also in the schools and colleges, for it is recommended by the great student-devotee Prahlāda Mahārāja in order to change the demoniac face of society.

kaumāra ācaret prājño
dharmān bhāgavatān iha
durlabhaṁ mānuṣaṁ janma
tad apy adhruvam artha-dam

(*Bhāg.* 7.6.1)

Disparity in human society is due to lack of principles in a godless civilization. There is God, or the Almighty One, from whom everything emanates, by whom everything is maintained and in whom everything is merged to rest. Material science has tried to find the ultimate source of creation very insufficiently, but it is a fact that there is one ultimate source of everything that be. This ultimate source is explained rationally and authoritatively in the beautiful *Bhāgavatam,* or *Śrīmad-Bhāgavatam.*

Śrīmad-Bhāgavatam is the transcendental science not only for knowing the ultimate source of everything but also for knowing our relation with Him and our duty toward perfection of the human society on the basis of this perfect knowledge. It is powerful reading matter in the Sanskrit language, and it is now rendered into English elaborately so that simply by a careful reading one will know God perfectly well, so much so that the reader will be sufficiently educated to defend himself from the onslaught of atheists. Over and above this, the reader will be able to convert others to accepting God as a concrete principle.

Śrīmad-Bhāgavatam begins with the definition of the ultimate source. It is a bona fide commentary on the *Vedānta-sūtra* by the same author, Śrīla Vyāsadeva, and gradually it develops into nine cantos up to the highest state of God realization. The only qualification one needs to study this great book of transcendental knowledge is to proceed step by step cautiously and not jump forward haphazardly as with an ordinary book. It should be gone through chapter by chapter, one after another. The reading matter is so arranged with the original Sanskrit text, its English transliteration, synonyms, translation and purports so that one is sure to become a God-realized soul at the end of finishing the first nine cantos.

The Tenth Canto is distinct from the first nine cantos because it deals directly with the transcendental activities of the Personality of Godhead, Śrī Kṛṣṇa. One will be unable to capture the effects of the Tenth Canto without going through the first nine cantos. The book is complete in twelve cantos, each independent, but it is good for all to read them in small installments one after another.

I must admit my frailties in presenting *Śrīmad-Bhāgavatam,* but still I am hopeful of its good reception by the thinkers and leaders of society on the strength of the following statement of *Śrīmad-Bhāgavatam* (1.5.11):

tad-vāg-visargo janatāgha-viplavo
yasmin prati-ślokam abaddhavaty api
nāmāny anantasya yaśo 'ṅkitāni yac
chṛṇvanti gāyanti gṛṇanti sādhavaḥ

"On the other hand, that literature which is full of descriptions of the transcendental glories of the name, fame, form and pastimes of the unlimited

Supreme Lord is a transcendental creation meant for bringing about a revolution in the impious life of a misdirected civilization. Such transcendental literature, even though irregularly composed, is heard, sung and accepted by purified men who are thoroughly honest."

Oṁ tat sat

A. C. Bhaktivedanta Swami

Introduction

"This *Bhāgavata Purāṇa* is as brilliant as the sun, and it has arisen just after the departure of Lord Kṛṣṇa to His own abode, accompanied by religion, knowledge, etc. Persons who have lost their vision due to the dense darkness of ignorance in the age of Kali shall get light from this *Purāṇa.*" (*Śrīmad-Bhāgavatam* 1.3.43)

The timeless wisdom of India is expressed in the *Vedas,* ancient Sanskrit texts that touch upon all fields of human knowledge. Originally preserved through oral tradition, the *Vedas* were first put into writing five thousand years ago by Śrīla Vyāsadeva, the "literary incarnation of God." After compiling the *Vedas,* Vyāsadeva set forth their essence in the aphorisms known as *Vedānta-sūtras. Śrīmad-Bhāgavatam (Bhāgavata Purāṇa)* is Vyāsadeva's commentary on his own *Vedānta-sūtras.* It was written in the maturity of his spiritual life under the direction of Nārada Muni, his spiritual master. Referred to as "the ripened fruit of the tree of Vedic literature," *Śrīmad-Bhāgavatam* is the most complete and authoritative exposition of Vedic knowledge.

After compiling the *Bhāgavatam,* Vyāsa imparted the synopsis of it to his son, the sage Śukadeva Gosvāmī. Śukadeva Gosvāmī subsequently recited the entire *Bhāgavatam* to Mahārāja Parīkṣit in an assembly of learned saints on the bank of the Ganges at Hastināpura (now Delhi). Mahārāja Parīkṣit was the emperor of the world and was a great *rājarṣi* (saintly king). Having received a warning that he would die within a week, he renounced his entire kingdom and retired to the bank of the Ganges to fast until death and receive spiritual enlightenment. The *Bhāgavatam* begins with Emperor Parīkṣit's sober inquiry to Śukadeva Gosvāmī: "You are the spiritual master of great saints and devotees. I am therefore begging you to show the way of perfection for all persons, and especially for one who is about to die. Please let me know what a man should hear, chant, remember and worship, and also what he should not do. Please explain all this to me."

Śukadeva Gosvāmī's answer to this question, and numerous other questions posed by Mahārāja Parīkṣit, concerning everything from the nature of the self to the origin of the universe, held the assembled sages in rapt attention continuously for the seven days leading up to the king's death. The sage Sūta Gosvāmī, who was present in that assembly when Śukadeva Gosvāmī first recited *Śrīmad-Bhāgavatam,* later repeated the *Bhāgavatam* before a gathering of sages in the forest of Naimiṣāraṇya. Those sages, concerned about the spiritual welfare of the people in general, had gathered to perform a long, continuous chain of sacrifices to counteract the degrading influence of the incipient age of Kali. In response to the sages' request that he speak the essence of Vedic wisdom, Sūta Gosvāmī repeated from memory the entire eighteen thousand verses of *Śrīmad-Bhāgavatam,* as spoken by Śukadeva Gosvāmī to Mahārāja Parīkṣit.

The reader of *Śrīmad-Bhāgavatam* hears Sūta Gosvāmī relate the questions of Mahārāja Parīkṣit and the answers of Śukadeva Gosvāmī. Also, Sūta Gosvāmī sometimes responds directly to questions put by Śaunaka Ṛṣi, the spokesman for the sages gathered at Naimiṣāraṇya. One therefore simultaneously hears two dialogues: one between Mahārāja Parīkṣit and Śukadeva Gosvāmī on the bank of the Ganges, and another at Naimiṣāraṇya between Sūta Gosvāmī and the sages at Naimiṣāraṇya forest, headed by Śaunaka Ṛṣi. Futhermore, while instructing King Parīkṣit, Śukadeva Gosvāmī often relates historical episodes and gives accounts of lengthy philosophical discussions between such great souls as Nārada Muni and Vasudeva. With this understanding of the history of the *Bhāgavatam,* the reader will easily be able to follow its intermingling of dialogues and events from various sources. Since philosophical wisdom, not chronological order, is most important in the text, one need only be attentive to the subject matter of *Śrīmad-Bhāgavatam* to appreciate fully its profound message.

The translators of this edition compare the *Bhāgavatam* to sugar candy—wherever you taste it, you will find it equally sweet and relishable. Therefore, to taste the sweetness of the *Bhāgavatam,* one may begin by reading any of its volumes. After such an introductory taste, however, the serious reader is best advised to go back to the First Canto and then proceed through the *Bhāgavatam,* canto after canto, in its natural order.

This edition of the *Bhāgavatam* is the first complete English translation of this important text with an elaborate commentary, and it is the first widely available to the English-speaking public. The first twelve volumes (Canto One through Canto Ten, Part One) are the product of the scholarly and devotional effort of His Divine Grace A. C. Bhaktivedanta Swami Prabhupāda, the founder-*ācārya* of the International Society for Krishna Consciousness and the world's most distinguished teacher of Indian religious and Philosophical thought.

Śrīla Prabhupāda began his *Śrīmad-Bhāgavatam* in mid-1962 in Vṛndavana, India, the land most sacred to Lord Kṛṣṇa. With no assistants and limited funds, but with an abundance of devotion and determination, he was able to publish the First Canto (then in three volumes) by early 1965. After coming to the United States later that year, Śrīla Prabhupāda continued his commentated translation of the *Bhāgavatam,* and over the next twelve years, while developing his growing Kṛṣṇa consciousness movement and traveling incessantly, he produced twenty-seven more volumes. These were all edited, illustrated, typeset, proofread and indexed by his disciples, members of the Bhaktivedanta Book Trust (BBT). Throughout all of these volumes (totaling twelve in the present edition), Śrīla Prabhupāda's pure devotion to Lord Kṛṣṇa, his consummate Sanskrit scholarship and his intimate familiarity with Vedic culture and thought, and with modern life, combine to reveal to the Western reader a magnificent exposition of this important classic.

After Śrīla Prabhupāda's departure from this world in 1977, his monumental work of translating and commenting on *Śrīmad-Bhāgavatam* was continued by his disciples, headed by Hridayānanda dāsa Goswami, Gopiparāṇadhana dāsa Adhikārī and Draviḍa dāsa Brahmacārī—all seasoned BBT workers. Relying on the same Sankrit editions of *Śrīmad-Bhāgavatam* that Śrīla Prabhupāda had used, Hridayānanda dāsa Goswami and Gopīparāṇadhana dāsa translated the Sanskrit text and added commentary. Then they turned over the manuscript to Draviḍa dāsa for final editing and production. In this way the concluding six volumes were published.

Readers will find this work of value for many reasons. For those interested in the classical roots of Indian civilization, it serves as a vast detailed reservoir of information on virtually every one of its aspects. For students of comparative philosophy and religion, the *Bhāgavatam* offers a penetrating view into the meaning of India's profound spiritual heritage. To sociologists and anthropologists, the *Bhāgavatam* reveals the practical workings of a peaceful, prosperous and scientifically organized Vedic culture, whose institutions were integrated on the basis of a highly developed spiritual world view. Students of literature will discover the *Bhāgavatam* to be a masterpiece of majestic poetry. For students of psychology, the text provides important perspectives on the nature of consciousness, human behavior and the philosophical study of identity. Finally, to those seeking spiritual insight, the *Bhāgavatam* offers simple and practical guidance for attainment of the highest self-knowledge and realization of the Absolute Truth. The entire multivolume text, presented by the Bhaktivedanta Book Trust, promises to occupy a significant place in the intellectual, cultural and spiritual life of modern man for a long time to come.

—The Publishers

CHAPTER ONE

The Degraded Dynasties of Kali-yuga

The Twelfth Canto of *Śrīmad-Bhāgavatam* begins with Śrīla Śukadeva Gosvāmī predicting the kings of the earth who will appear in the future during the age of Kali. Then he gives a description of the numerous faults of the age, after which the presiding goddess of the earth sarcastically berates the foolish members of the kingly order who perpetually try to conquer her. Next Śukadeva Gosvāmī explains the four varieties of material annihilation, and then he gives his final advice to Mahārāja Parīkṣit. Thereafter King Parīkṣit is bitten by the snake-bird Takṣaka and leaves this world. Sūta Gosvāmī concludes his narration of *Śrīmad-Bhāgavatam* to the sages at Naimiṣāraṇya forest by enumerating the teachers of the various branches of the *Vedas* and *Purāṇas,* relating the pious history of Mārkaṇḍeya Ṛṣi, glorifying the Supreme Lord in His universal form and in His expansion as the sun god, summarizing the topics discussed in this literature, and offering final benedictions and prayers.

The first chapter of this canto briefly describes the future kings of the dynasty of Magadha and how they become degraded because of the influence of the age of Kali. There were twenty kings who ruled in the family of Pūru, in the dynasty of the sun-god, counting from Uparicara Vasu to Purañjaya. After Purañjaya, the lineage of this dynasty will become corrupted. Following Purañjaya there will be five kings known as the Pradyotanas, who are then followed by the Śiśunāgas, the Mauryas, the Śuṅgas, the Kāṇvas, thirty kings of the Andhra nation, seven Ābhīras, ten Gardabhīs, sixteen Kaṅkas, eight Yavanas, fourteen Turuṣkas, ten Guruṇḍas, eleven Maulas, five Kilakilā monarchs and thirteen Bāhlikas. After this, different regions will be ruled over at the same time by seven Andhra kings, seven Kauśalas, the kings of Vidūra, and the Niṣadhas. Then the power of rulership in the countries of Magadha and so forth will fall to kings who are no better than *śūdras* and *mlecchas* and are totally absorbed in irreligion.

TEXTS 1–2

श्रीशुक उवाच
योऽन्त्यः पुरञ्जयो नाम भविष्यो बारहद्रथः ।
तस्यामात्यस्तु शुनको हत्वा स्वामिनमात्मजम् ॥ १ ॥
प्रद्योतसंज्ञं राजानं कर्ता यत् पालकः सुतः ।
विशाखयूपस्तत्पुत्रो भविता राजकस्ततः ॥ २ ॥

śrī-śuka uvāca
yo'ntyaḥ purañjayo nāma
bhaviṣyo bārahadrathaḥ
tasyāmātyas tu śunako
hatvā svāminam ātma-jam

pradyota-saṁjñaṁ rājānaṁ
kartā yat-pālakaḥ sutaḥ
viśākhayūpas tat-putro
bhavitā rājakas tataḥ

śrī śukaḥ uvāca — Śrī Śukadeva Gosvāmī said; *yaḥ*—who; *antyaḥ*—the final member (of the lineage described in the Ninth Canto); *purañjayaḥ*—Purañjaya (Ripuñjaya); *nāma* — named; *bhaviṣyaḥ* — will live in the future; *bārahadrathaḥ* — the descendant of Bṛhadratha; *tasya* — his; *amātyaḥ* — minister; *tu* — but; *śunakaḥ* — Śunaka; *hatvā* — killing; *svāminam* — his master; *ātma-jam* — his own son; *pradyota-saṁjñam* — named Pradyota; *rājānam* — the king; *kartā* — will make; *yat* — whose; *pālakaḥ* — named Pālaka; *sutaḥ* — the son; *viśākhayūpaḥ* — Viśākhayūpa; *tat-putraḥ* — the son of Pālaka; *bhavitā* — will be; *rājakaḥ* — Rājaka; *tataḥ* — then (coming as the son of Viśākhayūpa).

TRANSLATION

Śukadeva Gosvāmī said: The last king mentioned in our previous enumeration of the future rulers of the Māgadha dynasty was Purañjaya, who will take birth as the descendant of Bṛhadratha. Purañjaya's minister Śunaka will assassinate the king and install his own son, Pradyota, on the throne. The son of Pradyota will be Pālaka, his son will be Viśākhayūpa, and his son will be Rājaka.

PURPORT

The vicious political intrigue described here is symptomatic of the Age of Kali. In the Ninth Canto of this work, Śukadeva Gosvāmī describes how the great rulers of men descended from two royal dynasties, that of the sun and that of the moon. The Ninth Canto's description of Lord Rāmacandra, a most famous incarnation of God, occurs in this genealogical narration, and at the end of the Ninth Canto Śukadeva describes the forefathers of Lord Kṛṣṇa and Lord Balarāma. Finally, the appearance of Lord Kṛṣṇa and that of Lord Balarāma are mentioned within the context of the narration of the moon dynasty.

The Tenth Canto is devoted exclusively to a description of Lord Kṛṣṇa's childhood pastimes in Vṛndāvana, His teenage activities in Mathurā and His adult activities in Dvārakā. The famous epic *Mahābhārata* also describes the events of this period, focusing upon the five Pāṇḍava brothers and their activities in relation with Lord Kṛṣṇa and other leading historical figures, such as Bhīṣma, Dhṛtarāṣṭra, Droṇācārya and Vidura. Within the *Mahābhārata* is *Bhagavad-gītā,* in which Lord Kṛṣṇa is declared to be the Absolute Truth, the Supreme Personality of Godhead. *Śrīmad-Bhāgavatam,* of which we are presently translating the twelfth and final canto, is considered a more advanced literature than the *Mahābhārata* because throughout the entire work Lord Śrī Kṛṣṇa, the Absolute Truth and supreme source of all existence, is directly, centrally and irrefutably revealed. In fact, the First Canto of the *Bhāgavatam* describes how Śrī Vyāsadeva composed this great work because he was dissatisfied with his rather sporadic glorification of Lord Kṛṣṇa in the *Mahābhārata.*

Although *Śrīmad-Bhāgavatam* narrates the histories of many royal dynasties and the lives of innumerable kings, not until the description of the present age, the age of Kali, do we find a minister assassinating his own king and installing his son on the throne. This incident resembles Dhṛtarāṣṭra's attempt to assassinate the Pāṇḍavas and crown his son Duryodhana king. As the *Mahābhārata* describes, Lord Kṛṣṇa thwarted this attempt, but with the departure of the Lord for the spiritual sky, the age of Kali became fully manifested, ushering in political assassination within one's own house as a standard technique.

TEXT 3

नन्दिवर्धनस्तत्पुत्रः पञ्च प्रद्योतना इमे ।
अष्टत्रिंशोत्तरशतं भोक्ष्यन्ति पृथिवीं नृपाः ॥ ३ ॥

nandivardhanas tat-putraḥ
pañca pradyotanā ime
aṣṭa-triṁśottara-śataṁ
bhokṣyanti pṛthivīṁ nṛpāḥ

nandivardhanaḥ — Nandivardhana; *tat-putraḥ* — his son; *pañca* — five; *pradyotanāḥ* — Pradyotanas; *ime* — these; *aṣṭa-triṁśa* — thirty-eight; *uttara* — increased by; *śatam* — one hundred; *bhokṣyanti* — they will enjoy; *pṛthivīm* — the earth; *nṛpāḥ* — these kings.

TRANSLATION

The son of Rājaka will be Nandivardhana, and thus in the Pradyotana dynasty there will be five kings, who will enjoy the earth for 138 years.

TEXT 4

शिशुनागस्ततो भाव्यः काकवर्णस्तु तत्सुतः ।
क्षेमधर्मा तस्य सुतः क्षेत्रज्ञः क्षेमधर्मजः ॥ ४ ॥

śiśunāgas tato bhāvyaḥ
kākavarṇas tu tat-sutaḥ
kṣemadharmā tasya sutaḥ
kṣetrajñaḥ kṣemadharma-jaḥ

śiśunāgaḥ — Śiśunāga; *tataḥ* — then; *bhāvyaḥ* — will take birth; *kākavarṇaḥ* — Kākavarṇa; *tu* — and; *tat-sutaḥ* — his son; *kṣemadharmā* — Kṣemadharmā; *tasya* — of Kākavarṇa; *sutaḥ* — the son; *kṣetrajñaḥ* — Kṣetrajña; *kṣemadharma-jaḥ* — born to Kṣemadharmā.

TRANSLATION

Nandivardhana will have a son named Śiśunāga, and his son will be known as Kākavarṇa. The son of Kākavarṇa will be Kṣemadharmā, and the son of Kṣemadharmā will be Kṣetrajña.

TEXT 5

विधिसारः सुतस्तस्याजातशत्रुर्भविष्यति ।
दर्भकस्तत्सुतो भावी दर्भकस्याजयः स्मृतः ॥ ५ ॥

vidhisāraḥ sutas tasyā-
jātaśatrur bhaviṣyati
darbhakas tat-suto bhāvī
darbhakasyājayaḥ smṛtaḥ

vidhisāraḥ—Vidhisāra; *sutaḥ*—the son; *tasya* — of Kṣetrajña; *ajātaśatruḥ* —Ajātaśatru; *bhaviṣyati* — will be; *darbhakaḥ*—Darbhaka; *tat-sutaḥ*—the son of Ajātaśatru; *bhāvī*—will take birth; *darbhakasya* — of Darbhaka; *ajayaḥ* —Ajaya; *smṛtaḥ*—is remembered.

TRANSLATION

The son of Kṣetrajña will be Vidhisāra, and his son will be Ajātaśatru. Ajātaśatru will have a son named Darbhaka, and his son will be Ajaya.

TEXTS 6–8

नन्दिवर्धन आजेयो महानन्दिः सुतस्ततः ।
शिशुनागा दशैवैते सष्ट्युत्तरशतत्रयम् ॥ ६ ॥
समा भोक्ष्यन्ति पृथिवीं कुरुश्रेष्ठ कलौ नृपाः ।
महानन्दिसुतो राजन् शूद्रागर्भोद्भवो बली ॥ ७ ॥
महापद्मपतिः कश्चिन्नन्दः क्षत्रविनाशकृत् ।
ततो नृपा भविष्यन्ति शूद्रप्रायास्त्वधार्मिकाः ॥ ८ ॥

nandivardhana ājeyo
mahānandiḥ sutas tataḥ
śiśunāgā daśaivaite
saṣṭy-uttara-śata-trayam

samā bhokṣyanti pṛthivīṁ
kuru-śreṣṭha kalau nṛpāḥ
mahānandi-suto rājan
śūdrā-garbhodbhavo balī

mahāpadma-patiḥ kaścin
nandaḥ kṣatra-vināśa-kṛt
tato nṛpā bhaviṣyanti
śūdra-prāyās tv adhārmikāḥ

nandivardhanaḥ—Nandivardhana; *ājeyaḥ*—the son of Ajaya; *mahā-nandiḥ*—Mahānandi; *sutaḥ*—the son; *tataḥ*—then (following Nandivardhana); *śiśunāgāḥ*—the Śiśunāgas; *daśa* — ten; *eva* — indeed; *ete* — these; *saṣṭi* — sixty; *uttara* — increased by; *śata-trayam* — three hundred; *samāḥ* —years; *bhokṣyanti* — they will rule; *pṛthivīm* — the earth; *kuruśreṣṭha* — O best of the Kurus; *kalau* — in this age of Kali; *nṛpāḥ*—the kings; *mahānandi-sutaḥ*—the son of Mahānandi; *rājan* — O King Parīkṣit; *śūdrā-garbha* — in the womb of a *śūdra* woman; *udbhavaḥ*—taking birth; *balī*—powerful; *mahā-padma* — of an army, or wealth, measured in the millions; *patiḥ*—the master; *kaścit* — a certain; *nandaḥ*—Nanda; *kṣatra* — of the royal class; *vināśa-kṛt* — the destroyer; *tataḥ*—then; *nṛpāḥ*—the kings; *bhaviṣyanti* — will become; *śūdra-prāyāḥ*—no better than *śūdras; tu* — and; *adhārmikāḥ*—irreligious.

TRANSLATION

Ajaya will father a second Nandivardhana, whose son will be Mahānandi. O best of the Kurus, these ten kings of the Śiśunāga dynasty will rule the earth for a total of 360 years during the age of Kali. My dear Parīkṣit, King Mahānandi will father a very powerful son in the womb of a śūdra woman. He will be known as Nanda and will be the master of millions of soldiers and fabulous wealth. He will wreak havoc among the kṣatriyas, and from that time onward virtually all kings will be irreligious śūdras.

PURPORT

Here is a description of how authentic political authority degenerated and disintegrated throughout the world. There is a Supreme Godhead, and there are saintly, powerful men who have taken the role of government leaders and represented that Godhead on earth. With the advent of the age of Kali, however, this transcendental system of government collapsed, and unauthorized, uncivilized men gradually took the reins of power.

TEXT 9

स एकच्छत्रां पृथिवीमनुल्लङ्घितशासनः ।
शासिष्यति महापद्मो द्वितीय इव भार्गवः ॥ ९ ॥

sa eka-cchatrāṁ pṛthivīm
anullaṅghita-śāsanaḥ

śāsiṣyati mahāpadmo
dvitīya iva bhārgavaḥ

saḥ—he (Nanda); *eka-chatrām* — under a single leadership; *pṛthivīm* — the entire earth; *anullaṅghita* — undefied; *śāsanaḥ*—his rulership; *śāsiṣyati* — he will have sovereignty over; *mahāpadmaḥ*—the lord of Mahāpadma; *dvitīyaḥ*—a second; *iva* — as if; *bhārgavaḥ*—Paraśurāma.

TRANSLATION

That lord of Mahāpadma, King Nanda, will rule over the entire earth just like a second Paraśurāma, and no one will challenge his authority.

PURPORT

In the eighth verse of this chapter it was mentioned that King Nanda would destroy the remnants of the *kṣatriya* order. Therefore he is here compared to Lord Paraśurāma, who annihilated the *kṣatriya* class twenty-one times in a previous age.

TEXT 10

तस्य चाष्टौ भविष्यन्ति सुमाल्यप्रमुखाः सुताः ।
य इमां भोक्ष्यन्ति महीं राजानश्च शतं समाः ॥ १० ॥

tasya cāṣṭau bhaviṣyanti
sumālya-pramukhāḥ sutāḥ
ya imāṁ bhokṣyanti mahīṁ
rājānaś ca śataṁ samāḥ

tasya — of him (Nanda); *ca* — and; *aṣṭau* — eight; *bhaviṣyanti* — will take birth; *sumālya-pramukhāḥ*—headed by Sumālya; *sutāḥ*—sons; *ye* — who; *imām* — this; *bhokṣyanti* — will enjoy; *mahīm* — the earth; *rājānaḥ*— kings; *ca* — and; *śatam* — one hundred; *samāḥ*—years.

TRANSLATION

He will have eight sons, headed by Sumālya, who will control the earth as powerful kings for one hundred years.

TEXT 11

नव नन्दान् द्विजः कश्चित् प्रपन्नानुद्धरिष्यति ।
तेषामभावे जगतीं मौर्या भोक्ष्यन्ति वै कलौ ॥ ११ ॥

nava nandān dvijaḥ kaścit
prapannān uddhariṣyati
teṣām abhāve jagatīṁ
mauryā bhokṣyanti vai kalau

nava — nine; *nandān* — the Nandas (King Nanda and his eight sons); *dvijaḥ* — *brāhmaṇa; kaścit* — a certain; *prapannān* — trusting; *uddhariṣyati* — will uproot; *teṣām* — of them; *abhāve* — in the absence; *jagatīm* — the earth; *mauryāḥ* — the Maurya dynasty; *bhokṣyanti* — will rule over; *vai* — indeed; *kalau* — in this age, Kali-yuga.

TRANSLATION

A certain brāhmaṇa [Cāṇakya] will betray the trust of King Nanda and his eight sons and will destroy their dynasty. In their absence the Mauryas will rule the world as the age of Kali continues.

PURPORT

Śrīdhara Svāmī and Viśvanātha Cakravartī Ṭhākura both confirm that the *brāhmaṇa* mentioned here is Cāṇakya, also known as Kauṭilya or Vātsyāyana. The great historical narration *Śrīmad-Bhāgavatam,* which began with the events prior to the cosmic manifestation, now reaches into the realm of modern recorded history. Modern historians recognize both the Maurya dynasty and Candragupta, the king mentioned in the following verse.

TEXT 12

स एव चन्द्रगुप्तं वै द्विजो राज्येऽभिषेक्ष्यति ।
तत्सुतो वारिसारस्तु ततश्चाशोकवर्धनः ॥ १२ ॥

sa eva candraguptaṁ vai
dvijo rājye'bhiṣekṣyati
tat-suto vārisāras tu
tataś cāśokavardhanaḥ

His Divine Grace
A. C. Bhaktivedanta Swami Prabhupāda
Founder-Ācārya of ISKCON and greatest exponent of Kṛṣṇa consciousness in the modern world

The *Śrīmad-Bhāgavatam* accurately predicts the activities of Cāṇakya Paṇḍita, a learned *brāhmaṇa* who engineered the downfall of King Nanda of Magadha and enthroned Candragupta, thus founding the Maurya dynasty. (12.1.11–12)

At the end of the present age, Kali-yuga, the Supreme Lord will advent Himself in the form of Kalki in order to annihilate the degraded rulers of the earth. (12.2.20)

The Hare Kṛṣṇa movement is like a lifeboat rescuing the fallen souls from the dangerous ocean of the age of Kali. (12.3.52)

At the time of cosmic annihilation, a great fire flares up from the mouth of Lord Saṅkarṣaṇa, burning everything throughout the universe and then scorching the lifeless cosmic shell. (12.4.9)

The snake-bird Takṣaka came forward and bit King Parīkṣit, injecting him with a venom so powerful that it burned his body to ashes. (12.6.12–13)

To avenge the death of his father, Mahārāja Janamejaya had *brāhmaṇas* perform a mighty sacrifice in which he offered all the snakes in the world into the sacrificial fire. (12.6.16)

Śaunaka, the leader of the sages gathered at the forest of Naimiṣāraṇya, said to Sūta Gosvāmī, the speaker of *Śrīmad-Bhāgavatam*, "O Sūta, may you live a long life! O saintly one, best of speakers, please continue speaking to us. Indeed, only you can show men the path out of the ignorance in which they are wandering." Śaunaka then questioned Sūta

about the history of Mārkaṇḍeya Ṛṣi, a great sage who had survived the previous annihilation of the universe. Sūta Gosvāmī replied, "O great sage Śaunaka, your very question will help remove everyone's illusion, for it leads to topics of Lord Nārāyaṇa, which cleanse away the contamination of this Kali age." (12.8.1–6)

Despite all the temptations arranged by Cupid, Mārkaṇḍeya Ṛṣi remained fixed in meditation, defeating Cupid and his associates by burning them with his mystic potency. (12.8.26–29)

Desiring to bestow His mercy upon the saintly Mārkaṇḍeya Ṛṣi, the Supreme Personality of Godhead appeared before the sage in the forms of Nara and Nārāyaṇa. (12.8.32)

With great difficulty, Mārkaṇḍeya Ṛṣi moved about in the water of devastation for a long time, until he came upon a banyan tree. Lying upon a leaf of that tree was an infant boy glowing with a charming effulgence. (12.9.20–25)

Once while traveling through the sky upon his bull carrier, Lord Śiva came upon the great sage Mārkaṇḍeya seated in trance. (12.10.8)

Śrīla Vyāsadeva heard the transcendental knowledge of *Śrīmad-Bhāgavatam* from his spiritual master, Nārada Muni (shown above), who heard it from his father, Brahmā, the first created being in the universe. Brahmā had personally received this torchlight of knowledge from the Supreme Personality of Godhead Himself. In turn, Śrīla Vyāsadeva communicated the message of the *Bhāgavatam* to his son, Śukadeva

Gosvāmī, who spoke it to King Parīkṣit, Sūta Gosvāmī, a disciple of Śukadeva Gosvāmī was present when King Parīkṣit heard the *Bhāgavatam*, and later Sūta explained the same knowledge to the sages at Naimiṣāraṇya. This is the system for receiving transcendental knowledge. (12.13.19)

Lord Kṛṣṇa is supremely lovable because of His eternal, transcendental qualities. The beauty of this world is but a dim reflection of the unlimited beauty of the Lord. (12.13.11–12)

saḥ—he (Cāṇakya); *eva*—indeed; *candraguptam*—Prince Candragupta; *vai*—indeed; *dvijaḥ*—the *brāhmaṇa; rājye*—in the role of king; *abhiṣekṣyati*—will install; *tat*—of Candragupta; *sutaḥ*—the son; *vārisāraḥ*—Vārisāra; *tu*—and; *tataḥ*—following Vārisāra; *ca*—and; *aśokavardhanaḥ*—Aśokavardhana.

TRANSLATION

This brāhmaṇa will enthrone Candragupta, whose son will be named Vārisāra. The son of Vārisāra will be Aśokavardhana.

TEXT 13

सुयशा भविता तस्य संगतः सुयशःसुतः ।
शालिशूकस्ततस्तस्य सोमशर्मा भविष्यति ।
शतधन्वा ततस्तस्य भविता तद्बृहद्रथः ॥ १३ ॥

suyaśā bhavitā tasya
saṅgataḥ suyaśaḥ-sutaḥ
śāliśūkas tatas tasya
somaśarmā bhaviṣyati
śatadhanvā tatas tasya
bhavitā tad-bṛhadrathaḥ

suyaśāḥ—Suyaśā; *bhavitā*—will be born; *tasya*—of him (Aśokavardhana); *saṅgataḥ*—Saṅgata; *suyaśaḥ-sutaḥ*—the son of Suyaśā; *śāliśūkaḥ*—Śāliśūka; *tataḥ*—next; *tasya*—of him (Śāliśūka); *somaśarmā*—Somaśarmā; *bhaviṣyati*—will be; *śatadhanvā*—Śatadhanvā; *tataḥ*—next; *tasya*—of him (Somaśarmā); *bhavitā*—will be; *tat*—of him (Śatadhanvā); *bṛhadrathaḥ*—Bṛhadratha.

TRANSLATION

Aśokavardhana will be followed by Suyaśā, whose son will be Saṅgata. His son will be Śāliśūka, Śāliśūka's son will be Somaśarmā, and Somaśarmā's son will be Śatadhanvā. His son will be known as Bṛhadratha.

TEXT 14

मौर्या ह्येते दश नृपाः सप्तत्रिंशच्छतोत्तरम् ।
समा भोक्ष्यन्ति पृथिवीं कलौ कुरुकुलोद्वह ॥ १४ ॥

mauryā hy ete daśa nṛpāḥ
sapta-triṁśac-chatottaram
samā bhokṣyanti pṛthivīṁ
kalau kuru-kulodvaha

mauryāḥ—the Mauryas; *hi*— indeed; *ete*— these; *daśa*— ten; *nṛpāḥ*—kings; *sapta-triṁśat*— thirty-seven; *śata*— one hundred; *uttaram*— more than; *samāḥ*—years; *bhokṣyanti*— they will rule; *pṛthivīm*— the earth; *kalau*— in Kali-yuga; *kuru-kula*— of the Kuru dynasty; *udvaha*— O most eminent hero.

TRANSLATION

O best of the Kurus, these ten Maurya kings will rule the earth for 137 years of the Kali-yuga.

PURPORT

Although nine kings are mentioned by name, Daśaratha appeared after Sujyeṣṭha, before the rule of Saṅgata, and thus there are ten Maurya kings.

TEXTS 15–17

अग्निमित्रस्ततस्तस्मात् सुज्येष्ठो भविता ततः ।
वसुमित्रो भद्रकश्च पुलिन्दो भविता सुतः ॥ १५ ॥
ततो घोषः सुतस्तस्माद् वज्रमित्रो भविष्यति ।
ततो भागवतस्तस्माद् देवभूतिः कुरूद्वह ॥ १६ ॥
शुंगा दशैते भोक्ष्यन्ति भूमिं वर्षशताधिकम् ।
ततः काण्वानियं भूमिर्यास्यत्यल्पगुणान्नृप ॥ १७ ॥

agnimitras tatas tasmāt
sujyeṣṭho bhavitā tataḥ
vasumitro bhadrakaś ca
pulindo bhavitā sutaḥ

tato ghoṣaḥ sutas tasmād
vajramitro bhaviṣyati
tato bhāgavatas tasmād
devabhūtiḥ kurūdvaha

śuṅgā daśaite bhokṣyanti
bhūmiṁ varṣa-śatādhikam

tataḥ kāṇvān iyaṁ bhūmir
yāsyaty alpa-guṇān nṛpa

agnimitraḥ—Agnimitra; *tataḥ*—from Puṣpamitra, the general who will murder Bṛhadratha; *tasmāt* — from him (Agnimitra); *sujyeṣṭhaḥ*—Sujyeṣṭha; *bhavitā* — will be; *tataḥ*—from him; *vasumitraḥ*—Vasumitra; *bhadrakaḥ*—Bhadraka; *ca* — and; *pulindaḥ*—Pulinda; *bhavitā* — will be; *sutaḥ*—the son; *tataḥ*—from him (Pulinda); *ghoṣaḥ*—Ghoṣa; *sutaḥ*—the son; *tasmāt*—from him; *vajramitraḥ*—Vajramitra; *bhaviṣyati* — will be; *tataḥ*—from him; *bhāgavataḥ*—Bhāgavata; *tasmāt* — from him; *devabhūtiḥ*—Devabhūti; *kuru-udvaha* — O most eminent of the Kurus; *śuṅgāḥ*—the Śuṅgas; *daśa* — ten; *ete* — these; *bhokṣyanti* — will enjoy; *bhūmim* — the earth; *varṣa* — years; *śata* — one hundred; *adhikam* — more than; *tataḥ*—then; *kāṇvān* — the Kāṇva dynasty; *iyam* — this; *bhūmiḥ*—the earth; *yāsyati* — will come under the domain; *alpa-guṇān* — of few good qualities; *nṛpa* — O King Parīkṣit.

TRANSLATION

My dear King Parīkṣit, Agnimitra will follow as king, and then Sujyeṣṭha. Sujyeṣṭha will be followed by Vasumitra, Bhadraka, and the son of Bhadraka, Pulinda. Then the son of Pulinda, named Ghoṣa, will rule, followed by Vajramitra, Bhāgavata and Devabhūti. In this way, O most eminent of the Kuru heroes, ten Śuṅga kings will rule over the earth for more than one hundred years. Then the earth will come under the subjugation of the kings of the Kāṇva dynasty, who will manifest very few good qualities.

PURPORT

According to Śrīla Śrīdhara Svāmī, the Śuṅga dynasty began when General Puṣpamitra killed his king, Bṛhadratha, and assumed power. After Puṣpamitra came Agnimitra and the rest of the Śuṅga dynasty, which lasted for 112 years.

TEXT 18

शुंगं हत्वा देवभूतिं काण्वोऽमात्यस्तु कामिनम् ।
स्वयं करिष्यते राज्यं वसुदेवो महामतिः ॥ १८ ॥

śuṅgaṁ hatvā devabhūtiṁ
kāṇvo'mātyas tu kāminam

svayaṁ kariṣyate rājyaṁ
vasudevo mahā-matiḥ

śuṅgam — the Śuṅga king; *hatvā* — killing; *devabhūtim* — Devabhūti; *kāṇvaḥ*—the member of the Kāṇva family; *amātyaḥ*—his minister; *tu* — but; *kāminam* — lusty; *svayam* — himself; *kariṣyate* — will execute; *rājyam* — the rulership; *vasudevaḥ*—named Vasudeva; *mahā-matiḥ*—very intelligent.

TRANSLATION

Vasudeva, an intelligent minister coming from the Kāṇva family, will kill the last of the Śuṅga kings, a lusty debauchee named Devabhūti, and assume rulership himself.

PURPORT

Apparently, because King Devabhūti was lusty after the wives of other men, his minister killed him, assuming leadership and thus beginning the Kāṇva dynasty.

TEXT 19

तस्य पुत्रस्तु भूमित्रस्तस्य नारायणः सुतः ।
काण्वायना इमे भूमिं चत्वारिंशच्च पञ्च च ।
शतानि त्रीणि भोक्ष्यन्ति वर्षाणां च कलौ युगे ॥ १९ ॥

tasya putras tu bhūmitras
tasya nārāyaṇaḥ sutaḥ
kāṇvāyanā ime bhūmiṁ
catvāriṁśac ca pañca ca
śatāni trīṇi bhokṣyanti
varṣāṇāṁ ca kalau yuge

tasya — of him (Vasudeva); *putraḥ*—the son; *tu* — and; *bhūmitraḥ*—Bhūmitra; *tasya* — his; *nārāyaṇaḥ*—Nārāyaṇa; *sutaḥ*—the son; *kāṇva-ayanāḥ*—kings of the Kāṇva dynasty; *ime* — these; *bhūmim* — the earth; *catvāriṁśat* — forty; *ca* — and; *pañca* — five; *ca* — and; *śatāni* — hundreds; *trīṇi* — three; *bhokṣyanti* — they will rule; *varṣāṇām* — years; *ca* — and; *kalau yuge* — in the Kali-yuga.

TRANSLATION

The son of Vasudeva will be Bhūmitra, and his son will be Nārāyaṇa. These kings of the Kāṇva dynasty will rule the earth for 345 more years of the Kali-yuga.

TEXT 20

हत्वा काण्वं सुशर्माणं तद्भृत्यो वृषलो बली ।
गां भोक्ष्यत्यन्ध्रजातीयः कञ्चित्कालमसत्तमः ॥ २० ॥

hatvā kāṇvaṁ suśarmāṇaṁ
tad-bhṛtyo vṛṣalo balī
gāṁ bhokṣyaty andhra-jātīyaḥ
kañcit kālam asattamaḥ

hatvā — killing; *kāṇvam* — the Kāṇva king; *suśarmāṇam* — named Suśarmā; *tat-bhṛtyaḥ*—his own servant; *vṛṣalaḥ*—a low-class *śūdra; balī*— named Balī; *gām* — the earth; *bhokṣyati* — will rule; *andhra-jātīyaḥ*—of the Andhra race; *kañcit* — for some; *kālam* — time; *asattamaḥ*—most degraded.

TRANSLATION

The last of the Kāṇvas, Suśarmā, will be murdered by his own servant, Balī, a low-class śūdra of the Andhra race. This most degraded Mahārāja Balī will have control over the earth for some time.

PURPORT

Here is a further description of how uncultured men infiltrated government administration. The so-called king named Balī is described as *asattama,* a most impious, uncultured man.

TEXTS 21–26

कृष्णनामाथ तद्भ्राता भविता पृथिवीपतिः ।
श्रीशान्तकर्णस्तत्पुत्रः पौर्णमासस्तु तत्सुतः ॥ २१ ॥
लम्बोदरस्तु तत्पुत्रस्तस्माच्चिबिलको नृपः ।
मेघस्वातिश्चिबिलकादटमानस्तु तस्य च ॥ २२ ॥
अनिष्टकर्मा हालेयस्तलकस्तस्य चात्मजः ।
पुरीषभीरुस्तत्पुत्रस्ततो राजा सुनन्दनः ॥ २३ ॥

चकोरो बहवो यत्र शिवस्वातिररिन्दमः ।
तस्यापि गोमती पुत्रः पुरीमान् भविता ततः ॥ २४ ॥
मेदशिराः शिवस्कन्दो यज्ञश्रीस्तत्सुतस्ततः ।
विजयस्तत्सुतो भाव्यश्चन्द्रविज्ञः सलोमधिः ॥ २५ ॥
एते त्रिंशन्नृपतयश्चत्वार्यब्दशतानि च ।
षट्पञ्चाशच्च पृथिवीं भोक्ष्यन्ति कुरुनन्दन ॥ २६ ॥

kṛṣṇa-nāmātha tad-bhrātā
bhavitā pṛthivī-patiḥ
śrī-śāntakarṇas tat-putraḥ
paurṇamāsas tu tat-sutaḥ

lambodaras tu tat-putras
tasmāc cibilako nṛpaḥ
meghasvātiś cibilakād
aṭamānas tu tasya ca

aniṣṭakarmā hāleyas
talakas tasya cātma-jaḥ
purīṣabhīrus tat-putras
tato rājā sunandanaḥ

cakoro bahavo yatra
śivasvātir arin-damaḥ
tasyāpi gomatī putraḥ
purīmān bhavitā tataḥ

medaśirāḥ śivaskando
yajñaśrīs tat-sutas tataḥ
vijayas tat-suto bhāvyaś
candravijñaḥ sa-lomadhiḥ

ete triṁśan nṛpatayaś
catvāry abda-śatāni ca
ṣaṭ-pañcāśac ca pṛthivīṁ
bhokṣyanti kuru-nandana

kṛṣṇa-nāma — named Kṛṣṇa; *atha* — then; *tat* — of him (Balī); *bhrātā* — the brother; *bhavitā* — will become; *pṛthivī-patiḥ* — the master of the earth; *śrī-śāntakarṇaḥ* — Śrī Śāntakarṇa; *tat* — of Kṛṣṇa; *putraḥ* — the son; *pau-*

ṛṇamāsaḥ—Paurṇamāsa; *tu*—and; *tat-sutaḥ*—his son; *lambodaraḥ*—Lambodara; *tu*—and; *tat-putraḥ*—his son; *tasmāt*—from him (Lambodara); *cibilakaḥ*—Cibilaka; *nṛpaḥ*—the king; *meghasvātiḥ*—Meghasvāti; *cibilakāt*—from Cibilaka; *aṭamānaḥ*—Aṭamāna; *tu*—and; *tasya*—of him (Meghasvāti); *ca*—and; *aniṣṭakarmā*—Aniṣṭakarmā; *hāleyaḥ*—Hāleya; *talakaḥ*—Talaka; *tasya*—of him (Hāleya); *ca*—and; *ātma-jaḥ*—the son; *purīṣabhīruḥ*—Purīṣabhīru; *tat*—of Talaka; *putraḥ*—the son; *tataḥ*—then; *rājā*—the king; *sunandanaḥ*—Sunandana; *cakoraḥ*—Cakora; *bahavaḥ*—the Bahus; *yatra*—among whom; *śivasvātiḥ*—Śivasvāti; *arimdamaḥ*—the subduer of enemies; *tasya*—of him; *api*—also; *gomatī*—Gomatī; *putraḥ*—the son; *purīmān*—Purīmān; *bhavitā*—will be; *tataḥ*—from him (Gomatī); *medaśirāḥ*—Medaśirā; *śivaskandaḥ*—Śivaskanda; *yajñaśrīḥ*—Yajñaśrī; *tat*—of Śivaskanda; *sutaḥ*—the son; *tataḥ*—then; *vijayaḥ*—Vijaya; *tat-sutaḥ*—his son; *bhāvyaḥ*—will be; *candravijñaḥ*—Candravijña; *sa-lomadhiḥ*—along with Lomadhi; *ete*—these; *triṁśat*—thirty; *nṛ-patayaḥ*—kings; *catvāri*—four; *abda-śatāni*—centuries; *ca*—and; *ṣaṭ-pañcāsat*—fifty-six; *ca*—and; *pṛthivīm*—the world; *bhokṣyanti*—will rule; *kuru-nandana*—O favorite son of the Kurus.

TRANSLATION

The brother of Balī, named Kṛṣṇa, will become the next ruler of the earth. His son will be Śāntakarṇa, and his son will be Paurṇamāsa. The son of Paurṇamāsa will be Lambodara, who will father Mahārāja Cibilaka. From Cibilaka will come Meghasvāti, whose son will be Aṭamāna. The son of Aṭamāna will be Aniṣṭakarmā. His son will be Hāleya, and his son will be Talaka. The son of Talaka will be Purīṣabhīru, and following him Sunandana will become king. Sunandana will be followed by Cakora and the eight Bahus, among whom Śivasvāti will be a great subduer of enemies. The son of Śivasvāti will be Gomatī. His son will be Purīmān, whose son will be Medaśirā. His son will be Śivaskanda, and his son will be Yajñaśrī. The son of Yajñaśrī will be Vijaya, who will have two sons, Candravijña and Lomadhi. These thirty kings will enjoy sovereignty over the earth for a total of 456 years, O favorite son of the Kurus.

TEXT 27

सप्providedाभीरा आवभृत्या दश गर्दभिनो नृपाः ।
कंकाः षोडश भूपाला भविष्यन्त्यतिलोलुपाः ॥ २७ ॥

saptābhīrā āvabhṛtyā
daśa gardabhino nṛpāḥ
kaṅkāḥ ṣoḍaśa bhū-pālā
bhaviṣyanty ati-lolupāḥ

sapta — seven; *ābhīrāḥ*—Ābhīras; *āvabhṛtyāḥ*—of the city of Avabhṛti; *daśa* — ten; *gardabhinaḥ*—Gardabhīs; *nṛpāḥ*—kings; *kaṅkāḥ*—Kaṅkas; *ṣoḍaśa* — sixteen; *bhū-pālāḥ*—rulers of the earth; *bhaviṣyanti* — will be; *ati-lolupāḥ*—very greedy.

TRANSLATION

Then will follow seven kings of the Ābhīra race from the city of Avabhṛti, and then ten Gardabhīs. After them, sixteen kings of the Kaṅkas will rule and will be known for their excessive greed.

TEXT 28

ततोऽष्टौ यवना भाव्याश्चतुर्दश तुरुष्ककाः ।
भूयो दश गुरुण्डाश्च मौला एकादशैव तु ॥ २८ ॥

tato 'ṣṭau yavanā bhāvyāś
caturdaśa turuṣkakāḥ
bhūyo daśa guruṇḍāś ca
maulā ekādaśaiva tu

tataḥ—then; *aṣṭau* — eight; *yavanāḥ*—Yavanas; *bhāvyāḥ*—will be; *catuḥ-daśa* — fourteen; *turuṣkakāḥ*—Turuṣkas; *bhūyaḥ*—furthermore; *daśa* — ten; *guruṇḍāḥ*—Guruṇḍas; *ca* — and; *maulāḥ*—Maulas; *ekādaśa* — eleven; *eva* — indeed; *tu* — and.

TRANSLATION

Eight Yavanas will then take power, followed by fourteen Turuṣkas, ten Guruṇḍas and eleven kings of the Maula dynasty.

TEXTS 29–31

एते भोक्ष्यन्ति पृथिवीं दश वर्षशतानि च ।
नवाधिकां च नवतिं मौला एकादश क्षितिम् ॥ २९ ॥

भोक्ष्यन्त्यब्दशतान्यंग त्रीणि तैः संस्थिते ततः ।
किलकिलायां नृपतयो भूतनन्दोऽथ वगिंरिः ॥ ३० ॥
शिशुनन्दिश्च तद्भ्राता यशोनन्दिः प्रवीरकः ।
इत्येते वै वर्षशतं भविष्यन्त्यधिकानि षट् ॥ ३१ ॥

ete bhokṣyanti pṛthivīṁ
daśa varṣa-śatāni ca
navādhikāṁ ca navatiṁ
maulā ekādaśa kṣitim

bhokṣyanty abda-śatāny aṅga
trīṇi taiḥ saṁsthite tataḥ
kilakilāyāṁ nṛpatayo
bhūtanando'tha vaṅgiriḥ

śiśunandiś ca tad-bhrātā
yaśonandiḥ pravīrakaḥ
ity ete vai varṣa-śataṁ
bhaviṣyanty adhikāni ṣaṭ

ete — these; *bhokṣyanti* — will rule; *pṛthivīm* — the earth; *daśa* — ten; *varṣa-śatāni* — centuries; *ca* — and; *nava-adhikām* — plus nine; *ca* — and; *navatim* — ninety; *maulāḥ*—the Maulas; *ekādaśa* — eleven; *kṣitim* — the world; *bhokṣyanti* — will rule; *abda-śatāni* — centuries; *aṅga* — my dear Parīkṣit; *trīṇi* — three; *taiḥ*—they; *saṁsthite* — when they are all dead; *tataḥ* —then; *kilakilāyām* — in the city Kilakilā; *nṛ-patayaḥ*—kings; *bhūtanandaḥ* —Bhūtananda; *atha* — and then; *vaṅgiriḥ*—Vaṅgiri; *śiśunandiḥ*—Śiśunandi; *ca* — and; *tat* — his; *bhrātā* — brother; *yaśonandiḥ*—Yaśonandi; *pravīrakaḥ* —Pravīraka; *iti* — thus; *ete* — these; *vai* — indeed; *varṣa-śatam* — one hundred years; *bhaviṣyanti* — will be; *adhikāni* — plus; *ṣaṭ*—six.

TRANSLATION

These Ābhīras, Gardabhīs and Kaṅkas will enjoy the earth for 1,099 years, and the Maulas will rule for 300 years. When all of them have died off there will appear in the city of Kilakilā a dynasty of kings consisting of Bhūtananda, Vaṅgiri, Śiśunandi, Śiśunandi's brother Yaśonandi, and Pravīraka. These kings of Kilakilā will hold sway for a total of 106 years.

TEXTS 32–33

तेषां त्रयोदश सुता भवितारश्च बाह्लिकाः ।
पुष्पमित्रोऽथ राजन्यो दुर्मित्रोऽस्य तथैव च ॥३२॥
एककाला इमे भूपाः सप्तान्ध्राः सप्त कौशलाः ।
विदूरपतयो भाव्या निषधास्तत एव हि ॥३३॥

teṣāṁ trayodaśa sutā
bhavitāraś ca bāhlikāḥ
puṣpamitro'tha rājanyo
durmitro'sya tathaiva ca

eka-kālā ime bhū-pāḥ
saptāndhrāḥ sapta kauśalāḥ
vidūra-patayo bhāvyā
niṣadhās tata eva hi

teṣām — of them (Bhūtananda and the other kings of the Kilakilā dynasty); *trayodaśa* — thirteen; *sutāḥ* — sons; *bhavitāraḥ* — will be; *ca* — and; *bāhlikāḥ* — called the Bāhlikas; *puṣpamitraḥ* — Puṣpamitra; *atha* — then; *rājanyaḥ* — the king; *durmitraḥ* — Durmitra; *asya* — his (son); *tathā* — also; *eva* — indeed; *ca* — and; *eka-kālāḥ* — ruling at the same time; *ime* — these; *bhū-pāḥ* — kings; *sapta* — seven; *andhrāḥ* — Andhras; *sapta* — seven; *kauśalāḥ* — kings of Kauśala-deśa; *vidūra-patayaḥ* — rulers of Vidūra; *bhāvyāḥ* — will be; *niṣadhāḥ* — Niṣadhas; *tataḥ* — then (after the Bāhlikas); *eva hi* — indeed.

TRANSLATION

The Kilakilās will be followed by their thirteen sons, the Bāhlikas, and after them King Puṣpamitra, his son Durmitra, seven Andhras, seven Kauśalas and also kings of the Vidūra and Niṣadha provinces will separately rule in different parts of the world.

TEXT 34

मागधानां तु भविता विश्वस्फूर्जिः पुरञ्जयः ।
करिष्यत्यपरो वर्णान् पुलिन्दयदुमद्रकान् ॥३४॥

māgadhānāṁ tu bhavitā
viśvasphūrjiḥ purañjayaḥ

kariṣyaty aparo varṇān
pulinda-yadu-madrakān

māgadhānām — of the Magadha province; *tu* — and; *bhavitā* — there will be; *viśvasphūrjiḥ*—Viśvasphūrji; *purañjayaḥ*—King Purañjaya; *kariṣyati* — he will make; *aparaḥ*—being the replica of; *varṇān* — all the civilized classes of men; *pulinda-yadu-madrakān* — into outcastes such as the Pulindas, Yadus and Madrakas.

TRANSLATION

There will then appear a king of the Māgadhas named Viśvasphūrji, who will be like another Purañjaya. He will turn all the civilized classes into low-class, uncivilized men in the same category as the Pulindas, Yadus and Madrakas.

TEXT 35

प्रजाश्चाब्रह्मभूयिष्ठाः स्थापयिष्यति दुर्मतिः ।
वीर्यवान् क्षत्रमुत्साद्य पद्मवत्यां स वै पुरि ।
अनुगंगमाप्रयागं गुप्तां भोक्ष्यति मेदिनीम् ॥३५॥

prajāś cābrahma-bhūyiṣṭhāḥ
sthāpayiṣyati durmatiḥ
vīryavān kṣatram utsādya
padmavatyāṁ sa vai puri
anu-gaṅgam ā-prayāgaṁ
guptāṁ bhokṣyati medinīm

prajāḥ—the citizens; *ca* — and; *abrahma* — unbrahminical; *bhūyiṣṭhāḥ* —predominantly; *sthāpayiṣyati* — he will make; *durmatiḥ*—the unintelligent (Viśvasphūrji); *vīrya-vān* — powerful; *kṣatram* — the *kṣatriya* class; *utsādya* — destroying; *padmavatyām* — in Padmavatī; *saḥ*—he; *vai* — indeed; *puri* — in the city; *anu-gaṅgam* — from Gaṅgādvārā (Hardwar); *ā-prayāgam* — to Prayāga; *guptām* — protected; *bhokṣyati* — he will rule; *medinīm* — the earth.

TRANSLATION

Foolish King Viśvasphūrji will maintain all the citizens in ungodliness and will use his power to completely disrupt the kṣatriya order. From his

capital of Padmavatī he will rule that part of the earth extending from the source of the Gaṅgā to Prayāga.

TEXT 36

सौराष्ट्रावन्त्याभीराश्च शूरा अर्बुदमालवाः ।
व्रात्या द्विजा भविष्यन्ति शूद्रप्राया जनाधिपाः ॥ ३६ ॥

saurāṣṭrāvanty-ābhīrāś ca
śūrā arbuda-mālavāḥ
vrātyā dvijā bhaviṣyanti
śūdra-prāyā janādhipāḥ

śaurāṣṭra — residing in Śaurāṣṭra; *avantī*—in Avantī; *ābhīrāḥ*—and in Ābhīra; *ca* — and; *śūrāḥ*—residing in the Śūra province; *arbuda-mālavāḥ*—residing in Arbuda and Mālava; *vrātyāḥ*—deviated from all purificatory rituals; *dvijāḥ*—the *brāhmaṇas; bhaviṣyanti* — will become; *śūdra-prāyāḥ*—no better than *śūdras; jana-adhipāḥ*—the kings.

TRANSLATION

At that time the brāhmaṇas of such provinces as Śaurāṣṭra, Avantī, Ābhīra, Śūra, Arbuda and Mālava will forget all their regulative principles, and the members of the royal order in these places will become no better than śūdras.

TEXT 37

सिन्धोस्तटं चन्द्रभागां कौन्तीं काश्मीरमण्डलम् ।
भोक्ष्यन्ति शूद्रा व्रात्याद्या म्लेच्छाश्चाब्रह्मवर्चसः ॥ ३७ ॥

sindhos taṭaṁ candrabhāgāṁ
kauntīṁ kāśmīra-maṇḍalam
bhokṣyanti śūdrā vrātyādyā
mlecchāś cābrahma-varcasaḥ

sindhoḥ—of the river Sindhu; *taṭam* — the land on the shore; *candrabhāgām* — Candrabhāgā; *kauntīm* — Kauntī; *kāśmīra-maṇḍalam* — the region of Kāśmīra; *bhokṣyanti* — will rule; *śūdrāḥ*—*śūdras; vrātya-ādyāḥ*—*brāhmaṇas* who have fallen from the brahminical standard, and other disqualified men; *mlecchāḥ*—meat-eaters; *ca*—and; *abrahma-varcasaḥ*—lacking spiritual potency.

TRANSLATION

The land along the Sindhu River, as well as the districts of Candrabhāgā, Kauntī and Kāśmīra, will be ruled by śūdras, fallen brāhmaṇas and meat-eaters. Having given up the path of Vedic civilization, they will have lost all spiritual strength.

TEXT 38

तुल्यकाला इमे राजन् म्लेच्छप्रायाश्च भूभृतः ।
एतेऽधर्मानृतपराः फल्गुदास्तीव्रमन्यवः ॥ ३८ ॥

tulya-kālā ime rājan
mleccha-prāyāś ca bhū-bhṛtaḥ
ete'dharmānṛta-parāḥ
phalgu-dās tīvra-manyavaḥ

tulya-kālāḥ—ruling at the same time; *ime*—these; *rājan*—O King Parīkṣit; *mleccha-prāyāḥ*—mostly outcastes; *ca*—and; *bhū-bhṛtaḥ*—kings; *ete*—these; *adharma*—to irreligion; *anṛta*—and untruthfulness; *parāḥ*—dedicated; *phalgu-dāḥ*—giving little benefit to their subjects; *tīvra*—fierce; *manyavaḥ*—their anger.

TRANSLATION

There will be many such uncivilized kings ruling at the same time, O King Parīkṣit, and they will all be uncharitable, possessed of fierce tempers, and great devotees of irreligion and falsity.

TEXTS 39–40

स्त्रीबालगोद्विजघ्नाश्च परदारधनादृताः ।
उदितास्तमितप्राया अल्पसत्त्वाल्पकायुषः ॥ ३९ ॥
असंस्कृताः क्रियाहीना रजसा तमसावृताः ।
प्रजास्ते भक्षयिष्यन्ति म्लेच्छा राजन्यरूपिणः ॥ ४० ॥

strī-bāla-go-dvija-ghnāś ca
para-dāra-dhanādṛtāḥ

uditāsta-mita-prāyā
alpa-sattvālpakāyuṣaḥ

asaṁskṛtāḥ kriyā-hīnā
rajasā tamasāvṛtāḥ
prajās te bhakṣayiṣyanti
mlecchā rājanya-rūpiṇaḥ

strī—of women; *bāla* — children; *go* — cows; *dvija* — and *brāhmaṇas; ghnāḥ*—the murderers; *ca* — and; *para* — of other men; *dāra* — the wives; *dhana* — and money; *ādṛtāḥ*—showing interest in; *udita-asta-mita* — switching their moods from elated to depressed and then to moderate; *prāyāḥ* —for the most part; *alpa-sattva* — having little strength; *alpaka-āyuṣaḥ*— and short life spans; *asaṁskṛtāḥ*—not purified by Vedic rituals; *kriyā-hīnāḥ* —devoid of regulative principles; *rajasā* — by the mode of passion; *tamasā* — and by the mode of ignorance; *āvṛtāḥ*—covered over; *prajāḥ*—the citizens; *te* — they; *bhakṣayiṣyanti* — will virtually devour; *mlecchāḥ*—outcastes; *rājanya-rūpiṇaḥ*—appearing as kings.

TRANSLATION

These barbarians in the guise of kings will devour the citizenry, murdering innocent women, children, cows and brāhmaṇas and coveting the wives and property of other men. They will be erratic in their moods, have little strength of character and be very short-lived. Indeed, not purified by any Vedic rituals and lacking in the practice of regulative principles, they will be completely covered by the modes of passion and ignorance.

PURPORT

These verses give a concise, accurate description of the fallen leaders of this age.

TEXT 41

तन्नाथास्ते जनपदास्तच्छीलाचारवादिनः ।
अन्योन्यतो राजभिश्च क्षयं यास्यन्ति पीडिताः ॥ ४१ ॥

tan-nāthās te janapadās
tac-chīlācāra-vādinaḥ

anyonyato rājabhiś ca
kṣayaṁ yāsyanti pīḍitāḥ

tat-nāthāḥ—the subjects having these kings as rulers; *te*—they; *jana-padāḥ*—the residents of the cities; *tat*—of these kings; *śīla*—(imitating) the character; *ācāra*—behavior; *vādinaḥ*—and speech; *anyonyataḥ*—one another; *rājabhiḥ*—by the kings; *ca*—and; *kṣayam yāsyanti*—they will become ruined; *pīḍitāḥ*—tormented.

TRANSLATION

The citizens governed by these low-class kings will imitate the character, behavior and speech of their rulers. Harassed by their leaders and by each other, they will all suffer ruination.

PURPORT

At the end of the Ninth Canto of *Śrīmad-Bhāgavatam,* it is stated that Ripuñjaya, or Purañjaya, the first king mentioned in this chapter, ended his rule about one thousand years after the time of Lord Kṛṣṇa. Since Lord Kṛṣṇa appeared approximately five thousand years ago, Purañjaya must have appeared about four thousand years ago. That would mean that Viśvasphūrji, the last king mentioned, would have appeared approximately in the twelfth century of the Christian era.

Modern Western scholars have made the false accusation that Indian religious literature has no sense of chronological history. But the elaborate historical chronology described in this chapter certainly refutes that naive assessment.

Thus end the purports of the humble servants of His Divine Grace A.C. Bhaktivedanta Swami Prabhupāda to the Twelfth Canto, First Chapter, of the Śrīmad-Bhāgavatam, *entitled "The Degraded Dynasties of Kali-yuga."*

CHAPTER TWO

The Symptoms of Kali-yuga

This chapter relates that, when the bad qualities of the age of Kali will increase to an intolerable level, the Supreme Personality of Godhead will descend as Kalki to destroy those who are fixed in irreligion. After that, a new Satya-yuga will begin.

As the age of Kali progresses, all good qualities of men diminish and all impure qualities increase. Atheistic systems of so-called religion become predominant, replacing the codes of Vedic law. The kings become just like highway bandits, the people in general become dedicated to low occupations, and all the social classes become just like *śūdras.* All cows become like goats, all spiritual hermitages become like materialistic homes, and family ties extend no further than the immediate relationship of marriage.

When the age of Kali has almost ended, the Supreme Personality of Godhead will incarnate. He will appear in the village Śambhala, in the home of the exalted *brāhmaṇa* Viṣṇuyaśā, and will take the name Kalki. He will mount His horse Devadatta and, taking His sword in hand, will roam about the earth killing millions of bandits in the guise of kings. Then the signs of the next Satya-yuga will begin to appear. When the moon, sun and the planet Bṛhaspati enter simultaneously into one constellation and conjoin in the lunar mansion Puṣyā, Satya-yuga will begin. In the order of Satya, Tretā, Dvāpara and Kali, the cycle of four ages rotates in the society of living entities in this universe.

The chapter ends with a brief description of the future dynasties of the sun and moon coming from Vaivasvata Manu in the next Satya-yuga. Even now two saintly *kṣatriyas* are living who at the end of this Kali-yuga will reinitiate the pious dynasties of the sun god, Vivasvān, and the moon god, Candra. One of these kings is Devāpi, a brother of Mahārāja Śantanu, and the other is Maru, a descendant of Ikṣvāku. They are biding their time incognito in a village named Kalāpa.

TEXT 1

श्रीशुक उवाच

ततश्चानुदिनं धर्मः सत्यं शौचं क्षमा दया ।
कालेन बलिना राजन्नङ्क्ष्यत्यायुर्बलं स्मृतिः ॥ १ ॥

śrī-śuka uvāca
tataś cānu-dinaṁ dharmaḥ
satyaṁ śaucaṁ kṣamā dayā
kālena balinā rājan
naṅkṣyaty āyur balaṁ smṛtiḥ

śrī-śukaḥ uvāca — Śukadeva Gosvāmī said; *tataḥ*—then; *ca* — and; *anudinam* — day after day; *dharmaḥ*—religion; *satyam* — truth; *śaucam* — cleanliness; *kṣamā* — tolerance; *dayā* — mercy; *kālena* — by the force of time; *balinā* — strong; *rājan* — O King Parīkṣit; *naṅkṣyati* — will become ruined; *āyuḥ*—duration of life; *balam* — strength; *smṛtiḥ*—memory.

TRANSLATION

Śukadeva Gosvāmī said: Then, O King, religion, truthfulness, cleanliness, tolerance, mercy, duration of life, physical strength and memory will all diminish day by day because of the powerful influence of the age of Kali.

PURPORT

During the present age, Kali-yuga, practically all desirable qualities will gradually diminish, as described in this verse. For example, *dharma,* which indicates a respect for higher authority that leads one to obey religious principles, will diminish.

In the Western world, theologians have been unable to scientifically present the laws of God or, indeed, God Himself, and thus in Western intellectual history a rigid dichotomy has arisen between theology and science. In an attempt to resolve this conflict, some theologians have agreed to modify their doctrines so that they conform not only to proven scientific facts but even to pseudoscientific speculations and hypotheses, which, though unproven, are hypocritically included within the realm of "science." On the other hand, some fanatical theologians disregard the scientific method altogether and insist on the veracity of their antiquated, sectarian dogmas.

Thus bereft of systematic Vedic theology, material science has moved into the destructive realm of gross materialism, while speculative Western philosophy has drifted into the superficiality of relativistic ethics and inconclusive linguistic analysis. With so many of the best Western minds dedicated to materialistic analysis, naturally much of Western religious life, separated from the intellectual mainstream, is dominated by irrational fanaticism and unauthorized mystic and mystery cults. People have become so ignorant of the science of God that they often lump the Kṛṣṇa consciousness movement in with this odd assortment of fanciful attempts at theology and religion. Thus *dharma,* or true religion, which is strict and conscious obedience to God's law, is diminishing.

Satyam, truthfulness, is also diminishing, simply because people do not know what the truth is. Without knowing the Absolute Truth, one cannot clearly understand the real significance or purpose of life merely by amassing huge quantities of relative or hypothetical truths.

Kṣamā, tolerance or forgiveness, is diminishing as well, because there is no practical method by which people can purify themselves and thus become free of envy. Unless one is purified by chanting the holy names of the Lord in an authorized program of spiritual improvement, the mind will be overwhelmed by anger, envy and all sorts of small-mindedness. Thus *dayā,* mercy, is also decreasing. All living beings are eternally connected by their common participation in the divine existence of God. When this existential oneness is obscured through atheism and agnosticism, people are not inclined to be merciful to one another; they cannot recognize their self-interest in promoting the welfare of other living beings. In fact, people are no longer even merciful to themselves: they systematically destroy themselves through liquor, drugs, tobacco, meat-eating, sexual promiscuity and whatever other cheap gratificatory processes are available to them.

Because of all these self-destructive practices and the powerful influence of time, the average life span (*āyur*) is decreasing. Modern scientists, seeking to gain credibility among the mass of people, often publish statistics supposedly showing that science has increased the average duration of life. But these statistics do not take into account the number of people killed through the cruel practice of abortion. When we figure aborted children into the life expectancy of the total population, we find that the average duration of life has not at all increased in the age of Kali but is rather decreasing drastically.*

Balam, bodily strength, is also decreasing. The Vedic literature states that five thousand years ago, in the previous age, human beings — and even animals and plants — were larger and stronger. With the progress of the age of Kali, physical stature and strength will gradually diminish.

---

* According to the *United States Statistical Abstract* for 1984, there were about 3.7 million live births in the United states in 1982, and the average life expectancy at birth was 74.5 years. But when the 1.5 million abortions are added to the live births, the average life expectancy for *conceived* children falls to 53.0 years.

Certainly *smṛti,* memory, is weakening. In former ages human beings possessed superior memory, and they also did not encumber themselves with a terrible bureaucratic and technical society, as we have done. Thus essential information and abiding wisdom were preserved without recourse to writing. Of course, in the age of Kali things are dramatically different.

TEXT 2

वित्तमेव कलौ नृणां जन्माचारगुणोदयः ।
धर्मन्यायव्यवस्थायां कारणं बलमेव हि ॥ २ ॥

vittam eva kalau nṝṇāṁ
janmācāra-guṇodayaḥ
dharma-nyāya-vyavasthāyāṁ
kāraṇaṁ balam eva hi

vittam — wealth; *eva* — alone; *kalau* — in the age of Kali; *nṝṇām* — among men; *janma* — of good birth; *ācāra* — good behavior; *guṇa* — and good qualities; *udayaḥ*—the cause of manifestation; *dharma* — of religious duty; *nyāya* — and reason; *vyavasthāyām* — in the establishment; *kāraṇam* — the cause; *balam* — strength; *eva* — only; *hi* — indeed.

TRANSLATION

In Kali-yuga, wealth alone will be considered the sign of a man's good birth, proper behavior and fine qualities. And law and justice will be applied only on the basis of one's power.

PURPORT

In the age of Kali, a man is considered high class, middle class or low class merely according to his financial status, regardless of his knowledge, culture and behavior. In this age there are many great industrial and commercial cities with luxurious neighborhoods reserved for the wealthy. On beautiful tree-lined roads, within apparently aristocratic homes, it is not unusual to find many perverted, dishonest and sinful activities taking place. According to Vedic criteria, a man is considered high class if his behavior is enlightened, and his behavior is considered enlightened if his activities are dedicated to promoting the happiness of all creatures. Every living being is originally happy, because in all living bodies there is an eternal spiritual spark that partakes of the divine conscious nature of God. When our original spiritual awareness is revived, we become naturally blissful and satisfied in knowledge and peace. An enlightened, or educated, man should endeavor to revive his own spiritual understanding, and he should help others experience the same sublime consciousness.

The great Western philosopher Socrates stated that if a man is enlightened he will automatically act virtuously, and Śrīla Prabhupāda confirmed this fact. But in the Kali-yuga this obvious truth is disregarded, and the search for knowledge and virtue has been replaced by a vicious, animalistic competition for money. Those who prevail become the "top dogs" of modern society, and their consumer power grants them a reputation as most respectable, aristocratic and well educated.

This verse also states that in the age of Kali brute strength (*balam eva*) will determine law and "justice." We should keep in mind that in the progressive, Vedic culture, there was no artificial dichotomy between the spiritual and the public realms. All civilized people took it for granted that God is everywhere and that His laws are binding upon all creatures. The Sanskrit word *dharma,* therefore, indicates one's social, or public, obligation as well as one's religious duty. Thus responsibly caring for one's family is *dharma,* and engaging in the loving service of God is also *dharma.* This verse indicates, however, that in the age of Kali the principle of "might makes right" will hold sway.

In the first chapter of this canto we observed how this principle infiltrated India's past. Similarly, as the Western world achieved political, economic and technological hegemony over Asian lands, bogus propaganda was disseminated to the effect that Indian, and in general all non-Western, religion, theology and philosophy are somehow primitive and unscientific — mere mythology and superstition. Fortunately this arrogant, irrational view is now dissipating, and people all over the world are beginning to appreciate the staggering wealth of spiritual philosophy and science available in the Sanskrit literature of India. In other words, many intelligent people no longer consider traditional Western religion or empirical science, which has virtually superseded religion as the official Western dogma, necessarily authoritative merely because the West has politically and economically subdued other geographic and ethnic configurations of humanity. Thus there is now hope that spiritual issues can be contested and resolved on a philosophical level and not merely by a crude test of arms.

Next this verse points out that the rule of law will be applied unequally to the powerful and the powerless. Already in many nations justice is available only to those who can pay and fight for it. In a civilized state, every man, woman and child must have equal and rapid access to a fair system of laws. In modern times we sometimes refer to this as human rights. Certainly human rights are one of the more obvious casualties of the age of Kali.

TEXT 3

दाम्पत्येऽभिरुचिर्हेतुर्मायैव व्यावहारिके ।
स्त्रीत्वे पुंस्त्वे च हि रतिर्विप्रत्वे सूत्रमेव हि ॥ ३ ॥

dāmpatye 'bhirucir hetur
māyaiva vyāvahārike
strītve puṁstve ca hi ratir
vipratve sūtram eva hi

dām-patye — in the relationship of husband and wife; *abhiruciḥ*— superficial attraction; *hetuḥ*—the reason; *māyā* — deceit; *eva* — indeed; *vyāvahārike* — in business; *strītve* — in being a woman; *puṁstve* — in being a man; *ca* — and; *hi* — indeed; *ratiḥ*—sex; *vipratve* — in being a *brāhmaṇa; sūtram* — the sacred thread; *eva* — only; *hi* — indeed.

TRANSLATION

Men and women will live together merely because of superficial attraction, and success in business will depend on deceit. Womanliness and manliness will be judged according to one's expertise in sex, and a man will be known as a brāhmaṇa just by his wearing a thread.

PURPORT

Just as human life as a whole has a great and serious purpose — namely spiritual liberation — fundamental human institutions such as marriage and child-rearing should also be dedicated to that great objective. Unfortunately, in the present age the satisfaction of the sex impulse has become the overriding, if not the exclusive, reason for marriage.

The sexual impulse, which induces the male and female of almost every species to combine physically, and in higher species also emotionally, is ultimately not a natural urge, because it is based on the unnatural identification of the self with the body. Life itself is a spiritual phenomenon. It is the soul that lives and gives apparent life to the biological machine called the body. Consciousness is the soul's manifest energy, and thus consciousness, awareness itself, is originally an entirely spiritual event. When life, or consciousness, is confined within a biological machine and falsely mistakes itself to be that machine, material existence occurs and sex desire arises.

God intends human life to be an opportunity for us to rectify this illusory mode of existence and return to the vast satisfaction of pure, godly existence. But because our identification with the material body is a long historical affair, it is difficult for most people to immediately break free from the demands of the materially molded mind. Therefore the Vedic scriptures prescribe sacred marriage, in which a so-called man and a so-called woman may combine in a regulated, spiritual marriage sheltered by overarching religious injunctions. In this way the candidate for self-realization who has selected family life can derive adequate satisfaction for his senses and simultaneously please the Lord within his heart by obeying religious injunctions. The Lord then purifies him of material desire.

In Kali-yuga this deep understanding has been almost lost, and, as stated in this verse, men and women combine like animals, solely on the basis of mutual attraction to bodies made of flesh, bone, membrane, blood and so on. In other words, in our modern, godless society the weak, superficial intelligence of humanity rarely penetrates beyond the gross physical covering of the eternal soul, and thus family life has in most cases lost its highest purpose and value.

A corollary point established in this verse is that in the age of Kali a woman is considered "a good woman" if she is sexually attractive and, indeed, sexually efficient. Similarly, a sexually attractive man is "a good man." The best example of this superficiality is the incredible attention twentieth-century people give to materialistic movie stars, music stars and other prominent figures in the entertainment industry. In fact, pursuing sexual experiences with various types of bodies is similar to drinking old wine from new bottles. But few people in the Kali-yuga can understand this.

Finally, this verse states that in the age of Kali a man will become known as a priest, or *brāhmaṇa,* merely by wearing ceremonial dress. In India, *brāhmaṇas* wear a sacred thread, and in other parts of world members of the priestly class have other ornaments and symbols. But in the age of Kali the symbols alone will suffice to establish a person as a religious leader, despite his ignorance of God.

TEXT 4

लिंगमेवाश्रमख्यातावन्योन्यापत्तिकारणम् ।
अवृत्त्या न्यायदौर्बल्यं पाण्डित्ये चापलं वचः ॥ ४ ॥

liṅgam evāśrama-khyātāv
anyonyāpatti-kāraṇam
avṛttyā nyāya-daurbalyaṁ
pāṇḍitye cāpalaṁ vacaḥ

liṅgam — the external symbol; *eva* — merely; *āśrama-khyātau* — in knowing a person's spiritual order; *anyonya* — mutual; *āpatti* — of exchange; *kāraṇam* — the cause; *avṛttyā* — by lack of livelihood; *nyāya* — in credibility; *daurbalyam* — the weakness; *pāṇḍitye* — in scholarship; *cāpalam* — tricky; *vacaḥ*—words.

TRANSLATION

A person's spiritual position will be ascertained merely according to external symbols, and on that same basis people will change from one spiritual order to the next. A person's propriety will be seriously questioned if he does not earn a good living. And one who is very clever at juggling words will be considered a learned scholar.

PURPORT

The previous verse stated that in the age of Kali the priestly class will be recognized by external symbols alone, and this verse extends the same principle to the other orders of society, namely the political or military class, the business or productive class, and finally the laborer or artisan class.

Modern sociologists have demonstrated that in those societies chiefly governed by the Protestant ethic, poverty is considered a sign of indolence, dirtiness, stupidity, immorality and worthlessness. In a God-conscious society, however, many persons voluntarily decide to dedicate their lives not to material acquisition but rather to the pursuit of knowledge and spirituality. Thus a preference for the simple and the austere may indicate intelligence, self-control and sensitivity to the higher purpose of life. Of course, in itself poverty does not establish these virtues, but it may sometimes be the result of them. In the Kali-yuga, however, this possibility is often forgotten.

Intellectuality is another casualty of the bewildering age of Kali. Modern so-called philosophers and scientists have created a technical, esoteric terminology for each branch of learning, and when they give lectures people consider them learned simply because of their ability to speak that which no one else can understand. In Western culture, the Greek Sophists were among the first to systematically argue for rhetoric and "efficiency" above wisdom and purity, and sophistry certainly flourishes in the twentieth century. Modern universities have very little wisdom, though they do possess a virtual infinity of technical data. Although many modern thinkers are fundamentally ignorant of the higher, spiritual reality, they are, so to speak, "good talkers," and most people simply don't notice their ignorance.

TEXT 5

अनाढ्यतैवासाधुत्वे साधुत्वे दम्भ एव तु ।
स्वीकार एव चोद्वाहे स्नानमेव प्रसाधनम् ॥ ५ ॥

anāḍhyataivāsādhutve
sādhutve dambha eva tu
svīkāra eva codvāhe
snānam eva prasādhanam

anāḍhyatā — poverty; *eva* — simply; *asādhutve* — in one's being unholy; *sādhutve* — in virtue, or success; *dambhaḥ*—hypocrisy; *eva* — alone; *tu* — and; *svī-kāraḥ*—verbal acceptance; *eva* — alone; *ca* — and; *udvāhe* — in marriage; *snānam* — bathing with water; *eva* — alone; *prasādhanam* — cleaning and decorating of the body.

TRANSLATION

A person will be judged unholy if he does not have money, and hypocrisy will be accepted as virtue. Marriage will be arranged simply by verbal agreement, and a person will think he is fit to appear in public if he has merely taken a bath.

PURPORT

The word *dambha* indicates a self-righteous hypocrite — someone not so much concerned with *being* saintly as with *appearing* saintly. In the Age of Kali there is a rather large number of self-righteous, hypocritical religious fanatics claiming to have the only way, the only truth and the only light. In many Muslim countries this mentality has resulted in brutal repression of religious freedom and thus destroyed the opportunity for enlightened spiritual dialectic. Fortunately, in much of the Western world there is a system of free religious expression. Even in the West, however, self-righteous hypocrites consider sincere and saintly followers of other disciplines to be heathens and devils.

Western religious fanatics are usually addicted to many bad habits, such as smoking, drinking, sex, gambling and animal slaughter. Although the followers of the Kṛṣṇa consciousness movement strictly avoid illicit sex, intoxication, gambling and animal killing, and although they dedicate their lives to the constant glorification of God, self-righteous hypocrites claim that such strict austerity and devotion to God are "tricks of the devil." Thus the sinful are promoted as religious, and the saintly are decried as demonic. This pathetic incapacity to grasp the most rudimentary criteria of spirituality is a prominent symptom of Kali-yuga.

In this age, the institution of marriage will degenerate. Indeed, already a marriage certificate is sometimes cynically rejected as "a mere piece of paper." Forgetting the spiritual purpose of marriage and misunderstanding sex to be the goal of family life, lusty men and women directly engage in sexual affairs without the troublesome formalities and responsibilities of a legal relationship. Such foolish people argue that "sex is natural." But if sex is natural, pregnancy and childbirth are equally natural. And for the child it is certainly natural to be raised by a loving father and mother and in fact to have the same father and mother throughout his life. Psychological studies confirm that a child needs to be cared for by both his father and his mother, and thus it is obviously natural for sex to be accompanied by a permanent marriage arrangement. Hypocritical people justify unrestricted sex by saying "it is natural," but to avoid the natural consequence of sex — pregnancy — they use contraceptives, which certainly do not grow on trees. Indeed, contraceptives are not at all natural. Thus hypocrisy and foolishness abound in the age of Kali.

The verse concludes by saying that people will neglect to ornament their bodies properly in the present age. A human being should decorate his body with various religious ornaments. Vaiṣṇavas mark their bodies with *tilaka* blessed with the holy name of God. But in the age of Kali, religious and even material formalities are thoughtlessly discarded.

TEXT 6

दूरे वार्ययनं तीर्थं लावण्यं केशधारणम् ।
उदरंभरता स्वार्थः सत्यत्वे धाष्ट्र्यमेव हि ।
दाक्ष्यं कुटुम्बभरणं यशोऽर्थे धर्मसेवनम् ॥६॥

dūre vāry-ayanaṁ tīrthaṁ
lāvaṇyaṁ keśa-dhāraṇam
udaraṁ-bharatā svārthaḥ
satyatve dhārṣṭyam eva hi
dākṣyaṁ kuṭumba-bharaṇaṁ
yaśo'rthe dharma-sevanam

dūre — situated far away; *vāri* — of water; *ayanam* — a reservoir; *tīrtham* — holy place; *lāvaṇyam* — beauty; *keśa* — hair; *dhāraṇam* — carrying; *udaram-bharatā* — filling the belly; *sva-arthaḥ*—the goal of life; *satyatve* — in so-called truth; *dhārṣṭyam* — audacity; *eva* — simply; *hi* — indeed; *dākṣyam* — expertise; *kuṭumba-bharaṇam* — maintaining a family; *yaśaḥ*—fame; *arthe* — for the sake of; *dharma-sevanam* — observance of religious principles.

TRANSLATION

A sacred place will be taken to consist of no more than a reservoir of water located at a distance, and beauty will be thought to depend on one's hairstyle. Filling the belly will become the goal of life, and one who is audacious will be accepted as truthful. He who can maintain a family will be regarded as an expert man, and the principles of religion will be observed only for the sake of reputation.

PURPORT

In India there are many sacred places through which holy rivers flow. Foolish persons eagerly seek redemption from their sins by bathing in these rivers but do not take instruction from learned devotees of the Lord who reside in such places. One should go to a holy place seeking spiritual enlightenment and not just for ritualistic bathing.

In this age, people tirelessly arrange their hair in different styles, trying to enhance their facial beauty and sexuality. They do not know that actual beauty comes from within the heart, from the soul, and that only a person who is pure is truly attractive. As the difficulties of this age increase, filling one's belly will be the mark of success, and one who can maintain his own family will be considered brilliant in economic affairs. Religion will be practiced, if at all, only for the sake of reputation and without any essential understanding of the Supreme Personality of Godhead.

TEXT 7

एवं प्रजाभिर्दुष्टाभिराकीर्णे क्षितिमण्डले ।
ब्रह्मविट्क्षत्रशूद्राणां यो बली भविता नृपः ॥ ७ ॥

evaṁ prajābhir duṣṭābhir
ākīrṇe kṣiti-maṇḍale
brahma-viṭ-kṣatra-śūdrāṇāṁ
yo balī bhavitā nṛpaḥ

evam — in this way; *prajābhiḥ*—with populace; *duṣṭābhiḥ*—corrupted; *ākīrṇe* — being crowded; *kṣiti-maṇḍale* — the earth globe; *brahma* — among the *brāhmaṇas; viṭ*— *vaiśyas; kṣatra* — *kṣatriyas; śūdrāṇām* — and *śūdras; yaḥ*—whoever; *balī*—the strongest; *bhavitā* — he will become; *nṛpaḥ*—the king.

TRANSLATION

As the earth thus becomes crowded with a corrupt population, whoever among any of the social classes shows himself to be the strongest will gain political power.

TEXT 8

प्रजा हि लुब्धैराजन्यैर्निर्घृणैर्दस्युधर्मभिः ।
आच्छिन्नदारद्रविणा यास्यन्ति गिरिकाननम् ॥ ८ ॥

prajā hi lubdhai rājanyair
nirghṛṇair dasyu-dharmabhiḥ
ācchinna-dāra-draviṇā
yāsyanti giri-kānanam

prajāḥ—the citizens; *hi* — indeed; *lubdhaiḥ*—avaricious; *rājanyaiḥ*—by the royal order; *nirghṛṇaiḥ*—merciless; *dasyu* — of ordinary thieves; *dharmabhiḥ*—acting according to the nature; *ācchinna* — taken away; *dāra* — their wives; *draviṇāḥ*—and property; *yāsyanti* — they will go; *giri* — to the mountains; *kānanam* — and forests.

TRANSLATION

Losing their wives and properties to such avaricious and merciless rulers, who will behave no better than ordinary thieves, the citizens will flee to the mountains and forests.

TEXT 9

शाकमूलामिषक्षौद्रफलपुष्पाष्टिभोजनाः ।
अनावृष्ट्या विनङ्क्ष्यन्ति दुर्भिक्षकरपीडिताः ॥ ९ ॥

śāka-mūlāmiṣa-kṣaudra-
phala-puṣpāṣṭi-bhojanāḥ
anāvṛṣṭyā vinaṅkṣyanti
durbhikṣa-kara-pīḍitāḥ

śāka — leaves; *mūla* — roots; *āmiṣa* — meat; *kṣaudra* — wild honey; *phala* — fruits; *puṣpa* — flowers; *aṣṭi* — and seeds; *bhojanāḥ* — eating; *anāvṛṣṭyā* — because of drought; *vinaṅkṣyanti* — they will become ruined; *durbhikṣa* — by famine; *kara* — and taxation; *pīḍitāḥ* — tormented.

TRANSLATION

Harassed by famine and excessive taxes, people will resort to eating leaves, roots, flesh, wild honey, fruits, flowers and seeds. Struck by drought, they will become completely ruined.

PURPORT

Śrīmad-Bhāgavatam authoritatively describes the future of our planet. Just as a leaf disconnected from a plant or tree dries up, withers and disintegrates, when human society is disconnected from the Supreme Lord it withers up and disintegrates in violence and chaos. Despite our computers and rockets, if the Supreme Lord does not send rain we shall all starve.

TEXT 10

शीतवातातपप्रावृड्हिमैरन्योन्यतः प्रजाः ।
क्षुत्तृड्भ्यां व्याधिभिश्चैव सन्तप्स्यन्ते च चिन्तया ॥ १० ॥

śīta-vātātapa-prāvṛḍ-
himair anyonyataḥ prajāḥ

kṣut-tṛḍbhyāṁ vyādhibhiś caiva
santapsyante ca cintayā

śīta — by cold; *vāta* — wind; *ātapa* — the heat of the sun; *prāvṛt* — torrential rain; *himaiḥ* — and snow; *anyonyataḥ* — by quarrel; *prajāḥ* — the citizens; *kṣut* — by hunger; *tṛḍbhyām* — and thirst; *vyādhibhiḥ* — by diseases; *ca* — also; *eva* — indeed; *santapsyante* — they will suffer great distress; *ca* — and; *cintayā* — by anxiety.

TRANSLATION

The citizens will suffer greatly from cold, wind, heat, rain and snow. They will be further tormented by quarrels, hunger, thirst, disease and severe anxiety.

TEXT 11

त्रिंशद् विंशति वर्षाणि परमायुः कलौ नृणाम् ॥११॥

triṁśad viṁśati varṣāṇi
paramāyuḥ kalau nṛṇām

triṁśat — thirty; *viṁśati* — plus twenty; *varṣāṇi* — years; *parama-āyuḥ* — the maximum duration of life; *kalau* — in Kali-yuga; *nṛṇām* — of men.

TRANSLATION

The maximum duration of life for human beings in Kali-yuga will become fifty years.

TEXTS 12–16

क्षीयमाणेषु देहेषु देहिनां कलिदोषतः ।
वर्णाश्रमवतां धर्मे नष्टे वेदपथे नृणाम् ॥१२॥
पाषण्डप्रचुरे धर्मे दस्युप्रायेषु राजसु ।
चौर्यानृतवृथाहिंसानानावृत्तिषु वै नृषु ॥१३॥
शूद्रप्रायेषु वर्णेषु च्छागप्रायासु धेनुषु ।
गृहप्रायेष्वाश्रमेषु यौनप्रायेषु बन्धुषु ॥१४॥
अणुप्रायास्वोषधीषु शमीप्रायेषु स्थास्नुषु ।
विद्युत्प्रायेषु मेघेषु शून्यप्रायेषु सद्मसु ॥१५॥

इत्थं कलौ गतप्राये जनेषु खरधर्मिषु ।
धर्मत्राणाय सत्त्वेन भगवानवतरिष्यति ॥ १६ ॥

kṣīyamāṇeṣu deheṣu
dehināṁ kali-doṣataḥ
varṇāśramavatāṁ dharme
naṣṭe veda-pathe nṛṇām

pāṣaṇḍa-pracure dharme
dasyu-prāyeṣu rājasu
cauryānṛta-vṛthā-hiṁsā-
nānā-vṛttiṣu vai nṛṣu

śūdra-prāyeṣu varṇeṣu
cchāga-prāyāsu dhenuṣu
gṛha-prāyeṣv āśrameṣu
yauna-prāyeṣu bandhuṣu

aṇu-prāyāsv oṣadhīṣu
śamī-prāyeṣu sthāsnuṣu
vidyut-prāyeṣu megheṣu
śūnya-prāyeṣu sadmasu

itthaṁ kalau gata-prāye
janeṣu khara-dharmiṣu
dharma-trāṇāya sattvena
bhagavān avatariṣyati

kṣīyamāṇeṣu — having become smaller; *deheṣu* — the bodies; *dehinām* — of all living entities; *kali-doṣataḥ* — by the contamination of the age of Kali; *varṇa-āśrama-vatām* — of the members of *varṇāśrama* society; *dharme* — when their religious principles; *naṣṭe* — have been destroyed; *veda-pathe* — the path of the *Vedas; nṛṇām* — for all men; *pāṣaṇḍa-pracure* — mostly atheism; *dharme* — religion; *dasyu-prāyeṣu* — mostly thieves; *rājasu* — the kings; *caurya* — banditry; *anṛta* — lying; *vṛthā-hiṁsā* — useless slaughter; *nānā* — various; *vṛttiṣu* — their occupations; *vai* — indeed; *nṛṣu* — when men; *śūdra-prāyeṣu* — mostly low-class *śūdras; varṇeṣu* — the so-called social orders; *chāga-prāyāsu* — no better than goats; *dhenuṣu* — the cows; *gṛha-prāyeṣu* — just like materialistic homes; *āśrameṣu* — the spiritual hermitages; *yauna-prāyeṣu* — extending no further than marriage; *bandhuṣu* —

family ties; *aṇu-prāyāsu* — mostly very small; *oṣadhīṣu* — plants and herbs; *śamī-prāyeṣu* — just like *śamī* trees; *sthāsnuṣu* — all the trees; *vidyut-prāyeṣu* — always manifesting lightning; *megheṣu* — the clouds; *śūnya-prāyeṣu* — devoid of religious life; *sadmasu* — the homes; *ittham* — thus; *kalau* — when the age of Kali; *gata-prāye* — is almost finished; *janeṣu* — the people; *khara-dharmiṣu* — when they have assumed the characteristics of asses; *dharma-trāṇāya* — for the deliverance of religion; *sattvena* — in the pure mode of goodness; *bhagavān* — the Supreme Personality of Godhead; *avatariṣyati* — will descend.

TRANSLATION

By the time the age of Kali ends, the bodies of all creatures will be greatly reduced in size, and the religious principles of followers of varṇāśrama will be ruined. The path of the Vedas will be completely forgotten in human society, and so-called religion will be mostly atheistic. The kings will mostly be thieves, the occupations of men will be stealing, lying and needless violence, and all the social classes will be reduced to the lowest level of śūdras. Cows will be like goats, spiritual hermitages will be no different from mundane houses, and family ties will extend no further than the immediate bonds of marriage. Most plants and herbs will be tiny, and all trees will appear like dwarf śamī trees. Clouds will be full of lightning, homes will be devoid of piety, and all human beings will have become like asses. At that time, the Supreme Personality of Godhead will appear on the earth. Acting with the power of pure spiritual goodness, He will rescue eternal religion.

PURPORT

Significantly, these verses point out that most so-called religions in this age will be atheistic (*pāsaṇḍa-pracure dharme*). In confirmation of the *Bhāgavatam's* prediction, the United States Supreme Court has recently ruled that to be considered a religion a system of belief need not recognize a supreme being. Also, many atheistic, voidistic belief systems, often imported from the Orient, have attracted the attention of modern atheistic scientists, who expound on the similarities between Eastern and Western voidism in fashionable, esoteric books.

These verses vividly describe many unsavory symptoms of the age of Kali. Ultimately, at the end of this age, Lord Kṛṣṇa will descend as Kalki and remove the thoroughly demonic persons from the face of the earth.

TEXT 17

चराचरगुरोर्विष्णोरीश्वरस्याखिलात्मनः ।
धर्मत्राणाय साधूनां जन्म कर्मापनुत्तये ॥ १७ ॥

carācara-guror viṣṇor
īśvarasyākhilātmanaḥ
dharma-trāṇāya sādhūnāṁ
janma karmāpanuttaye

cara-acara — of all moving and nonmoving living beings; *guroḥ*—of the spiritual master; *viṣṇoḥ*—the Supreme Lord, Viṣṇu; *īśvarasya* — the Supreme Personality of Godhead; *akhila* — of all; *ātmanaḥ*—of the Supreme Soul; *dharma-trāṇāya* — for the protection of religion; *sādhūnām* — of saintly men; *janma* — the birth; *karma* — of their fruitive activities; *apanuttaye* — for the cessation.

TRANSLATION

Lord Viṣṇu — the Supreme Personality of Godhead, the spiritual master of all moving and nonmoving living beings, and the Supreme Soul of all — takes birth to protect the principles of religion and to relieve His saintly devotees from the reactions of material work.

TEXT 18

शम्भलग्राममुख्यस्य ब्राह्मणस्य महात्मनः ।
भवने विष्णुयशसः कल्किः प्रादुर्भविष्यति ॥ १८ ॥

śambhala-grāma-mukhyasya
brāhmaṇasya mahātmanaḥ
bhavane viṣṇuyaśasaḥ
kalkiḥ prādurbhaviṣyati

śambhala-grāma — in the village Śambhala; *mukhyasya* — of the chief citizen; *brāhmaṇasya* — of the *brāhmaṇa; mahā-ātmanaḥ*—the great soul; *bhavane* — in the home; *viṣṇuyaśasaḥ*—of Viṣṇuyaśā; *kalkiḥ*—Lord Kalki; *prādurbhaviṣyati* — will appear.

TRANSLATION

Lord Kalki will appear in the home of the most eminent brāhmaṇa of Śambhala village, the great soul Viṣṇuyaśā.

TEXTS 19–20

अश्वमाशुगमारुह्य देवदत्तं जगत्पतिः ।
असिनासाधुदमनमष्टैश्वर्यगुणान्वितः ॥ १९ ॥
विचरन्नाशुना क्षौण्यां हयेनाप्रतिमद्युतिः ।
नृपलिंगच्छदो दस्यून् कोटिशो निहनिष्यति ॥ २० ॥

aśvam āśu-gam āruhya
devadattaṁ jagat-patiḥ
asināsādhu-damanam
aṣṭaiśvarya-guṇānvitaḥ

vicarann āśunā kṣauṇyāṁ
hayenāpratima-dyutiḥ
nṛpa-liṅga-cchado dasyūn
koṭiśo nihaniṣyati

aśvam — His horse; *āśu-gam* — swift-traveling; *āruhya* — mounting; *devadattam* — named Devadatta; *jagat-patiḥ* — the Lord of the universe; *asinā* — with His sword; *asādhu-damanam* — (the horse who) subdues the unholy; *aṣṭa* — with eight; *aiśvarya* — mystic opulences; *guṇa* — and transcendental qualities of the Personality of Godhead; *anvitaḥ* — endowed; *vicaran* — traveling about; *āśunā* — swift; *kṣauṇyām* — upon the earth; *hayena* — by His horse; *apratima* — unrivaled; *dyutiḥ* — whose effulgence; *nṛpa-liṅga* — with the dress of kings; *chadaḥ* — disguising themselves; *dasyūn* — thieves; *koṭiśaḥ* — by the millions; *nihaniṣyati* — He will slaughter.

TRANSLATION

Lord Kalki, the Lord of the universe, will mount His swift horse Devadatta and, sword in hand, travel over the earth exhibiting His eight mystic opulences and eight special qualities of Godhead. Displaying His unequaled effulgence and riding with great speed, He will kill by the millions those thieves who have dared dress as kings.

PURPORT

These verses describe the thrilling pastimes of Lord Kalki. Anyone would be attracted by the sight of a powerful, beautiful man riding on a wonderful horse at lightning speed, chastising and devastating cruel, demonic people with the sword in His hand.

Of course, fanatical materialists may argue that this picture of Lord Kalki is a mere anthropomorphic creation of the human mind — a mythological deity created by people who need to believe in some superior being. But this argument is not logical, nor does it prove anything. It is merely the opinion of certain people. We need water, but that does not mean man creates water. We also need food, oxygen and many other things that we do not create. Since our general experience is that our needs correspond to available objects existing in the external world, that we appear to need a Supreme Lord would tend to indicate that in fact there is a Supreme Lord. In other words, nature endows us with a sense of need for things that actually exist and that are in fact necessary for our well-being. Similarly, we experience a need for God because we are in fact part of God and cannot live without Him. At the end of Kali-yuga this same God will appear as the mighty Kalki *avatāra* and beat the pollution out of the demons.

TEXT 21

अथ तेषां भविष्यन्ति मनांसि विशदानि वै ।
वासुदेवांगरागातिपुण्यगन्धानिलस्पृशाम् ।
पौरजानपदानां वै हतेष्वखिलदस्युषु ॥ २१ ॥

atha teṣāṁ bhaviṣyanti
manāṁsi viśadāni vai
vāsudevāṅga-rāgāti-
puṇya-gandhānila-spṛśām
paura-jānapadānāṁ vai
hateṣv akhila-dasyuṣu

atha — then; *teṣām* — of them; *bhaviṣyanti* — will become; *manāṁsi* — the minds; *viśadāni* — clear; *vai* — indeed; *vāsudeva* — of Lord Vāsudeva; *aṅga* — of the body; *rāga* — from the cosmetic decorations; *ati-puṇya* — most sacred; *gandha* — having the fragrance; *anila* — by the wind; *spṛśām* — of those who have been touched; *paura* — of the city-dwellers; *jāna-padānām* — and the residents of the smaller towns and villages; *vai* — indeed; *hateṣu* — when they have been killed; *akhila* — all; *dasyuṣu* — the rascal kings.

TRANSLATION

After all the impostor kings have been killed, the residents of the cities

and towns will feel the breezes carrying the most sacred fragrance of the sandalwood paste and other decorations of Lord Vāsudeva, and their minds will thereby become transcendentally pure.

PURPORT

Nothing can surpass the sublime experience of being dramatically rescued by a great hero who happens to be the Supreme Lord. The death of the demons at the end of Kali-yuga is accompanied by fragrant spiritual breezes, and thus the atmosphere becomes most enchanting.

TEXT 22

तेषां प्रजाविसर्गश्च स्थविष्ठः सम्भविष्यति ।
वासुदेवे भगवति सत्त्वमूर्तौ हृदि स्थिते ॥ २२ ॥

teṣāṁ prajā-visargaś ca
sthaviṣṭhaḥ sambhaviṣyati
vāsudeve bhagavati
sattva-mūrtau hṛdi sthite

teṣām — of them; *prajā* — of progeny; *visargaḥ* — the creation; *ca* — and; *sthaviṣṭhaḥ* — abundant; *sambhaviṣyati* — will be; *vāsudeve* — Lord Vāsudeva; *bhagavati* — the Supreme Personality of Godhead; *sattva-mūrtau* — in His transcendental form of pure goodness; *hṛdi* — in their hearts; *sthite* — when He is situated.

TRANSLATION

When Lord Vāsudeva, the Supreme Personality of Godhead, appears in their hearts in His transcendental form of goodness, the remaining citizens will abundantly repopulate the earth.

TEXT 23

यदावतीर्णो भगवान् कल्किर्धर्मपतिर्हरिः ।
कृतं भविष्यति तदा प्रजासूतिश्च सात्त्विकी ॥ २३ ॥

yadāvatīrṇo bhagavān
kalkir dharma-patir hariḥ
kṛtaṁ bhaviṣyati tadā
prajā-sūtiś ca sāttvikī

yadā — when; *avatīrṇaḥ* — incarnates; *bhagavān* — the Supreme Lord; *kalkiḥ* — Kalki; *dharma-patiḥ* — the master of religion; *hariḥ* — the Supreme Personality of Godhead; *kṛtam* — Satya-yuga; *bhaviṣyati* — will begin; *tadā* — then; *prajā-sūtiḥ* — the creation of progeny; *ca* — and; *sāttvikī* — in the mode of goodness.

TRANSLATION

When the Supreme Lord has appeared on earth as Kalki, the maintainer of religion, Satya-yuga will begin, and human society will bring forth progeny in the mode of goodness.

TEXT 24

यदा चन्द्रश्च सूर्यश्च तथा तिष्यबृहस्पती ।
एकराशौ समेष्यन्ति भविष्यति तदा कृतम् ॥ २४ ॥

yadā candraś ca sūryaś ca
tathā tiṣya-bṛhaspatī
eka-rāśau sameṣyanti
bhaviṣyati tadā kṛtam

yadā — when; *candraḥ* — the moon; *ca* — and; *sūryaḥ* — the sun; *ca* — and; *tathā* — also; *tiṣya* — the asterism Tiṣyā (more commonly known as Puṣyā, extending from 3° 20´ to 16° 40´ Cancer); *bṛhaspatī* — and the planet Jupiter; *eka-rāśau* — in the same constellation (Cancer); *sameṣyanti* — will enter simultaneously; *bhaviṣyati* — will be; *tadā* — then; *kṛtam* — Satya-yuga.

TRANSLATION

When the moon, the sun and Bṛhaspatī are together in the constellation Karkaṭa, and all three enter simultaneously into the lunar mansion Puṣyā — at that exact moment the age of Satya, or Kṛta, will begin.

TEXT 25

येऽतीता वर्तमाना ये भविष्यन्ति च पार्थिवाः ।
ते त उद्देशतः प्रोक्ता वंशीयाः सोमसूर्ययोः ॥ २५ ॥

ye'tītā vartamānā ye
bhaviṣyanti ca pārthivāḥ

te ta uddeśataḥ proktā
vaṁśīyāḥ soma-sūryayoḥ

ye — those who; *atītāḥ*—past; *vartamānāḥ*—present; *ye* — who; *bhaviṣyanti* — will be in the future; *ca* — and; *pārthivāḥ*—kings of the earth; *te te* — all of them; *uddeśataḥ*—by brief mention; *proktāḥ*—described; *vaṁśīyāḥ*—the members of the dynasties; *soma-sūryayoḥ*—of the sun god and the moon god.

TRANSLATION

Thus I have described all the kings — past, present and future — who belong to the dynasties of the sun and the moon.

TEXT 26

आरभ्य भवतो जन्म यावन्नन्दाभिषेचनम् ।
एतद् वर्षसहस्रं तु शतं पञ्चदशोत्तरम् ॥ २६ ॥

ārabhya bhavato janma
yāvan nandābhiṣecanam
etad varṣa-sahasraṁ tu
śataṁ pañcadaśottaram

ārabhya — beginning from; *bhavataḥ*—of your good self (Parīkṣit); *janma* — the birth; *yāvat* — up until; *nanda* — of King Nanda, the son of Mahānandi; *abhiṣecanam* — the coronation; *etat* — this; *varṣa* — years; *sahasram* — one thousand; *tu* — and; *śatam* — one hundred; *pañca-daśa-uttaram* — plus fifty.

TRANSLATION

From your birth up to the coronation of King Nanda, 1,150 years will pass.

PURPORT

Although Śukadeva Gosvāmī previously described approximately fifteen hundred years of royal dynasties, it is understood that some overlapping occurred between kings. Therefore the present chronological calculation should be taken as authoritative.

TEXTS 27–28

सप्तर्षीणां तु यौ पूर्वौ दृश्येते उदितौ दिवि ।
तयोस्तु मध्ये नक्षत्रं दृश्यते यत्समं निशि ॥ २७ ॥
तेनैव ऋषयो युक्तास्तिष्ठन्त्यब्दशतं नृणाम् ।
ते त्वदीये द्विजाः काल अधुना चाश्रिता मघाः ॥ २८ ॥

saptarṣīṇāṁ tu yau pūrvau
dṛśyete uditau divi
tayos tu madhye nakṣatraṁ
dṛśyate yat samaṁ niśi

tenaiva ṛṣayo yuktās
tiṣṭhanty abda-śataṁ nṛṇām
te tvadīye dvijāḥ kāla
adhunā cāśritā maghāḥ

sapta-ṛṣīṇām — of the constellation of the seven sages (the constellation known to Westerners as *Ursa Major*); *tu* — and; *yau* — which two stars; *pūrvau* — first; *dṛśyete* — are seen; *uditau* — risen; *divi* — in the sky; *tayoḥ* — of the two (named Pulaha and Kratu); *tu* — and; *madhye* — between; *nakṣatram* — the lunar mansion; *dṛśyate* — is seen; *yat* — which; *samam* — on the same line of celestial longitude, as their midpoint; *niśi* — in the night sky; *tena* — with that lunar mansion; *eva* — indeed; *ṛṣayaḥ* — the seven sages; *yuktāḥ* — are connected; *tiṣṭhanti* — they remain; *abda-śatam* — one hundred years; *nṛṇām* — of human beings; *te* — these seven sages; *tvadīye* — in your; *dvijāḥ* — the elevated *brāhmaṇas; kāle* — in the time; *adhunā* — now; *ca* — and; *āśritāḥ* — are situated; *maghāḥ* — in the asterism Maghā.

TRANSLATION

Of the seven stars forming the constellation of the seven sages, Pulaha and Kratu are the first to rise in the night sky. If a line running north and south were drawn through their midpoint, whichever of the lunar mansions this line passes through is said to be the ruling asterism of the constellation for that time. The Seven Sages will remain connected with that particular lunar mansion for one hundred human years. Currently, during your lifetime, they are situated in the nakṣatra called Maghā.

TEXT 29

विष्णोर्भगवतो भानुः कृष्णाख्योऽसौ दिवं गतः ।
तदाविशत्कलिर्लोकं पापे यद् रमते जनः ॥ २९ ॥

viṣṇor bhagavato bhānuḥ
kṛṣṇākhyo'sau divaṁ gataḥ
tadāviśat kalir lokaṁ
pāpe yad ramate janaḥ

viṣṇoḥ—of Viṣṇu; *bhagavataḥ*—the Supreme Personality of Godhead; *bhānuḥ*—the sun; *kṛṣṇa-ākhyaḥ*—known as Kṛṣṇa; *asau* — He; *divam* — to the spiritual sky; *gataḥ*—having returned; *tadā* — then; *aviśat* — entered; *kaliḥ*—the age of Kali; *lokam* — this world; *pāpe* — in sin; *yat* — in which age; *ramate* — take pleasure; *janaḥ*—the people.

TRANSLATION

The Supreme Lord, Viṣṇu, is brilliant like the sun and is known as Kṛṣṇa. When He returned to the spiritual sky, Kali entered this world, and people then began to take pleasure in sinful activities.

TEXT 30

यावत्स पादपद्माभ्यां स्पृशनास्ते रमापतिः ।
तावत्कलिर्वै पृथिवीं पराक्रन्तुं न चाशकत् ॥ ३० ॥

yāvat sa pāda-padmābhyāṁ
spṛśan āste ramā-patiḥ
tāvat kalir vai pṛthivīṁ
parākrantuṁ na cāśakat

yāvat — as long as; *saḥ*—He, Lord Śrī Kṛṣṇa; *pāda-padmābhyām* — with His lotus feet; *spṛśan* — touching; *āste* — remained; *ramā-patiḥ*—the husband of the goddess of fortune; *tāvat* — for that long; *kaliḥ*—the age of Kali; *vai* — indeed; *pṛthivīm* — the earth; *parākrantum* — to overcome; *na* — not; *ca* — and; *aśakat* — was able.

TRANSLATION

As long as Lord Śrī Kṛṣṇa, the husband of the goddess of fortune, touched the earth with His lotus feet, Kali was powerless to subdue this planet.

PURPORT

Although even during the time of Lord Kṛṣṇa's presence on earth Kali had entered the earth to a slight extent through the impious activities of Duryodhana and his allies, Lord Kṛṣṇa consistently suppressed Kali's influence. Kali could not flourish until Lord Kṛṣṇa had left the earth.

TEXT 31

यदा देवर्षयः सप्त मघासु विचरन्ति हि ।
तदा प्रवृत्तस्तु कलिर्द्वादशाब्दशतात्मकः ॥ ३१ ॥

yadā devarṣayaḥ sapta
maghāsu vicaranti hi
tadā pravṛttas tu kalir
dvādaśābda-śatātmakaḥ

yadā — when; *deva-ṛṣayaḥ sapta* — the seven sages among the demigods; *maghāsu* — in the lunar mansion Maghā; *vicaranti* — are traveling; *hi* — indeed; *tadā* — then; *pravṛttaḥ* — begins; *tu* — and; *kaliḥ* — the age of Kali; *dvādaśa* — twelve; *abda-śata* — centuries [These twelve hundred years of the demigods equal 432,000 earth years]; *ātmakaḥ* — consisting of.

TRANSLATION

When the constellation of the seven sages is passing through the lunar mansion Maghā, the age of Kali begins. It comprises twelve hundred years of the demigods.

TEXT 32

यदा मघाभ्यो यास्यन्ति पूर्वाषाढां महर्षयः ।
तदा नन्दात्प्रभृत्येष कलिर्वृद्धिं गमिष्यति ॥ ३२ ॥

yadā maghābhyo yāsyanti
pūrvāṣāḍhāṁ maharṣayaḥ
tadā nandāt prabhṛty eṣa
kalir vṛddhiṁ gamiṣyati

yadā — when; *maghābhyaḥ* — from Maghā; *yāsyanti* — they will go; *pūrva-āṣāḍhām* — to the next lunar mansion, Pūrvāṣāḍhā; *mahā-ṛṣayaḥ* — the seven great sages; *tadā* — then; *nandāt* — beginning from Nanda;

prabhṛti — and his descendants; *eṣaḥ* — this; *kaliḥ* — age of Kali; *vṛddhim* — maturity; *gamiṣyati* — will attain.

TRANSLATION

When the great sages of the Saptarṣi constellation pass from Maghā to Pūrvāṣāḍhā, Kali will have his full strength, beginning from King Nanda and his dynasty.

TEXT 33

यस्मिन् कृष्णो दिवं यातस्तस्मिन्नेव तदाहनि ।
प्रतिपन्नं कलियुगमिति प्राहुः पुराविदः ॥ ३३ ॥

yasmin kṛṣṇo divaṁ yātas
tasminn eva tadāhani
pratipannaṁ kali-yugam
iti prāhuḥ purā-vidaḥ

yasmin — on which; *kṛṣṇaḥ* — Lord Śrī Kṛṣṇa; *divam* — to the spiritual world; *yātaḥ* — gone; *tasmin* — on that; *eva* — same; *tadā* — then; *ahani* — day; *pratipannam* — obtained; *kali-yugam* — the age of Kali; *iti* — thus; *prāhuḥ* — they say; *purā* — of the past; *vidaḥ* — the experts.

TRANSLATION

Those who scientifically understand the past declare that on the very day that Lord Śrī Kṛṣṇa departed for the spiritual world, the influence of the age of Kali began.

PURPORT

Although technically Kali-yuga was to begin during the time of Lord Kṛṣṇa's presence on earth, this fallen age had to wait meekly for the departure of the Supreme Personality of Godhead.

TEXT 34

दिव्याब्दानां सहस्रान्ते चतुर्थे तु पुनः कृतम् ।
भविष्यति तदा नृणां मन आत्मप्रकाशकम् ॥ ३४ ॥

divyābdānāṁ sahasrānte
caturthe tu punaḥ kṛtam

bhaviṣyati tadā nṝṇāṁ
mana ātma-prakāśakam

divya — of the demigods; *abdānām* — years; *sahasra* — of one thousand; *ante* — at the end; *caturthe* — in the fourth age, Kali; *tu* — and; *punaḥ* — again; *kṛtam* — the Satya-yuga; *bhaviṣyati* — will be; *tadā* — then; *nṝṇām* — of men; *manaḥ* — the minds; *ātma-prakāśakam* — self-luminous.

TRANSLATION

After the one thousand celestial years of Kali-yuga, the Satya-yuga will manifest again. At that time the minds of all men will become self-effulgent.

TEXT 35

इत्येष मानवो वंशो यथा संख्यायते भुवि ।
तथा विट्शूद्रविप्राणां तास्ता ज्ञेया युगे युगे ॥ ३५ ॥

ity eṣa mānavo vaṁśo
yathā saṅkhyāyate bhuvi
tathā viṭ-śūdra-viprāṇāṁ
tās tā jñeyā yuge yuge

iti — thus (in the cantos of this *Śrīmad-Bhāgavatam*); *eṣaḥ* — this; *mānavaḥ* — descending from Vaivasvata Manu; *vaṁśaḥ* — the dynasty; *yathā* — as; *saṅkhyāyate* — it is enumerated; *bhuvi* — upon the earth; *tathā* — in the same way; *viṭ* — of the *vaiśyas; śūdra* — *śūdras; viprāṇām* — and *brāhmaṇas; tāḥ tāḥ* — the situations of each; *jñeyāḥ* — are to be understood; *yuge yuge* — in each age.

TRANSLATION

Thus I have described the royal dynasty of Manu, as it is known on this earth. One can similarly study the history of the vaiśyas, śūdras and brāhmaṇas living in the various ages.

PURPORT

Just as the dynasty of kings includes exalted and insignificant, virtuous and wicked monarchs, varieties of human character are found in the intellectual, commercial and laboring orders of society.

TEXT 36

एतेषां नामलिंगानां पुरुषाणां महात्मनाम् ।
कथामात्रावशिष्टानां कीर्तिरेव स्थिता भुवि ॥ ३६ ॥

eteṣāṁ nāma-liṅgānāṁ
puruṣāṇāṁ mahātmanām
kathā-mātrāvaśiṣṭānāṁ
kīrtir eva sthitā bhuvi

eteṣām — of these; *nāma* — their names; *liṅgānām* — which are the only means of remembering them; *puruṣāṇām* — of the personalities; *mahā-ātmanām* — who were great souls; *kathā* — the stories; *mātra* — merely; *avaśiṣṭānām* — whose remaining portion; *kīrtiḥ*—the glories; *eva* — only; *sthitā* — are present; *bhuvi* — on the earth.

TRANSLATION

These personalities, who were great souls, are now known only by their names. They exist only in accounts from the past, and only their fame remains on the earth.

PURPORT

Although one may consider oneself to be a great, powerful leader, he will ultimately end up as a name in a long list of names. In other words, it is useless to be attached to power and position in the material world.

TEXT 37

देवापिः शान्तनोर्भ्राता मरुश्चेक्ष्वाकुवंशजः ।
कलापग्राम आसाते महायोगबलान्वितौ ॥ ३७ ॥

devāpiḥ śāntanor bhrātā
maruś cekṣvāku-vaṁśa-jaḥ
kalāpa-grāma āsāte
mahā-yoga-balānvitau

devāpiḥ—Devāpi; *śāntanoḥ*—of Mahārāja Śāntanu; *bhrātā* — the brother; *maruḥ*—Maru; *ca* — and; *ikṣvāku-vaṁśa-jaḥ*—born in the dynasty of Ikṣvāku; *kalāpa-grāme* — in the village Kalāpa; *āsāte* — the two of them are living; *mahā* — great; *yoga-bala* — with mystic power; *anvitau* — endowed.

TRANSLATION

Devāpi, the brother of Mahārāja Śāntanu, and Maru, the descendant of Ikṣvāku, both possess great mystic strength and are living even now in the village of Kalāpa.

TEXT 38

ताविहैत्य कलेरन्ते वासुदेवानुशिक्षितौ ।
वर्णाश्रमयुतं धर्मं पूर्ववत् प्रथयिष्यतः ॥ ३८ ॥

tāv ihaitya kaler ante
vāsudevānuśikṣitau
varṇāśrama-yutaṁ dharmaṁ
pūrva-vat prathayiṣyataḥ

tau — they (Maru and Devāpi); *iha* — to human society; *etya* — returning; *kaleḥ*—of the age of Kali; *ante* — at the end; *vāsudeva* — by the Supreme Personality of Godhead, Vāsudeva; *anuśikṣitau* — instructed; *varṇa-āśrama* — the divine system of occupational and spiritual orders of society; *yutam* — comprising; *dharmam* — the code of eternal religion; *pūrva-vat* — just as previously; *prathayiṣyataḥ*—they will promulgate.

TRANSLATION

At the end of the age of Kali, these two kings, having received instruction directly from the Supreme Personality of Godhead, Vāsudeva, will return to human society and reestablish the eternal religion of man, characterized by the divisions of varṇa and āśrama, just as it was before.

PURPORT

According to this and the previous verse, the two great kings who will reestablish human culture after the end of Kali-yuga have already descended to the earth, where they are patiently waiting to render their devotional service to Lord Viṣṇu.

TEXT 39

कृतं त्रेता द्वापरं च कलिश्चेति चतुर्युगम् ।
अनेन क्रमयोगेन भुवि प्राणिषु वर्तते ॥ ३९ ॥

kṛtaṁ tretā dvāparaṁ ca
kaliś ceti catur-yugam
anena krama-yogena
bhuvi prāṇiṣu vartate

kṛtam — Satya-yuga; *tretā* — Tretā-yuga; *dvāparam* — Dvāpara-yuga; *ca* — and; *kaliḥ* — Kali-yuga; *ca* — and; *iti* — thus; *catuḥ-yugam* — the cycle of four ages; *anena* — by this; *krama* — sequential; *yogena* — pattern; *bhuvi* — in this world; *prāṇiṣu* — among living beings; *vartate* — goes on continuously.

TRANSLATION

The cycle of four ages — Satya, Tretā, Dvāpara and Kali — continues perpetually among living beings on this earth, repeating the same general sequence of events.

TEXT 40

राजन्नेते मया प्रोक्ता नरदेवास्तथापरे ।
भूमौ ममत्वं कृत्वान्ते हित्वेमां निधनं गताः ॥ ४० ॥

rājann ete mayā proktā
nara-devās tathāpare
bhūmau mamatvaṁ kṛtvānte
hitvemāṁ nidhanaṁ gatāḥ

rājan — O King Parīkṣit; *ete* — these; *mayā* — by me; *proktāḥ* — described; *nara-devāḥ* — kings; *tathā* — and; *apare* — other human beings; *bhūmau* — upon the earth; *mamatvam* — possessiveness; *kṛtvā* — exerting; *ante* — in the end; *hitvā* — giving up; *imām* — this world; *nidhanam* — destruction; *gatāḥ* — met.

TRANSLATION

My dear King Parīkṣit, all these kings I have described, as well as all other human beings, come to this earth and stake their claims, but ultimately they all must give up this world and meet their destruction.

TEXT 41

कृमिविड्भस्मसंज्ञान्ते राजनाम्नोऽपि यस्य च ।
भूतध्रुक् तत्कृते स्वार्थं किं वेद निरयो यतः ॥ ४१ ॥

kṛmi-viḍ-bhasma-saṁjñānte
rāja-nāmno'pi yasya ca
bhūta-dhruk tat-kṛte svārthaṁ
kiṁ veda nirayo yataḥ

kṛmi — of worms; *viṭ* — stool; *bhasma* — and ashes; *saṁjñā* — the designation; *ante* — in the end; *rāja-nāmnaḥ* — going by the name "king"; *api* — even though; *yasya* — of which (body); *ca* — and; *bhūta* — of living beings; *dhruk* — an enemy; *tat-kṛte* — for the sake of that body; *sva-artham* — his own best interest; *kim* — what; *veda* — does he know; *nirayaḥ* — punishment in hell; *yataḥ* — because of which.

TRANSLATION

Even though a person's body may now have the designation "king," in the end its name will be "worms," "stool" or "ashes." What can a person who injures other living beings for the sake of his body know about his own self-interest, since his activities are simply leading him to hell?

PURPORT

After death, the body may be buried and eaten by worms, or it may be thrown in the street or forest to be eaten by animals who will pass out its remnants as stool, or it may be burned and converted into ashes. Therefore one should not pave his way to hell by using his temporary body to injure the bodies of other living beings. In this verse the word *bhūta* includes nonhuman life forms, who are also creatures of God. One should give up all envious violence and learn to see God in everything by the process of Kṛṣṇa consciousness.

TEXT 42

कथं सेयमखण्डा भूः पूर्वैर्मे पुरुषैर्धृता ।
मत्पुत्रस्य च पौत्रस्य मत्पूर्वा वंशजस्य वा ॥ ४२ ॥

kathaṁ seyam akhaṇḍā bhūḥ
pūrvair me puruṣair dhṛtā
mat-putrasya ca pautrasya
mat-pūrvā vaṁśa-jasya vā

katham — how; *sā iyam* — this same; *akhaṇḍā* — unbounded; *bhūḥ* — earth; *pūrvaiḥ* — by the predecessors; *me* — my; *puruṣaiḥ* — by the personalities; *dhṛtā* — held in control; *mat-putrasya* — of my son; *ca* — and; *pautrasya* — of the grandson; *mat-pūrvā* — now under my sway; *vaṁśa-jasya* — of the descendant; *vā* — or.

TRANSLATION

[The materialistic king thinks:] "This unbounded earth was held by my predecessors and is now under my sovereignty. How can I arrange for it to remain in the hands of my sons, grandsons and other descendants ?"

PURPORT

This is an example of foolish possessiveness.

TEXT 43

तेजोऽबन्नमयं कायं गृहीत्वात्मतयाबुधाः ।
महीं ममतया चोभौ हित्वान्तेऽदर्शनं गताः ॥ ४३ ॥

tejo-'b-anna-mayaṁ kāyaṁ
gṛhītvātmatayābudhāḥ
mahīṁ mamatayā cobhau
hitvānte'darśanaṁ gatāḥ

tejaḥ—fire; *ap* — water; *anna* — and earth; *mayam* — composed of; *kāyam* — this body; *gṛhītvā* — accepting; *ātmatayā* — with the sense of "I"; *abudhāḥ*—the unintelligent; *mahīm* — this earth; *mamatayā* — with the sense of "my"; *ca* — and; *ubhau* — both; *hitvā* — giving up; *ante* — ultimately; *adarśanam* — disappearance; *gatāḥ*—they have obtained.

TRANSLATION

Although the foolish accept the body made of earth, water and fire as "me" and this earth as "mine," in every case they have ultimately abandoned both their body and the earth and passed away into oblivion.

PURPORT

Although the soul is eternal, our so-called family tradition and earthly fame will certainly pass into oblivion.

TEXT 44

ये ये भूपतयो राजन् भुञ्जते भुवमोजसा ।
कालेन ते कृताः सर्वे कथामात्राः कथासु च ॥ ४४ ॥

ye ye bhū-patayo rājan
bhuñjate bhuvam ojasā
kālena te kṛtāḥ sarve
kathā-mātrāḥ kathāsu ca

ye ye — whatever; *bhū-patayaḥ* — kings; *rājan* — O King Parīkṣit; *bhuñjate* — enjoy; *bhuvam* — the world; *ojasā* — with their power; *kālena* — by the force of time; *te* — they; *kṛtāḥ* — have been made; *sarve* — all; *kathā-mātrāḥ* — mere accounts; *kathāsu* — in various histories; *ca* — and.

TRANSLATION

My dear King Parīkṣit, all these kings who tried to enjoy the earth by their strength were reduced by the force of time to nothing more than historical accounts.

PURPORT

The word *rājan,* "O King," is significant in this verse. Parīkṣit Mahārāja was preparing to give up his body and go back home, back to Godhead, and Śukadeva Gosvāmī, his most merciful spiritual master, devastated any possible attachment that he might have to the position of king by showing the ultimate insignificance of such a position. By the causeless mercy of the spiritual master one is prepared to go back home, back to Godhead. The spiritual master teaches one to relax one's strong grip on material illusion and leave the kingdom of *māyā* behind. Although Śukadeva Gosvāmī speaks very bluntly within this chapter about the so-called glory of the material world, he is exhibiting the causeless mercy of the spiritual master, who takes his surrendered disciple back to the kingdom of Godhead, Vaikuṇṭha.

Thus end the purports of the humble servants of His Divine Grace A.C. Bhaktivedanta Swami Prabhupāda to the Twelfth Canto, Second Chapter, of the Śrīmad-Bhāgavatam, *entitled "The Symptoms of Kali-yuga."*

CHAPTER THREE

The Bhūmi-gītā

This chapter describes how the earth took note of the foolishness of the many kings bent on conquering her. It also describes how even though the age of Kali is full of faults, the glorification of the name of Lord Hari destroys them all.

Great kings, who are actually just playthings of death, desire to subdue their six internal enemies — the five senses and the mind — and afterward they imagine they will go on to conquer the earth and all its oceans. Seeing their false hopes, the earth simply laughs, for eventually they all must leave this planet and go elsewhere, as have all the great kings and monarchs of the past. Moreover, after usurping the earth or some part of it — which is actually unconquerable and must in every case be given up — fathers, sons, brothers, friends and relatives quarrel over it.

Thus the study of history naturally leads to the conclusion that all worldly achievements are temporary, and this conclusion should give rise to a sense of renunciation. Ultimately, the highest goal of life for any living entity is pure devotion to Lord Kṛṣṇa, which annihilates all inauspiciousness. In the age of Satya, religion was complete, still possessing its four legs of truth, mercy, austerity and charity. With the coming of each succeeding age, starting with Tretā, these religious qualities each diminish by one quarter. In Kali-yuga the legs of religion retain only one fourth of their power, and even that will be lost with the progress of the age. The mode of goodness is predominant during Satya-yuga, and the mode of passion is predominant during the Tretā-yuga. The mixed modes of passion and ignorance are predominant during Dvāpara-yuga, and in the age of Kali the mode of ignorance is predominant. Atheism, the smallness and inferiority of all things, and devotion to the genitals and belly are very much evident in the age of Kali. Living entities contaminated by the influence of Kali do not worship the Supreme Lord, Śrī Hari, even though they can be freed from all bondage and easily achieve the supreme destination simply by chanting the glories of His name and taking shelter of Him. But if somehow or other the Supreme Personality of Godhead becomes manifest within the hearts of the conditioned souls in Kali-yuga, then all faults of place, time and personality inherent in the age will be destroyed. Kali-yuga is an ocean of faults, but it possesses one great quality: simply by the chanting of the name of Kṛṣṇa, one can be delivered from material association and attain the Absolute Truth. All that was accomplished in the age of Satya by meditation, in the age of Tretā by sacrificial performances and in the age of Dvāpara by temple worship is easily gained during the Kali-yuga by the simple process of *hari-kīrtana.*

TEXT 1

श्रीशुक उवाच
दृष्ट्वात्मनि जये व्यग्रान्नृपान् हसति भूरियम् ।
अहो मा विजिगीषन्ति मृत्योः क्रीडनका नृपाः ॥ १ ॥

śrī-śuka uvāca
dṛṣṭvātmani jaye vyagrān
nṛpān hasati bhūr iyam
aho mā vijigīṣanti
mṛtyoḥ krīḍanakā nṛpāḥ

śrī-śukaḥ uvāca — Śrī Śukadeva Gosvāmī said; *dṛṣṭvā* — observing; *ātmani* — of herself; *jaye* — in conquest; *vyagrān* — busily engaged; *nṛpān* — the kings; *hasati* — she laughs; *bhūḥ*—the earth; *iyam* — this; *aho* — ah; *mā* — me; *vijigīṣanti* — they are desiring to conquer; *mṛtyoḥ*—of death; *krīḍanakāḥ*—playthings; *nṛpāḥ*—the kings.

TRANSLATION

Śukadeva Gosvāmī said: Seeing the kings of this earth busy trying to conquer her, the earth herself laughed. She said: "Just see how these kings, who are actually playthings in the hands of death, are desiring to conquer me."

TEXT 2

काम एष नरेन्द्राणां मोघः स्याद् विदुषामपि।
येन फेनोपमे पिण्डे येऽतिविश्रम्भिता नृपाः ॥ २ ॥

kāma eṣa narendrāṇāṁ
moghaḥ syād viduṣām api
yena phenopame piṇḍe
ye'ti-viśrambhitā nṛpāḥ

kāmaḥ—lust; *eṣaḥ*—this; *nara-indrāṇām*—of the rulers of men; *moghaḥ*—the failure; *syāt*—becomes; *viduṣām*—who are wise; *api*—even; *yena*—by which (lust); *phena-upame*—comparable to ephemeral bubbles; *piṇḍe*—in this lump; *ye*—who; *ati-viśrambhitāḥ*—perfectly trusting; *nṛpāḥ*—the kings.

TRANSLATION

"Great rulers of men, even those who are learned, meet frustration and failure because of material lust. Driven by lust, these kings place great hope and faith in the dead lump of flesh called the body, even though the material frame is as fleeting as bubbles of foam on water."

TEXTS 3–4

पूर्वं निर्जित्य षड्वर्गं जेष्यामो राजमन्त्रिणः ।
ततः सचिवपौराप्तकरीन्द्रानस्य कण्टकान् ॥ ३ ॥
एवं क्रमेण जेष्यामः पृथ्वीं सागरमेखलाम् ।
इत्याशाबद्धहृदया न पश्यन्त्यन्तिकेऽन्तकम् ॥ ४ ॥

pūrvaṁ nirjitya ṣaḍ-vargaṁ
jeṣyāmo rāja-mantriṇaḥ
tataḥ saciva-paurāpta-
karīndrān asya kaṇṭakān

evaṁ krameṇa jeṣyāmaḥ
pṛthvīṁ sāgara-mekhalām
ity āśā-baddha-hṛdayā
na paśyanty antike 'ntakam

pūrvam—first of all; *nirjitya*—conquering; *ṣaṭ-vargam*—the five senses and the mind; *jeṣyāmaḥ*—we will conquer; *rāja-mantriṇaḥ*—the royal ministers; *tataḥ*—then; *saciva*—the personal secretaries; *paura*—the citizens of the capital; *āpta*—the friends; *kari-indrān*—the elephant keepers; *asya*—ridding ourselves of; *kaṇṭakān*—the thorns; *evam*—in this way; *krameṇa*—gradually; *jeṣyāmaḥ*—we shall conquer; *pṛthvīm*—the earth; *sāgara*—the ocean; *mekhalām*—whose girdle; *iti*—thus thinking; *āśā*—by hopes; *baddha*—bound up; *hṛdayāḥ*—their hearts; *na paśyanti*—they do not see; *antike*—nearby; *antakam*—their own end.

TRANSLATION

"Kings and politicians imagine: 'First I will conquer my senses and mind; then I will subdue my chief ministers and rid myself of the thorn-pricks of my advisors, citizens, friends and relatives, as well as the keepers of my elephants. In this way I will gradually conquer the entire earth.' Because the hearts of these leaders are bound by great expectations, they fail to see death waiting nearby."

PURPORT

To satisfy their greed for power, determined politicians, dictators and military leaders undergo severe austerities and sacrifice, with much self-discipline. Then they lead their great nations in a struggle to control the sea, land, air and space. Although the politicians and their followers will soon be dead — since birth and death are all inevitable in this world — they persist in their frenetic struggle for ephemeral glory.

TEXT 5

समुद्रावरणां जित्वा मां विशन्त्यब्धिमोजसा ।
कियदात्मजयस्यैतन्मुक्तिरात्मजये फलम् ॥ ५ ॥

samudrāvaraṇāṁ jitvā
māṁ viśanty abdhim ojasā
kiyad ātma-jayasyaitan
muktir ātma-jaye phalam

samudra-āvaraṇām — bounded by the ocean; *jitvā* — having conquered; *mām* — me; *viśanti* — they enter; *abdhim* — the ocean; *ojasā* — by their strength; *kiyat* — how much; *ātma-jayasya* — of victory over the self; *etat* — this; *muktiḥ*—liberation; *ātma-jaye* — of victory over the self; *phalam* — the fruit.

TRANSLATION

"After conquering all the land on my surface, these proud kings forcibly enter the ocean to conquer the sea itself. What is the use of their self-control, which is aimed at political exploitation? The actual goal of self-control is spiritual liberation."

TEXT 6

यां विसृज्यैव मनवस्तत्सुताश्च कुरूद्वह ।
गता यथागतं युद्धे तां मां जेष्यन्त्यबुद्धयः ॥ ६ ॥

yāṁ visṛjyaiva manavas
tat-sutāś ca kurūdvaha
gatā yathāgataṁ yuddhe
tāṁ māṁ jeṣyanty abuddhayaḥ

yām — whom; *visṛjya* — giving up; *eva* — indeed; *manavaḥ* — human beings; *tat-sutāḥ* — their sons; *ca* — also; *kuru-udvaha* — O best of the Kurus; *gatāḥ* — gone away; *yathā-āgatam* — just as they had originally come; *yuddhe* — in battle; *tām* — that; *mām* — me, the earth; *jeṣyanti* — they try to conquer; *abuddhayaḥ* — unintelligent.

TRANSLATION

O best of the Kurus, the earth continued as follows: "Although in the past great men and their descendants have left me, departing from this world in the same helpless way they came into it, even today foolish men are trying to conquer me."

TEXT 7

मत्कृते पितृपुत्राणां भ्रातॄणां चापि विग्रहः ।
जायते ह्यसतां राज्ये ममताबद्धचेतसाम् ॥ ७ ॥

mat-kṛte pitṛ-putrāṇāṁ
bhrātṝṇāṁ cāpi vigrahaḥ
jāyate hy asatāṁ rājye
mamatā-baddha-cetasām

mat-kṛte — for the sake of me; *pitṛ-putrāṇām* — between fathers and sons; *bhrātṝṇām* — among brothers; *ca* — and; *api* — also; *vigrahaḥ* — conflict; *jāyate* — arises; *hi* — indeed; *asatām* — among the materialistic; *rājye* — for political rule; *mamatā* — by the sense of possession; *baddha* — bound up; *cetasām* — whose hearts.

TRANSLATION

"For the sake of conquering me, materialistic persons fight one another. Fathers oppose their sons, and brothers fight one another, because their hearts are bound to possessing political power."

TEXT 8

ममैवेयं मही कृत्स्ना न ते मूढेति वादिनः ।
स्पर्धमाना मिथो घ्नन्ति म्रियन्ते मत्कृते नृपाः ॥ ८ ॥

mamaiveyaṁ mahī kṛtsnā
na te mūḍheti vādinaḥ
spardhamānā mitho ghnanti
mriyante mat-kṛte nṛpāḥ

mama — mine; *eva* — indeed; *iyam* — this; *mahī* — land; *kṛtsnā* — entire; *na* — not; *te* — yours; *mūḍha* — you fool; *iti vādinaḥ* — thus speaking; *spardhamānāḥ* — quarreling; *mithaḥ* — each other; *ghnanti* — they kill; *mriyante* — they are killed; *mat-kṛte* — for my sake; *nṛpāḥ* — kings.

TRANSLATION

"Political leaders challenge one another: 'All this land is mine! It's not yours, you fool!' Thus they attack one another and die."

PURPORT

This verse describes with brilliant clarity the mundane political mentality that provokes innumerable conflicts in the world. For example, as we prepare this translation of *Śrīmad-Bhāgavatam,* British and Argentine military forces are bitterly fighting over the tiny Falkland Islands.

The fact is that the Supreme Lord is the proprietor of all land. Of course, even in a God-conscious world political boundaries exist. But in such a God-conscious atmosphere political tensions are greatly eased, and people of all lands welcome each other and respect each other's right to live in peace.

TEXTS 9–13

पृथुः पुरूरवा गाधिर्नहुषो भरतोऽर्जुनः ।
मान्धाता सगरो रामः खट्वांगो धुन्धुहा रघुः ॥ ९ ॥

तृणबिन्दुर्ययातिश्च शर्यातिः शन्तनुर्गयः ।
भगीरथः कुवलयाश्वः ककुत्स्थो नैषधो नृगः ॥ १० ॥
हिरण्यकशिपुर्वृत्रो रावणो लोकरावणः ।
नमुचिः शम्बरो भौमो हिरण्याक्षोऽथ तारकः ॥ ११ ॥
अन्ये च बहवो दैत्या राजानो ये महेश्वराः ।
सर्वे सर्वविदः शूराः सर्वे सर्वजितोऽजिताः ॥ १२ ॥
ममतां मय्यवर्तन्त कृत्वोच्चैर्मर्त्यधर्मिणः ।
कथावशेषाः कालेन ह्यकृतार्थाः कृता विभो ॥ १३ ॥

pṛthuḥ purūravā gādhir
nahuṣo bharato 'rjunaḥ
māndhātā sagaro rāmaḥ
khaṭvāṅgo dhundhuhā raghuḥ

tṛṇabindur yayātiś ca
śaryātiḥ śantanur gayaḥ
bhagīrathaḥ kuvalayāśvaḥ
kakutstho naiṣadho nṛgaḥ

hiraṇyakaśipur vṛtro
rāvaṇo loka-rāvaṇaḥ
namuciḥ śambaro bhaumo
hiraṇyākṣo 'tha tārakaḥ

anye ca bahavo daityā
rājāno ye maheśvarāḥ
sarve sarva-vidaḥ śūrāḥ
sarve sarva-jito 'jitāḥ

mamatāṁ mayy avartanta
kṛtvoccair martya-dharmiṇaḥ
kathāvaśeṣāḥ kālena
hy akṛtārthāḥ kṛtā vibho

pṛthuḥ purūravāḥ gādhiḥ—Mahārājas Pṛthu, Purūravā and Gādhi; *nahuṣaḥ bharataḥ arjunaḥ*—Nahuṣa, Bharata and Kārtavīrya Arjuna; *māndhātā sagaraḥ rāmaḥ*—Māndhātā, Sagara and Rāma; *khaṭvāṅgaḥ dhundhuhā raghuḥ*—Khaṭvāṅga, Dhundhuhā and Raghu; *tṛṇabinduḥ yayātiḥ ca*—

Tṛṇabindu and Yayāti; *śaryātiḥ śantanuḥ gayaḥ*—Śaryāti, Śantanu and Gaya; *bhagīrathaḥ kuvalayāśvaḥ*—Bhagīratha and Kuvalayāśva; *kakutsthaḥ naiṣadhaḥ nṛgaḥ*—Kakutstha, Naiṣadha and Nṛga; *hiraṇyakaśipuḥ vṛtraḥ*—Hiraṇyakaśipu and Vṛtrāsura; *rāvaṇaḥ*—Rāvaṇa; *loka-rāvaṇaḥ*—who made the whole world cry; *namuciḥ śambaraḥ bhaumaḥ*—Namuci, Śambara and Bhauma; *hiraṇyākṣaḥ*—Hiraṇyākṣa; *atha* — and; *tārakaḥ*—Tāraka; *anye* — others; *ca* — as well; *bahavaḥ*—many; *daityāḥ*—demons; *rājānaḥ*—kings; *ye* — who; *mahā-īśvarāḥ*—great controllers; *sarve* — all of them; *sarva-vidaḥ*—all-knowing; *śūrāḥ*—heroes; *sarve* — all; *sarva-jitaḥ*—all-conquering; *ajitāḥ*—unconquerable; *mamatām* — possessiveness; *mayi* — for me; *avartanta* — they lived; *kṛtvā* — expressing; *uccaiḥ*—to a great degree; *martya-dharmiṇaḥ*—subject to the laws of birth and death; *kathā-avaśeṣāḥ* —remaining merely as historical narrations; *kālena* — by the force of time; *hi* — indeed; *akṛta-arthāḥ*—incomplete in perfecting their desires; *kṛtāḥ*—they have been made; *vibho* — O Lord.

TRANSLATION

"Such kings as Pṛthu, Purūravā, Gādhi, Nahuṣa, Bharata, Kārtavīrya Arjuna, Māndhātā, Sagara, Rāma, Khaṭvāṅga, Dhundhuhā, Raghu, Tṛṇabindu, Yayāti, Śaryāti, Śantanu, Gaya, Bhagīratha, Kuvalayāśva, Kakutstha, Naiṣadha, Nṛga, Hiraṇyakaśipu, Vṛtra, Rāvaṇa, who made the whole world lament, Namuci, Śambara, Bhauma, Hiraṇyākṣa and Tāraka, as well as many other demons and kings who possessed great powers of control over others, were all full of knowledge, heroic, all-conquering and unconquerable. Nevertheless, O almighty Lord, although they lived their lives intensely trying to possess me, these kings were subject to the passage of time, which reduced them all to mere historical accounts. None of them could permanently establish their rule."

PURPORT

According to Śrīla Śrīdhara Svāmī, and as confirmed by Śrīla Viśvanātha Cakravartī Ṭhākura, the King Rāma mentioned here is not the incarnation of Godhead Rāmacandra. Pṛthu Mahārāja is understood to be an incarnation of the Supreme Personality of Godhead who completely exhibited the characteristics of an earthly king, claiming proprietorship over the entire earth. A saintly king like Pṛthu Mahārāja, however, controls the earth on behalf of the Supreme Personality of Godhead, whereas a demon such as Hiraṇyakaśipu or Rāvaṇa tries to exploit the earth for his personal sense gratification.

Nevertheless, both saintly kings and demons must leave the earth. In this way their political supremacy is ultimately neutralized by the force of time.

Modern political leaders cannot even temporarily control the entire earth, nor are their opulences and intelligence unlimited. Possessing hopelessly fragmented power, enjoying a minuscule life span, and lacking deep existential intelligence, modern leaders inevitably are symbols of frustration and misdirected ambition.

TEXT 14

कथा इमास्ते कथिता महीयसां
विताय लोकेषु यशः परेयुषाम् ।
विज्ञानवैराग्यविवक्षया विभो
वचोविभूतीर्न तु पारमार्थ्यम् ॥१४॥

kathā imās te kathitā mahīyasāṁ
vitāya lokeṣu yaśaḥ pareyuṣām
vijñāna-vairāgya-vivakṣayā vibho
vaco-vibhūtīr na tu pāramārthyam

kathāḥ—the narrations; *imāḥ*—these; *te*— unto you; *kathitāḥ*—have been spoken; *mahīyasām*— of great kings; *vitāya*— spreading; *lokeṣu*— throughout all the worlds; *yaśaḥ*—their fame; *pareyuṣām*— who have departed; *vijñāna*— transcendental knowledge; *vairāgya*— and renunciation; *vivakṣayā*— with the desire for teaching; *vibho*— O mighty Parīkṣit; *vacaḥ*—of words; *vibhūtīḥ*—the decoration; *na*— not; *tu*— but; *pārama-arthyam*— of the most essential purport.

TRANSLATION

Śukadeva Gosvāmī said: O mighty Parīkṣit, I have related to you the narrations of all these great kings, who spread their fame throughout the world and then departed. My real purpose was to teach transcendental knowledge and renunciation. Stories of kings lend power and opulence to these narrations but do not in themselves constitute the ultimate aspect of knowledge.

PURPORT

Since all the narrations of *Śrīmad-Bhāgavatam* bring the reader to the perfection of transcendental knowledge, they all give supreme spiritual lessons though apparently dealing with kings or other mundane subject matter. In relation with Kṛṣṇa, all ordinary topics become transcendental narrations, with the power to bring the reader to the perfection of life.

TEXT 15

यस्तूत्तमःश्लोकगुणानुवादः
संगीयतेऽभीक्ष्णममंगलघ्नः ।
तमेव नित्यं शृणुयादभीक्ष्णं
कृष्णेऽमलां भक्तिमभीप्समानः ॥ १५ ॥

yas tūttamaḥ-śloka-guṇānuvādaḥ
saṅgīyate'bhīkṣṇam amaṅgala-ghnaḥ
tam eva nityaṁ śṛṇuyād abhīkṣṇaṁ
kṛṣṇe'malāṁ bhaktim abhīpsamānaḥ

yaḥ—which; *tu* — on the other hand; *uttamaḥ-śloka* — of the Supreme Personality of Godhead, who is praised in transcendental verses; *guṇa* — of the qualities; *anuvādaḥ*—the recounting; *saṅgīyate* — is sung; *abhīkṣṇam* — always; *amaṅgala-ghnaḥ*—which destroys everything inauspicious; *tam* — that; *eva* — indeed; *nityam* — regularly; *śṛṇuyāt* — one should hear; *abhīkṣṇam* — constantly; *kṛṣṇe* — unto Lord Kṛṣṇa; *amalām* — untainted; *bhaktim* — devotional service; *abhīpsamānaḥ*—he who desires.

TRANSLATION

The person who desires pure devotional service to Lord Kṛṣṇa should hear the narrations of Lord Uttamaḥśloka's glorious qualities, the constant chanting of which destroys everything inauspicious. The devotee should engage in such listening in regular daily assemblies and should also continue his hearing throughout the day.

PURPORT

Since any topic related to Lord Kṛṣṇa is auspicious and transcendental, the direct narration of Lord Kṛṣṇa's own activities, political and nonpolitical, is certainly the supreme subject matter for hearing. The word *nityam* here indicates regulated cultivation of the topics of Lord Kṛṣṇa, and *abhīkṣṇam* indicates constant remembrance of such regulated spiritual experiences.

TEXT 16

श्रीराजोवाच
केनोपायेन भगवन् कलेर्दोषान् कलौ जनाः ।
विधमिष्यन्त्युपचितांस्तन्मे ब्रूहि यथा मुने ॥ १६ ॥

śrī-rājovāca
kenopāyena bhagavan
kaler doṣān kalau janāḥ
vidhamiṣyanty upacitāṁs
tan me brūhi yathā mune

śrī-rājā uvāca — King Parīkṣit said; *kena* — by what; *upāyena* — means; *bhagavan* — my dear lord; *kaleḥ* — of the age of Kali; *doṣān* — the faults; *kalau* — living in Kali-yuga; *janāḥ* — people; *vidhamiṣyanti* — will eradicate; *upacitān* — accumulated; *tat* — that; *me* — to me; *brūhi* — please explain; *yathā* — fittingly; *mune* — O sage.

TRANSLATION

King Parīkṣit said: My lord, how can persons living in the age of Kali rid themselves of the cumulative contamination of this age? O great sage, please explain this to me.

PURPORT

King Parīkṣit was a compassionate, saintly ruler. Thus, after hearing of the abominable qualities of the age of Kali, he naturally inquired as to how those born in this age can free themselves of its inherent contamination.

TEXT 17

युगानि युगधर्मांश्च मानं प्रलयकल्पयोः ।
कालस्येश्वररूपस्य गतिं विष्णोर्महात्मनः ॥ १७ ॥

yugāni yuga-dharmāṁś ca
mānaṁ pralaya-kalpayoḥ
kālasyeśvara-rūpasya
gatiṁ viṣṇor mahātmanaḥ

yugāni — the ages of the universal history; *yuga-dharmān* — the special qualities of each age; *ca* — and; *mānam* — the measurement; *pralaya* — of annihilation; *kalpayoḥ* — and of universal maintenance; *kālasya* — of time; *īśvara-rūpasya* — the representation of the Personality of Godhead; *gatim* — the movement; *viṣṇoḥ* — of Lord Viṣṇu; *mahā-ātmanaḥ* — the Supreme Soul.

TRANSLATION

Please explain the different ages of universal history, the special qualities of each age, the duration of cosmic maintenance and destruction, and the movement of time, which is the direct representation of the Supreme Soul, the Personality of Godhead, Lord Viṣṇu.

TEXT 18

श्रीशुक उवाच
कृते प्रवर्तते धर्मश्चतुष्पात्तज्जनैर्धृतः ।
सत्यं दया तपो दानमिति पादा विभोर्नृप ॥ १८ ॥

śrī-śuka uvāca
kṛte pravartate dharmaś
catuṣ-pāt taj-janair dhṛtaḥ
satyaṁ dayā tapo dānam
iti pādā vibhor nṛpa

śrī-śukaḥ uvāca — Śrī Śukadeva Gosvāmī said; *kṛte* — in the Satya-yuga, the age of truth; *pravartate* — exists; *dharmaḥ* — religion; *catuḥ-pāt* — with four legs; *tat* — of that age; *janaiḥ* — by the people; *dhṛtaḥ* — maintained; *satyam* — truth; *dayā* — mercy; *tapaḥ* — austerity; *dānam* — charity; *iti* — thus; *pādāḥ* — the legs; *vibhoḥ* — of mighty religion; *nṛpa* — O King.

TRANSLATION

Śukadeva Gosvāmī said: My dear King, in the beginning, during Satya-yuga, the age of truth, religion is present with all four of its legs intact and is carefully maintained by the people of that age. These four legs of powerful religion are truthfulness, mercy, austerity and charity.

PURPORT

Just as there are four seasons, there are four ages of the earth, each lasting hundreds of thousands of years. The first of these is Satya-yuga, when such good qualities as charity are prominent.

Actual charity, here referred to as *dānam*, is to award fearlessness and freedom to others, not to give them some material means of temporary pleasure or relief. Any material "charitable" arrangement will inevitably be crushed by the onward march of time. Thus only realization of one's eternal existence beyond the reach of time can make one fearless, and only freedom from material desire constitutes real freedom, for it enables one to escape the bondage of the laws of nature. Therefore real charity is to help people revive their eternal, spiritual consciousness.

Religion is here referred to as *vibhu*, "the mighty," because universal religious principles are not different from the Supreme Lord Himself and ultimately lead one to His kingdom. The qualities mentioned here — truthfulness, mercy, austerity and charity — are universal, nonsectarian aspects of pious life.

In the First Canto of *Śrīmad-Bhāgavatam*, the fourth leg of religion is listed as cleanliness. According to Śrīla Viśvanātha Cakravartī Ṭhākura, this is an alternative definition of the word *dānam* in the present context.

TEXT 19

सन्तुष्टाः करुणा मैत्राः शान्ता दान्तास्तितिक्षवः ।
आत्मारामाः समदृशः प्रायशः श्रमणा जनाः ॥ १९ ॥

santuṣṭāḥ karuṇā maitrāḥ
śāntā dāntās titikṣavaḥ
ātmārāmāḥ sama-dṛśaḥ
prāyaśaḥ śramaṇā janāḥ

santuṣṭāḥ—self-satisfied; *karuṇāḥ*—merciful; *maitrāḥ*—friendly; *śāntāḥ*—pacified; *dāntāḥ*—self-controlled; *titikṣavaḥ*—tolerant; *ātma-ārāmāḥ*—enthused from within; *sama-dṛśaḥ*—possessed of equal vision; *prāyaśaḥ*—for the most part; *śramaṇāḥ*—endeavoring diligently (for self-realization); *janāḥ*—the people.

TRANSLATION

The people of Satya-yuga are for the most part self-satisfied, merciful, friendly to all, peaceful, sober and tolerant. They take their pleasure from within, see all things equally and always endeavor diligently for spiritual perfection.

PURPORT

Sama-darśana, equal vision, is based on the perception of the Supreme Spirit behind all material variety and within all living entities.

TEXT 20

त्रेतायां धर्मपादानां तुर्यांशो हीयते शनैः ।
अधर्मपादैरनृतहिंसासन्तोषविग्रहैः ॥ २० ॥

tretāyāṁ dharma-pādānāṁ
turyāṁśo hīyate śanaiḥ
adharma-pādair anṛta-
hiṁṣāsantoṣa-vigrahaiḥ

tretāyām — in the second age; *dharma-pādānām* — of the legs of religion; *turya* — one fourth; *aṁśaḥ*—part; *hīyate* — is lost; *śanaiḥ*—gradually; *adharma-pādaiḥ*—by the legs of irreligion; *anṛta* — by falsity; *hiṁsā* — violence; *asantoṣa* — dissatisfaction; *vigrahaiḥ*—and quarrel.

TRANSLATION

In Tretā-yuga each leg of religion is gradually reduced by one quarter by the influence of the four pillars of irreligion — lying, violence, dissatisfaction and quarrel.

PURPORT

By falsity truth is diminished, by violence mercy is diminished, by dissatisfaction austerity is diminished, and by quarrel charity and cleanliness are diminished.

TEXT 21

तदा क्रियातपोनिष्ठा नातिहिंस्रा न लम्पटाः ।
त्रैवर्गिकास्त्रयीवृद्धा वर्णा ब्रह्मोत्तरा नृप ॥ २१ ॥

tadā kriyā-tapo-niṣṭhā
nāti-hiṁsrā na lampaṭāḥ
trai-vargikās trayī-vṛddhā
varṇā brahmottarā nṛpa

tadā — then (in the Tretā age); *kriyā* — to ritualistic ceremonies; *tapaḥ* — and to penances; *niṣṭhāḥ* — devoted; *na ati-hiṁsrāḥ* — not excessively violent; *na lampaṭāḥ* — not wantonly desiring sense gratification; *trai-vargikāḥ* — interested in the three principles of religiosity, economic development and sense gratification; *trayī* — by the three *Vedas; vṛddhāḥ* — made prosperous; *varṇāḥ* — the four classes of society; *brahma-uttarāḥ* — mostly *brāhmaṇas; nṛpa* — O King.

TRANSLATION

In the Tretā age people are devoted to ritual performances and severe austerities. They are not excessively violent or very lusty after sensual pleasure. Their interest lies primarily in religiosity, economic development and regulated sense gratification, and they achieve prosperity by following the prescriptions of the three Vedas. Although in this age society evolves into four separate classes, O King, most people are brāhmaṇas.

TEXT 22

तपःसत्यदयादानेष्वर्धं ह्रस्वति द्वापरे ।
हिंसातुष्ट्यनृतद्वेषैर्धर्मस्याधर्मलक्षणैः ॥ २२ ॥

tapaḥ-satya-dayā-dāneṣv
ardhaṁ hrasvati dvāpare
hiṁsātuṣṭy-anṛta-dveṣair
dharmasyādharma-lakṣaṇaiḥ

tapaḥ — of austerity; *satya* — truth; *dayā* — mercy; *dāneṣu* — and charity; *ardham* — one half; *hrasvati* — diminishes; *dvāpare* — in the age of Dvāpara; *hiṁsā* — by violence; *atuṣṭi* — dissatisfaction; *anṛta* — untruth; *dveṣaiḥ* — and hatred; *dharmasya* — of religion; *adharma-lakṣaṇaiḥ* — by the qualities of irreligion.

TRANSLATION

In Dvāpara-yuga the religious qualities of austerity, truth, mercy and charity are reduced to one half by their irreligious counterparts — dissatisfaction, untruth, violence and enmity.

TEXT 23

यशस्विनो महाशीलाः स्वाध्यायाध्ययने रताः ।
आढ्याः कुटुम्बिनो हृष्टा वर्णाः क्षत्रद्विजोत्तराः ॥ २३ ॥

yaśasvino mahā-śīlāḥ
svādhyāyādhyayane ratāḥ
āḍhyāḥ kuṭumbino hṛṣṭā
varṇāḥ kṣatra-dvijottarāḥ

yaśasvinaḥ—eager for glory; *mahā-śīlāḥ*—noble; *svādhyāya-adhyayane* —in study of the Vedic literature; *ratāḥ*—absorbed; *āḍhyāḥ*—endowed with opulence; *kuṭumbinaḥ*—having large families; *hṛṣṭāḥ*—joyful; *varṇāḥ*—the four classes of society; *kṣatra-dvija-uttarāḥ*—represented mostly by the *kṣatriyas* and *brāhmaṇas.*

TRANSLATION

In the Dvāpara age people are interested in glory and are very noble. They devote themselves to the study of the Vedas, possess great opulence, support large families and enjoy life with vigor. Of the four classes, the kṣatriyas and brāhmaṇas are most numerous.

TEXT 24

कलौ तु धर्मपादानां तुर्यांशोऽधर्महेतुभिः ।
एधमानैः क्षीयमाणो ह्यन्ते सोपि विनङ्क्ष्यति ॥ २४ ॥

kalau tu dharma-pādānāṁ
turyāṁśo'dharma-hetubhiḥ
edhamānaiḥ kṣīyamāṇo
hy ante so'pi vinaṅkṣyati

kalau — in the age of Kali; *tu* — and; *dharma-pādānām* — of the legs of religion; *turya-aṁśaḥ*—one fourth; *adharma* — of irreligion; *hetubhiḥ*—by the principles; *edhamānaiḥ*—which are increasing; *kṣīyamāṇaḥ*—decreasing; *hi* — indeed; *ante* — in the end; *saḥ*—that one quarter; *api* — also; *vinaṅkṣyati* — will be destroyed.

TRANSLATION

In the age of Kali only one fourth of the religious principles remains. That last remnant will continuously be decreased by the ever-increasing principles of irreligion and will finally be destroyed.

TEXT 25

तस्मिन् लुब्धा दुराचारा निर्दयाः शुष्कवैरिणः ।
दुर्भगा भूरितर्षाश्च शूद्रदासोत्तराः प्रजाः ॥ २५ ॥

tasmin lubdhā durācārā
nirdayāḥ śuṣka-vairiṇaḥ
durbhagā bhūri-tarṣāś ca
śūdra-dāsottarāḥ prajāḥ

tasmin — in that age; *lubdhāḥ*—greedy; *durācārāḥ*—ill-behaved; *nirdayāḥ*—merciless; *śuṣka-vairiṇaḥ*—prone to useless quarrel; *durbhagāḥ*—unfortunate; *bhūri-tarṣāḥ*—obsessed by many kinds of hankering; *ca* — and; *śūdra-dāsa-uttarāḥ*—predominantly low-class laborers and barbarians; *prajāḥ*—the people.

TRANSLATION

In the Kali age people tend to be greedy, ill-behaved and merciless, and they fight one another without good reason. Unfortunate and obsessed with material desires, the people of Kali-yuga are almost all śūdras and barbarians.

PURPORT

In this age, we can already observe that most people are laborers, clerks, fishermen, artisans or other kinds of workers within the *śūdra* category. Enlightened devotees of God and noble political leaders are extremely scarce, and even independent businessmen and farmers are a vanishing breed as huge business conglomerates increasingly convert them into subservient employees. Vast regions of the earth are already populated by barbarians and semibarbarous peoples, making the entire situation dangerous and bleak. The Kṛṣṇa consciousness movement is empowered to rectify the current dismal state of affairs. It is the only hope for the ghastly age called Kali-yuga.

TEXT 26

सत्त्वं रजस्तम इति दृश्यन्ते पुरुषे गुणाः ।
कालसञ्चोदितास्ते वै परिवर्तन्त आत्मनि ॥ २६ ॥

sattvaṁ rajas tama iti
dṛśyante puruṣe guṇāḥ
kāla-sañcoditās te vai
parivartanta ātmani

sattvam — goodness; *rajaḥ*—passion; *tamaḥ*—ignorance; *iti* — thus; *dṛśyante* — are seen; *puruṣe* — in a person; *guṇāḥ*—the modes of material nature; *kāla-sañcoditāḥ*—impelled by time; *te* — they; *vai* — indeed; *parivartante* — undergo permutation; *ātmani* — within the mind.

TRANSLATION

The material modes — goodness, passion and ignorance — whose permutations are observed within a person's mind, are set into motion by the power of time.

PURPORT

The four ages described in these verses are manifestations of various modes of material nature. The age of truth, Satya-yuga, manifests the predominance of material goodness, and Kali-yuga manifests the predominance of ignorance. According to Śrīla Viśvanātha Cakravartī Ṭhākura, within each age the other three ages occasionally manifest as sub-ages. Thus even within Satya-yuga a demon in the mode of ignorance may appear, and within the age of Kali the highest religious principles may flourish for some time. As described in *Śrīmad-Bhāgavatam,* the three modes of nature are present everywhere and in everything, but the predominant mode, or combination of modes, determines the general character of any material phenomenon. In each age, therefore, the three modes are present in varying proportions. The particular age represented by goodness (Satya), passion (Tretā), passion and ignorance (Dvāpara) or ignorance (Kali) exists within each of the other ages as a subfactor.

TEXT 27

प्रभवन्ति यदा सत्त्वे मनोबुद्धीन्द्रियाणि च ।
तदा कृतयुगं विद्याज्ज्ञाने तपसि यद् रुचिः ॥ २७ ॥

prabhavanti yadā sattve
mano-buddhīndriyāṇi ca
tadā kṛta-yugaṁ vidyāj
jñāne tapasi yad ruciḥ

prabhavanti — they are predominantly manifest; *yadā* — when; *sattve* — in the mode of goodness; *manaḥ*—the mind; *buddhi* — intelligence; *indriyāṇi* — senses; *ca* — and; *tadā* — then; *kṛta-yugam* — the age of Kṛta; *vidyāt* — should be understood; *jñāne* — in knowledge; *tapasi* — and austerity; *yat* — when; *ruciḥ*—pleasure.

TRANSLATION

When the mind, intelligence and senses are solidly fixed in the mode of goodness, that time should be understood as Satya-yuga, the age of truth. People then take pleasure in knowledge and austerity.

PURPORT

The word *kṛta* means "performed" or "executed." Thus in the age of truth all religious duties are duly performed, and people take great pleasure in spiritual knowledge and austerity. Even in the Kali-yuga, those who are situated in the mode of goodness take pleasure in the cultivation of spiritual knowledge and the regulated performance of austerity. This sublime state of existence is possible for one who has conquered sex desire.

TEXT 28

यदा कर्मसु काम्येषु भक्तिर्यशसि देहिनाम् ।
तदा त्रेता रजोवृत्तिरिति जानीहि बुद्धिमन् ॥ २८ ॥

yadā karmasu kāmyeṣu
bhaktir yaśasi dehinām
tadā tretā rajo-vṛttir
iti jānīhi buddhiman

yadā — when; *karmasu* — in duties; *kāmyeṣu* — based on selfish desire; *bhaktiḥ*—devotion; *yaśasi* — in honor; *dehinām* — of the embodied souls; *tadā* — then; *tretā* — the age of Tretā; *rajaḥ-vṛttiḥ*—predominated by activities in the mode of passion; *iti* — thus; *jānīhi* — you should understand; *buddhi-man* — O intelligent King Parīkṣit.

TRANSLATION

O most intelligent one, when the conditioned souls are devoted to their duties but have ulterior motives and seek personal prestige, you should understand such a situation to be the age of Tretā, in which the functions of passion are prominent.

TEXT 29

यदा लोभस्त्वसन्तोषो मानो दम्भोऽथ मत्सरः ।
कर्मणां चापि काम्यानां द्वापरं तद् रजस्तमः ॥ २९ ॥

yadā lobhas tv asantoṣo
māno dambho'tha matsaraḥ
karmaṇāṁ cāpi kāmyānāṁ
dvāparaṁ tad rajas-tamaḥ

yadā — when; *lobhaḥ* — greed; *tu* — indeed; *asantoṣaḥ* — dissatisfaction; *mānaḥ* — false pride; *dambhaḥ* — hypocrisy; *atha* — and; *matsaraḥ* — envy; *karmaṇām* — of activities; *ca* — and; *api* — also; *kāmyānām* — selfish; *dvāparam* — the age of Dvāpara; *tat* — that; *rajaḥ-tamaḥ* — predominated by a mixture of the modes of passion and ignorance.

TRANSLATION

When greed, dissatisfaction, false pride, hypocrisy and envy become prominent, along with attraction for selfish activities, such a time is the age of Dvāpara, dominated by the mixed modes of passion and ignorance.

TEXT 30

यदा मायानृतं तन्द्रा निद्रा हिंसा विषादनम् ।
शोकमोहौ भयं दैन्यं स कलिस्तामसः स्मृतः ॥ ३० ॥

yadā māyānṛtaṁ tandrā
nidrā hiṁsā viṣādanam
śoka-mohau bhayaṁ dainyaṁ
sa kalis tāmasaḥ smṛtaḥ

yadā — when; *māyā* — deceit; *anṛtam* — false speech; *tandrā* — sloth; *nidrā* — sleep and intoxication; *hiṁsā* — violence; *viṣādanam* — depression;

śoka — lamentation; *mohau* — and delusion; *bhayam* — fear; *dainyam* — poverty; *saḥ* — that; *kaliḥ* — the age of Kali; *tāmasaḥ* — in the mode of ignorance; *smṛtaḥ* — is considered.

TRANSLATION

When there is a predominance of cheating, lying, sloth, sleepiness, violence, depression, lamentation, bewilderment, fear and poverty, that age is Kali, the age of the mode of ignorance.

PURPORT

In Kali-yuga, people are almost exclusively devoted to gross materialism, with hardly any affinity for self-realization.

TEXT 31

तस्मात् क्षुद्रदृशो मर्त्याः क्षुद्रभाग्या महाशनाः ।
कामिनो वित्तहीनाश्च स्वैरिण्यश्च स्त्रियोऽसतीः ॥ ३१ ॥

tasmāt kṣudra-dṛśo martyāḥ
kṣudra-bhāgyā mahāśanāḥ
kāmino vitta-hīnāś ca
svairiṇyaś ca striyo 'satīḥ

tasmāt — due to these qualities of the age of Kali; *kṣudra-dṛśaḥ* — shortsighted; *martyāḥ* — human beings; *kṣudra-bhāgyāḥ* — unfortunate; *mahā-aśanāḥ* — excessive in their eating habits; *kāminaḥ* — full of lust; *vitta-hīnāḥ* — lacking wealth; *ca* — and; *svairiṇyaḥ* — independent in their social dealings; *ca* — and; *striyaḥ* — the women; *asatīḥ* — unchaste.

TRANSLATION

Because of the bad qualities of the age of Kali, human beings will become shortsighted, unfortunate, gluttonous, lustful and poverty-stricken. The women, becoming unchaste, will freely wander from one man to the next.

PURPORT

In the age of Kali certain pseudointellectuals, seeking individual freedom, support sexual promiscuity. In fact, identification of the self with the body and the pursuit of "individual freedom" in the body rather than in the soul are signs of the most dismal ignorance and slavery to lust. When women are unchaste, many children are born out of wedlock as products of lust. These children grow up in psychologically unfavorable circumstances, and a neurotic, ignorant society arises. Symptoms of this are already manifest throughout the world.

TEXT 32

दस्यूत्कृष्टा जनपदा वेदाः पाषण्डदूषिताः ।
राजानश्च प्रजाभक्षाः शिश्नोदरपरा द्विजाः ॥ ३२ ॥

dasyūtkṛṣṭā janapadā
vedāḥ pāṣaṇḍa-dūṣitāḥ
rājānaś ca prajā-bhakṣāḥ
śiśnodara-parā dvijāḥ

dasyu-utkṛṣṭāḥ—predominated by thieves; *jana-padāḥ*—the populated places; *vedāḥ*—the Vedic scriptures; *pāṣaṇḍa* — by atheists; *dūṣitāḥ*—contaminated; *rājānaḥ*—the political leaders; *ca* — and; *prajā-bhakṣāḥ*—consuming the populace; *śiśna-udara* — to the genitals and belly; *parāḥ*—dedicated; *dvijāḥ*—the *brāhmaṇas.*

TRANSLATION

Cities will be dominated by thieves, the Vedas will be contaminated by speculative interpretations of atheists, political leaders will virtually consume the citizens, and the so-called priests and intellectuals will be devotees of their bellies and genitals.

PURPORT

Many large cities are unsafe at night. For example, it is understood that no sane person will walk in New York's Central Park at night because he knows he will almost certainly be mugged. Apart from ordinary thieves, who abound in this age, large cities are filled with cutthroat businessmen, who enthusiastically convince people to purchase and consume useless or even harmful products. It has been well documented that beef, tobacco, liquor and many other modern products destroy one's physical health, what to speak of mental health, and yet modern capitalists do not hesitate to use every psychological trick in the book to convince people to consume these things. Modern cities are full of mental and atmospheric pollution, and even ordinary citizens are finding them unbearable.

This verse also points out that the teachings of the Vedic scriptures will be distorted in this age. Great universities teach courses on Hinduism in which Indian religion, despite limitless evidence to the contrary, is described as polytheistic and leading to an impersonal salvation. In fact, all Vedic literature is a unified whole, as stated by Lord Kṛṣṇa Himself in *Bhagavad-gītā* (15.15): *vedaiś ca sarvair aham eva vedyaḥ.* "By all the *Vedas* I [Kṛṣṇa] am to be known." All Vedic literature is meant for enlightening us about the Supreme Personal Absolute Truth — Viṣṇu, or Kṛṣṇa. Although known by many names and appearing in many forms, God is a single absolute entity, and He is a person. But this true Vedic understanding is hidden in the Kali-yuga.

In this verse Śukadeva astutely observes that "political leaders will virtually consume the citizens, and the so-called priests and intellectuals will be devotees of their bellies and genitals." How sadly true this statement is.

TEXT 33

अव्रता बटवोऽशौचा भिक्षवश्च कुटुम्बिनः ।
तपस्विनो ग्रामवासा न्यासिनोऽत्यर्थलोलुपाः ॥ ३३ ॥

avratā baṭavo 'śaucā
bhikṣavaś ca kuṭumbinaḥ
tapasvino grāma-vāsā
nyāsino 'tyartha-lolupāḥ

avratāḥ—failing to execute their vows; *baṭavaḥ*—the *brahmacārīs; aśaucāḥ*—unclean; *bhikṣavaḥ*—prone to begging; *ca* — and; *kuṭumbinaḥ* —the householders; *tapasvinaḥ*—those who have gone to the forest for austerities; *grāma-vāsāḥ*—village residents; *nyāsinaḥ*—the *sannyāsīs; atyartha-lolupāḥ*—excessively greedy for wealth.

TRANSLATION

The brahmacārīs will fail to execute their vows and become generally unclean, the householders will become beggars, the vānaprasthas will live in the villages, and the sannyāsīs will become greedy for wealth.

PURPORT

Brahmacarya, celibate student life, is practically nonexistent in the age of Kali. In America, many boys' schools have become coeducational because young men frankly refuse to live without the constant companionship of lusty young girls. Also, we have personally observed throughout the Western world that student residences are among the dirtiest places on earth, as predicted here by the word *aśaucāḥ.*

Concerning householder beggars, when devotees of the Lord go door to door distributing transcendental literature and requesting donations for the propagation of God's glories, irritated householders commonly reply, "Someone should give *me* a donation." Householders in Kali-yuga are not charitable. Instead, because of their miserly mentality, they become irritated when spiritual mendicants approach them.

In Vedic culture, at the age of fifty, couples retire to sacred places for austere life and spiritual perfection. In countries like America, however, retirement cities have been constructed wherein elderly people can make fools of themselves by wasting the last years of their lives playing golf, ping-pong and shuffleboard and by engaging in pathetic attempts at love affairs even while their bodies are horribly rotting and their minds are growing senile. This shameless abuse of the venerable last years of life denotes a stubborn unwillingness to acknowledge the actual purpose of human life and is certainly an offense against God.

The words *nyāsino 'tyartha-lolupāḥ* indicate that charismatic religious leaders, and even those who are not charismatic, will proclaim themselves prophets, saints and incarnations to cheat the innocent public and fatten their bank accounts. Therefore the International Society for Krishna Consciousness is working arduously to establish bona fide celibate student life, religious householder life, dignified and progressive retirement, and genuine spiritual leadership for the entire world. Today, May 9, 1982, in the sensual city of Rio de Janeiro, Brazil, we have awarded *sannyāsa,* the renounced order of life, to three young men, two Brazilians and one American, with the sincere hope that they will faithfully execute the rigid vows of renounced life and provide authentic spiritual leadership in South America.

TEXT 34

ह्रस्वकाया महाहारा भूर्यपत्या गतह्रियः ।
शश्वत् कटुकभाषिण्यश्चौर्यमायोरुसाहसाः ॥ ३४ ॥

hrasva-kāyā mahāhārā
bhūry-apatyā gata-hriyaḥ
śaśvat kaṭuka-bhāṣiṇyaś
caurya-māyoru-sāhasāḥ

hrasva-kāyāḥ—having dwarfed bodies; *mahā-āhārāḥ*—eating too much; *bhūri-apatyāḥ*—having many children; *gata-hriyaḥ*—losing their shyness; *śaśvat* — constantly; *kaṭuka* — harshly; *bhāṣiṇyaḥ*—speaking; *caurya* — exhibiting the tendencies of thievery; *māyā* — deceit; *uru-sāhasāḥ*—and great audacity.

TRANSLATION

Women will become much smaller in size, and they will eat too much, have more children than they can properly take care of, and lose all shyness. They will always speak harshly and will exhibit qualities of thievery, deceit and unrestrained audacity.

TEXT 35

पणयिष्यन्ति वै क्षुद्राः किराटाः कूटकारिणः ।
अनापद्यपि मंस्यन्ते वार्तां साधु जुगुप्सिताम् ॥ ३५ ॥

paṇayiṣyanti vai kṣudrāḥ
kirāṭāḥ kūṭa-kāriṇaḥ
anāpady api maṁsyante
vārtāṁ sādhu jugupsitām

paṇayiṣyanti — will engage in commerce; *vai* — indeed; *kṣudrāḥ*—petty; *kirāṭāḥ*—the merchants; *kūṭa-kāriṇaḥ*—indulging in cheating; *anāpadi* — when there is no emergency; *api* — even; *maṁsyante* — people will consider; *vārtām* — an occupation; *sādhu* — good; *jugupsitām* — which is actually contemptible.

TRANSLATION

Businessmen will engage in petty commerce and earn their money by cheating. Even when there is no emergency, people will consider any degraded occupation quite acceptable.

PURPORT

Although other occupations are available, people do not hesitate to work in coal mines, slaughterhouses, steel mills, deserts, floating oil rigs, submarines and other equally abominable situations. As also mentioned here, businessmen will consider cheating and lying to be a perfectly respectable way to do business. These are all symptoms of the age of Kali.

TEXT 36

पतिं त्यक्ष्यन्ति निर्द्रव्यं भृत्या अप्यखिलोत्तमम् ।
भृत्यं विपन्नं पतयः कौलं गाश्चापयस्विनीः ॥ ३६ ॥

patiṁ tyakṣyanti nirdravyaṁ
bhṛtyā apy akhilottamam
bhṛtyaṁ vipannaṁ patayaḥ
kaulaṁ gāś cāpayasvinīḥ

patim — a master; *tyakṣyanti* — they will abandon; *nirdravyam* — lacking property; *bhṛtyāḥ*—servants; *api* — even; *akhila-uttamam* — most excellent in personal qualities; *bhṛtyam* — a servant; *vipannam* — incapacitated; *patayaḥ*—masters; *kaulam* — belonging to the family for generations; *gāḥ* — cows; *ca* — and; *apayasvinīḥ*—which have stopped giving milk.

TRANSLATION

Servants will abandon a master who has lost his wealth, even if that master is a saintly person of exemplary character. Masters will abandon an incapacitated servant, even if that servant has been in the family for generations. Cows will be abandoned or killed when they stop giving milk.

PURPORT

In India, the cow is considered sacred not because Indian people are primitive worshipers of mythological totems but because Hindus intelligently understand that the cow is a mother. As children, nearly all of us were nourished with cow's milk, and therefore the cow is one of our mothers. Certainly one's mother is sacred, and therefore we should not kill the sacred cow.

TEXT 37

पितृभ्रातृसुहृज्ज्ञातीन् हित्वा सौरतसौहृदाः ।
ननान्दृश्यालसंवादा दीनाः स्त्रैणाः कलौ नराः ॥ ३७ ॥

pitṛ-bhrātṛ-suhṛj-jñātīn
hitvā saurata-sauhṛdāḥ
nanāndṛ-śyāla-saṁvādā
dīnāḥ straiṇāḥ kalau narāḥ

pitṛ—their fathers; *bhrātṛ*—brothers; *suhṛt* — well-wishing friends; *jñātīn* — and immediate relatives; *hitvā* — giving up; *saurata* — based on sexual relationships; *sauhṛdāḥ*—their conception of friendship; *nanāndṛ*—with their wives' sisters; *śyāla* — and wives' brothers; *saṁvādāḥ*—associating regularly; *dīnāḥ*—wretched; *straiṇāḥ*—effeminate; *kalau* — in Kali-yuga; *narāḥ*—the men.

TRANSLATION

In Kali-yuga men will be wretched and controlled by women. They will reject their fathers, brothers, other relatives and friends and will instead associate with the sisters and brothers of their wives. Thus their conception of friendship will be based exclusively on sexual ties.

TEXT 38

शूद्राः प्रतिग्रहीष्यन्ति तपोवेषोपजीविनः ।
धर्मं वक्ष्यन्त्यधर्मज्ञा अधिरुह्योत्तमासनम् ॥ ३८ ॥

śūdrāḥ pratigrahīṣyanti
tapo-veṣopajīvinaḥ
dharmaṁ vakṣyanty adharma-jñā
adhiruhyottamāsanam

śūdrāḥ—lowly, common workers; *pratigrahīṣyanti* — will accept religious charity; *tapaḥ*—by shows of austerity; *veṣa* — and by dressing as mendicants; *upajīvinaḥ*—earning their living; *dharmam* — the principles of religion; *vakṣyanti* — will speak about; *adharma-jñāḥ*—those who know nothing about religion; *adhiruhya* — mounting; *uttama-āsanam* — a high seat.

TRANSLATION

Uncultured men will accept charity on behalf of the Lord and will earn their livelihood by making a show of austerity and wearing a mendicant's dress. Those who know nothing about religion will mount a high seat and presume to speak on religious principles.

PURPORT

The epidemic of bogus *gurus,* swamis, priests and so forth is explicitly described here.

TEXTS 39–40

नित्यमुद्विग्नमनसो दुर्भिक्षकरकर्शिताः ।
निरन्ने भूतले राजननावृष्टिभयातुराः ॥ ३९ ॥
वासोऽन्नपानशयनव्यवायस्नानभूषणैः ।
हीनाः पिशाचसन्दर्शा भविष्यन्ति कलौ प्रजाः ॥ ४० ॥

nityam udvigna-manaso
durbhikṣa-kara-karśitāḥ
niranne bhū-tale rājan
anāvṛṣṭi-bhayāturāḥ

vāso-'nna-pāna-śayana-
vyavāya-snāna-bhūṣaṇaiḥ
hīnāḥ piśāca-sandarśā
bhaviṣyanti kalau prajāḥ

nityam — constantly; *udvigna* — agitated; *manasaḥ*—their minds; *durbhikṣa* — by famine; *kara* — and taxes; *karśitāḥ*—emaciated; *niranne* — when there is no food to be found; *bhū-tale* — upon the surface of the earth; *rājan* — O King Parīkṣit; *anāvṛṣṭi* — of drought; *bhaya* — because of fear; *āturāḥ*—anxious; *vāsaḥ*—clothing; *anna* — food; *pāna* — drink; *śayana* — rest; *vyavāya* — sex; *snāna* — bathing; *bhūṣaṇaiḥ*—and personal ornaments; *hīnāḥ*—lacking; *piśāca-sandarśāḥ*—appearing just like ghostly demons; *bhaviṣyanti* — they will become; *kalau* — in the age of Kali; *prajāḥ*— the people.

TRANSLATION

In the age of Kali, people's minds will always be agitated. They will become emaciated by famine and taxation, my dear King, and will always be disturbed by fear of drought. They will lack adequate clothing, food and drink, will be unable to properly rest, have sex or bathe themselves, and will have no ornaments to decorate their bodies. In fact, the people of Kali-yuga will gradually come to appear like ghostly, haunted creatures.

PURPORT

The symptoms described here are already prevalent in many countries of the world and will gradually spread to other places engulfed by impiety and materialism.

TEXT 41

कलौ काकिणिकेऽप्यर्थे विगृह्य त्यक्तसौहृदाः ।
त्यक्ष्यन्ति च प्रियान् प्राणान् हनिष्यन्ति स्वकानपि ॥ ४१ ॥

kalau kākiṇike'py arthe
vigṛhya tyakta-sauhṛdāḥ
tyakṣyanti ca priyān prāṇān
haniṣyanti svakān api

kalau — in the age of Kali; *kākiṇike* — of a small coin; *api* — even; *arthe* — for the sake; *vigṛhya* — developing enmity; *tyakta* — abandoning; *sauhṛdāḥ* — friendly relations; *tyakṣyanti* — they will reject; *ca* — and; *priyān* — dear; *prāṇān* — their own lives; *haniṣyanti* — they will kill; *svakān* — their own relatives; *api* — even.

TRANSLATION

In Kali-yuga men will develop hatred for each other even over a few coins. Giving up all friendly relations, they will be ready to lose their own lives and kill even their own relatives.

TEXT 42

न रक्षिष्यन्ति मनुजाः स्थविरौ पितरावपि ।
पुत्रान् भार्यां च कुलजां क्षुद्राः शिश्नोदरंभराः ॥ ४२ ॥

na rakṣiṣyanti manujāḥ
sthavirau pitarāv api
putrān bhāryāṁ ca kula-jāṁ
kṣudrāḥ śiśnodaraṁ-bharāḥ

na rakṣiṣyanti — they will not protect; *manujāḥ* — men; *sthavirau* — elderly; *pitarau* — parents; *api* — even; *putrān* — children; *bhāryām* — wife; *ca* — also; *kula-jām* — born of a proper family; *kṣudrāḥ* — petty; *śiśna-udaram* — their genitals and belly; *bharāḥ* — simply maintaining.

TRANSLATION

Men will no longer protect their elderly parents, their children or their respectable wives. Thoroughly degraded, they will care only to satisfy their own bellies and genitals.

PURPORT

In this age many people are already sending their elderly parents away to lonely, and often bizarre, old-age homes, although the elderly parents spent their entire lives serving their children.

Young children are also tormented in many ways in this age. Suicide among children has increased dramatically in recent years because they are being born not to loving, religious parents but to degraded, selfish men and women. In fact, children are often born because a birth-control pill, a prophylactic or some other contraceptive device malfunctioned. Under such conditions, it is very difficult nowadays for parents to morally guide their children. Generally ignorant of spiritual science, parents cannot lead their children on the path of liberation and thus fail to fulfill their primary responsibility in family life.

As predicted in this verse, adultery has become common, and people in general are extremely concerned with eating and sex, which they consider far more important than knowing the Absolute Truth.

TEXT 43

कलौ न राजन् जगतां परं गुरुं
त्रिलोकनाथानतपादपंकजम् ।
प्रायेण मर्त्या भगवन्तमच्युतं
यक्ष्यन्ति पाषण्डविभिन्नचेतसः ॥ ४३ ॥

kalau na rājan jagatāṁ paraṁ guruṁ
tri-loka-nāthānata-pāda-paṅkajam
prāyeṇa martyā bhagavantam acyutaṁ
yakṣyanti pāṣaṇḍa-vibhinna-cetasaḥ

kalau — in the age of Kali; *na* — not; *rājan* — O King; *jagatām* — of the universe; *param* — the supreme; *gurum* — spiritual master; *tri-loka* — of the three worlds; *nātha* — by the various masters; *ānata* — bowed down to; *pāda-paṅkajam* — whose lotus feet; *prāyeṇa* — for the most part; *martyāḥ* — human beings; *bhagavantam* — the Personality of Godhead; *acyutam* — Lord Acyuta; *yakṣyanti* — they will offer sacrifice; *pāṣaṇḍa* — by atheism; *vibhinna* — diverted; *cetasaḥ* — their intelligence.

TRANSLATION

O King, in the age of Kali people's intelligence will be diverted by atheism, and they will almost never offer sacrifice to the Supreme Personality of Godhead, who is the supreme spiritual master of the universe. Although the great personalities who control the three worlds all bow down to the lotus feet of the Supreme Lord, the petty and miserable human beings of this age will not do so.

PURPORT

The impulse to find the Absolute Truth, the source of all existence, has motivated philosophers, theologians and other intellectuals of various persuasions since time immemorial, and continues to do so today. However, soberly analyzing the ever-increasing plurality of so-called philosophies, religions, paths, ways of life and so on, we find that in almost all cases the ultimate objective is something impersonal or formless. But this idea of an impersonal or formless Absolute Truth has serious logical flaws. According to ordinary rules of logic, a particular effect should directly or indirectly embody the attributes, or nature, of its own cause. Thus that which has no personality or activity could hardly be the source of all personality and all activity.

Our irrepressible proclivity to philosophize about the ultimate truth often expresses itself through philosophical, scientific and mystical attempts to discover that from which everything emanates. This material world, which is a seemingly limitless network of interactive causes and effects, is certainly not the Absolute Truth, since scientific observation of material elements indicates that the stuff of this world, material energy, is endlessly transformed into different states and shapes. Therefore, one particular instance of material reality cannot be the ultimate source of all other things.

We may speculate that matter in some shape or other has always existed. This theory, however, is no longer attractive to modern cosmologists, such as those at the Massachusetts Institute of Technology. And even if we do posit that matter has always existed, we still must explain the source of consciousness if we want to satisfy our philosophical impulse toward discovering the Absolute Truth. Although modern empirical fanatics state that nothing is real except matter, everyone commonly experiences that consciousness is not the same kind of substance as a stone, a pencil or water. Awareness itself, in contradistinction to the objects of awareness, is not a physical entity but rather a process of perception and understanding. While there is ample evidence of a systematic interdependent relationship between matter and consciousness, there is no rigid empirical evidence whatsoever that matter is the *cause* of consciousness. Thus the theory that the material world has always existed and is therefore the ultimate truth does not scientifically or even intuitively explain the source of consciousness, which is the most fundamentally real aspect of our existence.

Furthermore, as demonstrated by Dr. Richard Thompson of the State University of New York at Binghamton and confirmed by several Nobel laureates in physics who have praised his work, the laws of nature governing the transformation of matter simply do not contain sufficiently complex information to account for the inconceivable complexity of events taking place within our own bodies and those of other life forms. In other words, not only do the material laws of nature fail to account for the existence of consciousness, but they cannot explain even the interaction of material elements at complex organic levels. Even Socrates, the first great Western philosopher, was disgusted with the attempt to establish ultimate causality in terms of mechanistic principles.

The heat and luminosity of the sun's rays demonstrate to the satisfaction of any rational man that the sun, the source of the rays, is certainly not a dark, cold globe but rather a reservoir of almost unlimited heat and light. Similarly, the innumerable instances of personality and personal consciousness within creation are more than adequate to demonstrate the existence, somewhere, of an unlimited reservoir of consciousness and personal behavior. In his dialogue *Philebus,* the Greek philosopher Plato argued that just as the material elements in our body are derived from a vast reservoir of material elements existing within the universe, our rational intelligence is also derived from a great cosmic intelligence existing within the universe, and this supreme intelligence is God, the creator. Unfortunately, in Kali-yuga many leading thinkers cannot understand this and instead deny that the Absolute Truth, the source of our personal consciousness, has consciousness and personality. This is as reasonable as saying that the sun is cold and dark.

In Kali-yuga, many people present cheap, stereotyped arguments, such as "If God had a body or personality, He would be limited." In this inadequate attempt at logic, a qualified term is falsely presented in a universal sense. What really should be said is, "If God had a *material* body or a *material* personality like those we have experienced, He would be limited." But we leave out the qualifying adjective *material* and make a pseudouniversal assertion, as if we understood the full range, within total reality, of bodies and personality.

Bhagavad-gītā, Śrīmad-Bhāgavatam and other Vedic literatures teach that the transcendental form and personality of the Absolute Truth are unlimited. Clearly, to be truly infinite God must be not only quantitatively but also qualitatively infinite. Unfortunately, in our mechanistic, industrial age we tend to define infinity only in its quantitative sense, and thus we fail to notice that an infinity of personal qualities is a necessary aspect of infinity. In other words, God must have infinite beauty, infinite wealth, infinite intelligence, infinite humor, infinite kindness, infinite anger and so on. Infinite is an absolute, and if anything we observe in this world is not contained, somehow or other, within our conception of the Absolute, then that conception is of something limited and not of the Absolute at all.

Only in Kali-yuga are there philosophers foolish enough to proudly define the most absolute of all terms — God — in materialistic, relative ways and then declare themselves enlightened thinkers. No matter how big our brain may be, we should have the common sense to place it at the feet of the Supreme Personality of Godhead.

TEXT 44

यन्नामधेयं म्रियमाण आतुरः
पतन् स्खलन् वा विवशो गृणन् पुमान् ।
विमुक्तकर्मार्गल उत्तमां गतिं
प्राप्नोति यक्ष्यन्ति न तं कलौ जनाः ॥ ४४ ॥

yan-nāmadheyaṁ mriyamāṇa āturaḥ
patan skhalan vā vivaśo gṛṇan pumān
vimukta-karmārgala uttamāṁ gatiṁ
prāpnoti yakṣyanti na taṁ kalau janāḥ

yat — whose; *nāmadheyam* — name; *mriyamāṇaḥ*—a person who is dying; *āturaḥ*—distressed; *patan* — collapsing; *skhalan* — voice faltering; *vā* — or; *vivaśaḥ*—helplessly; *gṛṇan* — chanting; *pumān* — a person; *vimukta* — freed; *karma* — of fruitive work; *argalaḥ*—from the chains; *uttamām* — the topmost; *gatim* — destination; *prāpnoti* — achieves; *yakṣyanti na* — they do not worship; *tam* — Him, the Personality of Godhead; *kalau* — in the age of Kali; *janāḥ*—people.

TRANSLATION

Terrified, about to die, a man collapses on his bed. Although his voice is faltering and he is hardly conscious of what he is saying, if he utters the holy name of the Supreme Lord he can be freed from the reaction of his fruitive work and achieve the supreme destination. But still people in the age of Kali will not worship the Supreme Lord.

PURPORT

You can lead a horse to water, but you cannot make him drink.

TEXT 45

पुंसां कलिकृतान् दोषान् द्रव्यदेशात्मसम्भवान् ।
सर्वान् हरति चित्तस्थो भगवान् पुरुषोत्तमः ॥ ४५ ॥

puṁsāṁ kali-kṛtān doṣān
dravya-deśātma-sambhavān
sarvān harati citta-stho
bhagavān puruṣottamaḥ

puṁsām — of men; *kali-kṛtān* — created by the influence of Kali; *doṣān* — the faults; *dravya* — objects; *deśa* — space; *ātma* — and personal nature; *sambhavān* — based upon; *sarvān* — all; *harati* — steals away; *citta-sthaḥ*— situated within the heart; *bhagavān* — the almighty Lord; *puruṣa-uttamaḥ*— the Supreme Person.

TRANSLATION

In the Kali-yuga, objects, places and even individual personalities are all polluted. The almighty Personality of Godhead, however, can remove all such contamination from the life of one who fixes the Lord within his mind.

TEXT 46

श्रुतः संकीर्तितो ध्यातः पूजितश्चादृतोऽपि वा ।
नृणां धुनोति भगवान् हृत्स्थो जन्मायुताशुभम् ॥ ४६ ॥

śrutaḥ saṅkīrtito dhyātaḥ
pūjitaś cādṛto'pi vā
nṛṇāṁ dhunoti bhagavān
hṛt-stho janmāyutāśubham

śrutaḥ—heard; *saṅkīrtitaḥ*—glorified; *dhyātaḥ*—meditated upon; *pūjitaḥ*—worshiped; *ca*—and; *ādṛtaḥ*—venerated; *api*—even; *vā*—or; *nṛṇām*—of men; *dhunoti*—cleanses away; *bhagavān*—the Supreme Personality of Godhead; *hṛt-sthaḥ*—seated within their hearts; *janma-ayuta*—of thousands of births; *aśubham*—the inauspicious contamination.

TRANSLATION

If a person hears about, glorifies, meditates upon, worships or simply offers great respect to the Supreme Lord, who is situated within the heart, the Lord will remove from his mind the contamination accumulated during many thousands of lifetimes.

TEXT 47

यथा हेम्नि स्थितो वह्निर्दुर्वर्णं हन्ति धातुजम् ।
एवमात्मगतो विष्णुर्योगिनामशुभाशयम् ॥ ४७ ॥

yathā hemni sthito vahnir
durvarṇaṁ hanti dhātu-jam
evam ātma-gato viṣṇur
yoginām aśubhāśayam

yathā—just as; *hemni*—in gold; *sthitaḥ*—situated; *vahniḥ*—fire; *durvarṇam*—the discoloration; *hanti*—destroys; *dhātu-jam*—due to the taint of other metals; *evam*—in the same way; *ātma-gataḥ*—having entered the soul; *viṣṇuḥ*—Lord Viṣṇu; *yoginām*—of the *yogīs; aśubha-āśayam*—the dirty mind.

TRANSLATION

Just as fire applied to gold removes any discoloration caused by traces of other metals, Lord Viṣṇu within the heart purifies the minds of the yogīs.

PURPORT

Although one may practice the mystic *yoga* system, his actual spiritual advancement is due to the mercy of the Supreme Lord within the heart; it is not directly the result of his austerity and meditation. If one becomes foolishly proud in the name of *yoga,* his spiritual position becomes ridiculous.

TEXT 48

विद्यातपःप्राणनिरोधमैत्री-
तीर्थाभिषेकव्रतदानजप्यैः ।
नात्यन्तशुद्धिं लभतेऽन्तरात्मा
यथा हृदिस्थे भगवत्यनन्ते ॥ ४८ ॥

vidyā-tapaḥ-prāṇa-nirodha-maitrī-
tīrthābhiṣeka-vrata-dāna-japyaiḥ
nātyanta-śuddhiṁ labhate 'ntarātmā
yathā hṛdi-sthe bhagavaty anante

vidyā — by worship of demigods; *tapaḥ* — austerities; *prāṇa-nirodha* — exercise of breath control; *maitrī* — compassion; *tīrtha-abhiṣeka* — bathing in holy places; *vrata* — strict vows; *dāna* — charity; *japyaiḥ* — and chanting of various *mantras; na* — not; *atyanta* — complete; *śuddhim* — purification; *labhate* — can achieve; *antaḥ-ātmā* — the mind; *yathā* — as; *hṛdi-sthe* — when He is present within the heart; *bhagavati* — the Personality of Godhead; *anante* — the unlimited Lord.

TRANSLATION

By one's engaging in the processes of demigod worship, austerities, breath control, compassion, bathing in holy places, strict vows, charity and chanting of various mantras, one's mind cannot attain the same absolute purification as that achieved when the unlimited Personality of Godhead appears within one's heart.

TEXT 49

तस्मात्सर्वात्मना राजन् हृदिस्थं कुरु केशवम् ।
म्रियमाणो ह्यवहितस्ततो यासि परां गतिम् ॥ ४९ ॥

tasmāt sarvātmanā rājan
hṛdi-sthaṁ kuru keśavam
mriyamāṇo hy avahitas
tato yāsi parāṁ gatim

tasmāt — therefore; *sarva-ātmanā* — with all endeavor; *rājan* — O King; *hṛdi-stham* — within your heart; *kuru* — make; *keśavam* — Lord Keśava;

mriyamāṇaḥ—dying; *hi*—indeed; *avahitaḥ*—concentrated; *tataḥ*—then; *yāsi*—you will go; *parām*—to the supreme; *gatim*—destination.

TRANSLATION

Therefore, O King, endeavor with all your might to fix the Supreme Lord Keśava within your heart. Maintain this concentration upon the Lord, and at the time of death you will certainly attain the supreme destination.

PURPORT

Although the Supreme Lord is always in the heart of every living being, the words *hṛdi-sthaṁ kuru keśavam* indicate that one should endeavor to realize the Lord's presence there and maintain this awareness at every moment. Parīkṣit Mahārāja is about to give up this world and is receiving final instructions from his spiritual master, Śukadeva Gosvāmī. In the context of the King's imminent departure, this verse has special significance.

TEXT 50

म्रियमाणैरभिध्येयो भगवान् परमेश्वरः ।
आत्मभावं नयत्यंग सर्वात्मा सर्वसंश्रयः ॥ ५० ॥

mriyamāṇair abhidhyeyo
bhagavān parameśvaraḥ
ātma-bhāvaṁ nayaty aṅga
sarvātmā sarva-saṁśrayaḥ

mriyamāṇaiḥ—by those who are dying; *abhidhyeyaḥ*—meditated upon; *bhagavān*—the Personality of Godhead; *parama-īśvaraḥ*—the Supreme Lord; *ātma-bhāvam*—their own true identity; *nayati*—leads them to; *aṅga*—my dear King; *sarva-ātmā*—the Supreme Soul; *sarva-saṁśrayaḥ*—the shelter of all beings.

TRANSLATION

My dear King, the Personality of Godhead is the ultimate controller. He is the Supreme Soul and the supreme shelter of all beings. When meditated upon by those about to die, He reveals to them their own eternal spiritual identity.

TEXT 51

कलेर्दोषनिधे राजन्नस्ति ह्येको महान् गुणः ।
कीर्तनादेव कृष्णस्य मुक्तसंगः परं व्रजेत् ॥ ५१ ॥

kaler doṣa-nidhe rājann
asti hy eko mahān guṇaḥ
kīrtanād eva kṛṣṇasya
mukta-saṅgaḥ paraṁ vrajet

kaleḥ—of the age of Kali; *doṣa-nidheḥ*—in the ocean of faults; *rājan*—O King; *asti*—there is; *hi*—certainly; *ekaḥ*—one; *mahān*—very great; *guṇaḥ*—good quality; *kīrtanāt*—by chanting; *eva*—certainly; *kṛṣṇasya*—of the holy name of Kṛṣṇa; *mukta-saṅgaḥ*—liberated from material bondage; *param*—to the transcendental spiritual kingdom; *vrajet*—one can go.

TRANSLATION

My dear King, although Kali-yuga is an ocean of faults, there is still one good quality about this age: Simply by chanting the Hare Kṛṣṇa mahā-mantra, one can become free from material bondage and be promoted to the transcendental kingdom.

PURPORT

After mentioning the innumerable faults of this age of Kali, Śukadeva Gosvāmī now mentions its one brilliant aspect. Just as one powerful king can kill innumerable thieves, one brilliant spiritual quality can destroy all the contamination of this age. It is impossible to overestimate the importance of chanting Hare Kṛṣṇa, Hare Kṛṣṇa, Kṛṣṇa Kṛṣṇa, Hare Hare/ Hare Rāma, Hare Rāma, Rāma Rāma, Hare Hare, especially in this fallen age.

TEXT 52

कृते यद्ध्यायतो विष्णुं त्रेतायां यजतो मखैः ।
द्वापरे परिचर्यायां कलौ तद्धरिकीर्तनात् ॥ ५२ ॥

kṛte yad dhyāyato viṣṇuṁ
tretāyāṁ yajato makhaiḥ
dvāpare paricaryāyāṁ
kalau tad dhari-kīrtanāt

kṛte — in the Satya-yuga; *yat* — which; *dhyāyataḥ*—from meditation; *viṣṇum* — on Lord Viṣṇu; *tretāyām* — in the Tretā-yuga; *yajataḥ*—from worshiping; *makhaiḥ*—by performing sacrifices; *dvāpare* — in the age of Dvāpara; *paricaryāyām* — by worshiping the lotus feet of Kṛṣṇa; *kalau* — in the age of Kali; *tat* — that same result (can be achieved); *hari-kīrtanāt* — simply by chanting the Hare Kṛṣṇa *mahā-mantra.*

TRANSLATION

Whatever result was obtained in Satya-yuga by meditating on Viṣṇu, in Tretā-yuga by performing sacrifices, and in Dvāpara-yuga by serving the Lord's lotus feet can be obtained in Kali-yuga simply by chanting the Hare Kṛṣṇa mahā-mantra.

PURPORT

A similar verse is found in the *Viṣṇu Purāṇa* (6.2.17), and also in the *Padma Purāṇa* (*Uttara-khaṇḍa* 72.25) and the *Bṛhan-nāradīya Purāṇa* (38.97):

dhyāyan kṛte yajan yajñais
tretāyāṁ dvāpare'rcayan
yad āpnoti tad āpnoti
kalau saṅkīrtya keśavam

"Whatever is achieved by meditation in Satya-yuga, by the performance of sacrifice in Tretā-yuga, and by the worship of Lord Kṛṣṇa's lotus feet in Dvāpara-yuga is obtained in the age of Kali simply by glorifying the name of Lord Keśava."

Śrīla Jīva Gosvāmī has further quoted from the *Brahma-vaivarta Purāṇa* concerning the degraded condition of people in Kali-yuga:

ataḥ kalau tapo-yoga-
vidyā-yajñādikāḥ kriyāḥ
sāṅgā bhavanti na kṛtāḥ
kuśalair api dehibhiḥ

"Thus in the age of Kali the practices of austerity, *yoga* meditation, Deity worship, sacrifice and so on, along with their various subsidiary functions, are not properly carried out, even by the most expert embodied souls."

Śrīla Jīva Gosvāmī has also cited the *Cātur-māsya-māhātmya* of the *Skanda Purāṇa* concerning the necessity of chanting Hare Kṛṣṇa in this age:

tathā caivottamaṁ loke
tapaḥ śrī-hari-kīrtanam
kalau yuge viśeṣeṇa
viṣṇu-prītyai samācaret

"In this way the most perfect penance to be executed in this world is the chanting of the name of Lord Śrī Hari. Especially in the age of Kali, one can satisfy the Supreme Lord Viṣṇu by performing *saṅkīrtana.*"

In conclusion, massive propaganda should be made all over the world to induce people to chant the Hare Kṛṣṇa *mantra,* by which human society can be rescued from the dangerous ocean of the age of Kali.

Thus end the purports of the humble servants of His Divine Grace A.C. Bhaktivedanta Swami Prabhupāda to the Twelfth Canto, Third Chapter, of the Śrīmad-Bhāgavatam, *entitled "The Bhūmi-gītā."*

CHAPTER FOUR

The Four Categories of Universal Annihilation

This chapter discusses the four kinds of annihilation (constant, occasional, material and final) and the chanting of the holy name of Lord Hari, which is the only means of stopping the cycle of material life.

One thousand cycles of four ages constitute one day of Brahmā, and each day of Brahmā, called a *kalpa,* contains within it the lifetimes of fourteen Manus. The duration of Brahmā's night is the same as that of his day. During his night Brahmā sleeps, and the three planetary systems meet destruction; this is the *naimittika,* or occasional, annihilation. When Brahmā's life span of one hundred years is finished, there occurs the *prākṛtika,* or total material, annihilation. At that time the seven elements of material nature, beginning with the *mahat,* and the entire universal egg composed of them are destroyed. When a person achieves knowledge of the Absolute, he understands factual reality. He perceives the entire created universe as separate from the Absolute and therefore unreal. That is called the *ātyantika,* or final, annihilation (liberation). At every moment time invisibly transforms the bodies of all created beings and all other manifestations of matter. This process of transformation causes the living entity to undergo the constant annihilation of birth and death. Those possessed of subtle vision state that all creatures, including Brahmā himself, are always subject to generation and annihilation. Material life means subjugation to birth and death, or generation and annihilation. The only boat suitable for crossing the ocean of material existence, which is otherwise impossible to cross, is the boat of submissive hearing of the nectarean pastimes of the Supreme Personality of Godhead.

TEXT 1

श्रीशुक उवाच

कालस्ते परमाण्वादिर्द्विपरार्धावधिर्नृप ।
कथितो युगमानं च शृणु कल्पलयावपि ॥ १ ॥

śrī-śuka uvāca
kālas te paramāṇv-ādir
dvi-parārdhāvadhir nṛpa
kathito yuga-mānaṁ ca
śṛṇu kalpa-layāv api

śrī-śukaḥ uvāca — Śrī Śukadeva Gosvāmī said; *kālaḥ*—time; *te* — to you; *parama-aṇu*—(the smallest fraction of time measured in terms of) the indivisible atom; *ādiḥ*—beginning with; *dvi-para-ardha* — the two halves of Brahmā's total life span; *avadhiḥ*—culminating in; *nṛpa* — O King Parīkṣit; *kathitaḥ*—has been described; *yuga-mānam* — the duration of the millennia; *ca* — and; *śṛṇu* — now hear; *kalpa* — Brahmā's day; *layau* — annihilation; *api* — also.

TRANSLATION

Śukadeva Gosvāmī said: My dear King, I have already described to you the measurements of time, beginning from the smallest fraction measured by the movement of a single atom up to the total life span of Lord Brahmā. I have also discussed the measurement of the different millennia of universal history. Now hear about the time of Brahmā's day and the process of annihilation.

TEXT 2

चतुर्युगसहस्रं तु ब्रह्मणो दिनमुच्यते ।
स कल्पो यत्र मनवश्चतुर्दश विशाम्पते ॥ २ ॥

catur-yuga-sahasraṁ tu
brahmaṇo dinam ucyate
sa kalpo yatra manavaś
caturdaśa viśām-pate

catuḥ-yuga — four ages; *sahasram* — one thousand; *tu* — indeed; *brahmaṇaḥ*—of Lord Brahmā; *dinam* — the day; *ucyate* — is said; *saḥ*—that; *kalpaḥ*—a *kalpa; yatra* — in which; *manavaḥ*—original progenitors of mankind; *caturdaśa* — fourteen; *viśām-pate* — O King.

TRANSLATION

One thousand cycles of four ages constitute a single day of Brahmā, known as a kalpa. In that period, O King, fourteen Manus come and go.

TEXT 3

तदन्ते प्रलयस्तावान् ब्राह्मी रात्रिरुदाहृता ।
त्रयो लोका इमे तत्र कल्पन्ते प्रलयाय हि ॥ ३ ॥

tad-ante pralayas tāvān
brāhmī rātrir udāhṛtā
trayo lokā ime tatra
kalpante pralayāya hi

tat-ante — after those (thousand cycles of ages); *pralayaḥ*—the annihilation; *tāvān* — of the same duration; *brāhmī*—of Brahmā; *rātriḥ*—the nighttime; *udāhṛtā* — is described; *trayaḥ*—the three; *lokāḥ*—worlds; *ime* — these; *tatra* — at that time; *kalpante* — are prone; *pralayāya* — to annihilation; *hi* — indeed.

TRANSLATION

After one day of Brahmā, annihilation occurs during his night, which is of the same duration. At that time all the three planetary systems are subject to destruction.

TEXT 4

एष नैमित्तिकः प्रोक्तः प्रलयो यत्र विश्वसृक् ।
शेतेऽनन्तासनो विश्वमात्मसात्कृत्य चात्मभूः ॥ ४ ॥

eṣa naimittikaḥ proktaḥ
pralayo yatra viśva-sṛk
śete'nantāsano viśvam
ātmasāt-kṛtya cātma-bhūḥ

eṣaḥ—this; *naimittikaḥ*—occasional; *proktaḥ*—is said; *pralayaḥ*—annihilation; *yatra* — in which; *viśva-sṛk* — the creator of the universe, the Supreme Lord, Nārāyaṇa; *śete* — lies down; *ananta-āsanaḥ*—upon the snakebed of Ananta Śeṣa; *viśvam* — the universe; *ātma-sāt-kṛtya* — absorbing within Himself; *ca* — also; *ātma-bhūḥ*—Lord Brahmā.

TRANSLATION

This is called the naimittika, or occasional, annihilation, during which the original creator, Lord Nārāyaṇa, lies down upon the bed of Ananta Śeṣa and absorbs the entire universe within Himself while Lord Brahmā sleeps.

TEXT 5

द्विपरार्धे त्वतिक्रान्ते ब्रह्मणः परमेष्ठिनः ।
तदा प्रकृतयः सप्त कल्पन्ते प्रलयाय वै ॥ ५ ॥

dvi-parārdhe tv atikrānte
brahmaṇaḥ parameṣṭhinaḥ
tadā prakṛtayaḥ sapta
kalpante pralayāya vai

dvi-parārdhe — two *parārdhas; tu* — and; *atikrānte* — when they have become completed; *brahmaṇaḥ*—of Lord Brahmā; *parame-sthinaḥ*—the most highly situated living entity; *tadā* — then; *prakṛtayaḥ*—the elements of nature; *sapta* — seven; *kalpante* — are subject; *pralayāya* — to destruction; *vai* — indeed.

TRANSLATION

When the two halves of the lifetime of Lord Brahmā, the most elevated created being, are complete, the seven basic elements of creation are annihilated.

TEXT 6

एष प्राकृतिको राजन् प्रलयो यत्र लीयते ।
अण्डकोषस्तु सङ्घातो विघात उपसाधिते ॥ ६ ॥

eṣa prākṛtiko rājan
pralayo yatra līyate
aṇḍa-koṣas tu saṅghāto
vighāta upasādite

eṣaḥ—this; *prākṛtikaḥ*—of the elements of material nature; *rājan* — O King Parīkṣit; *pralayaḥ*—the annihilation; *yatra* — in which; *līyate* — is dissolved; *aṇḍa-koṣaḥ*—the egg of the universe; *tu* — and; *saṅghātaḥ*—the amalgamation; *vighāte* — the cause of its disruption; *upasādite* — being encountered.

TRANSLATION

O King, upon the annihilation of the material elements, the universal egg, comprising the elemental amalgamation of creation, is confronted with destruction.

PURPORT

It is significant that Śukadeva Gosvāmī, the spiritual master of King Parīkṣit, is broadly discussing cosmic annihilation just before the death of his disciple. By attentively hearing the story of universal destruction, one can easily understand one's personal departure from this temporary world to be an insignificant incident within the gigantic scope of the total material manifestation. By his deep and relevant discussions of the creation of God, Śukadeva Gosvāmī, as an ideal spiritual master, is preparing his disciple for the moment of death.

TEXT 7

पर्जन्यः शतवर्षाणि भूमौ राजन् न वर्षति ।
तदा निरन्ने ह्यन्योन्यं भक्ष्यमाणाः क्षुधार्दिताः ।
क्षयं यास्यन्ति शनकैः कालेनोपद्रुताः प्रजाः ॥ ७ ॥

parjanyaḥ śata-varṣāṇi
bhūmau rājan na varṣati
tadā niranne hy anyonyaṁ
bhakṣyamāṇāḥ kṣudhārditāḥ
kṣayaṁ yāsyanti śanakaiḥ
kālenopadrutāḥ prajāḥ

parjanyaḥ—the clouds; *śata-varṣāṇi*—for one hundred years; *bhūmau*—upon the earth; *rājan*—my dear King; *na varṣati*—will not give rain; *tadā*—then; *niranne*—with the coming of famine; *hi*—indeed; *anyonyam*—one another; *bhakṣyamāṇāḥ*—eating; *kṣudhā*—by hunger; *arditāḥ*—distressed; *kṣayam*—to destruction; *yāsyanti*—they go; *śanakaiḥ*—gradually; *kālena*—by the force of time; *upadrutāḥ*—confounded; *prajāḥ*—the people.

TRANSLATION

As annihilation approaches, O King, there will be no rain upon the earth for one hundred years. Drought will lead to famine, and the starving populace will literally consume one another. The inhabitants of the earth, bewildered by the force of time, will gradually be destroyed.

TEXT 8

सामुद्रं दैहिकं भौमं रसं सांवर्तको रविः ।
रश्मिभिः पिबते घोरैः सर्वं नैव विमुञ्चति ॥ ८ ॥

sāmudraṁ daihikaṁ bhaumaṁ
rasaṁ sāṁvartako raviḥ
raśmibhiḥ pibate ghoraiḥ
sarvaṁ naiva vimuñcati

sāmudram — of the ocean; *daihikam* — of living bodies; *bhaumam* — of the earth; *rasam* — the juice; *sāṁvartakaḥ*—annihilating; *raviḥ*—the sun; *raśmibhiḥ*—with its rays; *pibate* — drinks up; *ghoraiḥ*—which are terrible; *sarvam* — all; *na* — nothing; *eva* — even; *vimuñcati* — gives.

TRANSLATION

The sun in its annihilating form will drink up with its terrible rays all the water of the ocean, of living bodies and of the earth itself. But the devastating sun will not give any rain in return.

TEXT 9

ततः संवर्तको वह्निः संकर्षणमुखोत्थितः ।
दहत्यनिलवेगोत्थः शून्यान् भूविवरानथ ॥ ९ ॥

tataḥ saṁvartako vahniḥ
saṅkarṣaṇa-mukhotthitaḥ
dahaty anila-vegotthaḥ
śūnyān bhū-vivarān atha

tataḥ—then; *saṁvartakaḥ*—of destruction; *vahniḥ*—the fire; *saṅkarṣaṇa* — of the Supreme Lord, Saṅkarṣaṇa; *mukha* — from the mouth; *utthitaḥ*—arisen; *dahati* — burns; *anila-vega* — by the force of the wind; *utthaḥ*—raised; *śūnyān* — empty; *bhū* — of the planets; *vivarān* — the crevices; *atha* — after that.

TRANSLATION

Next the great fire of annihilation will flare up from the mouth of Lord Saṅkarṣaṇa. Carried by the mighty force of the wind, this fire will burn throughout the universe, scorching the lifeless cosmic shell.

TEXT 10

उपर्यधः समन्ताच्च शिखाभिर्वह्निसूर्ययोः ।
दह्यमानं विभात्यण्डं दग्धगोमयपिण्डवत् ॥१०॥

upary adhaḥ samantāc ca
śikhābhir vahni-sūryayoḥ
dahyamānaṁ vibhāty aṇḍaṁ
dagdha-gomaya-piṇḍa-vat

upari — above; *adhaḥ* — and below; *samantāt* — in all directions; *ca* — and; *śikhābhiḥ* — with the flames; *vahni* — of the fire; *sūryayoḥ* — and of the sun; *dahyamānam* — being burned; *vibhāti* — glows; *aṇḍam* — the egg of the universe; *dagdha* — burned; *go-maya* — of cow dung; *piṇḍa-vat* — like a ball.

TRANSLATION

Burned from all sides — from above by the blazing sun and from below by the fire of Lord Saṅkarṣaṇa — the universal sphere will glow like a burning ball of cow dung.

TEXT 11

ततः प्रचण्डपवनो वर्षाणामधिकं शतम् ।
परः सांवर्तको वाति धूम्रं खं रजसावृतम् ॥११॥

tataḥ pracaṇḍa-pavano
varṣāṇām adhikaṁ śatam
paraḥ sāṁvartako vāti
dhūmraṁ khaṁ rajasāvṛtam

tataḥ — then; *pracaṇḍa* — terrible; *pavanaḥ* — a wind; *varṣāṇām* — of years; *adhikam* — more than; *śatam* — one hundred; *paraḥ* — great; *sāmvartakaḥ* — causing annihilation; *vāti* — blows; *dhūmram* — gray; *kham* — the sky; *rajasā* — with dust; *āvṛtam* — covered.

TRANSLATION

A great and terrible wind of destruction will begin to blow for more than one hundred years, and the sky, covered with dust, will turn gray.

TEXT 12

ततो मेघकुलान्यंग चित्रवर्णान्यनेकशः ।
शतं वर्षाणि वर्षन्ति नदन्ति रभसस्वनैः ॥ १२ ॥

tato megha-kulāny aṅga
citra varṇāny anekaśaḥ
śataṁ varṣāṇi varṣanti
nadanti rabhasa-svanaiḥ

tataḥ—then; *megha-kulāni* — the clouds; *aṅga* — my dear King; *citra-varṇāni* — of various colors; *anekaśaḥ*—numerous; *śatam* — one hundred; *varṣāṇi* — years; *varṣanti* — they pour down rain; *nadanti* — they thunder; *rabhasa-svanaiḥ*—with tremendous sounds.

TRANSLATION

After that, O King, groups of multicolored clouds will gather, roaring terribly with thunder, and will pour down floods of rain for one hundred years.

TEXT 13

तत एकोदकं विश्वं ब्रह्माण्डविवरान्तरम् ॥१३॥

tata ekodakaṁ viśvaṁ
brahmāṇḍa-vivarāntaram

tataḥ—then; *eka-udakam* — a single body of water; *viśvam* — the universe; *brahma-aṇḍa* — of the egg of creation; *vivara-antaram* — within.

TRANSLATION

At that time, the shell of the universe will fill up with water, forming a single cosmic ocean.

TEXT 14

तदा भूमेर्गन्धगुणं ग्रसन्त्याप उदप्लवे ।
ग्रस्तगन्धा तु पृथिवी प्रलयत्वाय कल्पते ॥ १४॥

tadā bhūmer gandha-guṇaṁ
grasanty āpa uda-plave

grasta-gandhā tu pṛthivī
pralayatvāya kalpate

tadā — then; *bhūmeḥ*—of the earth; *gandha-guṇam* — the perceptible quality of fragrance; *grasanti* — takes away; *āpaḥ*—the water; *uda-plave* — during the flooding; *grasta-gandhā* — deprived of its fragrance; *tu* — and; *pṛthivī*—the element earth; *pralayatvāya kalpate* — becomes unmanifest.

TRANSLATION

As the entire universe is flooded, the water will rob the earth of its unique quality of fragrance, and the element earth, deprived of its distinguishing quality, will be dissolved.

PURPORT

As clearly explained throughout *Śrīmad-Bhāgavatam,* the first element, sky, possesses the unique quality of sound. As creation expands, the second element, air, comes into being, and it possesses sound and touch. The third element, fire, possesses sound, touch and form, and the fourth element, water, possesses sound, touch, form and flavor. The earth possesses sound, touch, form, flavor and aroma. As each element loses its unique distinguishing quality, it naturally becomes indistinguishable from the more subtle elements and is thus effectively dissolved as a unique entity.

TEXTS 15–19

अपां रसमथो तेजस्ता लीयन्तेऽथ नीरसाः ।
ग्रसते तेजसो रूपं वायुस्तद्रहितं तदा ॥ १५ ॥
लीयते चानिले तेजो वायोः खं ग्रसते गुणम् ।
स वै विशति खं राजंस्ततश्च नभसो गुणम् ॥ १६ ॥
शब्दं ग्रसति भूतादिर्नभस्तमनु लीयते ।
तैजसश्चेन्द्रियाण्यंग देवान् वैकारिको गुणैः ॥ १७ ॥
महान् ग्रसत्यहंकारं गुणाः सत्त्वादयश्च तम् ।
ग्रसतेऽव्याकृतं राजन् गुणान् कालेन चोदितम् ॥ १८ ॥
न तस्य कालावयवैः परिणामादयो गुणाः ।
अनाद्यनन्तमव्यक्तं नित्यं कारणमव्ययम् ॥ १९ ॥

apāṁ rasam atho tejas
tā līyante'tha nīrasāḥ
grasate tejaso rūpaṁ
vāyus tad-rahitaṁ tadā

līyate cānile tejo
vāyoḥ khaṁ grasate guṇam
sa vai viśati khaṁ rājaṁs
tataś ca nabhaso guṇam

śabdaṁ grasati bhūtādir
nabhas tam anu līyate
taijasaś cendriyāṇy aṅga
devān vaikāriko guṇaiḥ

mahān grasaty ahaṅkāraṁ
guṇāḥ sattvādayaś ca tam
grasate'vyākṛtaṁ rājan
guṇān kālena coditam

na tasya kālāvayavaiḥ
pariṇāmādayo guṇāḥ
anādy anantam avyaktaṁ
nityaṁ kāraṇam avyayam

apām — of water; *rasam* — the taste; *atha* — then; *tejaḥ*—fire; *tāḥ*—that water; *līyante* — dissolves; *atha* — after this; *nīrasāḥ*—deprived of its quality of taste; *grasate* — takes away; *tejasaḥ*—of fire; *rūpam* — the form; *vāyuḥ*—the air; *tat-rahitam* — deprived of that form; *tadā* — then; *līyate* — merges; *ca* — and; *anile* — in wind; *tejaḥ*—fire; *vāyoḥ*—of the air; *kham* — the ether; *grasate* — takes away; *guṇam* — the perceptible quality (touch); *saḥ*—that air; *vai* — indeed; *viśati* — enters; *kham* — the ether; *rājan* — O King Parīkṣit; *tataḥ*—thereupon; *ca* — and; *nabhasaḥ*—of the ether; *guṇam* — the quality; *śabdam* — sound; *grasati* — takes away; *bhūta-ādiḥ*—the element of false ego in the mode of ignorance; *nabhaḥ*—the ether; *tam* — into that false ego; *anu* — subsequently; *līyate* — merges; *taijasaḥ*—false ego in the mode of passion; *ca* — and; *indriyāṇi* — the senses; *aṅga* — my dear King; *devān* — the demigods; *vaikārikaḥ*—false ego in the mode of goodness; *guṇaiḥ*—along with the manifest functions (of false ego); *mahān* — the *mahat-tattva; grasati* — seizes; *ahaṅkāram* — false ego; *guṇāḥ*—the basic modes of nature; *sattva-ādayaḥ*—goodness, passion and ignorance; *ca*—and; *tam*—that *mahat; grasate*—seizes; *avyākṛtam*—the unmanifest original form of nature; *rājan*—O King; *guṇān*—the three modes; *kālena*—by time; *coditam*—impelled; *na*—there are not; *tasya*—of that unmanifest nature; *kāla*—of time; *avayavaiḥ*—by the segments; *pariṇāma-ādayaḥ*—transformation and the other changes of visible matter (creation, growth and so on); *guṇāḥ*—such qualities; *anādi*—without beginning; *anantam*—without end; *avyaktam*—unmanifest; *nityam*—eternal; *kāraṇam*—the cause; *avyayam*—infallible.

TRANSLATION

The element fire then seizes the taste from the element water, which, deprived of its unique quality, taste, merges into fire. Air seizes the form inherent in fire, and then fire, deprived of form, merges into air. The element ether seizes the quality of air, namely touch, and that air enters into ether. Then, O King, false ego in ignorance seizes sound, the quality of ether, after which ether merges into false ego. False ego in the mode of passion takes hold of the senses, and false ego in the mode of goodness absorbs the demigods. Then the total mahat-tattva seizes false ego along with its various functions, and that mahat is seized by the three basic modes of nature—goodness, passion and ignorance. My dear King Parīkṣit, these modes are further overtaken by the original unmanifest form of nature, impelled by time. That unmanifest nature is not subject to the six kinds of transformation caused by the influence of time. Rather, it has no beginning and no end. It is the unmanifest, eternal and infallible cause of creation.

TEXTS 20–21

न यत्र वाचो न मनो न सत्त्वं
तमो रजो वा महदादयोऽमी ।
न प्राणबुद्धीन्द्रियदेवता वा
न सन्निवेशः खलु लोककल्पः ॥ २० ॥
न स्वप्नजाग्रन्न च तत्सुषुप्तं
न खं जलं भूरनिलोऽग्निरर्कः ।
संसुप्तवच्छून्यवदप्रतर्क्यं
तन्मूलभूतं पदमामनन्ति ॥ २१ ॥

na yatra vāco na mano na sattvaṁ
tamo rajo vā mahad-ādayo'mī
na prāṇa-buddhīndriya-devatā vā
na sanniveśaḥ khalu loka-kalpaḥ

na svapna-jāgran na ca tat suṣuptaṁ
na khaṁ jalaṁ bhūr anilo'gnir arkaḥ
saṁsupta-vac chūnya-vad apratarkyaṁ
tan mūla-bhūtaṁ padam āmananti

na — not; *yatra* — wherein; *vācaḥ*—speech; *na* — not; *manaḥ*—the mind; *na* — not; *sattvam* — the mode of goodness; *tamaḥ*—the mode of ignorance; *rajaḥ*—the mode of passion; *vā* — or; *mahat* — the *mahat-tattva; ādayaḥ*—and so on; *amī*—these elements; *na* — not; *prāṇa* — the vital air; *buddhi* — intelligence; *indriya* — the senses; *devatāḥ*—and the controlling demigods; *vā* — or; *na* — not; *sanniveśaḥ*—the particular construction; *khalu* — indeed; *loka-kalpaḥ*—of the arrangement of the planetary systems; *na* — not; *svapna* — sleep; *jāgrat* — waking condition; *na* — not; *ca* — and; *tat* — that; *suṣuptam* — deep sleep; *na* — not; *kham* — ether; *jalam* — water; *bhūḥ*—earth; *anilaḥ*—air; *agniḥ*—fire; *arkaḥ*—the sun; *saṁsupta-vat* — like one who is fast asleep; *śūnya-vat* — like a void; *apratarkyam* — inaccessible to logic; *tat* — that *pradhāna; mūla-bhūtam* — serving as the basis; *padam* — the substance; *āmananti* — great authorities say.

TRANSLATION

In the unmanifest stage of material nature, called pradhāna, there is no expression of words, no mind and no manifestation of the subtle elements beginning from the mahat, nor are there the modes of goodness, passion and ignorance. There is no life air or intelligence, nor any senses or demigods. There is no definite arrangement of planetary systems, nor are there present the different stages of consciousness — sleep, wakefulness and deep sleep. There is no ether, water, earth, air, fire or sun. The situation is just like that of complete sleep, or of voidness. Indeed, it is indescribable. Authorities in spiritual science explain, however, that since pradhāna is the original substance, it is the actual basis of material creation.

TEXT 22

लयः प्राकृतिको ह्येष पुरुषाव्यक्तयोर्यदा ।
शक्तयः सम्प्रलीयन्ते विवशाः कालविद्रुताः ॥ २२ ॥

layaḥ prākṛtiko hy eṣa
puruṣāvyaktayor yadā
śaktayaḥ sampralīyante
vivaśāḥ kāla-vidrutāḥ

layaḥ—the annihilation; *prākṛtikaḥ*—of the material elements; *hi*—indeed; *eṣaḥ*—this; *puruṣa*—of the Supreme Lord; *avyaktayoḥ*—and of His material nature in its unmanifest form; *yadā*—when; *śaktayaḥ*—the energies; *sampralīyante*—merge totally; *vivaśāḥ*—helpless; *kāla*—by time; *vidrutāḥ*—disarrayed.

TRANSLATION

This is the annihilation called prākṛtika, during which the energies belonging to the Supreme Person and His unmanifest material nature, disassembled by the force of time, are deprived of their potencies and merge together totally.

TEXT 23

बुद्धीन्द्रियार्थरूपेण ज्ञानं भाति तदाश्रयम् ।
दृश्यत्वाव्यतिरेकाभ्यामाद्यन्तवदवस्तु यत् ॥ २३ ॥

buddhīndriyārtha-rūpeṇa
jñānaṁ bhāti tad-āśrayam
dṛśyatvāvyatirekābhyām
ādy-antavad avastu yat

buddhi—of intelligence; *indriya*—the senses; *artha*—and the objects of perception; *rūpeṇa*—in the form; *jñānam*—the Absolute Truth; *bhāti*—manifests; *tat*—of these elements; *āśrayam*—the basis; *dṛśyatva*—because of being perceived; *avyatirekābhyām*—and because of being nondifferent from its own cause; *ādi-anta-vat*—which has a beginning and an end; *avastu*—is insubstantial; *yat*—whatever.

TRANSLATION

It is the Absolute Truth alone who manifests in the forms of intelligence, the senses and the objects of sense perception, and who is their ultimate basis. Whatever has a beginning and an end is insubstantial because of being an object perceived by limited senses and because of being nondifferent from its own cause.

PURPORT

The word *dṛśyatva* indicates that all subtle and gross material manifestations are made visible by the potency of the Supreme Lord and again become invisible, or unmanifest, at the time of annihilation. They are therefore in essence not separate from the source of their expansion and withdrawal.

TEXT 24

दीपश्चक्षुश्च रूपं च ज्योतिषो न पृथग् भवेत् ।
एवं धीः खानि मात्राश्च न स्युरन्यतमादृतात् ॥ २४॥

dīpaś cakṣuś ca rūpaṁ ca
jyotiṣo na pṛthag bhavet
evaṁ dhīḥ khāni mātrāś ca
na syur anyatamād ṛtāt

dīpaḥ—a lamp; *cakṣuḥ*—a perceiving eye; *ca*—and; *rūpam*—a perceived form; *ca*—and; *jyotiṣaḥ*—from the original element fire; *na*—not; *pṛthak*—distinct; *bhavet*—are; *evam*—in the same way; *dhīḥ*—intelligence; *khāni*—the senses; *mātrāḥ*—the perceptions; *ca*—and; *na syuḥ*—they are not; *anyatamāt*—which is itself completely distinct; *ṛtāt*—from the reality.

TRANSLATION

A lamp, the eye that views by the light of that lamp, and the visible form that is viewed are all basically nondifferent from the element fire. In the same way, intelligence, the senses and sense perceptions have no existence separate from the supreme reality, although that Absolute Truth remains totally distinct from them.

TEXT 25

बुद्धेर्जागरणं स्वप्नः सुषुप्तिरिति चोच्यते ।
मायामात्रं इदं राजन्नानात्वं प्रत्यगात्मनि ॥ २५॥

buddher jāgaraṇaṁ svapnaḥ
suṣuptir iti cocyate
māyā-mātram idaṁ rājan
nānātvaṁ pratyag-ātmani

buddheḥ—of intelligence; *jāgaraṇam* — waking consciousness; *svapnaḥ* —sleep; *suṣuptiḥ*—deep sleep; *iti* — thus; *ca* — and; *ucyate* — are called; *māyā-mātram* — merely illusion; *idam* — this; *rājan* — O King; *nānātvam* — the duality; *pratyak-ātmani* — experienced by the pure soul.

TRANSLATION

The three states of intelligence are called waking consciousness, sleep and deep sleep. But, my dear King, the variegated experiences created for the pure living entity by these different states are nothing more than illusion.

PURPORT

Pure Kṛṣṇa consciousness exists beyond the various stages of material awareness. Just as darkness vanishes in the presence of light, so illusory material intelligence, which is experienced as normal perception, dreaming and deep sleep, completely vanishes in the brilliant presence of pure Kṛṣṇa consciousness, the constitutional condition of every living entity.

TEXT 26

यथा जलधरा व्योम्नि भवन्ति न भवन्ति च ।
ब्रह्मणीदं तथा विश्वमवयव्युदयाप्ययात् ॥ २६ ॥

yathā jala-dharā vyomni
bhavanti na bhavanti ca
brahmaṇīdaṁ tathā viśvam
avayavy udayāpyayāt

yathā — just as; *jala-dharāḥ*—the clouds; *vyomni* — in the sky; *bhavanti* — are; *na bhavanti* — are not; *ca* — and; *brahmaṇi* — within the Absolute Truth; *idam* — this; *tathā* — similarly; *viśvam* — universe; *avayavi* — having parts; *udaya* — because of generation; *apyayāt* — and dissolution.

TRANSLATION

Just as clouds in the sky come into being and are then dispersed by the amalgamation and dissolution of their constituent elements, this material universe is created and destroyed within the Absolute Truth by the amalgamation and dissolution of its elemental, constituent parts.

TEXT 27

सत्यं ह्यवयवः प्रोक्तः सर्वावयविनामिह ।
विनार्थेन प्रतीयेरन् पटस्येवांग तन्तवः ॥ २७ ॥

satyaṁ hy avayavaḥ proktaḥ
sarvāvayavinām iha
vinārthena pratīyeran
paṭasyevāṅga tantavaḥ

satyam — real; *hi* — because; *avayavaḥ* — the ingredient cause; *proktaḥ* — is said to be; *sarva-avayavinām* — of all constituted entities; *iha* — in this created world; *vinā* — apart from; *arthena* — their manifest product; *pratīyeran* — they can be perceived; *paṭasya* — of a cloth; *iva* — as; *aṅga* — my dear King; *tantavaḥ* — the threads.

TRANSLATION

My dear King, it is stated [in the Vedānta-sūtra] that the ingredient cause that constitutes any manifested product in this universe can be perceived as a separate reality, just as the threads that make up a cloth can be perceived separately from their product.

TEXT 28

यत् सामान्यविशेषाभ्यामुपलभ्येत स भ्रमः ।
अन्योन्यापाश्रयात् सर्वमाद्यन्तवदवस्तु यत् ॥ २८ ॥

yat sāmānya-viśeṣābhyām
upalabhyeta sa bhramaḥ
anyonyāpāśrayāt sarvam
ādy-antavad avastu yat

yat — whatever; *sāmānya* — in terms of general cause; *viśeṣābhyām* — and specific product; *upalabhyeta* — is experienced; *saḥ* — that; *bhramaḥ* — is illusion; *anyonya* — mutual; *apāśrayāt* — because of dependence; *sarvam* — everything; *ādi-anta-vat* — subject to beginning and end; *avastu* — unreal; *yat* — which.

TRANSLATION

Anything experienced in terms of general cause and specific effect must be an illusion, because such causes and effects exist only relative to each other. Indeed, whatever has a beginning and an end is unreal.

PURPORT

The nature of a material cause cannot be perceived without perception of the effect. For example, the burning nature of fire cannot be perceived without observing the effect of fire, such as a burning object or ashes. Similarly, the saturating quality of water cannot be understood without observing the effect, a saturated cloth or paper. The organizational power of a man cannot be understood without observing the effect of his dynamic work, namely a solid institution. In this way, not only do effects depend upon their causes, but the perception of the cause also depends upon observation of the effect. Thus both are defined relatively and have a beginning and an end. The conclusion is that all such material causes and effects are essentially temporary and relative, and consequently illusory.

The Supreme Personality of Godhead, although the cause of all causes, has no beginning or end. Therefore He is neither material nor illusory. Lord Kṛṣṇa's opulences and potencies are absolute reality, beyond the interdependence of material cause and effect.

TEXT 29

विकारः ख्यायमानोऽपि प्रत्यगात्मानमन्तरा ।
न निरूप्योऽस्त्यणुरपि स्याच्चेच्चित्सम आत्मवत् ॥ २९ ॥

vikāraḥ khyāyamāno 'pi
pratyag-ātmānam antarā
na nirūpyo 'sty aṇur api
syāc cec cit-sama ātma-vat

vikāraḥ—the transformation of created existence; *khyāyamānaḥ*—appearing; *api*—although; *pratyak-ātmānam*—the Supreme Soul; *antarā*—without; *na*—not; *nirūpyaḥ*—conceivable; *asti*—is; *aṇuḥ*—a single atom; *api*—even; *syāt*—it is so; *cet*—if; *cit-samaḥ*—equally spirit; *ātma-vat*—remaining as it is, without change.

TRANSLATION

Although perceived, the transformation of even a single atom of material nature has no ultimate definition without reference to the Supreme Soul. To be accepted as factually existing, something must possess the same quality as pure spirit — eternal, unchanging existence.

PURPORT

A mirage of water appearing in the desert is actually a manifestation of light; the false appearance of water is a specific transformation of light. That which falsely appears as independent material nature is similarly a transformation of the Supreme Personality of Godhead. Material nature is the external potency of the Lord.

TEXT 30

न हि सत्यस्य नानात्वमविद्वान् यदि मन्यते ।
नानात्वं छिद्रयोर्यद्वज्ज्योतिषोर्वातयोरिव ॥ ३० ॥

na hi satyasya nānātvam
avidvān yadi manyate
nānātvaṁ chidrayor yadvaj
jyotiṣor vātayor iva

na — there is no; *hi* — indeed; *satyasya* — of the Absolute Truth; *nānātvam* — duality; *avidvān* — a person not in true knowledge; *yadi* — if; *manyate* — he thinks; *nānātvam* — the duality; *chidrayoḥ* — of the two skies; *yadvat* — just as; *jyotiṣoḥ* — of the two celestial lights; *vātayoḥ* — of the two winds; *iva* — as.

TRANSLATION

There is no material duality in the Absolute Truth. The duality perceived by an ignorant person is like the difference between the sky contained in an empty pot and the sky outside the pot, or the difference between the reflection of the sun in water and the sun itself in the sky, or the difference between the vital air within one living body and that within another body.

TEXT 31

यथा हिरण्यं बहुधा समीयते
नृभिः क्रियाभिर्व्यवहारवर्त्मसु ।
एवं वचोभिर्भगवानधोक्षजो
व्याख्यायते लौकिकवैदिकैर्जनैः ॥ ३१ ॥

yathā hiraṇyaṁ bahudhā samīyate
nṛbhiḥ kriyābhir vyavahāra-vartmasu
evaṁ vacobhir bhagavān adhokṣajo
vyākhyāyate laukika-vaidikair janaiḥ

yathā — just as; *hiraṇyam* — gold; *bahudhā* — in many forms; *samīyate* — appears; *nṛbhiḥ*—to men; *kriyābhiḥ*—in terms of different functions; *vyavahāra-vartmasu* — in ordinary usage; *evam* — similarly; *vacobhiḥ*—in varying terms; *bhagavān* — the Personality of Godhead; *adhokṣajaḥ*—the transcendental Lord, who is inconceivable to material senses; *vyākhyāyate* — is described; *laukika* — mundane; *vaidikaiḥ*—and Vedic; *janaiḥ*—by men.

TRANSLATION

According to their different purposes, men utilize gold in various ways, and gold is therefore perceived in various forms. In the same way, the Supreme Personality of Godhead, who is inaccessible to material senses, is described in various terms, both ordinary and Vedic, by different types of men.

PURPORT

All those who are not pure devotees of the Supreme Lord are basically trying to exploit the Lord and His energies. According to their strategy of exploitation, they conceive of and describe the Absolute Truth in various ways. In *Bhagavad-gītā* and *Śrīmad-Bhāgavatam* the Absolute Truth presents Himself as He actually is for the benefit of sincere people who do not foolishly try to conceptually manipulate the Supreme Godhead.

TEXT 32

यथा घनोऽर्कप्रभवोऽर्कदर्शितो
ह्यर्कांशभूतस्य च चक्षुषस्तमः ।

एवं त्वहं ब्रह्मगुणस्तदीक्षितो
ब्रह्मांशकस्यात्मन आत्मबन्धनः ॥ ३२ ॥

yathā ghano 'rka-prabhavo 'rka-darśito
hy arkāṁśa-bhūtasya ca cakṣuṣas tamaḥ
evaṁ tv ahaṁ brahma-guṇas tad-īkṣito
brahmāṁśakasyātmana ātma-bandhanaḥ

yathā — as; *ghanaḥ* — a cloud; *arka* — of the sun; *prabhavaḥ* — the product; *arka* — by the sun; *darśitaḥ* — made visible; *hi* — indeed; *arka* — of the sun; *aṁśa-bhūtasya* — which is the partial expansion; *ca* — and; *cakṣuṣaḥ* — of the eye; *tamaḥ* — darkness; *evam* — in the same way; *tu* — indeed; *aham* — false ego; *brahma-guṇaḥ* — a quality of the Absolute Truth; *tat-īkṣitaḥ* — visible through the agency of that Absolute Truth; *brahma-aṁśakasya* — of the partial expansion of the Absolute Truth; *ātmanaḥ* — of the *jīva* soul; *ātma-bandhanaḥ* — serving to obstruct perception of the Supreme Soul.

TRANSLATION

Although a cloud is a product of the sun and is also made visible by the sun, it nevertheless creates darkness for the viewing eye, which is another partial expansion of the sun. Similarly, material false ego, a particular product of the Absolute Truth made visible by the Absolute Truth, obstructs the individual soul, another partial expansion of the Absolute Truth, from realizing the Absolute Truth.

TEXT 33

घनो यदार्कप्रभवो विदीर्यते
चक्षुः स्वरूपं रविमीक्षते तदा ।
यदा ह्यहंकार उपाधिरात्मनो
जिज्ञासया नश्यति तर्ह्यनुस्मरेत् ॥ ३३ ॥

ghano yadārka-prabhavo vidīryate
cakṣuḥ svarūpaṁ ravim īkṣate tadā
yadā hy ahaṅkāra upādhir ātmano
jijñāsayā naśyati tarhy anusmaret

ghanaḥ — the cloud; *yadā* — when; *arka-prabhavaḥ* — the product of the sun; *vidīryate* — is torn apart; *cakṣuḥ* — the eye; *svarūpam* — in its real form;

ravim — the sun; *īkṣate* — sees; *tadā* — then; *yadā* — when; *hi* — indeed also; *ahaṅkāraḥ*—false ego; *upādhiḥ*—the superficial covering; *ātmanaḥ*— of the spirit soul; *jijñāsayā* — by spiritual inquiry; *naśyati* — is destroyed; *tarhi* — at that time; *anusmaret* — one gains his proper remembrance.

TRANSLATION

When the cloud originally produced from the sun is torn apart, the eye can see the actual form of the sun. Similarly, when the spirit soul destroys his material covering of false ego by inquiring into the transcendental science, he regains his original spiritual awareness.

PURPORT

Just as the sun can burn away the clouds that prevent one from seeing it, the Supreme Lord (and He alone) can remove the false ego that prevents one from seeing Him. There are some creatures, however, like owls, who are averse to seeing the sun. In the same way, those who are not interested in spiritual knowledge will never receive the privilege of seeing God.

TEXT 34

यदैवमेतेन विवेकहेतिना
मायामयाहंकरणात्मबन्धनम् ।
छित्त्वाच्युतात्मानुभवोऽवतिष्ठते
तमाहुरात्यन्तिकमंग सम्प्लवम् ॥ ३४॥

yadaivam etena viveka-hetinā
māyā-mayāhaṅkaraṇātma-bandhanam
chittvācyutātmānubhavo 'vatiṣṭhate
tam āhur ātyantikam aṅga samplavam

yadā — when; *evam* — in this way; *etena* — by this; *viveka* — of discrimination; *hetinā* — sword; *māyā-maya* — illusory; *ahaṅkaraṇa* — false ego; *ātma* — of the soul; *bandhanam* — the cause of bondage; *chittvā* — cutting off; *acyuta* — of the infallible; *ātma* — Supreme Soul; *anubhavaḥ*—realization; *avatiṣṭhate* — develops firmly; *tam* — that; *āhuḥ*— they call; *ātyantikam* — ultimate; *aṅga* — my dear King; *samplavam* — annihilation.

TRANSLATION

My dear Parīkṣit, when the illusory false ego that binds the soul has been cut off with the sword of discriminating knowledge and one has developed realization of Lord Acyuta, the Supreme Soul, this is called the ātyantika, or ultimate, annihilation of material existence.

TEXT 35

नित्यदा सर्वभूतानां ब्रह्मादीनां परन्तप ।
उत्पत्तिप्रलयावेके सूक्ष्मज्ञाः सम्प्रचक्षते ॥ ३५ ॥

nityadā sarva-bhūtānāṁ
brahmādīnāṁ parantapa
utpatti-pralayāv eke
sūkṣma-jñāḥ sampracakṣate

nityadā — constantly; *sarva-bhūtānām* — of all created beings; *brahma-ādīnām* — beginning with Lord Brahmā; *param-tapa* — O subduer of the enemies; *utpatti* — creation; *pralayau* — and annihilation; *eke* — some; *sūkṣma-jñāḥ* — expert knowers of subtle things; *sampracakṣate* — declare.

TRANSLATION

Experts in the subtle workings of nature, O subduer of the enemy, have declared that there are continuous processes of creation and annihilation that all created beings, beginning with Brahmā, constantly undergo.

TEXT 36

कालस्रोतोजवेनाशु ह्रियमाणस्य नित्यदा ।
परिणामिनामवस्थास्ता जन्मप्रलयहेतवः ॥ ३६ ॥

kāla-sroto-javenāśu
hriyamāṇasya nityadā
pariṇāminām avasthās tā
janma-pralaya-hetavaḥ

kāla — of time; *srotaḥ* — of the mighty current; *javena* — by the force; *āśu* — rapidly; *hriyamāṇasya* — of that which is being taken away; *nityadā* — constantly; *pariṇāminām* — of things subject to transformation; *avasthāḥ* —

the various conditions; *tāḥ*—they; *janma* — of birth; *pralaya* — and annihilation; *hetavaḥ*—the causes.

TRANSLATION

All material entities undergo transformation and are constantly and swiftly eroded by the mighty currents of time. The various stages of existence that material things exhibit are the perpetual causes of their generation and annihilation.

TEXT 37

अनाद्यन्तवतानेन कालेनेश्वरमूर्तिना ।
अवस्था नैव दृश्यन्ते वियति ज्योतिषामिव ॥ ३७ ॥

anādy-antavatānena
kāleneśvara-mūrtinā
avasthā naiva dṛśyante
viyati jyotiṣām iva

anādi-anta-vatā — without beginning or end; *anena* — by this; *kālena* — time; *īśvara* — of the Supreme Personality of Godhead; *mūrtinā* — the representation; *avasthāḥ*—the different stages; *na* — not; *eva* — indeed; *dṛśyante* — are seen; *viyati* — in outer space; *jyotiṣām* — of the moving planets; *iva* — just as.

TRANSLATION

These stages of existence created by beginningless and endless time, the impersonal representative of the Supreme Lord, are not visible, just as the infinitesimal momentary changes of position of the planets in the sky cannot be directly seen.

PURPORT

Although everyone knows that the sun is constantly moving in the sky, one cannot normally see the sun moving. Similarly, no one can directly perceive his hair or nails growing, although with the passing of time we perceive the fact of growth. Time, the potency of the Lord, is very subtle and powerful and is an insurmountable barrier to fools who are trying to exploit the material creation.

TEXT 38

नित्यो नैमित्तिकश्चैव तथा प्राकृतिको लयः ।
आत्यन्तिकश्च कथितः कालस्य गतिरीदृशी ॥ ३८ ॥

nityo naimittikaś caiva
tathā prākṛtiko layaḥ
ātyantikaś ca kathitaḥ
kālasya gatir īdṛśī

nityaḥ—continuous; *naimittikaḥ*—occasional; *ca*—and; *eva*—indeed; *tathā*—also; *prākṛtikaḥ*—natural; *layaḥ*—annihilation; *ātyantikaḥ*—final; *ca*—and; *kathitaḥ*—are described; *kālasya*—of time; *gatiḥ*—the progress; *īdṛśī*—like this.

TRANSLATION

In this way the progress of time is described in terms of the four kinds of annihilation—continuous, occasional, elemental and final.

TEXT 39

एताः कुरुश्रेष्ठ जगद्विधातुर्
नारायणस्याखिलसत्त्वधाम्नः ।
लीलाकथास्ते कथिताः समासतः
कार्त्स्न्येन नाजोऽप्यभिधातुमीशः ॥ ३९ ॥

etāḥ kuru-śreṣṭha jagad-vidhātur
nārāyaṇasyākhila-sattva-dhāmnaḥ
līlā-kathās te kathitāḥ samāsataḥ
kārtsnyena nājo'py abhidhātum īśaḥ

etāḥ—these; *kuru-śreṣtha*—O best of the Kurus; *jagat-vidhātuḥ*—of the creator of the universe; *nārāyaṇasya*—of Lord Nārāyaṇa; *akhila-sattva-dhāmnaḥ*—the reservoir of all existences; *līlā-kathāḥ*—the pastime narrations; *te*—to you; *kathitāḥ*—have been related; *samāsataḥ*—in summary; *kārtsnyena*—entirely; *na*—not; *ajaḥ*—unborn Brahmā; *api*—even; *abhidhātum*—to enumerate; *īśaḥ*—is capable.

TRANSLATION

O best of the Kurus, I have related to you these narrations of the pastimes of Lord Nārāyaṇa, the creator of this world and the ultimate reservoir of all existence, presenting them to you only in brief summary. Even Lord Brahmā himself would be incapable of describing them entirely.

TEXT 40

संसारसिन्धुमतिदुस्तरमुत्तितीर्षोर्
नान्यः प्लवो भगवतः पुरुषोत्तमस्य ।
लीलाकथारसनिषेवणमन्तरेण
पुंसो भवेद् विविधदुःखदवार्दितस्य ॥ ४० ॥

saṁsāra-sindhum ati-dustaram uttitīrṣor
nānyaḥ plavo bhagavataḥ puruṣottamasya
līlā-kathā-rasa-niṣevaṇam antareṇa
puṁso bhaved vividha-duḥkha-davārditasya

saṁsāra — of material existence; *sindhum* — the ocean; *ati-dustaram* — impossible to cross; *uttitīrṣoḥ*—for one who desires to cross; *na* — there is not; *anyaḥ*—any other; *plavaḥ*—boat; *bhagavataḥ*—of the Personality of Godhead; *puruṣa-uttamasya* — the Supreme Lord; *līlā-kathā* — of the narrations of the pastimes; *rasa* — to the transcendental taste; *niṣevaṇam* — the rendering of service; *antareṇa* — apart from; *puṁsaḥ*—for a person; *bhavet* — there can be; *vividha* — various; *duḥkha* — of material miseries; *dava* — by the fire; *arditasya* — who is distressed.

TRANSLATION

For a person who is suffering in the fire of countless miseries and who desires to cross the insurmountable ocean of material existence, there is no suitable boat except that of cultivating devotion to the transcendental taste for the narrations of the Supreme Personality of Godhead's pastimes.

PURPORT

Although it is not possible to completely describe the pastimes of the Lord, even a partial appreciation can save one from the unbearable miseries of material existence. The fever of material existence can be removed only by the medicine of the holy name and pastimes of the Supreme Lord, which are perfectly narrated in *Śrīmad-Bhāgavatam.*

TEXT 41

**पुराणसंहितामेतामृषिर्नारायणोऽव्ययः ।
नारदाय पुरा प्राह कृष्णद्वैपायनाय सः ॥ ४१ ॥**

purāṇa-saṁhitām etām
ṛṣir nārāyaṇo'vyayaḥ
nāradāya purā prāha
kṛṣṇa-dvaipāyanāya saḥ

purāṇa — of all the *Purāṇas; saṁhitām* — the essential compendium; *etām* — this; *ṛṣiḥ* — the great sage; *nārāyaṇaḥ* — Lord Nara-Nārāyaṇa; *avyayaḥ* — the infallible; *nāradāya* — to Nārada Muni; *purā* — previously; *prāha* — spoke; *kṛṣṇa-dvaipāyanāya* — to Kṛṣṇa Dvaipāyana Vedavyāsa; *saḥ* — he, Nārada.

TRANSLATION

Long ago this essential anthology of all the Purāṇas was spoken by the infallible Lord Nara-Nārāyaṇa Ṛṣi to Nārada, who then repeated it to Kṛṣṇa Dvaipāyana Vedavyāsa.

TEXT 42

**स वै मह्यं महाराज भगवान् बादरायणः ।
इमां भागवतीं प्रीतः संहितां वेदसम्मिताम् ॥ ४२ ॥**

sa vai mahyaṁ mahā-rāja
bhagavān bādarāyaṇaḥ
imāṁ bhāgavatīṁ prītaḥ
saṁhitāṁ veda-sammitām

saḥ — he; *vai* — indeed; *mahyam* — to me, Śukadeva Gosvāmī; *mahārāja* — O King Parīkṣit; *bhagavān* — the powerful incarnation of the Supreme Lord; *bādarāyaṇaḥ* — Śrīla Vyāsadeva; *imām* — this; *bhāgavatīm* — *Bhāgavata* scripture; *prītaḥ* — being satisfied; *saṁhitām* — the anthology; *veda-sammitām* — equal in status to the four *Vedas.*

TRANSLATION

My dear Mahārāja Parīkṣit, that great personality Śrīla Vyāsadeva taught me this same scripture, Śrīmad-Bhāgavatam, which is equal in stature to the four Vedas.

TEXT 43

इमां वक्ष्यत्यसौ सूत ऋषिभ्यो नैमिषालये ।
दीर्घसत्रे कुरुश्रेष्ठ सम्पृष्टः शौनकादिभिः ॥ ४३ ॥

imāṁ vakṣyaty asau sūta
ṛṣibhyo naimiṣālaye
dīrgha-satre kuru-śreṣṭha
sampṛṣṭaḥ śaunakādibhiḥ

imām — this; *vakṣyati* — will speak; *asau* — present before us; *sūtaḥ*— Sūta Gosvāmī; *ṛṣibhyaḥ*—to the sages; *naimiṣa-ālaye* — in the forest of Naimiṣa; *dīrgha-satre* — at the lengthy sacrificial performance; *kuru-śreṣṭha* — O best of the Kurus; *sampṛṣṭaḥ*—questioned; *śaunaka-ādibhiḥ*—by the assembly led by Śaunaka.

TRANSLATION

O best of the Kurus, the same Sūta Gosvāmī who is sitting before us will speak this Bhāgavatam to the sages assembled in the great sacrifice at Naimiṣāraṇya. This he will do when questioned by the members of the assembly, headed by Śaunaka.

Thus end the purports of the humble servants of His Divine Grace A.C. Bhaktivedanta Swami Prabhupāda to the Twelfth Canto, Fourth Chapter, of the Śrīmad-Bhāgavatam, *entitled "The Four Categories of Universal Annihilation."*

CHAPTER FIVE

Śukadeva Gosvāmī's Final Instructions to Mahārāja Parīkṣit

This chapter explains how King Parīkṣit's fear of death from the snake-bird Takṣaka was averted by Śukadeva Gosvāmī's brief instructions on the Absolute Truth.

Having in the last chapter described the four processes of annihilation that act in this material world, Śrīla Śukadeva Gosvāmī now reminds Parīkṣit Mahārāja how he had previously, in the Third Canto, discussed the measurement of time and of the various millennia of universal history. During a single day of Lord Brahmā, constituting one thousand cycles of four ages, fourteen different Manus rule and die. Thus death is unavoidable for every embodied being, but the soul itself never dies, being entirely distinct from the material body. Śrī Śukadeva Gosvāmī then states that in *Śrīmad-Bhāgavatam* he has repeatedly chanted the glories of the Supreme Soul, Lord Śrī Hari, from whose satisfaction Brahmā takes birth and from whose anger Rudra is born. The idea "I will die" is simply the mentality of animals, because the soul does not undergo the bodily phases of previous nonexistence, birth, existence and death. When the body's subtle mental covering is destroyed by transcendental knowledge, the soul within the body again exhibits his original identity. Just as the temporal existence of a lamp comes about by the combination of oil, the vessel, the wick and the fire, the material body comes about by the amalgamation of the three modes of nature. The material body appears at birth and displays life for some time. Finally, the combination of material modes dissolves, and the body undergoes death, a phenomenon similar to the extinguishing of a lamp. Śukadeva addresses the king, saying, "You should fix yourself in meditation upon Lord Vāsudeva, and thus the bite of the snake-bird will not affect you."

TEXT 1

श्रीशुक उवाच

अत्रानुवर्ण्यतेऽभीक्ष्णं विश्वात्मा भगवान् हरिः ।
यस्य प्रसादजो ब्रह्मा रुद्रः क्रोधसमुद्भवः ॥ १ ॥

śrī-śuka uvāca
atrānuvarṇyate 'bhīkṣṇaṁ
viśvātmā bhagavān hariḥ
yasya prasāda-jo brahmā
rudraḥ krodha-samudbhavaḥ

śrī-śukaḥ uvāca — Śrī Śukadeva Gosvāmī said; *atra* — in this *Śrīmad-Bhāgavatam; anuvarṇyate* — is elaborately described; *abhīkṣṇam* — repeatedly; *viśva-ātmā* — the soul of the entire universe; *bhagavān* — the Supreme Personality of Godhead; *hariḥ* — Lord Hari; *yasya* — of whom; *prasāda* — from the satisfaction; *jaḥ* — born; *brahmā* — Lord Brahmā; *rudraḥ* — Lord Śiva; *krodha* — from the anger; *samudbhavaḥ* — whose birth.

TRANSLATION

Śukadeva Gosvāmī said: This Śrīmad-Bhāgavatam has elaborately described in various narrations the Supreme Soul of all that be — the Personality of Godhead, Hari — from whose satisfaction Brahmā is born and from whose anger Rudra takes birth.

PURPORT

Śrīla Viśvanātha Cakravartī Ṭhākura has given a very elaborate summary of *Śrīmad-Bhāgavatam* in his commentary on this verse. The essence of the great *ācārya's* statement is that unconditional loving surrender to the Supreme Lord, Kṛṣṇa, as described by Śukadeva Gosvāmī, is the highest perfection of life. The exclusive purpose of *Śrīmad-Bhāgavatam* is to convince the conditioned soul to execute such surrender to the Lord and go back home, back to Godhead.

TEXT 2

त्वं तु राजन्मरिष्येति पशुबुद्धिमिमां जहि ।
न जातः प्रागभूतोऽद्य देहवत्त्वं न नङ्क्ष्यसि ॥ २ ॥

tvaṁ tu rājan mariṣyeti
paśu-buddhim imāṁ jahi
na jātaḥ prāg abhūto 'dya
deha-vat tvaṁ na naṅkṣyasi

tvam — you; *tu* — but; *rājan* — O King; *mariṣye* — I am about to die; *iti* — thus thinking; *paśu-buddhim* — animalistic mentality; *imām* — this; *jahi* — give up; *na* — not; *jātaḥ*—born; *prāk* — previously; *abhūtaḥ*—nonexistent; *adya* — today; *deha-vat* — like the body; *tvam* — you; *na naṅkṣyasi* — will not be destroyed.

TRANSLATION

O King, give up the animalistic mentality of thinking, "I am going to die." Unlike the body, you have not taken birth. There was not a time in the past when you did not exist, and you are not about to be destroyed.

PURPORT

At the end of the First Canto (1.19.15) King Parīkṣit stated:

taṁ mopajātaṁ pratiyantu viprā
gaṅgā ca devī dhṛta-cittam īśe
dvijopasṛṣṭaḥ kuhakas takṣako vā
daśatv alaṁ gāyata viṣṇu-gāthāḥ

"O *brāhmaṇas,* just accept me as a completely surrendered soul, and let Mother Ganges, the representative of the Lord, also accept me in that way, for I have already taken the lotus feet of the Lord into my heart. Let the snake-bird — or whatever magical thing the *brāhmaṇa* created — bite me at once. I only desire that you all continue singing the deeds of Lord Viṣṇu."

Even before hearing *Śrīmad-Bhāgavatam,* King Parīkṣit was a *mahā-bhāgavata,* a great and pure devotee of Lord Kṛṣṇa. There was actually no animalistic fear of death within the King, but for our sake Śukadeva Gosvāmī is speaking very strongly to his disciple, just as Lord Kṛṣṇa speaks strongly to Arjuna in *Bhagavad-gītā.*

TEXT 3

न भविष्यसि भूत्वा त्वं पुत्रपौत्रादिरूपवान् ।
बीजांकुरवद्देहादेर्व्यतिरिक्तो यथानलः ॥ ३ ॥

na bhaviṣyasi bhūtvā tvaṁ
putra-pautrādi-rūpavān
bījāṅkura-vad dehāder
vyatirikto yathānalaḥ

na bhaviṣyasi — you will not come into being; *bhūtvā* — becoming; *tvam* — you; *putra* — of children; *pautra* — grandchildren; *ādi* — and so on; *rūpa-vān* — assuming the forms; *bīja* — the seed; *aṅkura* — and the sprout; *vat* — like; *deha-ādeḥ* — from the material body and its paraphernalia; *vyatiriktaḥ* — distinct; *yathā* — as; *analaḥ* — the fire (from the wood).

TRANSLATION

You will not take birth again in the form of your sons and grandsons, like a sprout taking birth from a seed and then generating a new seed. Rather, you are entirely distinct from the material body and its paraphernalia, in the same way that fire is distinct from its fuel.

PURPORT

Sometimes one dreams of being reborn as the son of one's son, in the hope of perpetually remaining in the same material family. As stated in the *śruti-mantra, pitā putreṇa pitṛmān yoni-yonau:* "A father has a father in his son, because he may take birth as his own grandson." The purpose of *Śrīmad-Bhāgavatam* is spiritual liberation and not the foolish prolonging of the illusion of bodily identification. That is clearly stated in this verse.

TEXT 4

स्वप्ने यथा शिरश्छेदं पञ्चत्वाद्यात्मनः स्वयम् ।
यस्मात् पश्यति देहस्य तत आत्मा ह्यजोऽमरः ॥ ४ ॥

svapne yathā śiraś-chedaṁ
pañcatvādy ātmanaḥ svayam
yasmāt paśyati dehasya
tata ātmā hy ajo 'maraḥ

svapne — in a dream; *yathā* — as; *śiraḥ* — of one's head; *chedam* — the cutting off; *pañcatva-ādi* — the condition of being composed of the five material elements, and other material conditions; *ātmanaḥ* — one's own; *svayam* — oneself; *yasmāt* — because; *paśyati* — one sees; *dehasya* — of the body; *tataḥ* — therefore; *ātmā* — the soul; *hi* — certainly; *ajaḥ* — unborn; *amaraḥ* — immortal.

TRANSLATION

In a dream one can see his own head being cut off and thus understand that his actual self is standing apart from the dream experience. Similarly, while awake one can see that his body is a product of the five material elements. Therefore it is to be understood that the actual self, the soul, is distinct from the body it observes and is unborn and immortal.

TEXT 5

घटे भिन्ने घटाकाश आकाशः स्याद् यथा पुरा।
एवं देहे मृते जीवो ब्रह्म सम्पद्यते पुनः ॥ ५ ॥

ghaṭe bhinne ghaṭākāśa
ākāśaḥ syād yathā purā
evaṁ dehe mṛte jīvo
brahma sampadyate punaḥ

ghaṭe — a pot; *bhinne* — when it is broken; *ghaṭa-ākāśaḥ* — the sky within the pot; *ākāśaḥ* — sky; *syāt* — remains; *yathā* — as; *purā* — previously; *evam* — similarly; *dehe* — the body; *mṛte* — when it is given up, in the liberated condition; *jīvaḥ* — the individual soul; *brahma* — his spiritual status; *sampadyate* — attains; *punaḥ* — once again.

TRANSLATION

When a pot is broken, the portion of sky within the pot remains as the element sky, just as before. In the same way, when the gross and subtle bodies die, the living entity within resumes his spiritual identity.

TEXT 6

मनः सृजति वै देहान् गुणान् कर्माणि चात्मनः।
तन्मनः सृजते माया ततो जीवस्य संसृतिः ॥ ६ ॥

manaḥ sṛjati vai dehān
guṇān karmāṇi cātmanaḥ
tan manaḥ sṛjate māyā
tato jīvasya saṁsṛtiḥ

manaḥ — the mind; *sṛjati* — produces; *vai* — indeed; *dehān* — the material bodies; *guṇān* — the qualities; *karmāṇi* — the activities; *ca* — and; *āt-*

manaḥ—of the soul; *tat*— that; *manaḥ*—mind; *sṛjate*— produces; *māyā* — the illusory potency of the Supreme Lord; *tataḥ*—thus; *jīvasya*— of the individual living being; *saṁsṛtiḥ*—the material existence.

TRANSLATION

The material bodies, qualities and activities of the spirit soul are created by the material mind. That mind is itself created by the illusory potency of the Supreme Lord, and thus the soul assumes material existence.

TEXT 7

स्नेहाधिष्ठानवर्त्यग्निसंयोगो यावदीयते ।
तावद्दीपस्य दीपत्वमेवं देहकृतो भवः ।
रजःसत्त्वतमोवृत्त्या जायतेऽथ विनश्यति ॥ ७ ॥

snehādhiṣṭhāna-varty-agni-
saṁyogo yāvad īyate
tāvad dīpasya dīpatvam
evaṁ deha-kṛto bhavaḥ
rajaḥ-sattva-tamo-vṛttyā
jāyate 'tha vinaśyati

sneha— of the oil; *adhiṣṭhāna*— the vessel; *varti*— the wick; *agni*— and the fire; *saṁyogaḥ*—the combination; *yāvat*— to which extent; *īyate*— is seen; *tāvat*— to that extent; *dīpasya*— of the lamp; *dīpatvam*— the status of functioning as a lamp; *evam*— similarly; *deha-kṛtaḥ*—due to the material body; *bhavaḥ*—material existence; *rajaḥ-sattva-tamaḥ*—of the modes of passion, goodness and ignorance; *vṛttyā*— by the action; *jāyate*— arises; *atha*— and; *vinaśyati*— is destroyed.

TRANSLATION

A lamp functions as such only by the combination of its fuel, vessel, wick and fire. Similarly, material life, based on the soul's identification with the body, is developed and destroyed by the workings of material goodness, passion and ignorance, which are the constituent elements of the body.

TEXT 8

न तत्रात्मा स्वयंज्योतिर्यो व्यक्ताव्यक्तयोर्परः ।
आकाश इव चाधारो ध्रुवोऽनन्तोपमस्ततः ॥ ८ ॥

na tatrātmā svayaṁ-jyotir
yo vyaktāvyaktayoḥ paraḥ
ākāśa iva cādhāro
dhruvo'nantopamas tataḥ

na — not; *tatra* — there; *ātmā* — the soul; *svayam-jyotiḥ*—self-luminous; *yaḥ*—who; *vyakta-avyaktayoḥ*—from the manifest and the unmanifest (the gross and subtle bodies); *paraḥ*—different; *ākāśaḥ*—the sky; *iva* — as; *ca* — and; *ādhāraḥ*—the basis; *dhruvaḥ*—fixed; *ananta* — without end; *upamaḥ*—or comparison; *tataḥ*—thus.

TRANSLATION

The soul within the body is self-luminous and is separate from the visible gross body and invisible subtle body. It remains as the fixed basis of changing bodily existence, just as the ethereal sky is the unchanging background of material transformation. Therefore the soul is endless and without material comparison.

TEXT 9

एवमात्मानमात्मस्थमात्मनैवामृश प्रभो ।
बुद्ध्यानुमानगर्भिन्या वासुदेवानुचिन्तया ॥ ९ ॥

evam ātmānam ātma-stham
ātmanaivāmṛśa prabho
buddhyānumāna-garbhiṇyā
vāsudevānucintayā

evam — in this way; *ātmānam* — your true self; *ātma-stham* — situated within the bodily covering; *ātmanā* — with your mind; *eva* — indeed; *āmṛśa* — consider carefully; *prabho* — O master of the self (King Parīkṣit); *buddhyā* — with intelligence; *anumāna-garbhiṇyā* — conceived by logic; *vāsudeva-anucintayā* — with meditation upon Lord Vāsudeva.

TRANSLATION

My dear King, by constantly meditating upon the Supreme Lord, Vāsudeva, and by applying clear and logical intelligence, you should carefully consider your true self and how it is situated within the material body.

TEXT 10

चोदितो विप्रवाक्येन न त्वां धक्ष्यति तक्षकः ।
मृत्यवो नोपधक्ष्यन्ति मृत्यूनां मृत्युमीश्वरम् ॥ १० ॥

codito vipra-vākyena
na tvāṁ dhakṣyati takṣakaḥ
mṛtyavo nopadhakṣyanti
mṛtyūnāṁ mṛtyum īśvaram

coditaḥ — sent; *vipra-vākyena* — by the words of the *brāhmaṇa; na* — not; *tvām* — you; *dhakṣyati* — will burn; *takṣakaḥ* — the snake-bird Takṣaka; *mṛtyavaḥ* — the agents of death personified; *na upadhakṣyanti* — cannot burn; *mṛtyūnām* — of these causes of death; *mṛtyum* — the very death; *īśvaram* — the master of the self.

TRANSLATION

The snake-bird Takṣaka, sent by the curse of the brāhmaṇa, will not burn your true self. The agents of death will never burn such a master of the self as you, for you have already conquered all dangers on your path back to Godhead.

PURPORT

Real death is the covering of one's eternal Kṛṣṇa consciousness. For the soul, material illusion is just like death, but Parīkṣit Mahārāja had already destroyed all those dangers that threaten one's spiritual life, such as lust, envy and fear. Śukadeva Gosvāmī here congratulates the great saintly king, who, as a pure devotee of Lord Kṛṣṇa homeward bound to the spiritual sky, was far beyond the reach of death.

TEXTS 11–12

अहं ब्रह्म परं धाम ब्रह्माहं परमं पदम् ।
एवं समीक्ष्य चात्मानमात्मन्याधाय निष्कले ॥ ११ ॥
दशन्तं तक्षकं पादे लेलिहानं विषाननैः ।
न द्रक्ष्यसि शरीरं च विश्वं च पृथगात्मनः ॥ १२ ॥

ahaṁ brahma paraṁ dhāma
brahmāhaṁ paramaṁ padam

evaṁ samīkṣya cātmānam
ātmany ādhāya niṣkale

daśantaṁ takṣakaṁ pāde
lelihānaṁ viṣānanaiḥ
na drakṣyasi śarīraṁ ca
viśvaṁ ca pṛthag ātmanaḥ

aham — I; *brahma* — the Absolute Truth; *param* — supreme; *dhāma* — the abode; *brahma* — the Absolute Truth; *aham* — I; *paramam* — the supreme; *padam* — destination; *evam* — thus; *samīkṣya* — considering; *ca* — and; *ātmānam* — yourself; *ātmani* — in the Supreme Self; *ādhāya* — placing; *niṣkale* — which is free from material designation; *daśantam* — biting; *takṣakam* — Takṣaka; *pāde* — upon your foot; *lelihānam* — the snake, licking his lips; *viṣa-ānanaiḥ*—with his mouth full of poison; *na drakṣyasi* — you will not even notice; *śarīram* — your body; *ca* — and; *viśvam* — the entire material world; *ca* — and; *pṛthak* — separate; *ātmanaḥ*—from the self.

TRANSLATION

You should consider, "I am nondifferent from the Absolute Truth, the supreme abode, and that Absolute Truth, the supreme destination, is nondifferent from me." Thus resigning yourself to the Supreme Soul, who is free from all material misidentifications, you will not even notice the snake-bird Takṣaka when he approaches with his poison-filled fangs and bites your foot. Nor will you see your dying body or the material world around you, because you will have realized yourself to be separate from them.

TEXT 13

एतत्ते कथितं तात यदात्मा पृष्टवान्नृप ।
हरेर्विश्वात्मनश्चेष्टां किं भूयः श्रोतुमिच्छसि ॥ १३ ॥

etat te kathitaṁ tāta
yad ātmā pṛṣṭavān nṛpa
harer viśvātmanaś ceṣṭāṁ
kiṁ bhūyaḥ śrotum icchasi

etat — this; *te* — to you; *kathitam* — narrated; *tāta* — my dear Parīkṣit; *yat* — which; *ātmā* — you; *pṛṣṭavān* — inquired; *nṛpa* — O King; *hareḥ*—of the Supreme Personality of Godhead; *viśva-ātmanaḥ*—of the Soul of the universe; *ceṣṭām* — the pastimes; *kim* — what; *bhūyaḥ*—further; *śrotum* — to hear; *icchasi*— do you wish.

TRANSLATION

Beloved King Parīkṣit, I have narrated to you the topics you originally inquired about — the pastimes of Lord Hari, the Supreme Soul of the universe. Now, what more do you wish to hear?

PURPORT

In his commentary on this text, Śrīla Jīva Gosvāmī has elaborately demonstrated, by citing many *Bhāgavatam* verses, the exalted devotional position of King Parīkṣit, who was fully determined to fix his mind upon Lord Kṛṣṇa and go back home, back to Godhead.

Thus end the purports of the humble servants of His Divine Grace A.C. Bhaktivedanta Swami Prabhupāda to the Twelfth Canto, Fifth Chapter, of the Śrīmad-Bhāgavatam, *entitled "Śukadeva Gosvāmī's Final Instructions to Mahārāja Parīkṣit."*

CHAPTER SIX

Mahārāja Parīkṣit Passes Away

This chapter describes Mahārāja Parīkṣit's attainment of liberation, Mahārāja Janamejaya's performance of sacrifice for killing all snakes, the origin of the *Vedas,* and Śrīla Vedavyāsa's dividing of the Vedic literature.

After hearing the words of Śrī Śukadeva, Mahārāja Parīkṣit stated that by having listened to the *Bhāgavatam,* which is the compendium of the *Purāṇas* and which is full of the nectarean pastimes of the Supreme Personality of Godhead, Lord Uttamaḥśloka, Parīkṣit had attained the transcendental position of fearlessness and oneness with the Supreme. His ignorance had been dispelled, and by the mercy of Śrī Śukadeva he had gained sight of the supremely auspicious personal form of God, namely the Personality of Godhead, Śrī Hari. As a result, he had cast aside all fear of death. Śrī Parīkṣit Mahārāja then begged Śukadeva Gosvāmī to permit him to fix his heart upon the lotus feet of Lord Hari and give up his life. Granting this permission, Śrī Śukadeva rose and departed. Subsequently Mahārāja Parīkṣit, free of all doubts, sat down in yogic posture and merged himself in meditation upon the Supersoul. Then the snake-bird Takṣaka, arriving in the disguise of a *brāhmaṇa,* bit him, and the body of the saintly king immediately burned to ashes.

Janamejaya, the son of Parīkṣit, became very angry when he received news of his father's death, and he began a sacrificial performance for the purpose of destroying all the snakes. Even though Takṣaka received protection from Indra, he nevertheless became attracted by the *mantras* and was about to fall into the fire. Seeing this, Bṛhaspati, the son of Aṅgirā Ṛṣi, came and advised Mahārāja Janamejaya that Takṣaka could not be killed because he had drunk the nectar of the demigods. Furthermore, Aṅgirā said that all living entities must enjoy the fruits of their past activities. Therefore the king should give up this sacrifice. Janamejaya was thus convinced by the words of Bṛhaspati and stopped his sacrifice.

Thereafter Sūta Gosvāmī, in response to questions from Śrī Śaunaka, described the divisions of the *Vedas.* From the heart of the topmost demigod, Brahmā, came the subtle transcendental vibration, and from this subtle sound vibration arose the syllable *oṁ,* greatly potent and self-luminous. Using this *oṁkāra,* Lord Brahmā created the original *Vedas* and taught them to his sons, Marīci and others, who were all saintly leaders of the *brāhmaṇa* community. This body of Vedic knowledge was handed down through the disciplic succession of spiritual masters until the end of Dvāpara-yuga, when Lord Vyāsadeva divided it into four parts and instructed various schools of sages in these four *saṁhitās.* When the sage Yājñavalkya was rejected by his spiritual master, he had to give up all the Vedic *mantras* he had received from him. To obtain new *mantras* of the *Yajur Veda,* Yājñavalkya worshiped the Supreme Lord in the form of the sun-god. Śrī Sūryadeva subsequently fulfilled his prayer.

TEXT 1

सूत उवाच
एतन्निशम्य मुनिनाभिहितं परीक्षिद्
व्यासात्मजेन निखिलात्मदृशा समेन ।
तत्पादमूलमुपसृत्य नतेन मूर्ध्ना
बद्धाञ्जलिस्तमिदमाह स विष्णुरातः ॥ १ ॥

sūta uvāca
etan niśamya muninābhihitaṁ parīkṣid
vyāsātmajena nikhilātma-dṛśā samena
tat-pāda-mūlam upasṛtya natena mūrdhnā
baddhāñjalis tam idam āha sa viṣṇurātaḥ

sūtaḥ uvāca — Sūta Gosvāmī said; *etat* — this; *niśamya* — hearing; *muninā* — by the sage (Śukadeva); *abhihitam* — narrated; *parīkṣit* — Mahārāja Parīkṣit; *vyāsa-ātma-jena* — by the son of Vyāsadeva; *nikhila* — of all living beings; *ātma* — the Supreme Lord; *dṛśā* — who sees; *samena* — who is perfectly equipoised; *tat* — of him (Śukadeva); *pāda-mūlam* — to the lotus feet; *upasṛtya* — going up; *natena* — bowed down; *mūrdhnā* — with his head; *baddha-añjaliḥ* — his arms folded in supplication; *tam* — to him; *idam* — this; *āha* — said; *saḥ* — he; *viṣṇu-rātaḥ* — Parīkṣit, who while still in the womb had been protected by Lord Kṛṣṇa Himself.

TRANSLATION

Sūta Gosvāmī said: After hearing all that was narrated to him by the self-realized and equipoised Śukadeva, the son of Vyāsadeva, Mahārāja

Parīkṣit humbly approached his lotus feet. Bowing his head down upon the sage's feet, the King, who had lived his entire life under the protection of Lord Viṣṇu, folded his hands in supplication and spoke as follows.

PURPORT

According to Śrīla Viśvanātha Cakravartī Ṭhākura, some of the sages present while Śukadeva was instructing King Parīkṣit were impersonalist philosophers. Thus the word *samena* indicates that in the previous chapter Śukadeva Gosvāmī had spoken the philosophy of self-realization in a way pleasing to such intellectual *yogīs.*

TEXT 2

राजोवाच
सिद्धोऽस्म्यनुगृहीतोऽस्मि भवता करुणात्मना ।
श्रावितो यच्च मे साक्षादनादिनिधनो हरिः ॥ २ ॥

rājovāca
siddho 'smy anugṛhīto 'smi
bhavatā karuṇātmanā
śrāvito yac ca me sākṣād
anādi-nidhano hariḥ

rājā uvāca — King Parīkṣit said; *siddhaḥ* — fully successful; *asmi* — I am; *anugṛhītaḥ* — shown great mercy; *asmi* — I am; *bhavatā* — by your good self; *karuṇā-ātmanā* — who are full of mercy; *śrāvitaḥ* — has been described aurally; *yat* — because; *ca* — and; *me* — to me; *sākṣāt* — directly; *anādi* — who has no beginning; *nidhanaḥ* — or end; *hariḥ* — the Supreme Personality of Godhead.

TRANSLATION

Mahārāja Parīkṣit said: I have now achieved the purpose of my life, because a great and merciful soul like you has shown such kindness to me. You have personally spoken to me this narration of the Supreme Personality of Godhead, Hari, who is without beginning or end.

TEXT 3

नात्यद्भुतमहं मन्ये महतामच्युतात्मनाम् ।
अज्ञेषु तापतप्तेषु भूतेषु यदनुग्रहः ॥ ३ ॥

nāty-adbhutam ahaṁ manye
mahatām acyutātmanām
ajñeṣu tāpa-tapteṣu
bhūteṣu yad anugrahaḥ

na — not; *ati-adbhutam* — very surprising; *aham* — I; *manye* — think; *mahatām* — for the great souls; *acyuta-ātmanām* — whose minds are always absorbed in Lord Kṛṣṇa; *ajñeṣu* — upon the ignorant; *tāpa* — by the distresses of material life; *tapteṣu* — tormented; *bhūteṣu* — upon the conditioned souls; *yat* — which; *anugrahaḥ* — mercy.

TRANSLATION

I do not consider it at all amazing that great souls such as yourself, whose minds are always absorbed in the infallible Personality of Godhead, show mercy to the foolish conditioned souls, tormented as we are by the problems of material life.

TEXT 4

पुराणसंहितामेतामश्रौष्म भवतो वयम् ।
यस्यां खलूत्तमःश्लोको भगवाननुवर्ण्यते ॥ ४ ॥

purāṇa-saṁhitām etām
aśrauṣma bhavato vayam
yasyāṁ khalūttamaḥ-śloko
bhagavān anuvarṇyate

purāṇa-saṁhitām — essential summary of all the *Purāṇas; etām* — this; *aśrauṣma* — have heard; *bhavataḥ* — from you; *vayam* — we; *yasyām* — in which; *khalu* — indeed; *uttamaḥ-ślokaḥ* — who is always described in choice poetry; *bhagavān* — the Personality of Godhead; *anuvarṇyate* — is fittingly described.

TRANSLATION

I have heard from you this Śrīmad-Bhāgavatam, which is the perfect summary of all the Purāṇas and which perfectly describes the Supreme Lord, Uttamaḥśloka.

TEXT 5

भगवंस्तक्षकादिभ्यो मृत्युभ्यो न बिभेम्यहम् ।
प्रविष्टो ब्रह्म निर्वाणमभयं दर्शितं त्वया ॥ ५ ॥

bhagavaṁs takṣakādibhyo
mṛtyubhyo na bibhemy aham
praviṣṭo brahma nirvāṇam
abhayaṁ darśitaṁ tvayā

bhagavan — my lord; *takṣaka* — from the snake-bird Takṣaka; *ādibhyaḥ* — or other living entities; *mṛtyubhyaḥ* — from repeated deaths; *na bibhemi* — do not fear; *aham* — I; *praviṣṭaḥ* — having entered; *brahma* — the Absolute Truth; *nirvāṇam* — exclusive of everything material; *abhayam* — fearlessness; *darśitam* — shown; *tvayā* — by you.

TRANSLATION

My lord, I now have no fear of Takṣaka or any other living being, or even of repeated deaths, because I have absorbed myself in that purely spiritual Absolute Truth, which you have revealed and which destroys all fear.

TEXT 6

अनुजानीहि मां ब्रह्मन् वाचं यच्छाम्यधोक्षजे ।
मुक्तकामाशयं चेतः प्रवेश्य विसृजाम्यसून् ॥ ६ ॥

anujānīhi māṁ brahman
vācaṁ yacchāmy adhokṣaje
mukta-kāmāśayaṁ cetaḥ
praveśya visṛjāmy asūn

anujānīhi — please give your permission; *mām* — to me; *brahman* — O great *brāhmaṇa; vācam* — my speech (and all other sensory functions); *yacchāmi* — I shall place; *adhokṣaje* — within the Supreme Personality of Godhead; *mukta* — having given up; *kāma-āśayam* — all lusty desires; *cetaḥ* — my mind; *praveśya* — absorbing; *visṛjāmi* — I shall give up; *asūn* — my life air.

TRANSLATION

O brāhmaṇa, please give me permission to resign my speech and the functions of all my senses unto Lord Adhokṣaja. Allow me to

absorb my mind, purified of lusty desires, within Him and to thus give up my life.

PURPORT

Śukadeva Gosvāmī asked King Parīkṣit, "What more do you wish to hear?" Now the King replies that he has perfectly understood the message of *Śrīmad-Bhāgavatam* and that he is ready, without further discussion, to go back home, back to Godhead.

TEXT 7

अज्ञानं च निरस्तं मे ज्ञानविज्ञाननिष्ठया।
भवता दर्शितं क्षेमं परं भगवतः पदम् ॥ ७॥

ajñānaṁ ca nirastaṁ me
jñāna-vijñāna-niṣṭhayā
bhavatā darśitaṁ kṣemaṁ
paraṁ bhagavataḥ padam

ajñānam — ignorance; *ca* — also; *nirastam* — eradicated; *me* — my; *jñāna* — in knowledge of the Supreme Lord; *vijñāna* — and direct realization of His opulence and sweetness; *niṣṭhayā* — by becoming fixed; *bhavatā* — by you; *darśitam* — has been shown; *kṣemam* — all-auspicious; *param* — supreme; *bhagavataḥ* — of the Lord; *padam* — the Personality.

TRANSLATION

You have revealed to me that which is most auspicious, the supreme personal feature of the Lord. I am now fixed in knowledge and self-realization, and my ignorance has been eradicated.

TEXT 8

सूत उवाच
इत्युक्तस्तमनुज्ञाप्य भगवान् बादरायणिः।
जगाम भिक्षुभिः साकं नरदेवेन पूजितः ॥ ८॥

sūta uvāca
ity uktas tam anujñāpya
bhagavān bādarāyaṇiḥ

jagāma bhikṣubhiḥ sākaṁ
nara-devena pūjitaḥ

sūtaḥ uvāca — Śrī Sūta Gosvāmī said; *iti* — thus; *uktaḥ*—spoken to; *tam* — him; *anujñāpya* — giving permission; *bhagavān* — the powerful saint; *bādarāyaṇiḥ*—Śukadeva, the son of Bādarāyaṇa Vedavyāsa; *jagāma* — went away; *bhikṣubhiḥ*—the renounced sages; *sākam* — along with; *nara-devena* — by the King; *pūjitaḥ*—worshiped.

TRANSLATION

Sūta Gosvāmī said: Thus requested, the saintly son of Śrīla Vyāsadeva gave his permission to King Parīkṣit. Then, after being worshiped by the King and all the sages present, Śukadeva departed from that place.

TEXTS 9–10

परीक्षिदपि राजर्षिरात्मन्यात्मानमात्मना ।
समाधाय परं दध्यावस्पन्दासुर्यथा तरुः ॥ ९ ॥
प्राक्कूले बर्हिष्यासीनो गंगाकूल उदङ्मुखः ।
ब्रह्मभूतो महायोगी निःसंगश्छिन्नसंशयः ॥ १० ॥

parīkṣid api rājarṣir
ātmany ātmānam ātmanā
samādhāya paraṁ dadhyāv
aspandāsur yathā taruḥ

prāk-kūle barhiṣy āsīno
gaṅgā-kūla udaṅ-mukhaḥ
brahma-bhūto mahā-yogī
niḥsaṅgaś chinna-saṁśayaḥ

parīkṣit — Mahārāja Parīkṣit; *api* — furthermore; *rāja-ṛṣiḥ*—the great saintly King; *ātmani* — within his own spiritual identity; *ātmānam* — his mind; *ātmanā* — by his intelligence; *samādhāya* — placing; *param* — upon the Supreme; *dadhyau* — he meditated; *aspanda* — motionless; *asuḥ*—his living air; *yathā* — just as; *taruḥ*—a tree; *prāk-kūle* — with the tips of its stalks facing east; *barhiṣi* — upon *darbha* grass; *āsīnaḥ*—sitting; *gaṅgā-kūle* — on the bank of the Gaṅgā; *udak-mukhaḥ*—facing north; *brahma-bhūtaḥ*—in perfect realization of his true identity; *mahā-yogī*—the exalted mystic;

niḥsaṅgaḥ—free of all material attachment; *chinna* — broken off; *saṁśayaḥ* —all doubts.

TRANSLATION

Mahārāja Parīkṣit then sat down on the bank of the Ganges, upon a seat made of darbha grass with the tips of its stalks facing east, and turned himself toward the north. Having attained the perfection of yoga, he experienced full self-realization and was free of material attachment and doubt. The saintly King settled his mind within his spiritual self by pure intelligence and proceeded to meditate upon the Supreme Absolute Truth. His life air ceased to move, and he became as stationary as a tree.

TEXT 11

तक्षकः प्रहितो विप्राः क्रुद्धेन द्विजसूनुना ।
हन्तुकामो नृपं गच्छन् ददर्श पथि कश्यपम् ॥११॥

takṣakaḥ prahito viprāḥ
kruddhena dvija-sūnunā
hantu-kāmo nṛpaṁ gacchan
dadarśa pathi kaśyapam

takṣakaḥ—the snake-bird Takṣaka; *prahitaḥ*—sent; *viprāḥ*—O learned *brāhmaṇas; kruddhena* — who had been angered; *dvija* — of the sage Śamīka; *sūnunā* — by the son; *hantu-kāmaḥ*—desirous of killing; *nṛpam* — the King; *gacchan* — while going; *dadarśa* — he saw; *pathi* — upon the road; *kaśyapam* — Kaśyapa Muni.

TRANSLATION

O learned brāhmaṇas, the snake-bird Takṣaka, who had been sent by the angry son of a brāhmaṇa, was going toward the King to kill him when he saw Kaśyapa Muni on the path.

TEXT 12

तं तर्पयित्वा द्रविणैर्निवर्त्य विषहारिणम् ।
द्विजरूपप्रतिच्छन्नः कामरूपोऽदशन्नृपम् ॥१२॥

taṁ tarpayitvā draviṇair
nivartya viṣa-hāriṇam

dvija-rūpa-praticchannaḥ
kāma-rūpo 'daśan nṛpam

tam — him (Kaśyapa); *tarpayitvā* — gratifying; *draviṇaiḥ* — with valuable offerings; *nivartya* — stopping; *viṣa-hāriṇam* — an expert in counteracting poison; *dvija-rūpa* — in the form of a *brāhmaṇa; praticchannaḥ* — disguising himself; *kāma-rūpaḥ* — Takṣaka, who could assume any form he wished; *adaśat* — bit; *nṛpam* — King Parīkṣit.

TRANSLATION

Takṣaka flattered Kaśyapa by presenting him with valuable offerings and thereby stopped the sage, who was expert in counteracting poison, from protecting Mahārāja Parīkṣit. Then the snake-bird, who could assume any form he wished, disguised himself as a brāhmaṇa, approached the King and bit him.

PURPORT

Kaśyapa could counteract the poison of Takṣaka and demonstrated this power by bringing a palm tree back to life after Takṣaka had burned it to ashes by biting it with his fangs. According to the arrangement of destiny, Kaśyapa was diverted by Takṣaka, and the inevitable took place.

TEXT 13

ब्रह्मभूतस्य राजर्षेर्देहोऽहिगरलाग्निना ।
बभूव भस्मसात् सद्यः पश्यतां सर्वदेहिनाम् ॥ १३ ॥

brahma-bhūtasya rājarṣer
deho 'hi-garalāgninā
babhūva bhasmasāt sadyaḥ
paśyatāṁ sarva-dehinām

brahma-bhūtasya — of the fully self-realized; *rāja-ṛṣeḥ* — the saint among kings; *dehaḥ* — the body; *ahi* — of the snake; *garala* — from the poison; *agninā* — by the fire; *babhūva* — turned; *bhasma-sāt* — to ashes; *sadyaḥ* — immediately; *paśyatām* — while they were watching; *sarva-dehinām* — all embodied living beings.

TRANSLATION

While living beings all over the universe looked on, the body of the great self-realized saint among kings was immediately burned to ashes by the fire of the snake's poison.

TEXT 14

हाहाकारो महानासीद् भुवि खे दिक्षु सर्वतः ।
विस्मिता ह्यभवन् सर्वे देवासुरनरादयः ॥ १४ ॥

hāhā-kāro mahān āsīd
bhuvi khe dikṣu sarvataḥ
vismitā hy abhavan sarve
devāsura-narādayaḥ

hāhā-kāraḥ—a cry of lamentation; *mahān* — great; *āsīt* — there was; *bhuvi* — on the earth; *khe* — in the sky; *dikṣu* — in the directions; *sarvataḥ* —all about; *vismitāḥ*—amazed; *hi* — indeed; *abhavan* — they became; *sarve* — all; *deva* — the demigods; *asura* — demons; *nara* — human beings; *ādayaḥ*—and other creatures.

TRANSLATION

There arose a terrible cry of lamentation in all directions on the earth and in the heavens, and all the demigods, demons, human beings and other creatures were astonished.

TEXT 15

देवदुन्दुभयो नेदुर्गन्धर्वाप्सरसो जगुः ।
ववृषुः पुष्पवर्षाणि विबुधाः साधुवादिनः ॥ १५ ॥

deva-dundubhayo nedur
gandharvāpsaraso jaguḥ
vavṛṣuḥ puṣpa-varṣāṇi
vibudhāḥ sādhu-vādinaḥ

deva — of the demigods; *dundubhayaḥ*—the kettledrums; *neduḥ*—resounded; *gandharva-apsarasaḥ*—the Gandharvas and Apsarās; *jaguḥ*—sang; *vavṛṣuḥ*—they showered down; *puṣpa-varṣāṇi* — rains of flowers; *vibudhāḥ* —the demigods; *sādhu-vādinaḥ*—speaking praise.

TRANSLATION

Kettledrums sounded in the regions of the demigods, and the celestial Gandharvas and Apsarās sang. The demigods showered flowers and spoke words of praise.

PURPORT

Although lamenting at first, all learned persons, including the demigods, soon realized that a great soul had gone back home, back to Godhead. This was certainly a cause for celebration.

TEXT 16

जन्मेजयः स्वपितरं श्रुत्वा तक्षकभक्षितम् ।
यथाजुहाव संक्रुद्धो नागान् सत्रे सह द्विजैः ॥ १६ ॥

janmejayaḥ sva-pitaraṁ
śrutvā takṣaka-bhakṣitam
yathājuhāva saṅkruddho
nāgān satre saha dvijaiḥ

janmejayaḥ—King Janamejaya, the son of Parīkṣit; *sva-pitaram* — his own father; *śrutvā* — hearing; *takṣaka* — by Takṣaka, the snake-bird; *bhakṣitam* — bitten; *yathā* — properly; *ājuhāva* — offered as oblations; *saṅkruddhaḥ*— extremely angry; *nāgān* — the snakes; *satre* — in a great sacrifice; *saha* — along with; *dvijaiḥ*— *brāhmaṇas.*

TRANSLATION

Hearing that his father had been fatally bitten by the snake-bird, Mahārāja Janamejaya became extremely angry and had brāhmaṇas perform a mighty sacrifice in which he offered all the snakes in the world into the sacrificial fire.

TEXT 17

सर्पसत्रे समिद्धाग्नौ दह्यमानान्महोरगान् ।
दृष्टेन्द्रं भयसंविग्नस्तक्षकः शरणं ययौ ॥ १७ ॥

sarpa-satre samiddhāgnau
dahyamānān mahoragān

dṛṣṭvendraṁ bhaya-saṁvignas
takṣakaḥ śaraṇaṁ yayau

sarpa-satre — in the snake sacrifice; *samiddha* — blazing; *agnau* — in the fire; *dahyamānān* — being burned; *mahā-uragān* — the great serpents; *dṛṣṭvā* — seeing; *indram* — to Indra; *bhaya* — with fear; *saṁvignaḥ*—very disturbed; *takṣakaḥ*—Takṣaka; *śaraṇam* — for shelter; *yayau* — went.

TRANSLATION

When Takṣaka saw even the most powerful serpents being burned in the blazing fire of that snake sacrifice, he was overwhelmed with fear and approached Lord Indra for shelter.

TEXT 18

अपश्यंस्तक्षकं तत्र राजा पारीक्षितो द्विजान् ।
उवाच तक्षकः कस्मान्न दह्येतोरगाधमः ॥ १८ ॥

apaśyaṁs takṣakaṁ tatra
rājā pārīkṣito dvijān
uvāca takṣakaḥ kasmān
na dahyetoragādhamaḥ

apaśyan — not seeing; *takṣakam* — Takṣaka; *tatra* — there; *rājā* — the King; *pārīkṣitaḥ*—Janamejaya; *dvijān* — to the *brāhmaṇas; uvāca* — said; *takṣakaḥ*—Takṣaka; *kasmāt* — why; *na dahyeta* — has not been burned; *uraga* — of all the serpents; *adhamaḥ*—the lowest.

TRANSLATION

When King Janamejaya did not see Takṣaka entering his sacrificial fire, he said to the brāhmaṇas*:* Why is not Takṣaka, the lowest of all serpents, burning in this fire?

TEXT 19

तं गोपायति राजेन्द्र शक्रः शरणमागतम् ।
तेन संस्तम्भितः सर्पस्तस्मान्नाग्नौ पतत्यसौ ॥ १९ ॥

taṁ gopāyati rājendra
śakraḥ śaraṇam āgatam

tena saṁstambhitaḥ sarpas
tasmān nāgnau pataty asau

tam — him (Takṣaka); *gopāyati* — is hiding; *rāja-indra* — O best of kings; *śakraḥ* — Lord Indra; *śaraṇam* — for shelter; *āgatam* — who has approached; *tena* — by that Indra; *saṁstambhitaḥ* — kept; *sarpaḥ* — the snake; *tasmāt* — thus; *na* — not; *agnau* — into the fire; *patati* — does fall; *asau* — he.

TRANSLATION

The brāhmaṇas replied: O best of kings, the snake Takṣaka has not fallen into the fire because he is being protected by Indra, whom he has approached for shelter. Indra is holding him back from the fire.

TEXT 20

पारीक्षित इति श्रुत्वा प्राहर्त्विज उदारधीः ।
सहेन्द्रस्तक्षको विप्रा नाग्नौ किमिति पात्यते ॥ २० ॥

pārīkṣita iti śrutvā
prāhartvija udāra-dhīḥ
sahendras takṣako viprā
nāgnau kim iti pātyate

pārīkṣitaḥ — King Janamejaya; *iti* — these words; *śrutvā* — hearing; *prāha* — replied; *ṛtvijaḥ* — to the priests; *udāra* — broad; *dhīḥ* — whose intelligence; *saha* — along with; *indraḥ* — Indra; *takṣakaḥ* — Takṣaka; *viprāḥ* — O *brāhmaṇas; na* — not; *agnau* — into the fire; *kim* — why; *iti* — indeed; *pātyate* — is made to fall.

TRANSLATION

The intelligent King Janamejaya, hearing these words, replied to the priests: Then, my dear brāhmaṇas, why not make Takṣaka fall into the fire, along with his protector, Indra?

TEXT 21

तच्छ्रुत्वाजुहुवुर्विप्राः सहेन्द्रं तक्षकं मखे ।
तक्षकाशु पतस्वेह सहेन्द्रेण मरुत्वता ॥ २१ ॥

tac chrutvājuhuvur viprāḥ
sahendraṁ takṣakaṁ makhe
takṣakāśu patasveha
sahendreṇa marutvatā

tat — that; *śrutvā* — hearing; *ājuhuvuḥ*—they performed the ritual of offering oblation; *viprāḥ*—the *brāhmaṇa* priests; *saha* — along with; *indram* — King Indra; *takṣakam* — the snake-bird Takṣaka; *makhe* — into the sacrificial fire; *takṣaka* — O Takṣaka; *āśu* — quickly; *patasva* — you should fall; *iha* — here; *saha indreṇa* — together with Indra; *marut-vatā* — who is accompanied by all the demigods.

TRANSLATION

Hearing this, the priests then chanted this mantra for offering Takṣaka together with Indra as an oblation into the sacrificial fire: O Takṣaka, fall immediately into this fire, together with Indra and his entire host of demigods!

TEXT 22

इति ब्रह्मोदिताक्षेपैः स्थानादिन्द्रः प्रचालितः ।
बभूव सम्भ्रान्तमतिः सविमानः सतक्षकः ॥ २२ ॥

iti brahmoditākṣepaiḥ
sthānād indraḥ pracālitaḥ
babhūva sambhrānta-matiḥ
sa-vimānaḥ sa-takṣakaḥ

iti — thus; *brahma* — by the *brāhmaṇas; udita* — spoken; *ākṣepaiḥ*—by the insulting words; *sthānāt* — from his place; *indraḥ*—Lord Indra; *pracālitaḥ* —thrown; *babhūva* — became; *sambhrānta* — disturbed; *matiḥ*—in his mind; *sa-vimānaḥ*—along with his heavenly airplane; *sa-takṣakaḥ*—along with Takṣaka.

TRANSLATION

When Lord Indra, along with his airplane and Takṣaka, was suddenly thrown from his position by these insulting words of the brāhmaṇas, he became very disturbed.

TEXT 23

तं पतन्तं विमानेन सहतक्षकमम्बरात् ।
विलोक्याङ्गिरसः प्राह राजानं तं बृहस्पतिः ॥ २३ ॥

taṁ patantaṁ vimānena
saha-takṣakam ambarāt
vilokyāṅgirasaḥ prāha
rājānaṁ taṁ bṛhaspatiḥ

tam — him; *patantam* — falling; *vimānena* — in his airplane; *saha-takṣakam* — with Takṣaka; *ambarāt* — from the sky; *vilokya* — observing; *āṅgirasaḥ* — the son of Aṅgirā; *prāha* — spoke; *rājānam* — to the King (Janamejaya); *tam* — to him; *bṛhaspatiḥ* — Bṛhaspati.

TRANSLATION

Bṛhaspati, the son of Aṅgirā Muni, seeing Indra falling from the sky in his airplane along with Takṣaka, approached King Janamejaya and spoke to him as follows.

TEXT 24

नैष त्वया मनुष्येन्द्र वधमर्हति सर्पराट् ।
अनेन पीतममृतमथ वा अजरामरः ॥ २४ ॥

naiṣa tvayā manuṣyendra
vadham arhati sarpa-rāṭ
anena pītam amṛtam
atha vā ajarāmaraḥ

na — not; *eṣaḥ* — this snake-bird; *tvayā* — by you; *manuṣya-indra* — O great ruler of men; *vadham* — murder; *arhati* — deserves; *sarpa-rāṭ* — the king of snakes; *anena* — by him; *pītam* — has been drunk; *amṛtam* — the nectar of the demigods; *atha* — therefore; *vai* — certainly; *ajara* — free from the effects of old age; *amaraḥ* — virtually immortal.

TRANSLATION

O King among men, it is not fitting that this king of snakes meet death at your hands, for he has drunk the nectar of the immortal demigods.

Consequently he is not subject to the ordinary symptoms of old age and death.

TEXT 25

जीवितं मरणं जन्तोर्गतिः स्वेनैव कर्मणा ।
राजंस्ततोऽन्यो नास्त्यस्य प्रदाता सुखदुःखयोः ॥ २५ ॥

jīvitaṁ maraṇaṁ jantor
gatiḥ svenaiva karmaṇā
rājaṁs tato 'nyo nāsty asya
pradātā sukha-duḥkhayoḥ

jīvitam — the living; *maraṇam* — the dying; *jantoḥ*—of a living being; *gatiḥ*—the destination in his next life; *svena* — by his own; *eva* — only; *karmaṇā* — work; *rājan* — O King; *tataḥ*—than that; *anyaḥ*—another; *na asti* — there is not; *asya* — for him; *pradātā* — bestower; *sukha-duḥkhayoḥ*—of happiness and distress.

TRANSLATION

The life and death of an embodied soul and his destination in the next life are all caused by himself through his own activity. Therefore, O King, no other agent is actually responsible for creating one's happiness and distress.

PURPORT

Although King Parīkṣit apparently died by the bite of Takṣaka, it was Lord Kṛṣṇa Himself who brought the King back to the kingdom of God. Bṛhaspati wanted young King Janamejaya to see things from the spiritual point of view.

TEXT 26

सर्पचौराग्निविद्युद्भ्यः क्षुत्तृड्व्याध्यादिभिर्नृप ।
पञ्चत्वमृच्छते जन्तुर्भुंक्त आरब्धकर्म तत् ॥ २६ ॥

sarpa-caurāgni-vidyudbhyaḥ
kṣut-tṛḍ-vyādhy-ādibhir nṛpa
pañcatvam ṛcchate jantur
bhuṅkta ārabdha-karma tat

sarpa — from snakes; *caura* — thieves; *agni* — fire; *vidyudbhyaḥ* — and lightning; *kṣut* — from hunger; *tṛṭ* — thirst; *vyādhi* — disease; *ādibhiḥ* — and other agents; *nṛpa* — O King; *pañcatvam* — death; *ṛcchate* — obtains; *jantuḥ* — the conditioned living entity; *bhuṅkte* — he enjoys; *ārabdha* — already created by his past work; *karma* — the fruitive reaction; *tat* — that.

TRANSLATION

When a conditioned soul is killed by snakes, thieves, fire, lightning, hunger, disease or anything else, he is experiencing the reaction to his own past work.

PURPORT

According to Śrīla Viśvanātha Cakravartī Ṭhākura, King Parīkṣit obviously was not suffering the reaction of past *karma.* As a great devotee he was personally brought back home, back to Godhead, by the Lord.

TEXT 27

तस्मात् सत्रमिदं राजन् संस्थीयेताभिचारिकम् ।
सर्पा अनागसो दग्धा जनैर्दिष्टं हि भुज्यते ॥ २७ ॥

tasmāt satram idaṁ rājan
saṁsthīyetābhicārikam
sarpā anāgaso dagdhā
janair diṣṭaṁ hi bhujyate

tasmāt — therefore; *satram* — sacrifice; *idam* — this; *rājan* — O King; *saṁsthīyeta* — should be stopped; *ābhicārikam* — done with intent to harm; *sarpāḥ* — the serpents; *anāgasaḥ* — innocent; *dagdhāḥ* — burned; *janaiḥ* — by persons; *diṣṭam* — fate; *hi* — indeed; *bhujyate* — is suffered.

TRANSLATION

Therefore, my dear King, please stop this sacrificial performance, which was initiated with the intent of doing harm to others. Many innocent snakes have already been burned to death. Indeed, all persons must suffer the unforeseen consequences of their past activities.

PURPORT

Bṛhaspati here admits that although the snakes appeared to be innocent, by the Lord's arrangement they were also being punished for previous vicious activities.

TEXT 28

सूत उवाच
इत्युक्तः स तथेत्याह महर्षेर्मानयन् वचः ।
सर्पसत्रादुपरतः पूजयामास वाक्पतिम् ॥ २८ ॥

sūta uvāca
ity uktaḥ sa tathety āha
maharṣer mānayan vacaḥ
sarpa-satrād uparataḥ
pūjayām āsa vāk-patim

sūtaḥ uvāca — Sūta Gosvāmī said; *iti* — thus; *uktaḥ*—addressed; *saḥ*—he (Janamejaya); *tathā iti* — so be it; *āha* — he said; *mahā-ṛṣeḥ*—of the great sage; *mānayan* — honoring; *vacaḥ*—the words; *sarpa-satrāt* — from the snake sacrifice; *uparataḥ*—ceasing; *pūjayām āsa* — he worshiped; *vāk-patim* — Bṛhaspati, the master of eloquence.

TRANSLATION

Sūta Gosvāmī continued: Advised in this manner, Mahārāja Janamejaya replied, "So be it." Honoring the words of the great sage, he desisted from performing the snake sacrifice and worshiped Bṛhaspati, the most eloquent of sages.

TEXT 29

सैषा विष्णोर्महामायाबाध्ययालक्षणा यया ।
मुह्यन्त्यस्यैवात्मभूता भूतेषु गुणवृत्तिभिः ॥ २९ ॥

saiṣā viṣṇor mahā-māyā-
bādhyayālakṣaṇā yayā
muhyanty asyaivātma-bhūtā
bhūteṣu guṇa-vṛttibhiḥ

sā eṣā — this very; *viṣṇoḥ*—of the Supreme Lord, Viṣṇu; *mahā-māyā* — the illusory material energy; *abādhyayā* — by her who cannot be checked;

alakṣaṇā — indiscernible; *yayā* — by whom; *muhyanti* — become bewildered; *asya* — of the Lord; *eva* — indeed; *ātma-bhūtāḥ*—the part-and-parcel spirit souls; *bhūteṣu* — within their material bodies; *guṇa* — of the modes of nature; *vṛttibhiḥ*—by the functions.

TRANSLATION

This is indeed the Supreme Lord Viṣṇu's illusory energy, which is unstoppable and difficult to perceive. Although the individual spirit souls are part and parcel of the Lord, through the influence of this illusory energy they are bewildered by their identification with various material bodies.

PURPORT

The illusory energy of Lord Viṣṇu is so powerful that even the illustrious son of King Parīkṣit was temporarily misdirected. Because he was a devotee of Lord Kṛṣṇa, however, his bewilderment was quickly rectified. On the other hand, an ordinary, materialistic person without the special protection of the Lord plummets to the depths of material ignorance. Factually, materialistic persons are not interested in the protection of Lord Viṣṇu. Therefore their complete ruination is inevitable.

TEXTS 30–31

न यत्र दम्भीत्यभया विराजिता
मायात्मवादेऽसकृदात्मवादिभिः ।
न यद् विवादो विविधस्तदाश्रयो
मनश्च संकल्पविकल्पवृत्ति यत् ॥ ३० ॥
न यत्र सृज्यं सृजतोभयोः परं
श्रेयश्च जीवस्त्रिभिरन्वितस्त्वहम् ।
तदेतदुत्सादितबाध्यबाधकं
निषिध्य चोर्मीन् विरमेत तन्मुनिः ॥ ३१ ॥

na yatra dambhīty abhayā virājitā
māyātma-vāde 'sakṛd ātma-vādibhiḥ
na yad vivādo vividhas tad-āśrayo
manaś ca saṅkalpa-vikalpa-vṛtti yat

na yatra sṛjyaṁ sṛjatobhayoḥ paraṁ
śreyaś ca jīvas tribhir anvitas tv aham

tad etad utsādita-bādhya-bādhakaṁ
niṣidhya cormīn virameta tan muniḥ

na — not; *yatra* — in which; *dambhī*—he is a hypocrite; *iti* — thinking thus; *abhayā* — fearless; *virājitā* — visible; *māyā* — the illusory energy; *ātma-vāde* — when spiritual inquiry is being conducted; *asakṛt* — constantly; *ātma-vādibhiḥ*—by those who describe spiritual science; *na* — not; *yat* — in which; *vivādaḥ*—materialistic argument; *vividhaḥ*—taking many different forms; *tat-āśrayaḥ*—founded upon that illusory energy; *manaḥ*—the mind; *ca* — and; *saṅkalpa* — decision; *vikalpa* — and doubt; *vṛtti* — whose functions; *yat* — in which; *na* — not; *yatra* — in which; *sṛjyam* — the created products of the material world; *sṛjatā* — along with their causes; *ubhayoḥ*—by both; *param* — achieved; *śreyaḥ*—the benefits; *ca* — and; *jīvaḥ*—the living entity; *tribhiḥ*—with the three (modes of nature); *anvitaḥ*—joined; *tu* — indeed; *aham*—(conditioned by) false ego; *tat etat* — that indeed; *utsādita* — excluding; *bādhya* — the obstructed (conditioned living beings); *bādhakam* — and the obstructing (modes of material nature); *niṣidhya* — warding off; *ca* — and; *ūrmīn* — the waves (of false ego and so on); *virameta* — should take special pleasure; *tat* — in that; *muniḥ*—a sage.

TRANSLATION

But there exists a supreme reality, in which the illusory energy cannot fearlessly dominate, thinking, "I can control this person because he is deceitful." In that highest reality there are no illusory argumentative philosophies. Rather, there the true students of spiritual science constantly engage in authorized spiritual investigation. In that supreme reality there is no manifestation of the material mind, which functions in terms of alternating decision and doubt. Created material products, their subtle causes and the goals of enjoyment attained by their utilization do not exist there. Furthermore, in that supreme reality there is no conditioned spirit, covered by false ego and the three modes of nature. That reality excludes everything limited or limiting. One who is wise should therefore stop the waves of material life and enjoy within that Supreme Truth.

PURPORT

The illusory energy of the Lord, Māyā, can freely exert her influence over those who are hypocritical, deceitful and disobedient to the laws of God. Since the Personality of Godhead is free of all material qualities, Māyā herself becomes fearful in His presence. As stated by Lord Brahmā (*vilajjamānayā yasya sthātum īkṣa-pate 'muyā*): "Māyā herself is ashamed to stand face to face with the Supreme Lord."

In the supreme spiritual reality, useless academic wrangling is completely absent. As stated in *Śrīmad-Bhāgavatam* (6.4.31):

yac-chaktayo vadatāṁ vādināṁ vai
vivāda-saṁvāda-bhuvo bhavanti
kurvanti caiṣāṁ muhur ātma-mohaṁ
tasmai namo 'nanta-guṇāya bhūmne

"Let me offer my respectful obeisances unto the all-pervading Supreme Personality of Godhead, who possesses unlimited transcendental qualities. Acting from within the cores of the hearts of all philosophers, who propagate various views, He causes them to forget their own souls while sometimes agreeing and sometimes disagreeing among themselves. Thus He creates within this material world a situation in which they are unable to come to a conclusion. I offer my obeisances unto Him."

TEXT 32

परं पदं वैष्णवमामनन्ति तद्
यन्नेति नेतीत्यतदुत्सिसृक्षवः ।
विसृज्य दौरात्म्यमनन्यसौहृदा
हृदोपगुह्यावसितं समाहितैः ॥ ३२ ॥

paraṁ padaṁ vaiṣṇavam āmananti tad
yan neti netīty atad-utsisṛkṣavaḥ
visṛjya daurātmyam ananya-sauhṛdā
hṛdopaguhyāvasitaṁ samāhitaiḥ

param — the supreme; *padam* — situation; *vaiṣṇavam* — of Lord Viṣṇu; *āmananti* — they designate; *tat* — that; *yat* — which; *na iti na iti* — "not this, not this"; *iti* — thus analyzing; *atat* — everything extraneous; *utsisṛkṣavaḥ* — those who are desirous of giving up; *visṛjya* — rejecting; *daurātmyam* — petty materialism; *ananya* — placing nowhere else; *sauhṛdāḥ* — their affection; *hṛdā* — within their hearts; *upaguhya* — embracing Him; *avasitam* — who is captured; *samāhitaiḥ* — by those who meditate upon Him in trance.

TRANSLATION

Those who desire to give up all that is not essentially real move systematically, by negative discrimination of the extraneous, to the supreme position of Lord Viṣṇu. Giving up petty materialism, they offer their love exclusively to the Absolute Truth within their hearts and embrace that highest truth in fixed meditation.

PURPORT

The words *yan neti netīty atad-utsisṛkṣavaḥ* indicate the process of negative discrimination, by which one engaged in the search for essential and absolute truth systematically rejects all that is superfluous, superficial and relative. Throughout the world people have gradually rejected the ultimate validity of political, social and even religious truths, but because they lack Kṛṣṇa consciousness they remain bewildered and cynical. However, as clearly stated here, *paraṁ padaṁ vaiṣṇavam āmananti tat.* Those who actually desire perfect knowledge must not only reject the nonessential but must also ultimately understand the essential spiritual reality called *paraṁ padaṁ vaiṣṇavam:* the supreme destination, the abode of Lord Viṣṇu. *Padam* indicates both the status and the abode of the Supreme Personality of Godhead, which can be understood only by those who give up petty materialism and adopt the position of *ananya-sauhṛdam,* exclusive love for the Lord. Such exclusive love is not narrow-minded or sectarian, because all living entities, being within the Lord, are automatically served when one directly serves the supreme entity. This process of rendering the highest service to the Lord and to all living entities constitutes the science of Kṛṣṇa consciousness, which is taught throughout *Śrīmad-Bhāgavatam.*

TEXT 33

त एतदधिगच्छन्ति विष्णोर्यत् परमं पदम् ।
अहं ममेति दौर्जन्यं न येषां देहगेहजम् ॥ ३३ ॥

ta etad adhigacchanti
viṣṇor yat paramaṁ padam
ahaṁ mameti daurjanyaṁ
na yeṣāṁ deha-geha-jam

te — they; *etat* — this; *adhigacchanti* — come to know; *viṣṇoḥ* — of Lord Viṣṇu; *yat* — which; *paramam* — the supreme; *padam* — personal situation;

aham — I; *mama* — my; *iti* — thus; *daurjanyam* — the depravity; *na* — is not; *yeṣām* — for whom; *deha* — the body; *geha* — and home; *jam* — based upon.

TRANSLATION

Such devotees come to understand the supreme transcendental situation of the Personality of Godhead, Lord Viṣṇu, because they are no longer polluted by the concepts of "I" and "my," which are based on body and home.

TEXT 34

अतिवादांस्तितिक्षेत नावमन्येत कञ्चन ।
न चेमं देहमाश्रित्य वैरं कुर्वीत केनचित् ॥ ३४ ॥

ativādāṁs titikṣeta
nāvamanyeta kañcana
na cemaṁ deham āśritya
vairaṁ kurvīta kenacit

ati-vādān — insulting words; *titikṣeta* — one should tolerate; *na* — never; *avamanyeta* — one should disrespect; *kañcana* — anyone; *na ca* — nor; *imam* — this; *deham* — material body; *āśritya* — identifying with; *vairam* — enmity; *kurvīta* — one should have; *kenacit* — with anyone.

TRANSLATION

One should tolerate all insults and never fail to show proper respect to any person. Avoiding identification with the material body, one should not create enmity with anyone.

TEXT 35

नमो भगवते तस्मै कृष्णायाकुण्ठमेधसे ।
यत्पादाम्बुरुहध्यानात् संहितामध्यगामिमाम् ॥ ३५ ॥

namo bhagavate tasmai
kṛṣṇāyākuṇṭha-medhase
yat-pādāmburuha-dhyānāt
saṁhitām adhyagām imām

namaḥ — obeisances; *bhagavate* — to the Supreme Personality of Godhead; *tasmai* — to Him; *kṛṣṇāya* — Lord Śrī Kṛṣṇa; *akuṇṭha-medhase* — whose power is never impeded; *yat* — whose; *pāda-ambu-ruha* — upon the lotus feet; *dhyānāt* — by meditation; *saṁhitām* — the scripture; *adhyagām* — I have assimilated; *imām* — this.

TRANSLATION

I offer my obeisances to the Supreme Personality of Godhead, the invincible Lord Śrī Kṛṣṇa. Simply by meditating upon His lotus feet I have been able to study and appreciate this great literature.

TEXT 36

श्रीशौनक उवाच
पैलादिभिर्व्यासशिष्यैर्वेदाचार्यैर्महात्मभिः ।
वेदाश्च कथिता व्यस्ता एतत् सौम्याभिधेहि नः ॥ ३६ ॥

śrī-śaunaka uvāca
pailādibhir vyāsa-śiṣyair
vedācāryair mahātmabhiḥ
vedāś ca kathitā vyastā
etat saumyābhidhehi naḥ

śrī-śaunakaḥ uvāca — Śrī Śaunaka Ṛṣi said; *paila-ādibhiḥ* — by Paila and others; *vyāsa-śiṣyaiḥ* — the disciples of Śrīla Vyāsadeva; *veda-ācāryaiḥ* — the standard authorities of the *Vedas; mahā-ātmabhiḥ* — whose intelligence was very great; *vedāḥ* — the *Vedas; ca* — and; *kathitāḥ* — spoken; *vyastāḥ* — divided; *etat* — this; *saumya* — O gentle Sūta; *abhidhehi* — please narrate; *naḥ* — to us.

TRANSLATION

Śaunaka Ṛṣi said: O gentle Sūta, please narrate to us how Paila and the other greatly intelligent disciples of Śrīla Vyāsadeva, who are known as the standard authorities of Vedic wisdom, spoke and edited the Vedas.

TEXT 37

सूत उवाच
समाहितात्मनो ब्रह्मन् ब्रह्मणः परमेष्ठिनः ।
हृद्याकाशादभून्नादो वृत्तिरोधाद् विभाव्यते ॥ ३७ ॥

sūta uvāca
samāhitātmano brahman
brahmaṇaḥ parameṣṭhinaḥ
hṛdy ākāśād abhūn nādo
vṛtti-rodhād vibhāvyate

sūtaḥ uvāca — Sūta Gosvāmī said; *samāhita-ātmanaḥ*—whose mind was perfectly fixed; *brahman* — O *brāhmaṇa* (Śaunaka); *brahmaṇaḥ*—of Lord Brahmā; *parame-sthinaḥ*—the most elevated of living beings; *hṛdi* — within the heart; *ākāśāt* — from out of the sky; *abhūt* — arose; *nādaḥ*—the transcendental subtle sound; *vṛtti-rodhāt* — by stopping the functioning (of the ears); *vibhāvyate* — is perceived.

TRANSLATION

Sūta Gosvāmī said: O brāhmaṇa, first the subtle vibration of transcendental sound appeared from the sky of the heart of the most elevated Lord Brahmā, whose mind was perfectly fixed in spiritual realization. One can perceive this subtle vibration when one stops all external hearing.

PURPORT

Because *Śrīmad-Bhāgavatam* is the supreme Vedic literature, the sages headed by Śaunaka desired to trace out its source.

TEXT 38

यदुपासनया ब्रह्मन् योगिनो मलमात्मनः ।
द्रव्यक्रियाकारकाख्यं धूत्वा यान्त्यपुनर्भवम् ॥३८॥

yad-upāsanayā brahman
yogino malam ātmanaḥ
dravya-kriyā-kārakākhyaṁ
dhūtvā yānty apunar-bhavam

yat — of which (subtle form of the *Vedas*); *upāsanayā* — by the worship; *brahman* — O *brāhmaṇa; yoginaḥ*—mystic sages; *malam* — the contamination; *ātmanaḥ*—of the heart; *dravya* — substance; *kriyā* — activity; *kāraka* — and performer; *ākhyam* — designated as such; *dhūtvā* — cleansing away; *yānti* — they achieve; *apunaḥ-bhavam* — freedom from rebirth.

TRANSLATION

By worship of this subtle form of the Vedas, O brāhmaṇa, mystic sages cleanse their hearts of all contamination caused by impurity of substance, activity and doer, and thus they attain freedom from repeated birth and death.

TEXT 39

ततोऽभूत्त्रिवृद् ॐकारो योऽव्यक्तप्रभवः स्वराट् ।
यत्तल्लिंगं भगवतो ब्रह्मणः परमात्मनः ॥ ३९ ॥

tato 'bhūt tri-vṛd oṁkāro
yo 'vyakta-prabhavaḥ sva-rāṭ
yat tal liṅgaṁ bhagavato
brahmaṇaḥ paramātmanaḥ

tataḥ—from that; *abhūt* — came into being; *tri-vṛt* — threefold; *oṁkāraḥ* —the syllable *oṁ; yaḥ*—which; *avyakta* — not apparent; *prabhavaḥ*—its influence; *sva-rāṭ*—self-manifesting; *yat* — which; *tat* — that; *liṅgam* — the representation; *bhagavataḥ*—of the Supreme Personality of Godhead; *brahmaṇaḥ*—of the Absolute Truth in His impersonal aspect; *parama-ātmanaḥ* —and of the Supersoul.

TRANSLATION

From that transcendental subtle vibration arose the oṁkāra composed of three sounds. The oṁkāra has unseen potencies and manifests automatically within a purified heart. It is the representation of the Absolute Truth in all three of His phases — the Supreme Personality, the Supreme Soul and the supreme impersonal truth.

TEXTS 40–41

शृणोति य इमं स्फोटं सुप्तश्रोत्रे च शून्यदृक् ।
येन वाग् व्यज्यते यस्य व्यक्तिराकाश आत्मनः ॥ ४० ॥
स्वधाम्नो ब्राह्मणः साक्षाद् वाचकः परमात्मनः ।
स सर्वमन्त्रोपनिषद् वेदबीजं सनातनम् ॥ ४१ ॥

śṛṇoti ya imaṁ sphoṭaṁ
supta-śrotre ca śūnya-dṛk

yena vāg vyajyate yasya
vyaktir ākāśa ātmanaḥ

sva-dhāmno brahmaṇaḥ sākṣād
vācakaḥ paramātmanaḥ
sa sarva-mantropaniṣad
veda-bījaṁ sanātanam

śṛṇoti — hears; *yaḥ*—who; *imam* — this; *sphoṭam* — unmanifest and eternal subtle sound; *supta-śrotre* — when the sense of hearing is asleep; *ca* — and; *śūnya-dṛk* — devoid of material sight and other sensory functions; *yena* — by which; *vāk* — the expanse of Vedic sound; *vyajyate* — is elaborated; *yasya* — of which; *vyaktiḥ*—the manifestation; *ākāśe* — in the sky (of the heart); *ātmanaḥ*—from the soul; *sva-dhāmnaḥ*—who is His own origin; *brahmaṇaḥ*—of the Absolute Truth; *sākṣāt* — directly; *vācakaḥ*—the designating term; *parama-ātmanaḥ*—of the Supersoul; *saḥ*—that; *sarva* — of all; *mantra* — Vedic hymns; *upaniṣat* — the secret; *veda* — of the *Vedas; bījam* — the seed; *sanātanam* — eternal.

TRANSLATION

This oṁkāra, ultimately nonmaterial and imperceptible, is heard by the Supersoul without His possessing material ears or any other material senses. The entire expanse of Vedic sound is elaborated from oṁkāra, which appears from the soul, within the sky of the heart. It is the direct designation of the self-originating Absolute Truth, the Supersoul, and is the secret essence and eternal seed of all Vedic hymns.

PURPORT

The senses of a sleeping person do not function until he has awakened. Therefore, when a sleeping person is awakened by a noise, one may ask, "Who heard the noise?" The words *supta-śrotre* in this verse indicate that the Supreme Lord within the heart hears the sound and awakens the sleeping living entities. The Lord's sensory activities always function on a superior level. Ultimately, all sounds vibrate within the sky, and in the internal region of the heart there is a type of sky meant for the vibration of Vedic sounds. The seed, or source, of all Vedic sounds is the *oṁkāra.* This is confirmed by the Vedic statement *oṁ ity etad brahmaṇo nediṣṭhaṁ nāma.* The full elaboration of the Vedic seed sound is *Śrīmad-Bhāgavatam,* the greatest Vedic literature.

TEXT 42

तस्य ह्यासंस्त्रयो वर्णा अकाराद्या भृगूद्वह ।
धार्यन्ते यैस्त्रयो भावा गुणनामार्थवृत्तयः ॥ ४२ ॥

tasya hy āsaṁs trayo varṇā
a-kārādyā bhṛgūdvaha
dhāryante yais trayo bhāvā
guṇa-nāmārtha-vṛttayaḥ

tasya — of that *oṁkāra; hi* — indeed; *āsan* — came into being; *trayaḥ* — three; *varṇāḥ* — sounds of the alphabet; *a-kāra-ādyāḥ* — beginning with the letter *a; bhṛgu-udvaha* — O most eminent of the descendants of Bhṛgu; *dhāryante* — are sustained; *yaiḥ* — by which three sounds; *trayaḥ* — the threefold; *bhāvāḥ* — states of existence; *guṇa* — the qualities of nature; *nāma* — names; *artha* — goals; *vṛttayaḥ* — and states of consciousness.

TRANSLATION

Oṁkāra exhibited the three original sounds of the alphabet — A, U and M. These three, O most eminent descendant of Bhṛgu, sustain all the different threefold aspects of material existence, including the three modes of nature, the names of the Ṛg, Yajur and Sāma Vedas, the goals known as the Bhūr, Bhuvar and Svar planetary systems, and the three functional platforms called waking consciousness, sleep and deep sleep.

TEXT 43

ततोऽक्षरसमाम्नायमसृजद् भगवानजः ।
अन्तस्थोष्मस्वरस्पर्शह्रस्वदीर्घादिलक्षणम् ॥ ४३ ॥

tato 'kṣara-samāmnāyam
asṛjad bhagavān ajaḥ
antasthoṣma-svara-sparśa-
hrasva-dīrghādi-lakṣaṇam

tataḥ — from that *oṁkāra; akṣara* — of the different sounds; *samāmnāyam* — the total collection; *asṛjat* — created; *bhagavān* — the powerful demigod; *ajaḥ* — unborn Brahmā; *anta-stha* — as the semivowels; *uṣma* — sibilants; *svara* — vowels; *sparśa* — and consonant stops; *hrasva-dīrgha* — in short and long forms; *ādi* — and so on; *lakṣaṇam* — characterized.

TRANSLATION

From that oṁkāra Lord Brahmā created all the sounds of the alphabet — the vowels, consonants, semivowels, sibilants and others — distinguished by such features as long and short measure.

TEXT 44

तेनासौ चतुरो वेदांश्चतुर्भिर्वदनैर्विभुः ।
सव्याहृतिकान् सोंकारांश्चातुर्होत्रविवक्षया ॥ ४४ ॥

tenāsau caturo vedāṁś
caturbhir vadanair vibhuḥ
sa-vyāhṛtikān soṁkārāṁś
cātur-hotra-vivakṣayā

tena — with that body of sounds; *asau* — he; *caturaḥ*—the four; *vedān* — *Vedas; caturbhiḥ*—from his four; *vadanaiḥ*—faces; *vibhuḥ*—the all-powerful; *sa-vyāhṛtikān* — along with the *vyāhṛtis* (the invocations of the names of the seven planetary systems: *bhūḥ, bhuvaḥ, ṣvaḥ, mahaḥ, janaḥ, tapaḥ* and *satya*); *sa-oṁkārān* — along with the seed, *oṁ; cātuḥ-hotra* — the four aspects of ritual sacrifice performed by the priests of each of the four *Vedas; vivakṣayā* — with the desire of describing.

TRANSLATION

All-powerful Brahmā made use of this collection of sounds to produce from his four faces the four Vedas, which appeared together with the sacred oṁkāra and the seven vyāhṛti invocations. His intention was to propagate the process of Vedic sacrifice according to the different functions performed by the priests of each of the four Vedas.

TEXT 45

पुत्रानध्यापयत्तांस्तु ब्रह्मर्षीन् ब्रह्मकोविदान् ।
ते तु धर्मोपदेष्टारः स्वपुत्रेभ्यः समादिशन् ॥ ४५ ॥

putrān adhyāpayat tāṁs tu
brahmarṣīn brahma-kovidān
te tu dharmopadeṣṭāraḥ
sva-putrebhyaḥ samādiśan

putrān — to his sons; *adhyāpayat* — he taught; *tān* — those *Vedas; tu* — and; *brahma-ṛṣīn* — to the great sages among the *brāhmaṇas; brahma* — in the art of Vedic recitation; *kovidān* — who were very expert; *te* — they; *tu* — moreover; *dharma* — in religious rituals; *upadeṣṭāraḥ* — instructors; *sva-putrebhyaḥ* — to their own sons; *samādiśan* — imparted.

TRANSLATION

Brahmā taught these Vedas to his sons, who were great sages among the brāhmaṇas and experts in the art of Vedic recitation. They in turn took the role of ācāryas and imparted the Vedas to their own sons.

TEXT 46

ते परम्परया प्राप्तास्तत्तच्छिष्यैर्धृतव्रतैः ।
चतुर्युगेष्वथ व्यस्ता द्वापरादौ महर्षिभिः ॥ ४६ ॥

te paramparayā prāptās
tat-tac-chiṣyair dhṛta-vrataiḥ
catur-yugeṣv atha vyastā
dvāparādau maharṣibhiḥ

te — these *Vedas; paramparayā* — by continuous disciplic succession; *prāptāḥ* — received; *tat-tat* — of each succeeding generation; *śiṣyaiḥ* — by the disciples; *dhṛta-vrataiḥ* — who were firm in their vows; *catuḥ-yugeṣu* — throughout the four ages; *atha* — then; *vyastāḥ* — were divided; *dvāpara-ādau* — at the end of the Dvāpara millennium; *mahā-ṛṣibhiḥ* — by great authorities.

TRANSLATION

In this way, throughout the cycles of four ages, generation after generation of disciples — all firmly fixed in their spiritual vows — have received these Vedas by disciplic succession. At the end of each Dvāpara-yuga the Vedas are edited into separate divisions by eminent sages.

TEXT 47

क्षीणायुषः क्षीणसत्त्वान् दुर्मेधान् वीक्ष्य कालतः ।
वेदान् ब्रह्मर्षयो व्यस्यन् हृदिस्थाच्युतचोदिताः ॥ ४७ ॥

kṣīṇāyuṣaḥ kṣīṇa-sattvān
durmedhān vīkṣya kālataḥ
vedān brahmarṣayo vyasyan
hṛdi-sthācyuta-coditāḥ

kṣīṇa-āyuṣaḥ—their life span diminished; *kṣīṇa-sattvān* — their strength diminished; *durmedhān* — of less intelligence; *vīkṣya* — observing; *kālataḥ* —by the effect of time; *vedān* — the *Vedas; brahma-ṛṣayaḥ*—the chief sages; *vyasyan* — divided up; *hṛdi-stha* — sitting within their hearts; *acyuta* — by the infallible Personality of Godhead; *coditāḥ*—inspired.

TRANSLATION

Observing that people in general were diminished in their life span, strength and intelligence by the influence of time, great sages took inspiration from the Personality of Godhead sitting within their hearts and systematically divided the Vedas.

TEXTS 48–49

अस्मिन्नप्यन्तरे ब्रह्मन् भगवान लोकभावनः ।
ब्रह्मेशाद्यैर्लोकपालैर्याचितो धर्मगुप्तये ॥ ४८ ॥
पराशरात् सत्यवत्यामंशांशकलया विभुः ।
अवतीर्णो महाभाग वेदं चक्रे चतुर्विधम् ॥४९ ॥

asminn apy antare brahman
bhagavān loka-bhāvanaḥ
brahmeśādyair loka-pālair
yācito dharma-guptaye

parāśarāt satyavatyām
aṁśāṁśa-kalayā vibhuḥ
avatīrṇo mahā-bhāga
vedaṁ cakre catur-vidham

asmin — in this; *api* — also; *antare* — rule of Manu; *brahman* — O *brāhmaṇa* (Śaunaka); *bhagavān* — the Supreme Personality of Godhead; *loka* — of the universe; *bhāvanaḥ*—the protector; *brahma* — by Brahmā; *īśa* — Śiva; *ādyaiḥ*—and the others; *loka-pālaiḥ*—the rulers of the various planets; *yācitaḥ*—requested; *dharma-guptaye* — for the protection of the principles of religion; *parāśarāt* — by Parāśara Muni; *satyavatyām* — in the womb of Satyavatī; *aṁśa* — of His plenary expansion (Saṅkarṣaṇa); *aṁśa* — of the expansion (Viṣṇu); *kalayā* — as the partial expansion; *vibhuḥ*—the Lord; *avatīrṇaḥ*—descended; *mahā-bhāga* — O most fortunate one; *vedam* — the *Veda; cakre* — he made; *catuḥ-vidham* — in four parts.

TRANSLATION

O brāhmaṇa, in the present age of Vaivasvata Manu, the leaders of the universe, led by Brahmā and Śiva, requested the Supreme Personality of Godhead, the protector of all the worlds, to save the principles of religion. O most fortunate Śaunaka, the almighty Lord, exhibiting a divine spark of a portion of His plenary portion, then appeared in the womb of Satyavatī as the son of Parāśara. In this form, named Kṛṣṇa Dvaipāyana Vyāsa, he divided the one Veda into four.

TEXT 50

ऋगथर्वयजुःसाम्नां राशीरुद्धृत्य वर्गशः ।
चतस्रः संहिताश्चक्रे मन्त्रैर्मणिगणा इव ॥ ५० ॥

ṛg-atharva-yajuḥ-sāmnāṁ
rāśīr uddhṛtya vargaśaḥ
catasraḥ saṁhitāś cakre
mantrair maṇi-gaṇā iva

ṛk-atharva-yajuḥ-sāmnām — of the *Ṛg, Atharva, Yajur and Sāma Vedas*; *rāśīḥ*—the accumulation (*of mantras*); *uddhṛtya* — separating out; *vargaśaḥ* — in specific categories; *catasraḥ*—four; *saṁhitāḥ*—collections; *cakre* — he made; *mantraiḥ*—with the mantras; *maṇi-gaṇāḥ*—gems; *iva* — just as.

TRANSLATION

Śrīla Vyāsadeva separated the mantras of the Ṛg, Atharva, Yajur and Sāma Vedas into four divisions, just as one sorts out a mixed collection of jewels into piles. Thus he composed four distinct Vedic literatures.

PURPORT

When Lord Brahmā first spoke the four *Vedas* with his four mouths, the *mantras* were mixed together like an unsorted collection of various types of jewels. Śrīla Vyāsadeva sorted the Vedic *mantras* into four divisions (*saṁhitās*), which thus became the recognizable *Ṛg, Atharva, Yajur* and *Sāma Vedas.*

TEXT 51

तासां स चतुरः शिष्यानुपाहूय महामतिः ।
एकैकां संहितां ब्रह्मन्नेकैकस्मै ददौ विभुः ॥ ५१ ॥

tāsāṁ sa caturaḥ śiṣyān
upāhūya mahā-matiḥ
ekaikāṁ saṁhitāṁ brahmann
ekaikasmai dadau vibhuḥ

tāsām — of those four collections; *saḥ*—he; *caturaḥ*—four; *śiṣyān* — disciples; *upāhūya* — calling near; *mahā-matiḥ*—the powerfully intelligent sage; *eka-ekām* — one by one; *saṁhitām* — a collection; *brahman* — O *brāhmaṇa; eka-ekasmai* — to each of them; *dadau* — he gave; *vibhuḥ*—the powerful Vyāsadeva.

TRANSLATION

The most powerful and intelligent Vyāsadeva called four of his disciples, O brāhmaṇa, and entrusted to each of them one of these four saṁhitās.

TEXTS 52–53

पैलाय संहितामाद्यां बह्वृचाख्यां उवाच ह ।
वैशम्पायनसंज्ञाय निगदाख्यं यजुर्गणम् ॥ ५२ ॥
साम्नां जैमिनये प्राह तथा छन्दोगसंहिताम् ।
अथर्वांगिरसीं नाम स्वशिष्याय सुमन्तवे ॥ ५३ ॥

pailāya saṁhitām ādyāṁ
bahvṛcākhyāṁ uvāca ha
vaiśampāyana-saṁjñāya
nigadākhyaṁ yajur-gaṇam

sāmnāṁ jaiminaye prāha
tathā chandoga-saṁhitām
atharvāṅgirasīṁ nāma
sva-śiṣyāya sumantave

pailāya — to Paila; *saṁhitām* — the collection; *ādyām* — first (of the *Ṛg Veda*); *bahu-ṛca-ākhyām* — called *Bahvṛca; uvāca* — he spoke; *ha* — indeed; *vaiśampāyana-saṁjñāya* — to the sage named Vaiśampāyana; *nigada-ākhyam* — known as *Nigada; yajuḥ-gaṇam* — the collection of *Yajur mantras; sāmnām* — the *mantras* of the *Sāma Veda; jaiminaye* — to Jaimini; *prāha* — he spoke; *tathā* — and; *chandoga-saṁhitām* — the *saṁhitā* named *Chandoga; atharva-aṅgirasīm* — the *Veda* ascribed to the sages Atharva and Aṅgirā; *nāma* — indeed; *sva-śiṣyāya* — to his disciple; *sumantave* — Sumantu.

TRANSLATION

Śrīla Vyāsadeva taught the first saṁhitā, the Ṛg Veda, to Paila and gave this collection the name Bahvṛca. To the sage Vaiśampāyana he spoke the collection of Yajur mantras named Nigada. He taught the Sāma Veda mantras, designated as the Chandoga-saṁhitā, to Jaimini, and he spoke the Atharva Veda to his dear disciple Sumantu.

TEXTS 54–56

पैलः स्वसंहितामूचे इन्द्रप्रमितये मुनिः ।
बाष्कलाय च सोऽप्याह शिष्येभ्यः संहितां स्वकाम् ॥ ५४ ॥
चतुर्धा व्यस्य बोध्याय याज्ञवल्क्याय भार्गव ।
पराशरायाग्निमित्र इन्द्रप्रमितिरात्मवान् ॥ ५५ ॥
अध्यापयत् संहितां स्वां माण्डूकेयमृषिं कविम् ।
तस्य शिष्यो देवमित्रः सौभर्यादिभ्य ऊचिवान् ॥ ५६ ॥

pailaḥ sva-saṁhitām ūce
indrapramitaye muniḥ
bāṣkalāya ca so 'py āha
śiṣyebhyaḥ saṁhitāṁ svakām

caturdhā vyasya bodhyāya
yājñavalkyāya bhārgava
parāśarāyāgnimitra
indrapramitir ātmavān

adhyāpayat saṁhitāṁ svāṁ
māṇḍūkeyam ṛṣiṁ kavim

tasya śiṣyo devamitraḥ
saubhary-ādibhya ūcivān

pailaḥ—Paila; *sva-saṁhitām*—his own collection; *ūce*—spoke; *indrapramitaye*—to Indrapramiti; *muniḥ*—the sage; *bāṣkalāya*—to Bāṣkala; *ca*—and; *saḥ*—he (Bāṣkala); *api*—moreover; *āha*—spoke; *śiṣyebhyaḥ*—to his disciples; *saṁhitām*—the collection; *svakām*—his own; *caturdhā*—in four parts; *vyasya*—dividing; *bodhyāya*—to Bodhya; *yājñavalkyāya*—to Yājñavalkya; *bhārgava*—O descendant of Bhṛgu (Śaunaka); *parāśarāya*—to Parāśara; *agnimitre*—to Agnimitra; *indrapramitiḥ*—Indrapramiti; *ātmavān*—the self-controlled; *adhyāpayat*—taught; *saṁhitām*—the collection; *svām*—his; *māṇḍūkeyam*—to Māṇḍūkeya; *ṛṣim*—the sage; *kavim*—scholarly; *tasya*—of him (Māṇḍūkeya); *śiṣyaḥ*—the disciple; *devamitraḥ*—Devamitra; *saubhari-ādibhyaḥ*—to Saubhari and others; *ūcivān*—spoke.

TRANSLATION

After dividing his saṁhitā into two parts, the wise Paila spoke it to Indrapramiti and Bāṣkala. Bāṣkala further divided his collection into four parts, O Bhārgava, and instructed them to his disciples Bodhya, Yājñavalkya, Parāśara and Agnimitra. Indrapramiti, the self-controlled sage, taught his saṁhitā to the learned mystic Māṇḍūkeya, whose disciple Devamitra later passed down the divisions of the Ṛg Veda to Saubhari and others.

PURPORT

According to Śrīla Śrīdhara Svāmī, Māṇḍūkeya was the son of Indrapramiti, from whom he received Vedic knowledge.

TEXT 57

शाकल्यस्तत्सुतः स्वां तु पञ्चधा व्यस्य संहिताम् ।
वात्स्यमुद्गलशालीयगोखल्यशिशिरेष्वधात् ॥ ५७ ॥

śākalyas tat-sutaḥ svāṁ tu
pañcadhā vyasya saṁhitām
vātsya-mudgala-śālīya-
gokhalya-śiśireṣv adhāt

śākalyaḥ—Śākalya; *tat-sutaḥ*—the son of Māṇḍūkeya; *svām*—his own; *tu*—and; *pañcadhā*—in five parts; *vyasya*—dividing; *saṁhitām*—the collection; *vātsya-mudgala-śālīya* — to Vātsya, Mudgala and Śālīya; *gokhalya-śiśireṣu* — and to Gokhalya and Śiśira; *adhāt* — gave.

TRANSLATION

The son of Māṇḍūkeya, named Śākalya, divided his own collection into five, entrusting one subdivision each to Vātsya, Mudgala, Śālīya, Gokhalya and Śiśira.

TEXT 58

जातूकर्ण्यश्च तच्छिष्यः सनिरुक्तां स्वसंहिताम् ।
बलाकपैलजाबालविरजेभ्यो ददौ मुनिः ॥ ५८ ॥

jātūkarṇyaś ca tac-chiṣyaḥ
sa-niruktāṁ sva-saṁhitām
balāka-paila-jābāla-
virajebhyo dadau muniḥ

jātūkarṇyaḥ — Jātūkarṇya; *ca* — and; *tat-śiṣyaḥ* — the disciple of Śākalya; *sa-niruktām* — along with a glossary explaining obscure terms; *sva-saṁhitām* — the collection he received; *balāka-paila-jābāla-virajebhyaḥ* — to Balāka, Paila, Jābāla and Viraja; *dadau* — passed down; *muniḥ* — the sage.

TRANSLATION

The sage Jātūkarṇya was also a disciple of Śākalya, and after dividing the saṁhitā he received from Śākalya into three parts, he added a fourth section, a Vedic glossary. He taught one of these parts to each of four disciples — Balāka, the second Paila, Jābāla and Viraja.

TEXT 59

बाष्कलिः प्रतिशाखाभ्यो वालखिल्याख्यसंहिताम् ।
चक्रे वालायनिर्भज्यः काशारश्चैव तां दधुः ॥ ५९ ॥

bāṣkaliḥ prati-śākhābhyo
vālakhilyākhya-saṁhitām
cakre vālāyanir bhajyaḥ
kāśāraś caiva tāṁ dadhuḥ

bāṣkaliḥ — Bāṣkali, the son of Bāṣkala; *prati-śākhābhyaḥ* — from all the different branches; *vālakhilya-ākhya* — entitled *Vālakhilya; saṁhitām* — the collection; *cakre* — he made; *vālāyaniḥ*—Vālāyani; *bhajyaḥ*—Bhajya; *kāśāraḥ* —Kāśāra; *ca* — and; *eva* — indeed; *tām* — that; *dadhuḥ*—they accepted.

TRANSLATION

Bāṣkali assembled the Vālakhilya-saṁhitā, a collection from all the branches of the Ṛg Veda. This collection was received by Vālāyani, Bhajya and Kāśāra.

PURPORT

According to Śrīla Śrīdhara Svāmī, Vālāyani, Bhajya and Kāśāra belonged to the Daitya community.

TEXT 60

बह्वृचाः संहिता ह्येता एभिर्ब्रह्मर्षिभिर्धृताः ।
श्रुत्वैतच्छन्दसां व्यासं सर्वपापैः प्रमुच्यते ॥ ६० ॥

bahvṛcāḥ saṁhitā hy etā
ebhir brahmarṣibhir dhṛtāḥ
śrutvaitac-chandasāṁ vyāsaṁ
sarva-pāpaiḥ pramucyate

bahu-ṛcāḥ—of the *Ṛg Veda; saṁhitāḥ*—the collections; *hi* — indeed; *etāḥ*—these; *ebhiḥ*—by these; *brahma-ṛṣibhiḥ*—saintly *brāhmaṇas; dhṛtāḥ* —maintained through disciplic succession; *śrutvā* — hearing; *etat* — their; *chandasām* — of the sacred verses; *vyāsam* — the process of division; *sarva-pāpaiḥ*—from all sins; *pramucyate* — one becomes delivered.

TRANSLATION

Thus these various saṁhitās of the Ṛg Veda were maintained through disciplic succession by these saintly brāhmaṇas. Simply by hearing of this distribution of the Vedic hymns, one will be freed from all sins.

TEXT 61

वैशम्पायनशिष्या वै चरकाध्वर्यवोऽभवन् ।
यच्चेरुर्ब्रह्महत्यांहः क्षपणं स्वगुरोर्व्रतम् ॥ ६१ ॥

vaiśampāyana-śiṣyā vai
carakādhvaryavo 'bhavan

yac cerur brahma-hatyāṁhaḥ
kṣapaṇaṁ sva-guror vratam

vaiśampāyana-śiṣyāḥ—the disciples of Vaiśampāyana; *vai*— indeed; *caraka* — named the Carakas; *adhvaryavaḥ*—authorities of the *Atharva Veda; abhavan* — became; *yat* — because; *ceruḥ*—they executed; *brahma-hatyā* — due to the killing of a *brāhmaṇa; aṁhaḥ*—of the sin; *kṣapaṇam* — the expiation; *sva-guroḥ*—for their own *guru; vratam* — the vow.

TRANSLATION

The disciples of Vaiśampāyana became authorities in the Atharva Veda. They were known as the Carakas because they executed strict vows to free their guru from his sin of killing a brāhmaṇa.

TEXT 62

याज्ञवल्क्यश्च तच्छिष्य आहाहो भगवन् कियत् ।
चरितेनाल्पसाराणां चरिष्येऽहं सुदुश्चरम् ॥ ६२ ॥

yājñavalkyaś ca tac-chiṣya
āhāho bhagavan kiyat
caritenālpa-sārāṇāṁ
cariṣye 'haṁ su-duścaram

yājñavalkyaḥ—Yājñavalkya; *ca* — and; *tat-śiṣyaḥ*—the disciple of Vaiśampāyana; *āha* — said; *aho* — just see; *bhagavan* — O master; *kiyat* — how much value; *caritena* — with the endeavor; *alpa-sārāṇām* — of these weak fellows; *cariṣye* — shall execute; *aham* — I; *su-duścaram* — that which is very difficult to perform.

TRANSLATION

Once Yājñavalkya, one of the disciples of Vaiśampāyana, said: O master, how much benefit will be derived from the feeble endeavors of these weak disciples of yours? I will personally perform some outstanding penance.

TEXT 63

इत्युक्तो गुरुरप्याह कुपितो याह्यलं त्वया ।
विप्रावमन्त्रा शिष्येण मदधीतं त्यजाश्विति ॥ ६३ ॥

ity ukto gurur apy āha
kupito yāhy alaṁ tvayā
viprāvamantrā śiṣyeṇa
mad-adhītaṁ tyajāśv iti

iti — thus; *uktaḥ* — addressed; *guruḥ* — his spiritual master; *api* — indeed; *āha* — said; *kupitaḥ* — angry; *yāhi* — go away; *alam* — enough; *tvayā* — with you; *vipra-avamantrā* — the insulter of *brāhmaṇas; śiṣyeṇa* — such a disciple; *mat-adhītam* — what has been taught by me; *tyaja* — give up; *āśu* — immediately; *iti* — thus.

TRANSLATION

Addressed thus, the spiritual master Vaiśampāyana became angry and said: Go away from here! Enough of you, O disciple who insults brāhmaṇas! Furthermore, you must immediately give back everything I have taught you.

PURPORT

Śrī Vaiśampāyana was angry because one of his disciples, Yājñavalkya, was insulting the other disciples, who were, after all, qualified *brāhmaṇas.* Just as a father is disturbed when one son mistreats the father's other children, the spiritual master is very displeased if a proud disciple insults or mistreats the *guru's* other disciples.

TEXTS 64–65

देवरातसुतः सोऽपि छर्दित्वा यजुषां गणम् ।
ततो गतोऽथ मुनयो ददृशुस्तान् यजुर्गणान् ॥ ६४ ॥
यजूंषि तित्तिरा भूत्वा तल्लोलुपतयाददुः ।
तैत्तिरीया इति यजुःशाखा आसन् सुपेशलाः ॥ ६५ ॥

devarāta-sutaḥ so 'pi
charditvā yajuṣāṁ gaṇam
tato gato 'tha munayo
dadṛśus tān yajur-gaṇān

yajūṁṣi tittirā bhūtvā
tal-lolupatayādaduḥ

taittirīyā iti yajuḥ-
śākhā āsan su-peśalāḥ

devarāta-sutaḥ—the son of Devarāta (Yājñavalkya); *saḥ*—he; *api*—indeed; *charditvā*—vomiting; *yajuṣām*—of the *Yajur Veda; gaṇam*—the collected *mantras; tataḥ*—from there; *gataḥ*—having gone; *atha*—then; *munayaḥ*—the sages; *dadṛśuḥ*—saw; *tān*—those; *yajuḥ-gaṇān*—*yajur-mantras; yajūṁsi*—these *yajurs; tittirāḥ*—partridges; *bhūtvā*—becoming; *tat*—for those *mantras; lolupatayā*—with greedy desire; *ādaduḥ*—picked them up; *taittirīyāḥ*—known as *Taittirīya; iti*—thus; *yajuḥ-śākhāḥ*—branches of the *Yajur Veda; āsan*—came into being; *su-peśalāḥ*—most beautiful.

TRANSLATION

Yājñavalkya, the son of Devarāta, then vomited the mantras of the Yajur Veda and went away from there. The assembled disciples, looking greedily upon these yajur hymns, assumed the form of partridges and picked them all up. These divisions of the Yajur Veda therefore became known as the most beautiful Taittirīya-saṁhitā, the hymns collected by partridges [tittirāḥ].

PURPORT

According to Śrīla Śrīdhara Svāmī, it is improper for a *brāhmaṇa* to collect what has been vomited, and so the powerful *brāhmaṇa* disciples of Vaiśampāyana assumed the form of *tittiras,* partridges, and collected the valuable *mantras.*

TEXT 66

याज्ञवल्क्यस्ततो ब्रह्मंश्छन्दांस्यधि गवेषयन् ।
गुरोरविद्यमानानि सूपतस्थेऽर्कमीश्वरम् ॥ ६६ ॥

yājñavalkyas tato brahmaṁś
chandāṁsy adhi gaveṣayan
guror avidyamānāni
sūpatasthe 'rkam īśvaram

yājñavalkyaḥ—Yājñavalkya; *tataḥ*—thereafter; *brahman*—O *brāhmaṇa; chandāṁsi*—*mantras; adhi*—additional; *gaveṣayan*—seeking out; *guroḥ*

—to his spiritual master; *avidyamānāni* — not known; *su-upatasthe* — he carefully worshiped; *arkam* — the sun; *īśvaram* — the powerful controller.

TRANSLATION

My dear brāhmaṇa Śaunaka, Yājñavalkya then desired to find out new yajur-mantras unknown to even his spiritual master. With this in mind he offered attentive worship to the powerful lord of the sun.

TEXT 67

श्रीयाज्ञवल्क्य उवाच

ॐ नमो भगवते आदित्यायाखिलजगतामात्मस्वरूपेण काल-
स्वरूपेण चतुर्विधभूतनिकायानां ब्रह्मादिस्तम्बपर्यन्तानामन्तर्हृदयेषु
बहिरपि चाकाश इवोपाधिनाव्यवधीयमानो भवानेक एव क्षणलव-
निमेषावयवोपचितसंवत्सरगणेनापामादानविसर्गाभ्यामिमां लोक-
यात्रामनुवहति ॥ ६७ ॥

śrī-yājñavalkya uvāca

oṁ namo bhagavate ādityāyākhila-jagatām ātma-svarūpeṇa kāla- svarū-peṇa catur-vidha-bhūta-nikāyānāṁ brahmādi-stamba-paryantānām antar-hṛdayeṣu bahir api cākāśa ivopādhināvyavadhīyamāno bhavān eka eva kṣaṇa-lava-nimeṣāvayavopacita-saṁvatsara-gaṇenāpām ādāna- visargāb-hyām imāṁ loka-yātrām anuvahati.

śrī-yājñavalkyaḥ uvāca — Śrī Yājñavalkya said; *oṁ namaḥ*—I offer my respectful obeisances; *bhagavate* — to the Personality of Godhead; *ādityāya* — appearing as the sun god; *akhila-jagatām* — of all the planetary systems; *ātma-svarūpeṇa* — in the form of the Supersoul; *kāla-svarūpeṇa* — in the form of time; *catuḥ-vidha* — of four kinds; *bhūta-nikāyānām* — of all the living beings; *brahma-ādi* — beginning from Lord Brahmā; *stamba-paryantānām* — and extending down to the blades of grass; *antaḥ-hṛdayeṣu* — within the recesses of their hearts; *bahiḥ*—externally; *api* — also; *ca* — and; *ākāśaḥ iva* — in the same way as the sky; *upādhinā* — by material designations; *avyavadhīyamānaḥ*—not being covered; *bhavān* — yourself; *ekaḥ*—alone; *eva* — indeed; *kṣaṇa-lava-nimeṣa* — the *kṣaṇa, lava* and *nimeṣa* (the smallest fractions of time); *avayava* — by these fragments; *upacita* — collected together; *saṁvatsara-gaṇena* — by the years; *apām* — of the water;

ādāna — by taking away; *visargābhyām* — and giving; *imām* — this; *loka* — of the universe; *yātrām* — the maintenance; *anuvahati* — carries out.

TRANSLATION

Śrī Yājñavalkya said: I offer my respectful obeisances to the Supreme Personality of Godhead appearing as the sun. You are present as the controller of the four kinds of living entities, beginning from Brahmā and extending down to the blades of grass. Just as the sky is present both inside and outside every living being, you exist both within the hearts of all as the Supersoul and externally in the form of time. Just as the sky cannot be covered by the clouds present within it, you are never covered by any false material designation. By the flow of years, which are made up of the tiny fragments of time called kṣaṇas, lavas and nimeṣas, you alone maintain this world, drying up the waters and giving them back as rain.

PURPORT

This prayer is not offered to the sun god as an independent or autonomous entity but rather to the Supreme Personality of Godhead, represented by His powerful expansion the solar deity.

TEXT 68

यदु ह वाव विबुधर्षभ सवितरदस्तपत्यनुसवनमहरहराम्नायविधि
नोपतिष्ठमानानामखिलदुरितवृजिनबीजावभर्जन भगवतः समभिधी-
महि तपन मण्डलम् ॥ ६८ ॥

yad u ha vāva vibudharṣabha savitar adas tapaty anusavanam ahar
ahar āmnāya-vidhinopatiṣṭhamānānām akhila-durita-vṛjina-
bījāvabharjana bhagavataḥ samabhidhīmahi tapana maṇḍalam.

yat — which; *u ha vāva* — indeed; *vibudha-ṛṣabha* — O chief of the demigods; *savitaḥ* — O lord of the sun; *adaḥ* — that; *tapati* — is glowing; *anusavanam* — at each of the junctures of the day (sunrise, noon and sunset); *ahaḥ ahaḥ* — each day; *āmnāya-vidhinā* — by the Vedic path, as passed down through disciplic succession; *upatiṣṭhamānānām* — of those who are engaged in offering prayer; *akhila-durita* — all sinful activities; *vṛjina* — the consequent suffering; *bīja* — and the original seed of such; *avabharjana* — O you who burn; *bhagavataḥ* — of the mighty controller; *samabhidhīmahi* — I meditate with full attention; *tapana* — O glowing one; *maṇḍalam* — upon the sphere.

TRANSLATION

O glowing one, O powerful lord of the sun, you are the chief of all the demigods. I meditate with careful attention on your fiery globe, because for those who offer prayers to you three times daily according to the Vedic method passed down through authorized disciplic succession, you burn away all sinful activities, all consequent suffering and even the original seed of desire.

TEXT 69

य इह वाव स्थिरचरनिकराणां निजनिकेतनानां मनइन्द्रियासुगणान्अनात्मनः स्वयमात्मान्तर्यामी प्रचोदयति ॥ ६९ ॥

ya iha vāva sthira-cara-nikarāṇāṁ nija-niketanānāṁ mana-indriyāsu-gaṇān anātmanaḥ svayam ātmāntar-yāmī pracodayati.

yaḥ — who; *iha* — in this world; *vāva* — indeed; *sthira-cara-nikarāṇām* — of all the nonmoving and moving living beings; *nija-niketanānām* — who depend on your shelter; *manaḥ-indriya-asu-gaṇān* — the mind, senses and vital air; *anātmanaḥ* — which are nonliving matter; *svayam* — yourself; *ātma* — in their hearts; *antaḥ-yāmī* — the indwelling lord; *pracodayati* — inspires to activity.

TRANSLATION

You are personally present as the indwelling lord in the hearts of all moving and nonmoving beings, who depend completely on your shelter. Indeed, you animate their material minds, senses and vital airs to act.

TEXT 70

य एवेमं लोकमतिकरालवदनान्धकारसंज्ञाजगरग्रहगिलितं मृतकमिव विचेतनमवलोक्यानुकम्पया परमकारुणिक ईक्षयैवोत्थाप्याहरहरनुसवनं श्रेयसि स्वधर्माख्यात्मावस्थाने प्रवर्तयति ॥ ७० ॥

ya evemaṁ lokam ati-karāla-vadanāndhakāra-saṁjñājagara-graha-gilitaṁ mṛtakam iva vicetanam avalokyānukampayā parama-kāruṇika īkṣayaivotthāpyāhar ahar anusavanaṁ śreyasi sva-dharmākhyātmāva-sthāne pravartayati.

yaḥ—who; *eva* — alone; *imam* — this; *lokam* — world; *ati-karāla* — very fearful; *vadana* — the mouth of which; *andhakāra-saṁjña* — known as darkness; *ajagara* — by the python; *graha* — seized; *gilitam* — and swallowed; *mṛtakam* — dead; *iva* — as if; *vicetanam* — unconscious; *avalokya* — by glancing; *anukampayā* — mercifully; *parama-kāruṇikaḥ*—supremely magnanimous; *īkṣayā* — by casting his glance; *eva* — indeed; *utthāpya* — raising them up; *ahaḥ ahaḥ*—day after day; *anu-savanam* — at the three sacred junctures of the day; *śreyasi* — in the ultimate benefit; *sva-dharma-ākhya* — known as the soul's proper duty; *ātma-avasthāne* — in the inclination toward spiritual life; *pravartayati* — engages.

TRANSLATION

The world has been seized and swallowed by the python of darkness in its horrible mouth and has become unconscious, as if dead. But mercifully glancing upon the sleeping people of the world, you raise them up with the gift of sight. Thus you are most magnanimous. At the three sacred junctures of each day, you engage the pious in the path of ultimate good, inducing them to perform religious duties that situate them in their spiritual position.

PURPORT

According to Vedic culture, the three higher classes of society (the intellectual, political and mercantile sections) are formally connected with the spiritual master by initiation and receive the Gāyatrī *mantra.* This purifying *mantra* is chanted three times daily — at sunrise, noon and sunset. Auspicious moments for the performance of spiritual duties are calculated according to the sun's path in the sky, and this systematic scheduling of spiritual duties is here attributed to the sun as the representative of God.

TEXT 71

अवनिपतिरिवासाधूनां भयमुदीरयन्नटति परित आशापालैस्तत्र तत्र कमलकोशाञ्जलिभिरुपहृतार्हणः ॥ ७१ ॥

avani-patir ivāsādhūnāṁ bhayam udīrayann aṭati parita āśā-pālais
tatra tatra kamala-kośāñjalibhir upahṛtārhaṇaḥ.

avani-patiḥ—a king; *iva* — as; *asādhūnām* — of the unholy; *bhayam* — fear; *udīrayan* — creating; *aṭati* — travels about; *paritaḥ*—all around; *āśā-pālaiḥ*—by the controlling deities of the directions; *tatra tatra* — here and there; *kamala-kośa* — holding lotus flowers; *añjalibhiḥ*—with folded palms; *upahṛta* — offered; *arhaṇaḥ*—honorable presentations.

TRANSLATION

Just like an earthly king, you travel about everywhere spreading fear among the unholy as the powerful deities of the directions offer you in their folded palms lotus flowers and other respectful presentations.

TEXT 72

अथ ह भगवंस्तव चरणनलिनयुगलं त्रिभुवनगुरुभिरभिवन्दितमहम्
अयातयामयजुष्काम उपसरामीति ॥ ७२ ॥

atha ha bhagavaṁs tava caraṇa-nalina-yugalaṁ tri-bhuvana-gurubhir abhivanditam aham ayāta-yāma-yajuṣ-kāma upasarāmīti.

atha — thus; *ha* — indeed; *bhagavan* — O lord; *tava* — your; *caraṇa-nalina-yugalam* — two lotus feet; *tri-bhuvana* — of the three worlds; *gurubhiḥ*—by the spiritual masters; *abhivanditam* — honored; *aham* — I; *ayāta-yāma* — unknown to anyone else; *yajuḥ-kāmaḥ*—desiring to have the *yajur-mantras; upasarāmi* — am approaching with worship; *iti* — thus.

TRANSLATION

Therefore, my lord, I am prayerfully approaching your lotus feet, which are honored by the spiritual masters of the three worlds, because I hope to receive from you mantras of the Yajur Veda unknown to anyone else.

TEXT 73

सूत उवाच
एवं स्तुतः स भगवान् वाजिरूपधरो रविः ।
यजूंष्ययातयामानि मुनयेऽदात्प्रसादितः ॥ ७३ ॥

sūta uvāca
evaṁ stutaḥ sa bhagavān
vāji-rūpa-dharo raviḥ

yajūṁṣy ayāta-yāmāni
munaye 'dāt prasāditaḥ

sūtaḥ uvāca — Sūta Gosvāmī said; *evam* — in this way; *stutaḥ* — offered glorification; *saḥ* — he; *bhagavān* — the powerful demigod; *vāji-rūpa* — the form of a horse; *dharaḥ* — assuming; *raviḥ* — the sun god; *yajūṁṣi* — *yajur-mantras; ayāta-yāmāni* — never learned by any other mortal; *munaye* — to the sage; *adāt* — presented; *prasāditaḥ* — being satisfied.

TRANSLATION

Sūta Gosvāmī said: Satisfied by such glorification, the powerful sun god assumed the form of a horse and presented to the sage Yājñavalkya yajur-mantras previously unknown in human society.

TEXT 74

यजुर्भिरकरोच्छाखा दश पञ्च शतैर्विभुः ।
जगृहुर्वाजसन्यस्ताः काण्वमाध्यन्दिनादयः ॥ ७४ ॥

yajurbhir akaroc chākhā
daśa pañca śatair vibhuḥ
jagṛhur vājasanyas tāḥ
kāṇva-mādhyandinādayaḥ

yajurbhiḥ — with the *yajur-mantras; akarot* — he made; *śākhāḥ* — branches; *daśa* — ten; *pañca* — plus five; *śataiḥ* — with the hundreds; *vibhuḥ* — the powerful; *jagṛhuḥ* — they accepted; *vāja-sanyaḥ* — produced from the hairs of the horse's mane and thus known as *Vājasaneyī; tāḥ* — them; *kāṇva-mādhyandina-ādayaḥ* — the disciples of Kāṇva and Mādhyandina, and other *ṛṣis.*

TRANSLATION

From these countless hundreds of mantras of the Yajur Veda, the powerful sage compiled fifteen new branches of Vedic literature. These became known as the Vājasaneyi-saṁhitā because they were produced from the hairs of the horse's mane, and they were accepted in disciplic succession by the followers of Kāṇva, Mādhyandina and other ṛṣis.

TEXT 75

जैमिनेः समगस्यासीत् सुमन्तुस्तनयो मुनिः ।
सुत्वांस्तु तत्सुतस्ताभ्यामेकैकां प्राह संहिताम् ॥ ७५ ॥

jaimineḥ sama-gasyāsīt
sumantus tanayo muniḥ
sutvāṁs tu tat-sutas tābhyām
ekaikāṁ prāha saṁhitām

jaimineḥ — of Jaimini; *sāma-gasya* — the singer of the *Sāma Veda; āsīt* — there was; *sumantuḥ* — Sumantu; *tanayaḥ* — the son; *muniḥ* — the sage (Jaimini); *sutvān* — Sutvān; *tu* — and; *tat-sutaḥ* — the son of Sumantu; *tābhyām* — to each of them; *eka-ekām* — one of each of the two parts; *prāha* — he spoke; *saṁhitām* — collection.

TRANSLATION

Jaimini Ṛṣi, the authority of the Sāma Veda, had a son named Sumantu, and the son of Sumantu was Sutvān. The sage Jaimini spoke to each of them a different part of the Sāma-veda-saṁhitā.

TEXTS 76–77

सुकर्मा चापि तच्छिष्यः सामवेदतरोर्महान् ।
सहस्रसंहिताभेदं चक्रे साम्नां ततो द्विज ॥ ७६ ॥
हिरण्यनाभः कौशल्यः पौष्यञ्जिश्च सुकर्मणः ।
शिष्यौ जगृहतुश्चान्य आवन्त्यो ब्रह्मवित्तमः ॥ ७७ ॥

sukarmā cāpi tac-chiṣyaḥ
sāma-veda-taror mahān
sahasra-saṁhitā-bhedaṁ
cakre sāmnāṁ tato dvija

hiraṇyanābhaḥ kauśalyaḥ
pauṣyañjiś ca sukarmaṇaḥ
śiṣyau jagṛhatuś cānya
āvantyo brahma-vittamaḥ

sukarmā — Sukarmā; *ca* — and; *api* — indeed; *tat-śiṣyaḥ* — the disciple of Jaimini; *sāma-veda-taroḥ* — of the tree of the *Sāma Veda; mahān* — the great thinker; *sahasra-saṁhitā* — of one thousand collections; *bhedam* — a division; *cakre* — he made; *sāmnām* — of the *sāma-mantras; tataḥ*—and then; *dvija* — O *brāhmaṇa* (Śaunaka); *hiraṇyanābhaḥ kauśalyaḥ*— Hiraṇyanābha, the son of Kuśala; *pauṣyañjiḥ*—Pauṣyañji; *ca* — and; *sukarmaṇaḥ*—of Sukarmā; *śiṣyau* — the two disciples; *jagṛhatuḥ*—took; *ca* — and; *anyaḥ*—another; *āvantyaḥ*— Āvantya; *brahma-vit-tamaḥ*—most perfectly realized in knowledge of the Absolute Truth.

TRANSLATION

Sukarmā, another disciple of Jaimini, was a great scholar. He divided the mighty tree of the Sāma Veda into one thousand saṁhitās. Then, O brāhmaṇa, three disciples of Sukarmā — Hiraṇyanābha, the son of Kuśala; Pauṣyañji; and Āvantya, who was very advanced in spiritual realization — took charge of the sāma-mantras.

TEXT 78

उदीच्याः सामगाः शिष्या आसन् पञ्चशतानि वै ।
पौष्यञ्ज्यावन्त्ययोश्चापि तांश्च प्राच्यान् प्रचक्षते ॥ ७८ ॥

udīcyāḥ sāma-gāḥ śiṣyā
āsan pañca-śatāni vai
pauṣyañjy-āvantyayoś cāpi
tāṁś ca prācyān pracakṣate

udīcyāḥ—belonging to the north; *sāma-gāḥ*—the singer of the *Sāma Veda; śiṣyāḥ*—the disciples; *āsan* — there were; *pañca-śatāni* — five hundred; *vai* — indeed; *pauṣyañji-āvantyayoḥ*—of Pauṣyañji and Āvantya; *ca* — and; *api* — indeed; *tān* — they; *ca* — also; *prācyān* — easterners; *pracakṣate* — are called.

TRANSLATION

The five hundred disciples of Pauṣyañji and Āvantya became known as the northern singers of the Sāma Veda, and in later times some of them also became known as eastern singers.

TEXT 79

लौगाक्षिर्मांगलिः कुल्यः कुशीदः कुक्षिरेव च ।
पौश्यञ्जिशिष्या जगृहुः संहितास्ते शतं शतम् ॥ ७९ ॥

laugākṣir māṅgaliḥ kulyaḥ
kuśīdaḥ kukṣir eva ca
pauṣyañji-śiṣyā jagṛhuḥ
saṁhitās te śataṁ śatam

laugākṣiḥ māṅgaliḥ kulyaḥ—Laugākṣi, Māṅgali and Kulya; *kuśīdaḥ kukṣiḥ*—Kuśīda and Kukṣi; *eva*—indeed; *ca*—also; *pauṣyañji-śiṣyāḥ*—disciples of Pauṣyañji; *jagṛhuḥ*—they took; *saṁhitāḥ*—collections; *te*—they; *śatam śatam*—each one hundred.

TRANSLATION

Five other disciples of Pauṣyañji, namely Laugākṣi, Māṅgali, Kulya, Kuśīda and Kukṣi, each received one hundred saṁhitās.

TEXT 80

कृतो हिरण्यनाभस्य चतुर्विंशति संहिताः ।
शिष्य ऊचे स्वशिष्येभ्यः शेषा आवन्त्य आत्मवान् ॥ ८० ॥

kṛto hiraṇyanābhasya
catur-viṁśati saṁhitāḥ
śiṣya ūce sva-śiṣyebhyaḥ
śeṣā āvantya ātmavān

kṛtaḥ—Kṛta; *hiraṇyanābhasya*—of Hiraṇyanābha; *catuḥ-viṁśati*—twenty-four; *saṁhitāḥ*—collections; *śiṣyaḥ*—the disciple; *ūce*—spoke; *sva-śiṣyebhyaḥ*—to his own disciples; *śeṣāḥ*—the remaining (collections); *āvantyaḥ*—Āvantya; *ātma-vān*—the self-controlled.

TRANSLATION

Kṛta, the disciple of Hiraṇyanābha, spoke twenty-four saṁhitās to his own disciples, and the remaining collections were passed down by the self-realized sage Āvantya.

Thus end the purports of the humble servants of His Divine Grace A.C. Bhaktivedanta Swami Prabhupāda to the Twelfth Canto, Sixth Chapter, of the Śrīmad-Bhāgavatam, *entitled "Mahārāja Parīkṣit Passes Away."*

CHAPTER SEVEN

The Purāṇic Literatures

In this chapter Śrī Sūta Gosvāmī describes the expansion of the branches of the *Atharva Veda,* enumerates the compilers of the *Purāṇas* and explains the characteristics of a *Purāṇa.* He then lists the eighteen major *Purāṇas* and finishes his account by stating that any person who hears about these matters from someone in a proper disciplic succession will acquire spiritual potency.

TEXT 1

सूत उवाच
अथर्ववित् सुमन्तुश्च शिष्यमध्यापयत् स्वकाम् ।
संहितां सोऽपि पथ्याय वेददर्शाय चोक्तवान् ॥१॥

sūta uvāca
atharva-vit sumantuś ca
śiṣyam adhyāpayat svakām
saṁhitāṁ so'pi pathyāya
vedadarśāya coktavān

sūtaḥ uvāca — Sūta Gosvāmī said; *atharva-vit* — the expert knower of the *Atharva Veda; sumantuḥ*—Sumantu; *ca* — and; *śiṣyam* — to his disciple; *adhyāpayat* — instructed; *svakām* — his own; *saṁhitām* — collection; *saḥ*— he, the disciple of Sumantu; *api* — also; *pathyāya* — to Pathya; *vedadarśāya* — to Vedadarśa; *ca* — and; *uktavān* — spoke.

TRANSLATION

Sūta Gosvāmī said: Sumantu Ṛṣi, the authority on the Atharva Veda, taught his saṁhitā to his disciple Kabandha, who in turn spoke it to Pathya and Vedadarśa.

PURPORT

As confirmed in the *Viṣṇu Purāṇa:*

atharva-vedaṁ sa muniḥ
sumantur amita-dyutiḥ

śiṣyam adhyāpayām āsa
kabandhaṁ so'pi ca dvidhā
kṛtvā tu vedadarśāya
tathā pathyāya dattavān

"That sage Sumantu, whose brilliance was immeasurable, taught the *Atharva Veda* to his disciple Kabandha. Kabandha in turn divided it into two parts and passed them down to Vedadarśa and Pathya."

TEXT 2

शौक्लायनिर्ब्रह्मबलिर्मोदोषः पिप्पलायनिः ।
वेददर्शस्य शिष्यास्ते पथ्यशिष्यानथो शृणु ।
कुमुदः शुनको ब्रह्मन् जाजलिश्चाप्यथर्ववित् ॥ २ ॥

śauklāyanir brahmabalir
modoṣaḥ pippalāyaniḥ
vedadarśasya śiṣyās te
pathya-śiṣyān atho śṛṇu
kumudaḥ śunako brahman
jājaliś cāpy atharva-vit

śauklāyaniḥ brahmabaliḥ—Śauklāyani and Brahmabali; *modoṣaḥ pippalāyaniḥ*—Modoṣa and Pippalāyani; *vedadarśasya* — of Vedadarśa; *śiṣyāḥ* —the disciples; *te* — they; *pathya-śiṣyān* — the disciples of Pathya; *atho* — furthermore; *śṛṇu* — please hear; *kumudaḥ śunakaḥ*—Kumuda and Śunaka; *brahman* — O *brāhmaṇa,* Śaunaka; *jājaliḥ*—Jājali; *ca* — and; *api* — also; *atharva-vit* — full in knowledge of the *Atharva Veda.*

TRANSLATION

Śauklāyani, Brahmabali, Modoṣa and Pippalāyani were disciples of Vedadarśa. Hear from me also the names of the disciples of Pathya. My dear brāhmaṇa, they are Kumuda, Śunaka and Jājali, all of whom knew the Atharva Veda very well.

PURPORT

According to Śrīla Śrīdhara Svāmī, Vedadarśa divided his edition of the *Atharva Veda* into four parts and instructed them to his four disciples. Pathya divided his edition into three parts and instructed it to the three disciples mentioned here.

TEXT 3

बभ्रुः शिष्योऽथांगिरसः सैन्धवायन एव च ।
अधीयेतां संहिते द्वे सावर्णाद्यास्तथापरे ॥ ३ ॥

babhruḥ śiṣyo 'thāṅgirasaḥ
saindhavāyana eva ca
adhīyetāṁ saṁhite dve
sāvarṇādyās tathāpare

babhruḥ—Babhru; *śiṣyaḥ*—the disciple; *atha* — then; *aṅgirasaḥ*—of Śunaka (also known as Aṅgirā); *saindhavāyanaḥ*—Saindhavāyana; *eva* — indeed; *ca* — also; *adhīyetām* — they learned; *saṁhite* — collections; *dve* — two; *sāvarṇa* — Sāvarṇa; *ādyāḥ*—headed by; *tathā* — similarly; *apare* — other disciples.

TRANSLATION

Babhru and Saindhavāyana, disciples of Śunaka, studied the two divisions of their spiritual master's compilation of the Atharva Veda. Saindhavāyana's disciple Sāvarṇa and disciples of other great sages also studied this edition of the Atharva Veda.

TEXT 4

नक्षत्रकल्पः शान्तिश्च कश्यपागिंरसादयः ।
एते आथर्वणाचार्याः शृणु पौराणिकान्मुने ॥ ४ ॥

nakṣatrakalpaḥ śāntiś ca
kaśyapāṅgirasādayaḥ
ete ātharvaṇācāryāḥ
śṛṇu paurāṇikān mune

nakṣatrakalpaḥ—Nakṣatrakalpa; *śāntiḥ*—Śāntikalpa; *ca* — also; *kaśyapa-āṅgirasa-ādayaḥ*—Kaśyapa, Āṅgirasa and others; *ete* — these; *ātharvaṇa-ācāryāḥ*—spiritual masters of the *Atharva Veda; śṛṇu* — now hear; *paurāṇikān* — the authorities of the *Purāṇas; mune* — O sage, Śaunaka.

TRANSLATION

Nakṣatrakalpa, Śāntikalpa, Kaśyapa, Āṅgirasa and others were also among the ācāryas of the Atharva Veda. Now, O sage, listen as I name the authorities on Purāṇic literature.

TEXT 5

त्रय्यारुणिः कश्यपश्च सावर्णिरकृतव्रणः ।
वैशम्पायनहारीतौ षड् वै पौराणिका इमे ॥ ५ ॥

trayyāruṇiḥ kaśyapaś ca
sāvarṇir akṛtavraṇaḥ
vaiśampāyana-hārītau
ṣaḍ vai paurāṇikā ime

trayyāruṇiḥ kaśyapaḥ ca — Trayyāruṇi and Kaśyapa; *sāvarṇiḥ akṛta-vraṇaḥ* — Sāvarṇi and Akṛtavraṇa; *vaiśampāyana-hārītau* — Vaiśampāyana and Hārīta; *ṣaṭ* — six; *vai* — indeed; *paurāṇikāḥ* — spiritual masters of the *Purāṇas; ime* — these.

TRANSLATION

Trayyāruṇi, Kaśyapa, Sāvarṇi, Akṛtavraṇa, Vaiśampāyana and Hārīta are the six masters of the Purāṇas.

TEXT 6

अधीयन्त व्यासशिष्यात् संहितां मत्पितुर्मुखात् ।
एकैकामहमेतेषां शिष्यः सर्वाः समध्यगाम् ॥ ६ ॥

adhīyanta vyāsa-śiṣyāt
saṁhitāṁ mat-pitur mukhāt
ekaikām aham eteṣāṁ
śiṣyaḥ sarvāḥ samadhyagām

adhīyanta — they have learned; *vyāsa-śiṣyāt* — from the disciple of Vyāsadeva (Romaharṣaṇa); *saṁhitām* — the collection of the *Purāṇas; mat-pituḥ* — of my father; *mukhāt* — from the mouth; *eka-ekām* — each learning one portion; *aham* — I; *eteṣām* — of these; *śiṣyaḥ* — the disciple; *sarvāḥ* — all the collections; *samadhyagām* — I have thoroughly learned.

TRANSLATION

Each of them studied one of the six anthologies of the Purāṇas from my father, Romaharṣaṇa, who was a disciple of Śrīla Vyāsadeva. I became the disciple of these six authorities and thoroughly learned all their presentations of Purāṇic wisdom.

TEXT 7

कश्यपोऽहं च सावर्णी रामशिष्योऽकृतव्रणः ।
अधीमहि व्यासशिष्याच्चत्वारो मूलसंहिताः ॥ ७ ॥

kaśyapo 'haṁ ca sāvarṇī
rāma-śiṣyo 'kṛtavraṇaḥ
adhīmahi vyāsa-śiṣyāc
catvāro mūla-saṁhitāḥ

kaśyapaḥ—Kaśyapa; *aham*—I; *ca*—and; *sāvarṇiḥ*—Sāvarṇi; *rāma-śiṣyaḥ*—a disciple of Rāma; *akṛtvraṇaḥ*—namely Akṛtavraṇa; *adhīmahi*—we have assimilated; *vyāsa-śiṣyāt*—from the disciple of Vyāsa (Romaharṣaṇa); *catvāraḥ*—four; *mūla-saṁhitāḥ*—basic collections.

TRANSLATION

Romaharṣaṇa, a disciple of Vedavyāsa, divided the Purāṇas into four basic compilations. The sage Kaśyapa and I, along with Sāvarṇi and Akṛtavraṇa, a disciple of Rāma, learned these four divisions.

TEXT 8

पुराणलक्षणं ब्रह्मन् ब्रह्मर्षिभिर्निरूपितम् ।
शृणुष्व बुद्धिमाश्रित्य वेदशास्त्रानुसारतः ॥ ८ ॥

purāṇa-lakṣaṇaṁ brahman
brahmarṣibhir nirūpitam
śṛṇuṣva buddhim āśritya
veda-śāstrānusārataḥ

purāṇa-lakṣaṇam—the characteristics of a *Purāṇa; brahman*—O *brāhmaṇa,* Śaunaka; *brahma-ṛṣibhiḥ*—by great learned *brāhmaṇas; nirūpitam*—

ascertained; *śṛṇuṣva* — please hear; *buddhim* — intelligence; *āśritya* — resorting to; *veda-śāstra* — the Vedic scriptures; *anusārataḥ*—in accordance with.

TRANSLATION

O Śaunaka, please hear with attention the characteristics of a Purāṇa, which have been defined by the most eminent learned brāhmaṇas in accordance with Vedic literature.

TEXTS 9–10

सर्गोऽस्याथ विसर्गश्च वृत्तिरक्षान्तराणि च ।
वंशो वंशानुचरितं संस्था हेतुरपाश्रयः ॥ ९ ॥
दशभिर्लक्षणैर्युक्तं पुराणं तद्विदो विदुः ।
केचित् पञ्चविधं ब्रह्मन्महदल्पव्यवस्थया ॥ १० ॥

sargo 'syātha visargaś ca
vṛtti-rakṣāntarāṇi ca
vaṁśo vaṁśānucaritaṁ
saṁsthā hetur apāśrayaḥ

daśabhir lakṣaṇair yuktaṁ
purāṇaṁ tad-vido viduḥ
kecit pañca-vidhaṁ brahman
mahad-alpa-vyavasthayā

sargaḥ—the creation; *asya* — of this universe; *atha* — then; *visargaḥ*— the secondary creation; *ca* — and; *vṛtti* — maintenance; *rakṣā* — protection by sustenance; *antarāṇi* — the reigns of the Manus; *ca* — and; *vaṁśaḥ*—the dynasties of great kings; *vaṁśa-anucaritam* — the narrations of their activities; *saṁsthā* — the annihilation; *hetuḥ*—the motivation (for the living entities' involvement in material activities); *apāśrayaḥ*—the supreme shelter; *daśabhiḥ*—with the ten; *lakṣaṇaiḥ*—characteristics; *yuktam* — endowed; *purāṇam* — a *Purāṇa; tat* — of this matter; *vidaḥ*—those who know; *viduḥ* —they know; *kecit* — some authorities; *pañca-vidham* — fivefold; *brahman* — O *brāhmaṇa; mahat* — of great; *alpa* — and lesser; *vyavasthayā* — according to the distinction.

TRANSLATION

O brāhmaṇa, authorities on the matter understand a Purāṇa to contain ten characteristic topics: the creation of this universe, the subsequent creation of worlds and beings, the maintenance of all living beings, their sustenance, the rule of various Manus, the dynasties of great kings, the activities of such kings, annihilation, motivation and the supreme shelter. Other scholars state that the great Purāṇas deal with these ten topics, while lesser Purāṇas may deal with five.

PURPORT

The ten subjects of a great *Purāṇa* are also described in the Second Canto of *Śrīmad-Bhāgavatam* (2.10.1):

śrī-śuka uvāca
atra sargo visargaś ca
sthānaṁ poṣaṇam ūtayaḥ
manvantareśānukathā
nirodho muktir āśrayaḥ

"Śrī Śukadeva Gosvāmī said: In the *Śrīmad-Bhāgavatam* there are ten divisions of statements regarding the following: the creation of the universe, subcreation, planetary systems, protection by the Lord, the creative impetus, the change of Manus, the science of God, returning home (back to Godhead), liberation and the *summum bonum*."

According to Śrīla Jīva Gosvāmī, *Purāṇas* such as *Śrīmad-Bhāgavatam* deal with these ten topics, whereas lesser *Purāṇas* deal with only five. As stated in Vedic literature:

sargaś ca pratisargaś ca
vaṁśo manvantarāṇi ca
vaṁśānucaritaṁ ceti
purāṇaṁ pañca-lakṣaṇam

"Creation, secondary creation, the dynasties of kings, the reigns of Manus and the activities of various dynasties are the five characteristics of a *Purāṇa*." *Purāṇas* covering five categories of knowledge are understood to be secondary Purāṇic literature.

Śrīla Jīva Gosvāmī has explained that the ten principal topics of *Śrīmad-Bhāgavatam* are found within each of the twelve cantos. One should not try to assign each of the ten topics to a particular canto. Nor should the *Śrīmad-*

Bhāgavatam be artificially interpreted to show that it deals with the topics successively. The simple fact is that all aspects of knowledge important to human beings, summarized in the ten categories mentioned above, are described with various degrees of emphasis and analysis throughout the *Śrīmad-Bhāgavatam.*

TEXT 11

अव्याकृतगुणक्षोभान्महतस्त्रिवृतोऽहमः ।
भूतसूक्ष्मेन्द्रियार्थानां सम्भवः सर्ग उच्यते ॥ ११ ॥

avyākṛta-guṇa-kṣobhān
mahatas tri-vṛto'hamaḥ
bhūta-sūkṣmendriyārthānāṁ
sambhavaḥ sarga ucyate

avyākṛta — of the unmanifest stage of nature; *guṇa-kṣobhāt* — by the agitation of the modes; *mahataḥ*—from the basic *mahat-tattva; tri-vṛtaḥ*—threefold; *ahamaḥ*—from the false ego; *bhūta-sūkṣma* — of the subtle forms of perception; *indriya* — of the senses; *arthānām* — and the objects of sense perception; *sambhavaḥ*—the generation; *sargaḥ*—creation; *ucyate* — is called.

TRANSLATION

From the agitation of the original modes within the unmanifest material nature, the mahat-tattva arises. From the mahat-tattva comes the element false ego, which divides into three aspects. This threefold false ego further manifests as the subtle forms of perception, as the senses and as the gross sense objects. The generation of all these is called creation.

TEXT 12

पुरुषानुगृहीतानामेतेषां वासनामयः ।
विसर्गोऽयं समाहारो बीजाद् बीजं चराचरम् ॥ १२ ॥

puruṣānugṛhītānām
eteṣāṁ vāsanā-mayaḥ
visargo'yaṁ samāhāro
bījād bījaṁ carācaram

puruṣa — of the Supreme Personality of Godhead in His pastime role of creation; *anugṛhītānām* — which have received the mercy; *eteṣām* — of these elements; *vāsanā-mayaḥ* — consisting predominantly of the remnants of past desires of the living entities; *visargaḥ* — the secondary creation; *ayam* — this; *samāhāraḥ* — manifest amalgamation; *bījāt* — from a seed; *bījam* — another seed; *cara* — moving beings; *acaram* — and nonmoving beings.

TRANSLATION

The secondary creation, which exists by the mercy of the Lord, is the manifest amalgamation of the desires of the living entities. Just as a seed produces additional seeds, activities that promote material desires in the performer produce moving and nonmoving life forms.

PURPORT

Just as a seed grows into a tree that produces thousands of new seeds, material desire develops into fruitive activity that stimulates thousands of new desires within the heart of the conditioned soul. The word *puruṣānugṛhītānām* indicates that by the mercy of the Supreme Lord one is allowed to desire and act in this world.

TEXT 13

वृत्तिर्भूतानि भूतानां चराणामचराणि च ।
कृता स्वेन नृणां तत्र कामाच्चोदनयापि वा ॥ १३ ॥

vṛttir bhūtāni bhūtānāṁ
carāṇām acarāṇi ca
kṛtā svena nṛṇāṁ tatra
kāmāc codanayāpi vā

vṛttiḥ — the sustenance; *bhūtāni* — living beings; *bhūtānām* — of living beings; *carāṇām* — of those that move; *acarāṇi* — those that do not move; *ca* — and; *kṛtā* — executed; *svena* — by one's own conditioned nature; *nṛṇām* — for human beings; *tatra* — therein; *kāmāt* — out of lust; *codanayā* — in pursuit of Vedic injunction; *api* — indeed; *vā* — or.

TRANSLATION

Vṛtti means the process of sustenance, by which the moving beings live upon the nonmoving. For a human, vṛtti specifically means acting for

one's livelihood in a manner suited to his personal nature. Such action may be carried out either in pursuit of selfish desire or in accordance with the law of God.

TEXT 14

रक्षाच्युतावतारेहा विश्वस्यानु युगे युगे ।
तिर्यङ्मर्त्यर्षिदेवेषु हन्यन्ते यैस्त्रयीद्विषः ॥ १४ ॥

rakṣācyutāvatāreha
viśvasyānu yuge yuge
tiryaṅ-martyarṣi-deveṣu
hanyante yais trayī-dviṣaḥ

rakṣā — protection; *acyuta-avatāra* — of the incarnations of Lord Acyuta; *īhā* — the activities; *viśvasya* — of this universe; *anu yuge yuge* — in each age; *tiryak* — among the animals; *martya* — human beings; *ṛṣi* — sages; *deveṣu* — and demigods; *hanyante* — are killed; *yaiḥ* — by which incarnations; *trayī-dviṣaḥ* — the Daityas, who are enemies of Vedic culture.

TRANSLATION

In each age, the infallible Lord appears in this world among the animals, human beings, sages and demigods. By His activities in these incarnations He protects the universe and kills the enemies of Vedic culture.

PURPORT

The protective activities of the Lord, indicated by the word *rakṣā,* constitute one of the ten fundamental topics of a *Mahā-purāṇa,* or a great Purāṇic literature.

TEXT 15

मन्वन्तरं मनुर्देवा मनुपुत्राः सुरेश्वराः ।
ऋषयोऽशांवताराश्च हरेः षड्विधमुच्यते ॥ १५ ॥

manvantaraṁ manur devā
manu-putrāḥ sureśvarāḥ
ṛṣayo 'ṁśāvatārāś ca
hareḥ ṣaḍ-vidham ucyate

manu-antaram — the reign of each Manu; *manuḥ*—the Manu; *devāḥ*—the demigods; *manu-putrāḥ*—the sons of Manu; *sura-īśvarāḥ*—the different Indras; *ṛṣayaḥ*—the chief sages; *aṁśa-avatārāḥ*—the incarnations of portions of the Supreme Lord; *ca* — and; *hareḥ*—of Lord Hari; *ṣaṭ-vidham* — sixfold; *ucyate* — is said.

TRANSLATION

In each reign of Manu, six types of personalities appear as manifestations of Lord Hari: the ruling Manu, the chief demigods, the sons of Manu, Indra, the great sages and the partial incarnations of the Supreme Personality of Godhead.

TEXT 16

राज्ञां ब्रह्मप्रसूतानां वंशस्त्रैकालिकोऽन्वयः ।
वंशानुचरितं तेषां वृत्तं वंशधराश्च ये ॥ १६ ॥

rājñāṁ brahma-prasūtānāṁ
vaṁśas trai-kāliko 'nvayaḥ
vaṁśānucaritaṁ teṣāṁ
vṛttaṁ vaṁśa-dharāś ca ye

rājñām — of the kings; *brahma-prasūtānām* — born originally from Brahmā; *vaṁśaḥ*—dynasty; *trai-kālikaḥ*—extending into the three phases of time (past, present and future); *anvayaḥ*—the series; *vaṁśa-anucaritam* — histories of the dynasties; *teṣām* — of these dynasties; *vṛttam* — the activities; *vaṁśa-dharāḥ*—the prominent members of the dynasties; *ca* — and; *ye* — which.

TRANSLATION

Dynasties are lines of kings originating with Lord Brahmā and extending continuously through past, present and future. The accounts of such dynasties, especially of their most prominent members, constitute the subject of dynastic history.

TEXT 17

नैमित्तिकः प्राकृतिको नित्य आत्यन्तिको लयः ।
संस्थेति कविभिः प्रोक्तश्चतुर्धास्य स्वभावतः ॥ १७ ॥

naimittikaḥ prākṛtiko
nitya ātyantiko layaḥ
saṁstheti kavibhiḥ proktaś
caturdhāsya svabhāvataḥ

naimittikaḥ—occasional; *prākṛtikaḥ*—elemental; *nityaḥ*—continuous; *ātyantikaḥ*—ultimate; *layaḥ*—annihilation; *saṁsthā* — the dissolution; *iti* — thus; *kavibhiḥ*—by learned scholars; *proktaḥ*—described; *caturdhā* — in four aspects; *asya* — of this universe; *svabhāvataḥ*—by the inherent energy of the Supreme Personality of Godhead.

TRANSLATION

There are four types of cosmic annihilation — occasional, elemental, continuous and ultimate — all of which are effected by the inherent potency of the Supreme Lord. Learned scholars have designated this topic dissolution.

TEXT 18

हेतुर्जीवोऽस्य सर्गादेरविद्याकर्मकारकः ।
यं चानुशायिनं प्राहुरव्याकृतमुतापरे ॥ १८ ॥

hetur jīvo 'sya sargāder
avidyā-karma-kārakaḥ
yaṁ cānuśāyinaṁ prāhur
avyākṛtam utāpare

hetuḥ—the cause; *jīvaḥ*—the living being; *asya* — of this universe; *sarga-ādeḥ*—of the creation, maintenance and destruction; *avidyā* — out of ignorance; *karma-kārakaḥ*—the performer of material activities; *yam* — whom; *ca* — and; *anuśāyinam* — the underlying personality; *prāhuḥ*—they call; *avyākṛtam* — the unmanifest; *uta* — indeed; *apare* — others.

TRANSLATION

Out of ignorance the living being performs material activities and thereby becomes in one sense the cause of the creation, maintenance and destruction of the universe. Some authorities call the living being the personality underlying the material creation, while others say he is the unmanifest self.

PURPORT

The Supreme Lord Himself creates, maintains and annihilates the cosmos. However, such activities are performed in response to the desires of conditioned souls, who are described herein as *hetu,* or the cause of cosmic activity. The Lord creates this world to facilitate the conditioned soul's attempt to exploit nature and ultimately to facilitate his self-realization.

Since conditioned souls cannot perceive their own constitutional identity, they are described here as *avyākṛtam,* or unmanifest. In other words, the living entity cannot perceive his real form unless he is completely Kṛṣṇa conscious.

TEXT 19

व्यतिरेकान्वयो यस्य जाग्रत्स्वप्नसुषुप्तिषु ।
मायामयेषु तद् ब्रह्म जीववृत्तिष्वपाश्रयः ॥ १९ ॥

vyatirekānvayo yasya
jāgrat-svapna-suṣuptiṣu
māyā-mayeṣu tad brahma
jīva-vṛttiṣv apāśrayaḥ

vyatireka — the presence as separate; *anvayaḥ*— and as conjoint; *yasya* — of which; *jāgrat* — within waking consciousness; *svapna* — sleep; *suṣuptiṣu* — and deep sleep; *māyā-mayeṣu* — within the products of the illusory energy; *tat* — that; *brahma* — the Absolute Truth; *jīva-vṛttiṣu* — within the functions of the living entities; *apāśrayaḥ*— the unique shelter.

TRANSLATION

The Supreme Absolute Truth is present throughout all the stages of awareness — waking consciousness, sleep and deep sleep — throughout all the phenomena manifested by the illusory energy, and within the functions of all living entities, and He also exists separate from all these. Thus situated in His own transcendence, He is the ultimate and unique shelter.

TEXT 20

पदार्थेषु यथा द्रव्यं सन्मात्रं रूपनामसु ।
बीजादिपञ्चतान्तासु ह्यवस्थासु युतायुतम् ॥ २० ॥

padārtheṣu yathā dravyaṁ
san-mātraṁ rūpa-nāmasu
bījādi-pañcatāntāsu
hy avasthāsu yutāyutam

pada-artheṣu — within material objects; *yathā* — just as; *dravyam* — the basic substance; *sat-mātram* — the sheer existence of things; *rūpa-nāmasu* — among their forms and names; *bīja-ādi* — beginning from the seed (i.e., from the time of conception); *pañcatā-antāsu* — ending with death; *hi* — indeed; *avasthāsu* — throughout the various phases of bodily existence; *yuta-ayutam* — both conjoined and separate.

TRANSLATION

Although a material object may assume various forms and names, its essential ingredient is always present as the basis of its existence. Similarly, both conjointly and separately, the Supreme Absolute Truth is always present with the created material body throughout its phases of existence, beginning with conception and ending with death.

PURPORT

Moist clay can be molded into various shapes and named "waterpot," "flowerpot" or "storage pot." Despite the various names and forms, the essential ingredient, earth, is constantly present. Similarly, the Supreme Lord is present throughout a material body's stages of bodily existence. The Lord is identical with material nature, being its ultimate generating source. At the same time, the unique Supreme Being exists separately, aloof in His own abode.

TEXT 21

विरमेत यदा चित्तं हित्वा वृत्तित्रयं स्वयम् ।
योगेन वा तदात्मानं वेदेहाया निवर्तते ॥ २१ ॥

virameta yadā cittaṁ
hitvā vṛtti-trayaṁ svayam
yogena vā tadātmānaṁ
vedehāyā nivartate

virameta — desists; *yadā* — when; *cittam* — the mind; *hitvā* — giving up; *vṛtti-trayam* — the functions of material life in the three phases of waking, sleep and deep sleep; *svayam* — automatically; *yogena* — by regulated spiritual practice; *vā* — or; *tadā* — then; *ātmānam* — the Supreme Soul; *veda* — he knows; *īhāyāḥ*— from material endeavor; *nivartate* — he ceases.

TRANSLATION

Either automatically or because of one's regulated spiritual practice, one's mind may stop functioning on the material platform of waking consciousness, sleep and deep sleep. Then one understands the Supreme Soul and withdraws from material endeavor.

PURPORT

As stated in *Śrīmad-Bhāgavatam* (3.25.33), *jarayaty āśu yā kośaṁ nigīrṇam analo yathā:* "*Bhakti,* devotional service, dissolves the subtle body of the living entity without separate endeavor, just as fire in the stomach digests all that we eat." The subtle material body is inclined to exploit nature through sex, greed, false pride and madness. Loving service to the Lord, however, dissolves the stubborn false ego and lifts one to pure blissful consciousness, Kṛṣṇa consciousness, the sublime perfection of existence.

TEXT 22

एवं लक्षणलक्ष्याणि पुराणानि पुराविदः ।
मुनयोऽष्टादश प्राहुः क्षुल्लकानि महान्ति च ॥ २२ ॥

evaṁ lakṣaṇa-lakṣyāṇi
purāṇāni purā-vidaḥ
munayo 'ṣṭādaśa prāhuḥ
kṣullakāni mahānti ca

evam — in this way; *lakṣaṇa-lakṣyāṇi* — symptomized by their characteristics; *purāṇāni* — the *Purāṇas; purā-vidaḥ*— those who are expert in such ancient histories; *munayaḥ*— the sages; *aṣṭādaśa* — eighteen; *prāhuḥ*— say; *kṣullakāni* — minor; *mahānti* — great; *ca* — also.

TRANSLATION

Sages expert in ancient histories have declared that the Purāṇas, according to their various characteristics, can be divided into eighteen major Purāṇas and eighteen secondary Purāṇas.

TEXTS 23–24

ब्राह्मं पाद्मं वैष्णवं च शैवं लैंगं सगारुडं ।
नारदीयं भागवतमाग्नेयं स्कान्दसंज्ञितम् ॥ २३ ॥
भविष्यं ब्रह्मवैवर्तं मार्कण्डेयं सवामनम् ।
वाराहं मात्स्यं कौर्मं च ब्रह्माण्डाख्यमिति त्रिषट् ॥ २४ ॥

brāhmaṁ pādmaṁ vaiṣṇavaṁ ca
śaivaṁ laiṅgaṁ sa-gāruḍaṁ
nāradīyaṁ bhāgavatam
āgneyaṁ skānda-saṁjñitam

bhaviṣyaṁ brahma-vaivartaṁ
mārkaṇḍeyaṁ sa-vāmanam
vārāhaṁ mātsyaṁ kaurmaṁ ca
brahmāṇḍākhyam iti tri-ṣaṭ

brāhmam — the *Brahma Purāṇa; pādmam* — the *Padma Purāṇa*; *vaiṣṇavam* — the *Viṣṇu Purāṇa;* ca — and; *śaivam* — the *Śiva Purāṇa; laiṅgam* — the *Liṅga Purāṇa; sa-gāruḍam* — along with the *Garuḍa Purāṇa; nāradīyam* — the *Nārada Purāṇa; bhāgavatam* — the *Bhāgavata Purāṇa; āgneyam* — the *Agni Purāṇa; skānda* — the *Skanda Purāṇa; saṁjñitam* — known as; *bhaviṣyam* — the *Bhaviṣya Purāṇa; brahma-vaivartam* — the *Brahma-vaivarta Purāṇa; mārkaṇḍeyam* — the *Mārkaṇḍeya Purāṇa; sa-vāmanam* — together with the *Vāmana Purāṇa; vārāham* — the *Varāha Purāṇa; mātsyam* — the *Matsya Purāṇa; kaurmam* — the *Kūrma Purāṇa; ca* — and; *brahmāṇḍa-ākhyam* — known as the *Brahmāṇḍa Purāṇa; iti* — thus; *tri-ṣaṭ* — three times six.

TRANSLATION

The eighteen major Purāṇas are the Brahmā, Padma, Viṣṇu, Śiva, Liṅga, Garuḍa, Nārada, Bhāgavata, Agni, Skanda, Bhaviṣya, Brahma-vaivarta, Mārkaṇḍeya, Vāmana, Varāha, Matsya, Kūrma and Brahmāṇḍa Purāṇas.

PURPORT

Śrīla Jīva Gosvāmī has quoted from the *Varāha Purāṇa, Śiva Purāṇa* and *Matsya Purāṇa* in confirmation of the above two verses.

TEXT 25

ब्रह्मन्निदं समाख्यातं शाखाप्रणयनं मुनेः ।
शिष्यशिष्यप्रशिष्याणां ब्रह्मतेजोविवर्धनम् ॥ २५ ॥

brahmann idaṁ samākhyātaṁ
śākhā-praṇayanaṁ muneḥ
śiṣya-śiṣya-praśiṣyāṇāṁ
brahma-tejo-vivardhanam

brahman — O *brāhmaṇa; idam* — this; *samākhyātam* — thoroughly described; *śākhā-praṇayanam* — the expansion of the branches; *muneḥ*—of the sage (Śrīla Vyāsadeva); *śiṣya* — of the disciples; *śiṣya-praśiṣyāṇām* — and the subsequent disciples of his disciples; *brahma-tejaḥ*—spiritual potency; *vivardhanam* — which increases.

TRANSLATION

I have thoroughly described to you, O brāhmaṇa, the expansion of the branches of the Vedas by the great sage Vyāsadeva, his disciples and the disciples of his disciples. One who listens to this narration will increase in spiritual strength.

Thus end the purports of the humble servants of His Divine Grace A.C. Bhaktivedanta Swami Prabhupāda to the Twelfth Canto, Seventh Chapter, of the Śrīmad-Bhāgavatam, *entitled "The Purāṇic Literatures."*

CHAPTER EIGHT

Mārkaṇḍeya's Prayers to Nara-Nārāyaṇa Ṛṣi

This chapter describes how Mārkaṇḍeya Ṛṣi performed austerities, defeated by his potency Cupid and all his associates, and offered prayers to Lord Śrī Hari in His forms of Nara and Nārāyaṇa.

Śrī Śaunaka was confused about the extraordinarily long life span of Śrī Mārkaṇḍeya, who had taken birth in Śaunaka's own dynasty yet who had moved about alone in the ocean of devastation millions of years previously and seen a wonderful young child lying upon a banyan leaf. It seemed to Śaunaka that Mārkaṇḍeya had lived through two days of Brahmā, and he asked Śrī Sūta Gosvāmī to explain this.

Suta Gosvāmī replied that the sage Mārkaṇḍeya, after receiving the purificatory ritual of brahminical initiation from his father, had fixed himself in the vow of lifelong celibacy. He then worshiped the Supreme Lord Hari for six lifetimes of Manu. In the seventh *manvantara,* Lord Indra sent Kāmadeva (Cupid) and his associates to interrupt the sage's austerities. But Mārkaṇḍeya Ṛṣi defeated them by the potency generated from his penance.

Then, to show mercy to Mārkaṇḍeya, Lord Śrī Hari appeared before him in the form of Nara-Nārāyaṇa. Śrī Mārkaṇḍeya prostrated himself in obeisance and then worshiped the Lords by offering Them comfortable seats, water for washing Their feet, and other respectful presentations. He then prayed, "O Almighty Lord, You bring to life the vital air of all creatures, and You also protect the three worlds, vanquish distress and award liberation. You never allow those who have taken shelter of You to be defeated by any kind of misery. Attaining Your lotus feet is the only auspicious goal for the conditioned souls, and service to You fulfills all their desires. Your pastimes, enacted in the mode of pure goodness, can award everyone salvation from material life. Therefore those who are intelligent worship Your personal form of pure goodness named Śrī Nārāyaṇa, along with Nara, who represents Your unalloyed devotee."

"The living entity bewildered by illusion can directly understand You if he receives the knowledge presented in the *Vedas* and promulgated by You, the spiritual master of the entire universe. Even great thinkers like Brahmā are simply bewildered when they try to understand Your identity by struggling on the path of *sāṅkhya-yoga.* You Yourself manifest the proponents of Sāṅkhya and other philosophies, and thus Your true personal identity remains hidden beneath the designative covering of the *jīva* soul. I offer my homage to You, the Mahāpuruṣa."

TEXT 1

श्रीशौनक उवाच
सूत जीव चिरं साधो वद नो वदतां वर ।
तमस्यपारे भ्रमतां नृणां त्वं पारदर्शनः ॥ १ ॥

śrī-śaunaka uvāca
sūta jīva ciraṁ sādho
vada no vadatāṁ vara
tamasy apāre bhramatāṁ
nṝṇāṁ tvaṁ pāra-darśanaḥ

śrī-śaunakaḥ uvāca — Śrī Śaunaka said; *sūta* — O Sūta Gosvāmī; *jīva* — may you live; *ciram* — for a long time; *sādho* — O saint; *vada* — please speak; *naḥ*—to us; *vadatām* — of speakers; *vara* — O you who are the best; *tamasi* — in darkness; *apāre* — unbounded; *bhramatām* — who are wandering; *nṝṇām* — for men; *tvam* — you; *pāra-darśanaḥ*—the seer of the opposite shore.

TRANSLATION

Śrī Śaunaka said: O Sūta, may you live a long life! O saintly one, best of speakers, please continue speaking to us. Indeed, only you can show men the path out of the ignorance in which they are wandering.

PURPORT

According to Śrīla Jīva Gosvāmī, the sages saw that Sūta Gosvāmī was about to end his narration of *Śrīmad-Bhāgavatam,* and thus they urged him to first tell the story of Mārkaṇḍeya Ṛṣi.

TEXTS 2–5

आहुश्चिरायुषमृषिं मृकण्डुतनयं जनाः ।
यः कल्पान्ते ह्युर्वरितो येन ग्रस्तमिदं जगत् ॥ २ ॥

स वा अस्मत्कुलोत्पन्नः कल्पेऽस्मिन् भार्गवर्षभः ।
नैवाधुनापि भूतानां सम्प्लवः कोऽपि जायते ॥ ३ ॥
एक एवार्णवे भ्राम्यन् ददर्श पुरुषं किल ।
वटपत्रपुटे तोकं शयानं त्वेकमद्भुतम् ॥ ४ ॥
एष नः संशयो भूयान् सूत कौतूहलं यतः ।
तं नश्छिन्धि महायोगिन् पुराणेष्वपि सम्मतः ॥ ५ ॥

āhuś cirāyuṣam ṛṣiṁ
mṛkaṇḍu-tanayaṁ janāḥ
yaḥ kalpānte hy urvarito
yena grastam idaṁ jagat

sa vā asmat-kulotpannaḥ
kalpe'smin bhārgavarṣabhaḥ
naivādhunāpi bhūtānāṁ
samplavaḥ ko 'pi jāyate

eka evārṇave bhrāmyan
dadarśa puruṣaṁ kila
vaṭa-patra-puṭe tokaṁ
śayānaṁ tv ekam adbhutam

eṣa naḥ saṁśayo bhūyān
sūta kautūhalaṁ yataḥ
taṁ naś chindhi mahā-yogin
purāṇeṣv api sammataḥ

āhuḥ—they say; *cira-āyuṣam* — having an extraordinarily long life span; *ṛṣim* — the sage; *mṛkaṇḍu-tanayam* — the son of Mṛkaṇḍu; *janāḥ*—people; *yaḥ*—who; *kalpa-ante* — at the end of the day of Lord Brahmā; *hi* — indeed; *urvaritaḥ*—remaining alone; *yena* — by which (annihilation); *grastam* — seized; *idam* — this; *jagat* — entire universe; *saḥ*—he, Mārkaṇḍeya; *vai* — indeed; *asmat-kula* — in my own family; *utpannaḥ*—born; *kalpe* — in the day of Brahmā; *asmin* — this; *bhārgava-ṛṣabhaḥ*—the most eminent descendant of Bhṛgu Muni; *na* — not; *eva* — certainly; *adhunā* — in our age; *api* — even; *bhūtānām* — of all creation; *samplavaḥ*—annihilation by flood; *kaḥ*— any; *api* — at all; *jāyate* — has arisen; *ekaḥ*—alone; *eta* — indeed; *arṇave* — in the great ocean; *bhrāmyan* — wandering; *dadarśa* — he saw; *puruṣam* —

a personality; *kila* — it is said; *vaṭa-patra* — of a banyan leaf; *puṭe* — within the fold; *tokam* — an infant boy; *śayānam* — lying; *tu* — but; *ekam* — one; *adbhutam* — wonderful; *eṣaḥ* — this; *naḥ* — our; *saṁśayaḥ* — doubt; *bhūyān* — great; *sūta* — O Sūta Gosvāmī; *kautūhalam* — curiosity; *yataḥ* — due to which; *tam* — that; *naḥ* — for us; *chindhi* — please cut; *mahā-yogin* — O great *yogī; purāṇeṣu* — of the *Purāṇas; api* — indeed; *sammataḥ* — universally accepted (as the expert knower).

TRANSLATION

Authorities say that Mārkaṇḍeya Ṛṣi, the son of Mṛkaṇḍu, was an exceptionally long-lived sage who was the only survivor at the end of Brahmā's day, when the entire universe was merged in the flood of annihilation. But this same Mārkaṇḍeya Ṛṣi, the foremost descendant of Bhṛgu, took birth in my own family during the current day of Brahmā, and we have not yet seen any total annihilation in this day of Brahmā. Also, it is well known that Mārkaṇḍeya, while wandering helplessly in the great ocean of annihilation, saw in those fearful waters a wonderful personality — an infant boy lying alone within the fold of a banyan leaf. O Sūta, I am most bewildered and curious about this great sage, Mārkaṇḍeya Ṛṣi. O great yogī, you are universally accepted as the authority on all the Purāṇas. Therefore kindly dispel my confusion.

PURPORT

Lord Brahmā's day, consisting of his 12 hours, lasts 4 billion 320 million years, and his night is of the same duration. Apparently Mārkaṇḍeya lived throughout one such day and night and in the following day of Brahmā continued living as the same Mārkaṇḍeya. It seems that when annihilation occurred during Brahmā's night, the sage wandered throughout the fearful waters of destruction and saw within those waters an extraordinary personality lying on a banyan leaf. All of these mysteries concerning. Mārkaṇḍeya will be clarified by Sūta Gosvāmī at the request of the great sages.

TEXT 6

सूत उवाच

प्रश्नस्त्वया महर्षेऽयं कृतो लोकभ्रमापहः ।
नारायणकथा यत्र गीता कलिमलापहा ॥ ६ ॥

sūta uvāca
praśnas tvayā maharṣe'yaṁ
kṛto loka-bhramāpahaḥ
nārāyaṇa-kathā yatra
gītā kali-malāpahā

sūtaḥ uvāca — Sūta Gosvāmī said; *praśnaḥ* — question; *tvayā* — by you; *mahā-ṛṣe* — O great sage, Śaunaka; *ayam* — this; *kṛtaḥ* — made; *loka* — of the entire world; *bhrama* — the delusion; *apahaḥ* — which takes away; *nārāyaṇa-kathā* — discussion of the Supreme Lord, Nārāyaṇa; *yatra* — in which; *gītā* — is sung; *kali-mala* — the contamination of the present age of Kali; *apahā* — removing.

TRANSLATION

Sūta Gosvāmī said: O great sage Śaunaka, your very question will help remove everyone's illusion, for it leads to the topics of Lord Nārāyaṇa, which cleanse away the contamination of this Kali age.

TEXTS 7–11

प्राप्तद्विजातिसंस्कारो मार्कण्डेयः पितुः क्रमात् ।
छन्दांस्यधीत्य धर्मेण तपःस्वाध्यायसंयुतः ॥ ७ ॥
बृहद्व्रतधरः शान्तो जटिलो वल्कलाम्बरः ।
बिभ्रत्कमण्डलुं दण्डमुपवीतं समेखलम् ॥ ८ ॥
कृष्णाजिनं साक्षसूत्रं कुशांश्च नियमर्द्धये ।
अग्न्यर्कगुरुविप्रात्मस्वर्चयन् सन्ध्ययोर्हरिम् ॥ ९ ॥
सायं प्रातः स गुरवे भैक्ष्यमाहृत्य वाग्यतः ।
बुभुजे गुर्वनुज्ञातः सकृन्नो चेदुपोषितः ॥ १० ॥
एवं तपःस्वाध्यायपरो वर्षाणामयुतायुतम् ।
आराधयन् हृषीकेशं जिग्ये मृत्युं सुदुर्जयम् ॥ ११ ॥

prāpta-dvijāti-saṁskāro
mārkaṇḍeyaḥ pituḥ kramāt
chandāṁsy adhītya dharmeṇa
tapaḥ-svādhyāya-saṁyutaḥ

bṛhad-vrata-dharaḥ śānto
jaṭilo valkalāmbaraḥ

bibhrat kamaṇḍaluṁ daṇḍam
upavītaṁ sa-mekhalam

kṛṣṇājinaṁ sākṣa-sūtraṁ
kuśāṁś ca niyamarddhaye
agny-arka-guru-viprātmasv
arcayan sandhyayor harim

sāyaṁ prātaḥ sa gurave
bhaikṣyam āhṛtya vāg-yataḥ
bubhuje gurv-anujñātaḥ
sakṛn no ced upoṣitaḥ

evaṁ tapaḥ-svādhyāya-paro
varṣāṇām ayutāyutam
ārādhayan hṛṣīkeśaṁ
jigye mṛtyuṁ su-durjayam

prāpta — having received; *dvi-jāti* — of second birth; *saṁskāraḥ*—the purificatory rituals; *mārkaṇḍeyaḥ*—Mārkaṇḍeya; *pituḥ*—from his father; *kramāt* — bv proper sequence; *chandāṁsi* — the Vedic hymns; *adhītya* — studying; *dharmeṇa* — along with regulative principles; *tapaḥ*—in austerities; *svādhyāya* — and study; *saṁyutaḥ*—full; *bṛhat-vrata* — the great vow of lifelong celibacy; *dharaḥ*—maintaining; *śāntaḥ*—peaceful; *jaṭilaḥ*—with matted hair; *valkala-ambaraḥ*—wearing bark as his clothing; *bibhrat* — carrying; *kamaṇḍalum* — a waterpot; *daṇḍam* — a mendicant's staff; *upavītam* — the sacred thread; *sa-mekhalam* — along with the ritual belt of a *brahmacārī; kṛṣṇa-ajinam* — the skin of a black deer; *sa-akṣa-sūtram* — and prayer beads made of lotus seeds; *kuśān* — *kuśa* grass; *ca* — also; *niyama-ṛddhaye* — to facilitate his spiritual progress; *agni* — in the form of fire; *arka* — the sun; *guru* — the spiritual master; *vipra* — the *brāhmaṇas; ātmasu* — and the Supersoul; *arcayan* — worshiping; *sandhyayoḥ*—at the beginning and the end of the day; *harim* — the Supreme Personality of Godhead; *sāyam* — in the evening; *prātaḥ*—in the early morning; *saḥ*—he; *gurave* — unto his spiritual master; *bhaikṣyam* — alms obtained by begging; *āhṛtya* — bringing; *vāk-yataḥ*—with controlled speech; *bubhuje* — he partook; *guru-anujñātaḥ*—invited by his spiritual master; *sakṛt* — once; *na* — not (invited); *u* — indeed; *cet* — if; *upoṣitaḥ*—fasting; *evam* — in this way; *tapaḥ-svādhyāya-paraḥ*—dedicated to austerities and studies of the Vedic literature;

varṣāṇām — years; *ayuta-ayutam* — ten thousand times ten thousand; *ārādhayan* — worshiping; *hṛṣīka-īśam* — the supreme master of the senses, Lord Viṣṇu; *jigye* — he conquered; *mṛtyum* — death; *su-durjayam* — impossible to conquer.

TRANSLATION

After being purified by his father's performance of the prescribed rituals leading to Mārkaṇḍeya's brahminical initiation, Mārkaṇḍeya studied the Vedic hymns and strictly observed the regulative principles. He became advanced in austerity and Vedic knowledge and remained a lifelong celibate. Appearing most peaceful with his matted hair and his clothing made of bark, he furthered his spiritual progress by carrying the mendicant's waterpot, staff, sacred thread, brahmacārī belt, black deerskin, lotus-seed prayer beads and bundles of kuśa grass. At the sacred junctures of the day he regularly worshiped the Supreme Personality of Godhead in five forms — the sacrificial fire, the sun, his spiritual master, the brāhmaṇas and the Supersoul within his heart. Morning and evening he would go out begging, and upon returning he would present all the food he had collected to his spiritual master. Only when his spiritual master invited him would he silently take his one meal of the day; otherwise he would fast. Thus devoted to austerity and Vedic study, Mārkaṇḍeya Ṛṣi worshiped the supreme master of the senses, the Personality of Godhead, for countless millions of years, and in this way he conquered unconquerable death.

TEXT 12

ब्रह्मा भृगुर्भवो दक्षो ब्रह्मपुत्राश्च येऽपरे ।
नृदेवपितृभूतानि तेनासन्नतिविस्मिताः ॥ १२ ॥

brahmā bhṛgur bhavo dakṣo
brahma-putrāś ca ye'pare
nṛ-deva-pitṛ-bhūtāni
tenāsann ati-vismitāḥ

brahmā — Lord Brahmā; *bhṛguḥ* — Bhṛgu Muni; *bhavaḥ* — Lord Śiva; *dakṣaḥ* — Prajāpati Dakṣa; *brahma-putrāḥ* — the great sons of Brahmā; *ca* — and; *ye* — who; *apare* — others; *nṛ* — human beings; *deva* — demigods; *pitṛ*

—forefathers; *bhūtāni*— and ghostly spirits; *tena*— with that (conquest of death); *āsan*— they all became; *ati-vismitāḥ*—extremely amazed.

TRANSLATION

Lord Brahmā, Bhṛgu Muni, Lord Śiva, Prajāpati Dakṣa, the great sons of Brahmā, and many others among the human beings, demigods, forefathers and ghostly spirits — all were astonished by the achievement of Mārkaṇḍeya Ṛṣi.

TEXT 13

इत्थं बृहद्व्रतधरस्तपःस्वाध्यायसंयमैः ।
दध्यावधोक्षजं योगी ध्वस्तक्लेशान्तरात्मना ॥ १३ ॥

itthaṁ bṛhad-vrata-dharas
tapaḥ-svādhyāya-saṁyamaiḥ
dadhyāv adhokṣajaṁ yogī
dhvasta-kleśāntarātmanā

ittham— in this manner; *bṛhat-vrata-dharaḥ*—maintaining the vow of celibacy, *brahmacarya; tapaḥ-svādhyāya-saṁyamaiḥ*—by his austerities, study of the *Vedas* and regulative principles; *dadhyau*— he meditated; *adhokṣajam*— upon the transcendental Lord; *yogī*—the *yogī; dhvasta*— destroyed; *kleśa*— all troubles; *antaḥ-ātmanā*— with his introspective mind.

TRANSLATION

In this way the devotional mystic Mārkaṇḍeya maintained rigid celibacy through penance, study of the Vedas and self-discipline. With his mind thus free of all disturbances, he turned it inward and meditated on the Supreme Personality of Godhead, who lies beyond the material senses.

TEXT 14

तस्यैवं युञ्जतश्चित्तं महायोगेन योगिनः ।
व्यतीयाय महान् कालो मन्वन्तरषडात्मकः ॥ १४ ॥

tasyaivaṁ yuñjataś cittaṁ
mahā-yogena yoginaḥ
vyatīyāya mahān kālo
manvantara-ṣaḍ-ātmakaḥ

tasya — he; *evam* — thus; *yuñjataḥ*—while fixing; *cittam* — his mind; *mahā-yogena* — by powerful practice of *yoga; yoginaḥ*—the mystic sage; *vyatīyāya* — passed by; *mahān* — a great; *kālaḥ*—period of time; *manu-antara* — lifetimes of Manu; *ṣaṭ*—six; *ātmakaḥ*—consisting of.

TRANSLATION

While the mystic sage thus concentrated his mind by powerful yoga practice, the tremendous period of six lifetimes of Manu passed by.

TEXT 15

एतत् पुरन्दरो ज्ञात्वा सप्तमेऽस्मिन् किलान्तरे ।
तपोविशङ्कितो ब्रह्मन्नारेभे तद्विघातनम् ॥ १५ ॥

etat purandaro jñātvā
saptame'smin kilāntare
tapo-viśaṅkito brahmann
ārebhe tad-vighātanam

etat — this; *purandaraḥ*—Lord Indra; *jñātvā* — learning; *saptame* — in the seventh; *asmin* — this; *kila* — indeed; *antare* — reign of Manu; *tapaḥ*— of the austerities; *viśaṅkitaḥ*—becoming fearful; *brahman* — O *brāhmaṇa* Śaunaka; *ārebhe* — he set into motion; *tat* — of that austeritv; *vighātanam* — obstruction.

TRANSLATION

O brāhmaṇa, during the seventh reign of Manu, the current age, Lord Indra came to know of Mārkaṇḍeya's austerities and became fearful of his growing mystic potency. Thus he tried to impede the sage's penance.

TEXT 16

गन्धर्वाप्सरसः कामं वसन्तमलयानिलौ ।
मुनये प्रेषयामास रजस्तोकमदौ तथा ॥ १६ ॥

gandharvāpsarasaḥ kāmaṁ
vasanta-malayānilau
munaye preṣayām āsa
rajas-toka-madau tathā

gandharva-apsarasaḥ — the celestial singers and dancing girls; *kāmam* — Cupid; *vasanta* — the spring season; *malaya-anilau* — and the refreshing breeze from the Malaya Hills; *munaye* — to the sage; *preṣayām āsa* — he sent; *rajaḥ-toka* — the child of passion, greed; *madau* — and intoxication; *tathā* — also.

TRANSLATION

To ruin the sage's spiritual practice, Lord Indra sent Cupid, beautiful celestial singers, dancing girls, the season of spring and the sandalwood-scented breeze from the Malaya Hills, along with greed and intoxication personified.

TEXT 17

ते वै तदाश्रमं जग्मुर्हिमाद्रेः पार्श्व उत्तरे ।
पुष्पभद्रा नदी यत्र चित्राख्या च शिला विभो ॥ १७ ॥

te vai tad-āśramaṁ jagmur
himādreḥ pārśva uttare
puṣpabhadrā nadī yatra
citrākhyā ca śilā vibho

te — they; *vai* — indeed; *tat* — of Mārkaṇḍeya Ṛṣi; *āśramam* — to the hermitage; *jagmuḥ* — went; *hima-adreḥ* — of the Himālaya Mountains; *pārśve* — to the side; *uttare* — on the north; *puṣpabhadrā nadī* — the Puṣpabhadrā River; *yatra* — where; *citrā-ākhyā* — named Citrā; *ca* — and; *śilā* — the peak; *vibho* — O powerful Śaunaka.

TRANSLATION

O most powerful Śaunaka, they went to Mārkaṇḍeya's hermitage, on the northern side of the Himālaya Mountains where the Puṣpabhadrā River passes by the famous peak Citrā.

TEXTS 18–20

तदाश्रमपदं पुण्यं पुण्यद्रुमलताञ्चितम् ।
पुण्यद्विजकुलाकीर्णं पुण्यामलजलाशयम् ॥ १८ ॥
मत्तभ्रमरसंगीतं मत्तकोकिलकूजितम् ।
मत्तबर्हिनटाटोपं मत्तद्विजकुलाकुलम् ॥ १९ ॥

वायुः प्रविष्ट आदाय हिमनिर्झरशीकरान् ।
सुमनोभिः परिष्वक्तो ववावुत्तम्भयन् स्मरम् ॥ २० ॥

tad-āśrama-padaṁ puṇyaṁ
puṇya-druma-latāñcitam
puṇya-dvija-kulākīrṇaṁ
puṇyāmala-jalāśayam

matta-bhramara-saṅgītaṁ
matta-kokila-kūjitam
matta-barhi-naṭāṭopaṁ
matta-dvija-kulākulam

vāyuḥ praviṣṭa ādāya
hima-nirjhara-śīkarān
sumanobhiḥ pariṣvakto
vavāv uttambhayan smaram

tat — his; *āśrama-padam* — place of hermitage; *puṇyam* — pious; *puṇya* — pious; *druma* — with trees; *latā* — and creepers; *añcitam* — specially marked; *puṇya* — pious; *dvija* — of *brāhmaṇa* sages; *kula* — with the groups; *ākīrṇam* — brimming; *puṇya* — pious; *amala* — spotless; *jala-āśayam* — having reservoirs of water; *matta* — maddened; *bhramara* — of bees; *saṅgītam* — with singing; *matta* — maddened; *kokila* — of cuckoos; *kūjitam* — with cooing; *matta* — maddened; *barhi* — of peacocks; *naṭa-āṭopam* — with the frenzy of dancing; *matta* — maddened; *dvija* — of birds; *kula* — with the families; *ākulam* — filled; *vāyuḥ* — the wind of the Malaya Hills; *praviṣṭaḥ* — entering; *ādāya* — taking up; *hima* — chilling; *nirjhara* — of the waterfalls; *śīkarān* — the drops of mist; *sumanobhiḥ* — by the flowers; *pariṣvaktaḥ* — being embraced; *vavau* — blew; *uttambhayan* — evoking; *smaram* — Cupid.

TRANSLATION

Groves of pious trees decorated the holy āśrama of Mārkaṇḍeya Ṛṣi, and many saintly brāhmaṇas lived there, enjoying the abundant pure, sacred ponds. The āśrama resounded with the buzzing of intoxicated bees and the cooing of excited cuckoos, while jubilant peacocks danced about. Indeed, many families of maddened birds crowded that hermitage. The springtime breeze sent by Lord Indra entered there, carrying cooling drops

of spray from nearby waterfalls. Fragrant from the embrace of forest flowers, that breeze entered the hermitage and began evoking the lusty spirit of Cupid.

TEXT 21

उद्यच्चन्द्रनिशावक्त्रः प्रवालस्तबकालिभिः ।
गोपद्रुमलताजालैस्तत्रासीत् कुसुमाकरः ॥ २१ ॥

udyac-candra-niśā-vaktraḥ
pravāla-stabakālibhiḥ
gopa-druma-latā-jālais
tatrāsīt kusumākaraḥ

udyat — rising; *candra* — with the moon; *niśā* — nighttime; *vaktraḥ* — whose face; *pravāla* — of new sprouts; *stabaka* — and blossoms; *ālibhiḥ* — with rows; *gopa* — being hidden; *druma* — of the trees; *latā* — and creepers; *jālaiḥ* — along with the multitude; *tatra* — there; *āsīt* — appeared; *kusuma-ākaraḥ* — the spring season.

TRANSLATION

Springtime then appeared in Mārkaṇḍeya's āśrama. Indeed, the evening sky, glowing with the light of the rising moon, became the very face of spring, and sprouts and fresh blossoms virtually covered the multitude of trees and creepers.

TEXT 22

अन्वीयमानो गन्धर्वैर्गीतवादित्रयूथकैः ।
अदृश्यतात्तचापेषुः स्वःस्त्रीयूथपतिः स्मरः ॥ २२ ॥

anvīyamāno gandharvair
gīta-vāditra-yūthakaiḥ
adṛśyatātta-cāpeṣuḥ
svaḥ-strī-yūtha-patiḥ smaraḥ

anvīyamānaḥ — being followed; *gandharvaiḥ* — by Gandharvas; *gīta* — of singers; *vāditra* — and players of musical instruments; *yūthakaiḥ* — by companies; *adṛśyata* — was seen; *ātta* — holding up; *cāpa-iṣuḥ* — his bow and arrows; *svaḥ-strī-yūtha* — of hoardes of heavenly women; *patiḥ* — the master; *smaraḥ* — Cupid.

TRANSLATION

Cupid, the master of many heavenly women, then came there holding his bow and arrows. He was followed by groups of Gandharvas playing musical instruments and singing.

TEXT 23

हुत्वाग्निं समुपासीनं ददृशुः शक्रकिंकराः ।
मीलिताक्षं दुराधर्षं मूर्तिमन्तमिवानलम् ॥ २३ ॥

hutvāgniṁ samupāsīnaṁ
dadṛśuḥ śakra-kiṅkarāḥ
mīlitākṣaṁ durādharṣaṁ
mūrtimantam ivānalam

hutvā — having offered oblations; *agnim* — to the sacrificial fire; *samupāsīnam* — sitting in yogic meditation; *dadṛśuḥ* — they saw; *śakra* — of Indra; *kiṅkarāḥ* — the servants; *mīlita* — closed; *akṣam* — his eyes; *durādharṣam* — invincible; *mūrti-mantam* — personified; *iva* — as if; *analam* — fire.

TRANSLATION

These servants of Indra found the sage sitting in meditation, having just offered his prescribed oblations into the sacrificial fire. His eyes closed in trance, he seemed invincible, like fire personified.

TEXT 24

ननृतुस्तस्य पुरतः स्त्रियोऽथो गायका जगुः ।
मृदंगवीणापणवैर्वाद्यं चक्रुर्मनोरमम् ॥ २४ ॥

nanṛtus tasya purataḥ
striyo 'tho gāyakā jaguḥ
mṛdaṅga-vīṇā-paṇavair
vādyaṁ cakrur mano-ramam

nanṛtuḥ — danced; *tasya* — of him; *purataḥ* — in front; *striyaḥ* — women; *atha u* — and furthermore; *gāyakāḥ* — singers; *jaguḥ* — sang; *mṛdaṅga* —

with drums; *vīṇā* — stringed instruments; *paṇavaiḥ*—and cymbals; *vādyam* — instrumental music; *cakruḥ*—they made; *manaḥ-ramam* — charming.

TRANSLATION

The women danced before the sage, and the celestial singers sang to the charming accompaniment of drums, cymbals and vīṇās.

TEXT 25

सन्दधेऽस्त्रं स्वधनुषि कामः पञ्चमुखं तदा ।
मधुर्मनो रजस्तोक इन्द्रभृत्या व्यकम्पयन् ॥ २५ ॥

sandadhe 'straṁ sva-dhanuṣi
kāmaḥ pañca-mukhaṁ tadā
madhur mano rajas-toka
indra-bhṛtyā vyakampayan

sandadhe — he fixed; *astram* — the weapon; *sva-dhanuṣi* — upon his bow; *kāmaḥ*—Cupid; *pañca-mukham* — having five heads (sight, sound, smell, touch and taste); *tadā* — then; *madhuḥ*—spring; *manaḥ*—the mind of the sage; *rajaḥ-tokaḥ*—the child of passion, greed; *indra-bhṛtyāḥ*—the servants of Indra; *vyakampayan* — attempted to agitate.

TRANSLATION

While the son of passion [greed personified], spring and the other servants of Indra all tried to agitate Mārkaṇḍeya's mind, Cupid drew his five-headed arrow and fixed it upon his bow.

TEXTS 26–27

क्रीडन्त्याः पुञ्जिकस्थल्याः कन्दुकैः स्तनगौरवात् ।
भृशमुद्विग्नमध्यायाः केशविस्रंसितस्रजः ॥ २६ ॥
इतस्ततो भ्रमद्दृष्टेश्चलन्त्या अनु कन्दुकम् ।
वायुर्जहार तद्वासः सूक्ष्मं त्रुटितमेखलम् ॥ २७ ॥

krīḍantyāḥ puñjikasthalyāḥ
kandukaiḥ stana-gauravāt
bhṛśam udvigna-madhyāyāḥ
keśa-visraṁsita-srajaḥ

itas tato bhramad-dṛṣṭeś
calantyā anu kandukam
vāyur jahāra tad-vāsaḥ
sūkṣmaṁ truṭita-mekhalam

krīḍantyāḥ—who was playing; *puñjikasthalyāḥ*—of the Apsarā named Puñjikasthalī; *kandukaiḥ*—with a number of balls; *stana*—of her breasts; *gauravāt*—because of the great weight; *bhṛśam*—very much; *udvigna*—overburdened; *madhyāyāḥ*—whose waist; *keśa*—from her hair; *visraṁsita*—falling; *srajaḥ*—the flower garland; *itaḥ tataḥ*—here and there; *bhramat*—wandering; *dṛṣṭeḥ*—whose eyes; *calantyāḥ*—who was running about; *anu kandukam*—after her ball; *vāyuḥ*—the wind; *jahāra*—stole away; *tat-vāsaḥ*—her garment; *sūkṣmam*—fine; *truṭita*—loosened; *mekhalam*—the belt.

TRANSLATION

The Apsarā Puñjikasthalī made a show of playing with a number of toy balls. Her waist seemed weighed down by her heavy breasts, and the wreath of flowers in her hair became disheveled. As she ran about after the balls, glancing here and there, the belt of her thin garment loosened, and suddenly the wind blew her clothes away.

TEXT 28

विससर्ज तदा बाणं मत्वा तं स्वजितं स्मरः ।
सर्वं तत्राभवन्मोघमनीशस्य यथोद्यमः ॥ २८ ॥

visasarja tadā bāṇaṁ
matvā taṁ sva-jitaṁ smaraḥ
sarvaṁ tatrābhavan mogham
anīśasya yathodyamaḥ

visasarja—shot; *tadā*—then; *bāṇam*—the arrow; *matvā*—thinking; *tam*—him; *sva*—by himself; *jitam*—conquered; *smaraḥ*—Cupid; *sarvam*—all this; *tatra*—directed at the sage; *abhavat*—became; *mogham*—futile; *anīśasya*—of an atheist disbeliever; *yathā*—just as; *udyamaḥ*—the endeavors.

TRANSLATION

Cupid, thinking he had conquered the sage, then shot his arrow. But all these attempts to seduce Mārkaṇḍeya proved futile, just like the useless endeavors of an atheist.

TEXT 29

त इत्थमपकुर्वन्तो मुनेस्तत्तेजसा मुने ।
दह्यमाना निववृतुः प्रबोध्याहिमिवार्भकाः ॥ २९ ॥

ta ittham apakurvanto
munes tat-tejasā mune
dahyamānā nivavṛtuḥ
prabodhyāhim ivārbhakāḥ

te — they; *ittham* — in this way; *apakurvantaḥ*—trying to do harm; *muneḥ*—to the sage; *tat* — his; *tejasā* — by the potency; *mune* — O sage (Śaunaka); *dahyamānāḥ*—feeling burned; *nivavṛtuḥ*—they desisted; *prabodhya* — having awakened; *ahim* — a snake; *iva* — as if; *arbhakāḥ*—children.

TRANSLATION

O learned Śaunaka, while Cupid and his followers tried to harm the sage, they felt themselves being burned alive by his potency. Thus they stopped their mischief, just like children who have aroused a sleeping snake.

TEXT 30

इतीन्द्रानुचरैर्ब्रह्मन् धर्षितोऽपि महामुनिः ।
यन्नागादहमो भावं न तच्चित्रं महत्सु हि ॥ ३० ॥

itīndrānucarair brahman
dharṣito 'pi mahā-muniḥ
yan nāgād ahamo bhāvaṁ
na tac citraṁ mahatsu hi

iti — thus; *indra-anucaraiḥ*—by the followers of Indra; *brahman* — O *brāhmaṇa; dharṣitaḥ*—impudently attacked; *api* — although; *mahā-muniḥ* —the elevated sage; *yat* — that; *na agāt* — he did not succumb; *ahamaḥ*—

of false ego; *bhāvam* — to the transformation; *na* — not; *tat* — that; *citram* — surprising; *mahatsu* — for great souls; *hi* — indeed.

TRANSLATION

O brāhmaṇa, the followers of Lord Indra had impudently attacked the saintly Mārkaṇḍeya, yet he did not succumb to any influence of false ego. For great souls such tolerance is not at all surprising.

TEXT 31

दृष्ट्वा निस्तेजसं कामं सगणं भगवान् स्वराट् ।
श्रुत्वानुभावं ब्रह्मर्षेर्विस्मयं समगात्परम् ॥ ३१ ॥

dṛṣṭvā nistejasaṁ kāmaṁ
sa-gaṇaṁ bhagavān svarāṭ
śrutvānubhāvaṁ brahmarṣer
vismayaṁ samagāt param

dṛṣṭvā — seeing; *nistejasam* — deprived of his power; *kāmam* — Cupid; *sa-gaṇam* — along with his associates; *bhagavān* — the powerful lord; *sva-rāṭ* — King Indra; *śrutvā* — and hearing; *anubhāvam* — the influence; *brahma-ṛṣeḥ* — of the sage among the *brāhmaṇas; vismayam* — astonishment; *samagāt* — he attained; *param* — great.

TRANSLATION

The mighty King Indra was most astonished when he heard of the mystic prowess of the exalted sage Mārkaṇḍeya and saw how Cupid and his associates had become powerless in his presence.

TEXT 32

तस्यैवं युञ्जतश्चित्तं तपःस्वाध्यायसंयमैः ।
अनुग्रहायाविरासीन्नरनारायणो हरिः ॥ ३२ ॥

tasyaivaṁ yuñjataś cittaṁ
tapaḥ-svādhyāya-saṁyamaiḥ
anugrahāyāvirāsīn
nara-nārāyaṇo hariḥ

tasya — while he, Mārkaṇḍeya; *evam* — in this way; *yuñjataḥ*—was fixing; *cittam* — his mind; *tapaḥ*—by austerity; *svādhyāya* — study of the *Vedas; saṁyamaiḥ*—and regulative principles; *anugrahāya* — for showing mercy; *āvirāsīt* — made Himself manifest; *nara-nārāyaṇaḥ*—exhibiting the forms of Nara and Nārāyaṇa; *hariḥ*—the Supreme Personality of Godhead.

TRANSLATION

Desiring to bestow His mercy upon the saintly Mārkaṇḍeya, who had perfectly fixed his mind in self-realization through penance, Vedic study and observance of regulative principles, the Supreme Personality of Godhead personally appeared before the sage in the forms of Nara and Nārāyaṇa.

TEXTS 33–34

तौ शुक्लकृष्णौ नवकञ्जलोचनौ
चतुर्भुजौ रौरववल्कलाम्बरौ ।
पवित्रपाणी उपवीतकं त्रिवृत्
कमण्डलुं दण्डमृजुं च वैणवम् ॥ ३३ ॥
पद्माक्षमालामुत जन्तुमार्जनं
वेदं च साक्षात्तप एव रूपिणौ ।
तपत्तडिद्वर्णपिशंगरोचिषा
प्रांशू दधानौ विबुधर्षभार्चितौ ॥ ३४ ॥

tau śukla-kṛṣṇau nava-kañja-locanau
catur-bhujau raurava-valkalāmbarau
pavitra-pāṇī upavītakaṁ tri-vṛt
kamaṇḍaluṁ daṇḍam ṛjuṁ ca vaiṇavam

padmākṣa-mālām uta jantu-mārjanaṁ
vedaṁ ca sākṣāt tapa eva rūpiṇau
tapat-taḍid-varṇa-piśaṅga-rociṣā
prāṁśū dadhānau vibudharṣabhārcitau

tau — the two of Them; *śukla-kṛṣṇau* — one white and the other black; *nava-kañja* — like blooming lotus flowers; *locanau* — Their eyes; *catuḥ-bhujau* — having four arms; *raurava* — black deerskin; *valkala* — and bark; *am-*

barau — as Their clothing; *pavitra* — most purifying; *pāṇī*—Their hands; *upavītakam* — sacred thread; *tri-vṛt* — threefold; *kamaṇḍalum* — waterpot; *daṇḍam* — staff; *ṛjum* — straight; *ca* — and; *vaiṇavam* — made of bamboo; *padma-akṣa* — of lotus seeds; *mālām* — prayer beads; *uta* — and; *jantu-mār-janam* — which purifies all living beings; *vedam* — the *Vedas* (represented by bundles of *darbha* grass); *ca* — and; *sākṣāt* — directly; *tapaḥ*—austerity; *eva* — indeed; *rūpiṇau* — personified; *tapat* — blazing; *taḍit* — lightning; *varṇa* — the color; *piśaṅga* — yellowish; *rociṣā* — with Their effulgence; *prāṁśū* — very tall; *dadhānau* — bearing; *vibudha-ṛṣabha* — by the chief of the demigods; *arcitau* — worshiped.

TRANSLATION

One of Them was of a whitish complexion, the other blackish, and They both had four arms. Their eyes resembled the petals of blooming lotuses, and They wore garments of black deerskin and bark, along with the three-stranded sacred thread. In Their hands, which were most purifying, They carried the mendicant's waterpot, straight bamboo staff and lotus-seed prayer beads, as well as the all-purifying Vedas in the symbolic form of bundles of darbha grass. Their bearing was tall and Their yellow effulgence the color of radiant lightning. Appearing as austerity personified, They were being worshiped by the foremost demigods.

TEXT 35

ते वै भगवतो रूपे नरनारायणावृषी ।
दृष्ट्वोत्थायादरेणोच्चैर्ननामांगेन दण्डवत् ॥ ३५ ॥

te vai bhagavato rūpe
nara-nārāyaṇāv ṛṣī
dṛṣṭvotthāyādareṇoccair
nanāmāṅgena daṇḍa-vat

te — They; *vai* — indeed; *bhagavataḥ*—of the Personality of Godhead; *rūpe* — the personal manifestations; *nara-nārāyaṇau* — Nara and Nārāyaṇa; *ṛṣī*—the two sages; *dṛṣṭvā* — seeing; *utthāya* — standing up; *ādareṇa* — with respect; *uccaiḥ*—great; *nanāma* — bowed down; *aṅgena* — with his entire body; *daṇḍa-vat* — just like a stick.

TRANSLATION

These two sages, Nara and Nārāyaṇa, were the direct personal forms of the Supreme Lord. When Mārkaṇḍeya Ṛṣi saw Them, he immediately stood up and then with great respect offered Them obeisances by falling down flat on the ground like a stick.

TEXT 36

स तत्सन्दर्शनानन्दनिर्वृतात्मेन्द्रियाशयः ।
हृष्टरोमाश्रुपूर्णाक्षो न सेहे तावुदीक्षितुम् ॥ ३६ ॥

sa tat-sandarśanānanda-
nirvṛtātmendriyāśayaḥ
hṛṣṭa-romāśru-pūrṇākṣo
na sehe tāv udīkṣitum

saḥ—he, Mārkaṇḍeya; *tat* — of Them; *sandarśana* — because of seeing; *ānanda* — by the ecstasy; *nirvṛta* — pleased; *ātma* — whose body; *indriya* — senses; *āśayaḥ*—and mind; *hṛṣṭa* — standing on end; *romā* — his bodily hairs; *aśru* — with tears; *pūrṇa* — filled; *akṣaḥ*—his eyes; *na sehe* — he was unable; *tau* — upon them; *udīkṣitum* — to glance.

TRANSLATION

The ecstasy of seeing Them completely satisfied Mārkaṇḍeya's body, mind and senses and caused the hairs on his body to stand on end and his eyes to fill with tears. Overwhelmed, Mārkaṇḍeya found it difficult to look at Them.

TEXT 37

उत्थाय प्राञ्जलिः प्रह्व औत्सुक्यादाश्लिषन्निव ।
नमो नम इतीशानौ बभाषे गद्‌गदाक्षरम् ॥ ३७ ॥

utthāya prāñjaliḥ prahva
autsukyād āśliṣann iva
namo nama itīśānau
babhāṣe gadgadākṣaram

utthāya — standing up; *prāñjaliḥ*—with folded hands; *prahvaḥ*—humble; *autsukyāt* — out of eagerness; *āśliṣan* — embracing; *iva* — as if; *namaḥ*

—obeisances; *namaḥ*—obeisances; *iti*—thus; *īśānau*—to the two Lords; *babhāṣe*—he spoke; *gadgada*—choking with ecstasy; *akṣaram*—the syllables.

TRANSLATION

Standing with his hands folded in supplication and his head bowed in humility, Mārkaṇḍeya felt such eagerness that he imagined he was embracing the two Lords. In a voice choked with ecstasy, he repeatedly said, "I offer You my humble obeisances."

TEXT 38

तयोरासनमादाय पादयोरवनिज्य च ।
अर्हणेनानुलेपेन धूपमाल्यैरपूजयत् ॥ ३८ ॥

tayor āsanam ādāya
pādayor avanijya ca
arhaṇenānulepena
dhūpa-mālyair apūjayat

tayoḥ—to Them; *āsanam*—sitting places; *ādāya*—offering; *pādayoḥ*—Their feet; *avanijya*—bathing; *ca*—and; *arhaṇena*—with suitable respectful offerings; *anulepena*—by anointing Them with sandalwood pulp and other fragrant substances; *dhūpa*—with incense; *mālyaiḥ*—and flower garlands; *apūjayat*—he worshiped.

TRANSLATION

He gave Them sitting places and washed Their feet, and then he worshiped Them with presentations of arghya, sandalwood pulp, fragrant oils, incense and flower garlands.

TEXT 39

सुखमासनमासीनौ प्रसादाभिमुखौ मुनी ।
पुनरानम्य पादाभ्यां गरिष्ठाविदमब्रवीत् ॥ ३९ ॥

sukham āsanam āsīnau
prasādābhimukhau munī
punar ānamya pādābhyāṁ
gariṣṭhāv idam abravīt

sukham — comfortably; *āsanam* — on sitting places; *āsīnau* — seated; *prasāda* — mercy; *abhimukhau* — ready to give; *munī*— to the Lord's incarnation as the two sages; *punaḥ*— again; *ānamya* — bowing down; *pādābhyām* — at Their feet; *gariṣṭhau* — to the supremely worshipable; *idam* — this; *abravīt* — he spoke.

TRANSLATION

Mārkaṇḍeya Ṛṣi once again bowed down at the lotus feet of those two most worshipable sages, who were sitting at ease, ready to bestow all mercy upon him. He then addressed Them as follows.

TEXT 40

श्रीमार्कण्डेय उवाच

किं वर्णये तव विभो यदुदीरितोऽसुः
संस्पन्दते तमनु वाङ्मनइन्द्रियाणि ।
स्पन्दन्ति वै तनुभृतामजशर्वयोश्च
स्वस्याप्यथापि भजतामसि भावबन्धुः ॥ ४० ॥

śrī-mārkaṇḍeya uvāca
kiṁ varṇaye tava vibho yad-udīrito 'suḥ
saṁspandate tam anu vāṅ-mana-indriyāṇi
spandanti vai tanu-bhṛtām aja-śarvayoś ca
svasyāpy athāpi bhajatām asi bhāva-bandhuḥ

śrī-mārkaṇḍeyaḥ uvāca — Śrī Mārkaṇḍeya said; *kim* — what; *varṇaye* — shall I describe; *tava* — about You; *vibho* — O Almighty Lord; *yat* — by whom; *udīritaḥ*— moved; *asuḥ*— the vital air; *saṁspandate* — comes to life; *tam anu* — following it; *vāk* — the power of speech; *manaḥ*— the mind; *indriyāṇi* — and the senses; *spandanti* — begin to act; *vai* — indeed; *tanu-bhṛtām* — of all embodied living beings; *aja-śarvayoḥ*— of Lord Brahmā and Lord Śiva; *ca* — as well; *svasya* — of myself; *api* — also; *atha api* — nevertheless; *bhajatām* — for those who are worshiping; *asi* — You become; *bhāva-bandhuḥ* — the intimate loving friend.

TRANSLATION

Śrī Mārkaṇḍeya said: O Almighty Lord, how can I possibly describe You? You awaken the vital air, which then impels the mind, senses and power

of speech to act. This is true for all ordinary conditioned souls and even for great demigods like Brahmā and Śiva. So it is certainly true for me. Nevertheless, You become the intimate friend of those who worship You.

TEXT 41

मूर्ती इमे भगवतो भगवंस्त्रिलोक्याः
क्षेमाय तापविरमाय च मृत्युजित्यै ।
नाना बिभर्ष्यवितुमन्यतनूर्यथेदं
सृष्ट्वा पुनर्ग्रससि सर्वमिवोर्णनाभिः ॥ ४१ ॥

mūrtī ime bhagavato bhagavaṁs tri-lokyāḥ
kṣemāya tāpa-viramāya ca mṛtyu-jityai
nānā bibharṣy avitum anya-tanūr yathedaṁ
sṛṣṭvā punar grasasi sarvam ivorṇanābhiḥ

mūrtī—the two personal forms; *ime*—these; *bhagavataḥ*—of the Supreme Personality of Godhead; *bhagavan*—O Lord; *tri-lokyāḥ*—of all the three worlds; *kṣemāya*—for the ultimate benefit; *tāpa*—of material misery; *viramāya*—for the cessation; *ca*—and; *mṛtyu*—of death; *jityai*—for the conquest; *nānā*—various; *bibharṣi*—You manifest; *avitum*—for the purpose of protecting; *anya*—other; *tanūḥ*—transcendental bodies; *yathā*—just as; *idam*—this universe; *sṛṣṭvā*—having created; *punaḥ*—once again; *grasasi*—You swallow up; *sarvam*—entirely; *iva*—just like; *ūrṇa-nābhiḥ*—a spider.

TRANSLATION

O Supreme Personality of Godhead, these two personal forms of Yours have appeared to bestow the ultimate benefit for the three worlds — the cessation of material misery and the conquest of death. My Lord, although You create this universe and then assume many transcendental forms to protect it, You also swallow it up, just like a spider who spins and later withdraws its web.

TEXT 42

तस्यावितुः स्थिरचरेशितुरङ्घ्रिमूलं
यत्स्थं न कर्मगुणकालरजः स्पृशन्ति ।

यद् वै स्तुवन्ति निनमन्ति यजन्त्यभीक्ष्णं
ध्यायन्ति वेदहृदया मुनयस्तदाप्त्यै ॥ ४२ ॥

tasyāvituḥ sthira-careśitur aṅghri-mūlaṁ
yat-sthaṁ na karma-guṇa-kāla-rajaḥ spṛśanti
yad vai stuvanti ninamanti yajanty abhīkṣṇaṁ
dhyāyanti veda-hṛdayā munayas tad-āptyai

tasya — of Him; *avituḥ* — the protector; *sthira-cara* — of the stationary and moving living beings; *īśituḥ* — the supreme controller; *aṅghri-mūlam* — the soles of His lotus feet; *yat-stham* — one who is situated at which; *na* — do not; *karma-guṇa-kāla* — of material work, material qualities and time; *rajaḥ* — the contamination; *spṛśanti* — touch; *yat* — whom; *vai* — indeed; *stuvanti* — praise; *ninamanti* — bow down to; *yajanti* — worship; *abhīkṣṇam* — at every moment; *dhyāyanti* — meditate upon; *veda-hṛdayāḥ* — who have assimilated the essence of the *Vedas; munayaḥ* — sages; *tat-āptyai* — for the purpose of achieving Him.

TRANSLATION

Because You are the protector and the supreme controller of all moving and nonmoving beings, anyone who takes shelter of Your lotus feet can never be touched by the contamination of material work, material qualities or time. Great sages who have assimilated the essential meaning of the Vedaṣ offer their prayers to You. To gain Your association, they bow down to You at every opportunity and constantly worship You and meditate upon You.

TEXT 43

नान्यं तवाङ्घ्र्युपनयादपवर्गमूर्तेः
क्षेमं जनस्य परितोभिय ईश विद्मः ।
ब्रह्मा बिभेत्यलमतो द्विपरार्धधिष्ण्यः
कालस्य ते किमुत तत्कृतभौतिकानाम् ॥ ४३ ॥

nānyaṁ tavāṅghry-upanayād apavarga-mūrteḥ
kṣemaṁ janasya parito-bhiya īśa vidmaḥ
brahmā bibhety alam ato dvi-parārdha-dhiṣṇyaḥ
kālasya te kim uta tat-kṛta-bhautikānām

na anyam — no other; *tava* — Your; *aṅghri* — of the lotus feet; *upanayāt* — than the attainment; *apavarga-mūrteḥ*—who are liberation personified; *kṣemam* — benefit; *janasya* — for the person; *paritaḥ*—on all sides; *bhiyaḥ* —who is fearful; *īśa* — O Lord; *vidmaḥ*—do we know; *brahmā* — Lord Brahmā; *bibheti* — is afraid; *alam* — very much; *ataḥ*—on account of this; *dvi-parārdha* — the entire duration of the universe; *dhiṣṇyaḥ*—the period of whose reign; *kālasya* — because of time; *te* — Your feature; *kim uta* — then what to speak; *tat-kṛta* — created by him, Brahmā; *bhautikānām* — of the mundane creatures.

TRANSLATION

My dear Lord, even Lord Brahmā, who enjoys his exalted position for the entire duration of the universe, fears the passage of time. Then what to speak of those whom Brahmā creates, the conditioned souls. They encounter fearful dangers at every step of their lives. I do not know of any relief from this fear except shelter at Your lotus feet, which are the very form of liberation.

TEXT 44

तद्वै भजाम्यृतधियस्तव पादमूलं
हित्वेदमात्मच्छदि चात्मगुरोः परस्य ।
देहाद्यपार्थमसदन्त्यमभिज्ञमात्रं
विन्देत ते तर्हि सर्वमनीषितार्थम् ॥ ४४ ॥

tad vai bhajāmy ṛta-dhiyas tava pāda-mūlaṁ
hitvedam ātma-cchadi cātma-guroḥ parasya
dehādy apārtham asad antyam abhijña-mātraṁ
vindeta te tarhi sarva-manīṣitārtham

tat — therefore; *vai* — indeed; *bhajāmi* — I worship; *ṛta-dhiyaḥ*—of Him whose intelligence always perceives the truth; *tava* — of You; *pāda-mūlam* — the soles of the lotus feet; *hitvā* — giving up; *idam* — this; *ātma-chadi* — covering of the self; *ca* — and; *ātma-guroḥ*—of the master of the soul; *parasya* — who is the Supreme Truth; *deha-ādi* — the material body and other false designations; *apārtham* — useless; *asat* — insubstantial; *antyam* — temporary; *abhijña-mātram* — only imagined to have a separate existence; *vindeta* — one obtains; *te* — from You; *tarhi* — then; *sarva* — all; *manīṣita* — desired; *artham* — objects.

TRANSLATION

Therefore I worship Your lotus feet, having renounced my identification with the material body and everything else that covers my true self. These useless, insubstantial and temporary coverings are merely presumed to be separate from You, whose intelligence encompasses all truth. By attaining You — the Supreme Godhead and the master of the soul — one attains everything desirable.

PURPORT

One who falsely identifies himself as the material body or mind automatically feels entitled to exploit the material world. But when we realize our eternal spiritual nature and Lord Kṛṣṇa's supreme proprietorship over all that be, we renounce our false enjoying propensity by the strength of spiritual knowledge.

TEXT 45

सत्त्वं रजस्तम इतीश तवात्मबन्धो
मायामयाः स्थितिलयोदयहेतवोऽस्य ।
लीला धृता यदपि सत्त्वमयी प्रशान्त्यै
नान्ये नृणां व्यसनमोहभियश्च याभ्याम् ॥ ४५ ॥

sattvaṁ rajas tama itīśa tavātma-bandho
māyā-mayāḥ sthiti-layodaya-hetavo'sya
līlā dhṛtā yad api sattva-mayī praśāntyai
nānye nṛṇāṁ vyasana-moha-bhiyaś ca yābhyām

sattvam — goodness; *rajaḥ* — passion; *tamaḥ* — ignorance; *iti* — the modes of nature thus termed; *īśa* — O Lord; *tava* — Your; *ātma-bandho* — O supreme friend of the soul; *māyā-mayāḥ* — produced from Your personal energy; *sthiti-laya-udaya* — of maintenance, destruction and creation; *hetavaḥ* — the causes; *asya* — of this universe; *līlāḥ* — as pastimes; *dhṛtāḥ* — assumed; *yat api* — although; *sattva-mayī* — that which is in the mode of goodness; *praśāntyai* — for liberation; *na* — not; *anye* — the other two; *nṛṇām* — for persons; *vyasana* — danger; *moha* — bewilderment; *bhiyaḥ* — and fear; *ca* — also; *yābhyām* — from which.

TRANSLATION

O my Lord, O supreme friend of the conditioned soul, although for the creation, maintenance and annihilation of this world You accept the modes of goodness, passion and ignorance, which constitute Your illusory potency, You specifically employ the mode of goodness to liberate the conditioned souls. The other two modes simply bring them suffering, illusion and fear.

PURPORT

The words *līlā dhṛtāḥ* indicate that the creative activities of Lord Brahmā, the destructive activities of Lord Śiva and the sustaining functions of Lord Viṣṇu are all pastimes of the Absolute Truth, Lord Kṛṣṇa. But ultimately only Lord Viṣṇu can award liberation from the clutches of material illusion, as indicated by the words *sattva-mayī praśāntyai.*

Our passionate and ignorant activities cause great suffering, illusion and fear for us and others; therefore they should be given up. One should become firmly situated in the mode of goodness and live peacefully on the spiritual platform. The essence of goodness is to renounce selfish interest in all one's activities and thus dedicate one's entire being to the Supreme Being, Lord Kṛṣṇa, who is the source of our existence.

TEXT 46

तस्मात्तवेह भगवन्नथ तावकानां
शुक्लां तनुं स्वदयितां कुशला भजन्ति ।
यत् सात्वताः पुरुषरूपमुशन्ति सत्त्वं
लोको यतोऽभयमुतात्मसुखं न चान्यत् ॥ ४६ ॥

tasmāt taveha bhagavann atha tāvakānāṁ
śuklāṁ tanuṁ sva-dayitāṁ kuśalā bhajanti
yat sātvatāḥ puruṣa-rūpam uśanti sattvaṁ
loko yato'bhayam utātma-sukhaṁ na cānyat

tasmāt — therefore; *tava* — Your; *iha* — in this world; *bhagavan* — O Supreme Lord; *atha* — and; *tāvakānām* — of Your devotees; *śuklām* — transcendental; *tanum* — the personal form; *sva-dayitām* — most dear to them; *kuśalāḥ*—those who are expert in spiritual knowledge; *bhajanti* — worship; *yat* — because; *sātvatāḥ*—the great devotees; *puruṣa* — of the original Personality of Godhead; *rūpam* — the form; *uśanti* — consider; *sattvam* — the mode of goodness; *lokaḥ*—the spiritual world; *yataḥ*—from which; *abhayam* — fearlessness; *uta* — and; *ātma-sukham* — the happiness of the soul; *na* — not; *ca* — and; *anyat* — any other.

TRANSLATION

O Lord, because fearlessness, spiritual happiness and the kingdom of God are all achieved through the mode of pure goodness, Your devotees consider this mode, but never passion and ignorance, to be a direct manifestation of You, the Supreme Personality of Godhead. Intelligent persons thus worship Your beloved transcendental form, composed of pure goodness, along with the spiritual forms of Your pure devotees.

PURPORT

Intelligent persons do not worship the demigods, who represent the modes of passion and ignorance. Lord Brahmā represents passion, Lord Śiva represents ignorance, and demigods such as Indra also represent the modes of material nature. But Lord Viṣṇu, or Nārāyaṇa, represents pure spiritual goodness, which brings one realization of the spiritual world, freedom from fear, and spiritual bliss. Such benefits can never be derived from impure, material goodness, for it is always mixed with the modes of passion and ignorance. As clearly indicated in this verse, the transcendental form of God is fully constituted of eternal spiritual goodness and thus has no tinge of the material mode of goodness, passion or ignorance.

TEXT 47

तस्मै नमो भगवते पुरुषाय भूम्ने
विश्वाय विश्वगुरवे परदैवताय ।
नारायणाय ऋषये च नरोत्तमाय
हंसाय संयतगिरे निगमेश्वराय ॥ ४७ ॥

tasmai namo bhagavate puruṣāya bhūmne
viśvāya viśva-gurave para-daivatāya
nārāyaṇāya ṛṣaye ca narottamāya
haṁsāya saṁyata-gire nigameśvarāya

tasmai — to Him; *namaḥ*—my obeisances; *bhagavate* — to the Godhead; *puruṣāya* — the Supreme Person; *bhūmne* — the all-pervading one; *viśvāya*

— the all-inclusive manifestation of the universe; *viśva-gurave* — the spiritual master of the universe; *para-daivatāya* — the supremely worshipable Deity; *nārāyaṇāya* — to Lord Nārāyaṇa; *ṛṣaye* — the sage; *ca* — and; *nara-uttamāya* — to the best of human beings; *haṁsāya* — situated in perfect purity; *saṁyata-gire* — who has controlled his speech; *nigama-īśvarāya* — the master of the Vedic scriptures.

TRANSLATION

I offer my humble obeisances to Him, the Supreme Personality of Godhead. He is the all-pervading and all-inclusive form of the universe, as well as its spiritual master. I bow down to Lord Nārāyaṇa, the supremely worshipable Deity appearing as a sage, and also to the saintly Nara, the best of human beings, who is fixed in perfect goodness, fully in control of his speech, and the propagator of the Vedic literatures.

TEXT 48

यं वै न वेद वितथाक्षपथैर्भ्रमद्धीः
सन्तं स्वकेष्वसुषु हृद्यपि दृक्पथेषु ।
तन्माययावृतमतिः स उ एव साक्षाद्
आद्यस्तवाखिलगुरोरुपसाद्य वेदम् ॥ ४८ ॥

yaṁ vai na veda vitathākṣa-pathair bhramad-dhīḥ
santaṁ svakeṣv asuṣu hṛdy api dṛk-patheṣu
tan-māyayāvṛta-matiḥ sa u eva sākṣād
ādyas tavākhila-guror upasādya vedam

yam — whom; *vai* — indeed; *na veda* — does not recognize; *vitatha* — deceptive; *akṣa-pathaiḥ* — by methods of empirical perception; *bhramat* — becoming diverted; *dhīḥ* — whose intelligence; *santam* — present; *svakeṣu* — within one's own; *asuṣu* — senses; *hṛdi* — within the heart; *api* — even; *dṛk-patheṣu* — among perceived objects of the external world; *tat-māyayā* — by His illusory potency; *āvṛta* — covered over; *matiḥ* — his understanding; *saḥ* — he; *u* — even; *eva* — indeed; *sākṣāt* — directly; *ādyaḥ* — originally (in ignorance); *tava* — of You; *akhila-guroḥ* — the spiritual master of all living beings; *upasādya* — obtaining; *vedam* — the knowledge of the *Vedas.*

TRANSLATION

A materialist, his intelligence perverted by the action of his deceptive senses, cannot recognize You at all, although You are always present within his own senses and heart and also among the objects of his perception. Yet even though one's understanding has been covered by Your illusory potency, if one obtains Vedic knowledge from You, the supreme spiritual master of all, he can directly understand You.

TEXT 49

यद्दर्शनं निगम आत्मरहःप्रकाशं
मुह्यन्ति यत्र कवयोऽजपरा यतन्तः ।
तं सर्ववादविषयप्रतिरूपशीलं
वन्दे महापुरुषमात्मनिगूढबोधम् ॥ ४९ ॥

yad-darśanaṁ nigama ātma-rahaḥ-prakāśaṁ
muhyanti yatra kavayo'ja-parā yatantaḥ
taṁ sarva-vāda-viṣaya-pratirūpa-śīlaṁ
vande mahā-puruṣam ātma-nigūḍha-bodham

yat — of whom; *darśanam* — the vision; *nigame* — in the *Vedas; ātma* — of the Supreme Soul; *rahaḥ*— the mystery; *prakāśam* — which reveals; *muhyanti* — become bewildered; *yatra* — about which; *kavayaḥ*— great learned authorities; *aja-parāḥ*— headed by Brahmā; *yatantaḥ*— endeavoring; *tam* — to Him; *sarva-vāda* — of all different philosophies; *viṣaya* — the subject matter; *pratirūpa* — adjusting itself as suitable; *śīlam* — whose personal nature; *vande* — I offer my homage; *mahā-puruṣam* — to the Supreme Personality of Godhead; *ātma* — from the spirit soul; *nigūḍha* — hidden; *bodham* — understanding.

TRANSLATION

My dear Lord, the Vedic literatures alone reveal confidential knowledge of Your supreme personality, and thus even such great scholars as Lord Brahmā himself are bewildered in their attempt to understand You through empirical methods. Each philosopher understands You according to his particular speculative conclusions. I worship that Supreme Person, knowledge of whom is hidden by the bodily designations covering the conditioned soul's spiritual identity.

PURPORT

Even great demigods like Brahmā are bewildered in their speculative attempts to understand the Supreme Personality of Godhead. Each philosopher is covered by a unique combination of the modes of nature and thus describes the Supreme Truth according to his own material conditioning. Therefore even strenuous empirical endeavor will never bring one to the conclusion of all knowledge. The highest knowledge is Kṛṣṇa, the Supreme Personality of Godhead, and one can understand Him only by fully surrendering to Him and serving Him with love. This is why Mārkaṇḍeya Ṛṣi states here, *vande mahā-puruṣam:* "I simply worship that Supreme Personality." Those who try to worship God but at the same time continue speculating or acting fruitively will attain only mixed and bewildering results. To be pure a devotee must give up all fruitive activity and mental speculation; in that way his loving service to the Lord will yield perfect knowledge of the Supreme. Only this perfection can satisfy the eternal soul.

Thus end the purports of the humble servants of His Divine Grace A.C. Bhaktivedanta Swami Prabhupāda to the Twelfth Canto, Eighth Chapter, of the Śrīmad-Bhāgavatam, *entitled "Mārkaṇḍeya's Prayers to Nara-Nārāyaṇa Ṛṣi."*

CHAPTER NINE

Mārkaṇḍeya Ṛṣi Sees the Illusory Potency of the Lord

This chapter describes Mārkaṇḍeya Ṛṣi's vision of the Supreme Personality of Godhead's illusory energy.

Satisfied by the prayers Śrī Mārkaṇḍeya had offered, the Supreme Lord told him to ask for a benediction, and the sage said he wanted to see the Lord's illusory energy. The Supreme Lord Śrī Hari, present before Mārkaṇḍeya in the form of Nara-Nārāyaṇa, replied, "So be it," and then left for Badarikāśrama. One day, as Śrī Mārkaṇḍeya was offering his evening prayers, the water of devastation suddenly flooded the three worlds. With great difficulty Mārkaṇḍeya moved about all alone in this water for a long time, until he came upon a banyan tree. Lying upon a leaf of that tree was an infant boy glowing with a charming effulgence. As Mārkaṇḍeya moved toward the leaf, he was pulled by the boy's inhalation and, just like a mosquito, drawn within His body.

Inside the boy's body, Mārkaṇḍeya was amazed to see the entire universe just as it had been before the annihilation. After a moment the sage was carried out by the force of the child's exhalation and hurled back into the ocean of annihilation. Then, seeing that the child on the leaf was actually Śrī Hari, the transcendental Lord situated within his own heart, Śrī Mārkaṇḍeya tried to embrace Him. But at that moment Lord Hari, the master of all mystic power, disappeared. Then the waters of annihilation disappeared as well, and Śrī Mārkaṇḍeya found himself in his own *āśrama,* just as before.

TEXT 1

सूत उवाच
संस्तुतो भगवानित्थं मार्कण्डेयेन धीमता।
नारायणो नरसखः प्रीत आह भृगूद्वहम् ॥१॥

sūta uvāca
saṁstuto bhagavān itthaṁ
mārkaṇḍeyena dhīmatā
nārāyaṇo nara-sakhaḥ
prīta āha bhṛgūdvaham

sūtaḥ uvāca — Sūta Gosvāmī said; *saṁstutaḥ*— properly glorified; *bhagavān* — the Supreme Lord; *ittham* — in this way; *mārkaṇḍeyena* — by Mārkaṇḍeya; *dhī-matā* — the intelligent sage; *nārāyaṇaḥ*— Lord Nārāyaṇa; *nara-sakhaḥ*— the friend of Nara; *prītaḥ*— satisfied; *āha* — spoke; *bhṛgu-udvaham* — to the most eminent descendant of Bhṛgu.

TRANSLATION

Sūta Gosvāmī said: The Supreme Lord Nārāyaṇa, the friend of Nara, was satisfied by the proper glorification offered by the intelligent sage Mārkaṇḍeya. Thus the Lord addressed that excellent descendant of Bhṛgu.

TEXT 2

श्रीभगवानुवाच

भो भो ब्रह्मर्षिवर्योऽसि सिद्ध आत्मसमाधिना ।
मयि भक्त्यानपायिन्या तपःस्वाध्यायसंयमैः ॥ २ ॥

śrī-bhagavān uvāca
bho bho brahmarṣi-varyo 'si
siddha ātma-samādhinā
mayi bhaktyānapāyinyā
tapaḥ-svādhyāya-saṁyamaiḥ

śrī-bhagavān uvāca — the Supreme Personality of Godhead said; *bhoḥ bhoḥ*— dear sage; *brahma-ṛṣi* — of all learned *brāhmaṇas; varyaḥ*— the best; *asi* — you are; *siddhaḥ*— perfect; *ātma-samādhinā* — by fixed meditation upon the Self; *mayi* — directed toward Me; *bhaktyā* — by devotional service; *anapāyinyā* — undeviating; *tapaḥ*— by austerities; *svādhyāya* — study of the *Vedas; saṁyamaiḥ*— and regulative principles.

TRANSLATION

The Supreme Personality of Godhead said: My dear Mārkaṇḍeya, you are indeed the best of all learned brāhmaṇas. You have perfected your life by practicing fixed meditation upon the Supreme Soul, as well as by focusing upon Me your undeviating devotional service, your austerities, your study of the Vedas and your strict adherence to regulative principles.

TEXT 3

वयं ते परितुष्टाः स्म त्वद्बृहद्व्रतचर्यया ।
वरं प्रतीच्छ भद्रं ते वरदोऽस्मि त्वदीप्सितम् ॥ ३ ॥

vayaṁ te parituṣṭāḥ sma
tvad-bṛhad-vrata-caryayā
varaṁ pratīccha bhadraṁ te
vara-do 'smi tvad-īpsitam

vayam — We; *te* — with you; *parituṣṭāḥ*— perfectly satisfied; *sma* — have become; *tvat* — your; *bṛhat-vrata* — of the vow of lifelong celibacy; *caryayā* — by performance; *varam* — a benediction; *pratīccha* — please choose; *bhadram* — all good; *te* — unto you; *vara-daḥ*— the giver of benedictions; *asmi* — I am; *tvat-īpsitam* — desired by you.

TRANSLATION

We are perfectly satisfied with your practice of lifelong celibacy. Please choose whatever benediction you desire, since I can grant your wish. May you enjoy all good fortune.

PURPORT

Śrīla Viśvanātha Cakravartī Ṭhākura explains that the Lord used the plural form in the beginning of this verse — "We are satisfied" — because He was referring to Himself along with Śiva and Umā, who will later be glorified by Mārkaṇḍeya. The Lord then used the singular — "I am the bestower of benedictions" — because ultimately only Lord Nārāyaṇa (Kṛṣṇa) can award the highest perfection of life, eternal Kṛṣṇa consciousness.

TEXT 4

श्रीऋषिरुवाच
जितं ते देवदेवेश प्रपन्नार्तिहराच्युत ।
वरेणैतावतालं नो यद् भवान् समदृश्यत ॥ ४ ॥

śrī-ṛṣir uvāca
jitaṁ te deva-deveśa
prapannārti-harācyuta
vareṇaitāvatālaṁ no
yad bhavān samadṛśyata

śrī-ṛṣiḥ uvāca — the sage said; *jitam* — are victorious; *te* — You; *deva-deva-īśa* — O Lord of lords; *prapanna* — of one who is surrendered; *ārti-hara* — O remover of all distress; *acyuta* — O infallible one; *vareṇa* — with the benediction; *etāvatā* — this much; *alam* — enough; *naḥ*—by us; *yat* — that; *bhavān* — Your good self; *samadṛśyata* — has been seen.

TRANSLATION

The sage said: O Lord of lords, all glories to You! O Lord Acyuta, You remove all distress for the devotees who surrender unto You. That you have allowed me to see You is all the benediction I want.

TEXT 5

गृहीत्वाजादयो यस्य श्रीमत्पादाब्जदर्शनम् ।
मनसा योगपक्वेन स भवान्मेऽक्षिगोचरः ॥ ५ ॥

gṛhītvājādayo yasya
śrīmat-pādābja-darśanam
manasā yoga-pakvena
sa bhavān me'kṣi-gocaraḥ

gṛhītvā — receiving; *aja-ādayaḥ*—(became) Brahmā and others; *yasya* — whose; *śrīmat* — all-opulent; *pāda-abja* — of the lotus feet; *darśanam* — the sight; *manasā* — by the mind; *yoga-pakvena* — matured in *yoga* practice; *saḥ*—He; *bhavān* — Yourself; *me* — my; *akṣi* — to the eyes; *go-caraḥ*—perceptible.

TRANSLATION

Such demigods as Lord Brahmā achieved their exalted positions simply by seeing Your beautiful lotus feet after their minds had become mature in yoga practice. And now, my Lord, You have personally appeared before me.

PURPORT

Mārkaṇḍeya Ṛṣi points out that exalted demigods like Lord Brahmā achieved their positions simply by glimpsing the Lord's lotus feet, and yet Mārkaṇḍeya Ṛṣi was now able to see Lord Kṛṣṇa's entire body. Thus he could not even imagine the extent of his good fortune.

TEXT 6

अथाप्यम्बुजपत्राक्ष पुण्यश्लोकशिखामणे ।
द्रक्ष्ये मायां यया लोकः सपालो वेद सद्भिदाम् ॥ ६ ॥

athāpy ambuja-patrākṣa
puṇya-śloka-śikhāmaṇe
drakṣye māyāṁ yayā lokaḥ
sa-pālo veda sad-bhidām

atha api — nonetheless; *ambuja-patra* — like the petals of a lotus; *akṣa* — O You whose eyes; *puṇya-śloka* — of famous personalities; *śikhāmaṇe* — O crest jewel; *drakṣye* — I desire to see; *māyām* — the illusory energy; *yayā* — by which; *lokaḥ* — the entire world; *sa-pālaḥ* — along with its ruling demigods; *veda* — considers; *sat* — of the absolute reality; *bhidām* — material differentiation.

TRANSLATION

O lotus-eyed Lord, O crest jewel of renowned personalities, although I am satisfied simply by seeing You, I do wish to see Your illusory potency, by whose influence the entire world, together with its ruling demigods, considers reality to be materially variegated.

PURPORT

A conditioned soul sees the material world to be constituted of independent, separate entities. Actually, all things are united, being potencies of the Supreme Lord. Mārkaṇḍeya Ṛṣi is curious to witness the exact process by which *māyā,* the Lord's bewildering potency, casts living beings into illusion.

TEXT 7

सूत उवाच
इतीडितोऽर्चितः काममृषिणा भगवान्मुने ।
तथेति स स्मयन् प्रागाद् बदर्याश्रममीश्वरः ॥ ७ ॥

sūta uvāca
itīḍito 'rcitaḥ kāmam
ṛṣiṇā bhagavān mune
tatheti sa smayan prāgād
badary-āśramam īśvaraḥ

sūtaḥ uvāca — Sūta Gosvāmī said; *iti* — in these words; *īḍitaḥ*—glorified; *arcitaḥ*—worshiped; *kāmam* — satisfactorily; *ṛṣiṇā* — by the sage Mārkaṇḍeya; *bhagavān* — the Personality of Godhead; *mune* — O wise Śaunaka; *tathā iti*—"so be it"; *saḥ*—He; *smayan* — smiling; *prāgāt* — departed; *badarī-āśramam* — for the hermitage Badarikāśrama; *īśvaraḥ*—the Supreme Lord.

TRANSLATION

Sūta Gosvāmī said: O wise Śaunaka, thus satisfied by Mārkaṇḍeya's praise and worship, the Supreme Personality of Godhead, smiling, replied, "So be it," and then departed for His hermitage at Badarikāśrama.

PURPORT

The words *bhagavān* and *īśvara* in this verse refer to the Supreme Lord in His incarnation as the twin sages Nara and Nārāyaṇa. According to Śrīla Viśvanātha Cakravartī Ṭhākura, the Supreme Lord smiled ruefully, because He prefers that His pure devotees stay away from His illusory energy. Curiosity to see the illusory energy of the Lord sometimes develops into sinful material desire. Nonetheless, to please His devotee Mārkaṇḍeya, the Lord granted his request, just as a father who cannot convince his son to give up pursuing a harmful desire may let him experience some painful reaction so that he will then voluntarily desist. Thus, understanding what would soon happen to Mārkaṇḍeya, the Lord smiled as He prepared to display the illusory potency to him.

TEXTS 8–9

तमेव चिन्तयन्नर्थमृषिः स्वाश्रम एव सः ।
वसन्नग्न्यर्कसोमाम्बुभूवायुवियदात्मसु ॥ ८ ॥
ध्यायन् सर्वत्र च हरिं भावद्रव्यैरपूजयत् ।
क्वचित् पूजां विसस्मार प्रेमप्रसरसम्प्लुतः ॥ ९ ॥

tam eva cintayann artham
ṛṣiḥ svāśrama eva saḥ
vasann agny-arka-somāmbu-
bhū-vāyu-viyad-ātmasu

dhyāyan sarvatra ca hariṁ
bhāva-dravyair apūjayat

kvacit pūjāṁ visasmāra
prema-prasara-samplutaḥ

tam — that; *eva* — indeed; *cintayan* — thinking of; *artham* — the goal; *ṛṣiḥ*—the sage Mārkaṇḍeya; *sva-āśrame* — at his own hermitage; *eva* — indeed; *saḥ*—he; *vasan* — remaining; *agni* — in the fire; *arka* — the sun; *soma* — the moon; *ambu* — the water; *bhū* — the earth; *vāyu* — the wind; *viyat* — the lightning; *ātmasu* — and in his own heart; *dhyāyan* — meditating; *sarvatra* — in all circumstances; *ca* — and; *harim* — upon Lord Hari; *bhāva-dravyaiḥ*—with paraphernalia conceived in his mind; *apūjayat* — he offered worship; *kvacit* — sometimes; *pūjām* — the worship; *visasmāra* — he forgot; *prema* — of pure love of God; *prasara* — in the flood; *samplutaḥ*—being drowned.

TRANSLATION

Thinking always of his desire to see the Lord's illusory energy, the sage remained in his āśrama, meditating constantly upon the Lord within fire, the sun, the moon, water, the earth, air, lightning and his own heart and worshiping Him with paraphernalia conceived in his mind. But sometimes, overwhelmed by waves of love for the Lord, Mārkaṇḍeya would forget to perform his regular worship.

PURPORT

It is apparent from these verses that Mārkaṇḍeya Ṛṣi was a great devotee of Lord Kṛṣṇa; therefore he wanted to see the illusory energy of the Lord not to fulfill some material ambition but to learn how His potency is working.

TEXT 10

तस्यैकदा भृगुश्रेष्ठ पुष्पभद्रातटे मुनेः ।
उपासीनस्य सन्ध्यायां ब्रह्मन् वायुरभून्महान् ॥१०॥

tasyaikadā bhṛgu-śreṣṭha
puṣpabhadrā-taṭe muneḥ
upāsīnasya sandhyāyāṁ
brahman vāyur abhūn mahān

tasya — while he; *ekadā* — one day; *bhṛgu-śreṣṭha* — O best of the descendants of Bhṛgu; *puṣpabhadrā-taṭe* — on the bank of the river Puṣpabhadrā; *muneḥ*—the sage; *upāsīnasya* — was performing worship; *sandhyāyām* — at the juncture of the day; *brahman* — O *brāhmaṇa; vāyuḥ*—a wind; *abhūt* — arose; *mahān* — great.

TRANSLATION

O brāhmaṇa Śaunaka, best of the Bhṛgus, one day while Mārkaṇḍeya was performing his evening worship on the bank of the Puṣpabhadrā, a great wind suddenly arose.

TEXT 11

तं चण्डशब्दं समुदीरयन्तं
बलाहका अन्वभवन् करालाः ।
अक्षस्थविष्ठा मुमुचुस्तडिद्भिः
स्वनन्त उच्चैरभि वर्षधाराः ॥ ११ ॥

taṁ caṇḍa-śabdaṁ samudīrayantaṁ
balāhakā anv abhavan karālāḥ
akṣa-sthaviṣṭhā mumucus taḍidbhiḥ
svananta uccair abhi varṣa-dhārāḥ

tam — that wind; *caṇḍa-śabdam* — a terrible sound; *samudīrayantam* — which was creating; *balāhakāḥ*—clouds; *anu* — following it; *abhavan* — appeared; *karālāḥ*—fearful; *akṣa* — like wagon wheels; *sthaviṣṭhāḥ*—solid; *mumucuḥ*—they released; *taḍidbhiḥ*—along with lightning; *svanantaḥ*—resounding; *uccaiḥ*—greatly; *abhi* — in all directions; *varṣa* — of rain; *dhārāḥ*—torrents.

TRANSLATION

That wind created a terrible sound and brought in its wake fearsome clouds that were accompanied by lightning and roaring thunder and that poured down on all sides torrents of rain as heavy as wagon wheels.

TEXT 12

ततो व्यदृश्यन्त चतुःसमुद्राः
समन्ततः क्ष्मातलमाग्रसन्तः ।
समीरवेगोर्मिभिरुग्रनक्र-
महाभयावर्तगभीरघोषाः ॥ १२ ॥

tato vyadṛśyanta catuḥ samudrāḥ
samantataḥ kṣmā-talam āgrasantaḥ
samīra-vegormibhir ugra-nakra-
mahā-bhayāvarta-gabhīra-ghoṣāḥ

tataḥ—then; *vyadṛśyanta*—appeared; *catuḥ samudrāḥ*—the four oceans; *samantataḥ*—on all sides; *kṣmā-talam*—the surface of the earth; *āgrasantaḥ*—swallowing up; *samīra*—of the wind; *vega*—impelled by the force; *ūrmibhiḥ*—with their waves; *ugra*—terrible; *nakra*—with sea monsters; *mahā-bhaya*—very fearful; *āvarta*—with whirlpools; *gabhīra*—grave; *ghoṣāḥ*—with sounds.

TRANSLATION

Then the four great oceans appeared on all sides, swallowing up the surface of the earth with their wind-tossed waves. In these oceans were terrible sea monsters, fearful whirlpools and ominous rumblings.

TEXT 13

अन्तर्बहिश्चाद्भिरतिद्युभिः खरैः
शतह्रदाभिरुपतापितं जगत् ।
चतुर्विधं वीक्ष्य सहात्मना मुनिर्
जलाप्लुतां क्ष्मां विमनाः समत्रसत् ॥ १३ ॥

antar bahiś cādbhir ati-dyubhiḥ kharaiḥ
śatahradābhir upatāpitaṁ jagat
catur-vidhaṁ vīkṣya sahātmanā munir
jalāplutāṁ kṣmāṁ vimanāḥ samatrasat

antaḥ—internally; *bahiḥ*—externally; *ca*—and; *adbhiḥ*—by the water; *ati-dyubhiḥ*—rising higher than the sky; *kharaiḥ*—by the fierce (winds); *śata-hradābhiḥ*—by lightning bolts; *upatāpitam*—greatly distressed; *jagat*—all the inhabitants of the universe; *catuḥ-vidham*—of four varieties (those who have taken birth from embryos, from eggs, from seeds and from perspiration); *vīkṣya*—seeing; *saha*—along with; *ātmanā*—himself; *muniḥ*—the sage; *jala*—by the water; *āplutām*—flooded; *kṣmām*—the earth; *vimanāḥ*—perplexed; *samatrasat*—he became fearful.

TRANSLATION

The sage saw all the inhabitants of the universe, including himself, tormented within and without by the harsh winds, the bolts of lightning, and the great waves rising beyond the sky. As the whole earth flooded, he grew perplexed and fearful.

PURPORT

Here the word *catur-vidham* refers to the four sources of birth for conditioned souls: embryos, eggs, seeds and perspiration.

TEXT 14

तस्यैवमुद्वीक्षत ऊर्मिभीषणः
प्रभञ्जनाघूर्णितवार्महार्णवः ।
आपूर्यमाणो वरषद्भिरम्बुदैः
क्ष्मामप्यधाद् द्वीपवर्षाद्रिभिः समम् ॥१४॥

tasyaivam udvīkṣata ūrmi-bhīṣaṇaḥ
prabhañjanāghūrṇita-vār mahārṇavaḥ
āpūryamāṇo varaṣadbhir ambudaiḥ
kṣmām apyadhād dvīpa-varṣādribhiḥ samam

tasya — while he; *evam* — in this way; *udvīkṣataḥ*—was looking on; *urmi* — with its waves; *bhīṣaṇaḥ*—frightening; *prabhañjana* — by hurricane winds; *āghūrṇita* — swirled around; *vāḥ*—its water; *mahā-arṇavaḥ*—the great ocean; *āpūryamānaḥ*—becoming filled; *varaṣadbhiḥ*—with rain; *ambu-daiḥ*—by the clouds; *kṣmām* — the earth; *apyadhāt* — covered over; *dvīpa* — with its islands; *varṣa* — continents; *adribhiḥ*—and mountains; *samam* — together.

TRANSLATION

Even as Mārkaṇḍeya looked on, the rain pouring down from the clouds filled the ocean more and more until that great sea, its waters violently whipped into terrifying waves by hurricanes, covered up all the earth's islands, mountains and continents.

TEXT 15

सक्ष्मान्तरिक्षं सदिवं सभागणं
त्रैलोक्यमासीत् सह दिग्भिराप्लुतम् ।
स एक एवोर्वरितो महामुनिर्
बभ्राम विक्षिप्य जटा जडान्धवत् ॥१५॥

sa-kṣmāntarikṣaṁ sa-divaṁ sa-bhā-gaṇaṁ
trai-lokyam āsīt saha digbhir āplutam
sa eka evorvarito mahā-munir
babhrāma vikṣipya jaṭā jaḍāndha-vat

sa — along with; *kṣmā* — the earth; *antarikṣam* — and outer space; *sa-divam* — along with the heavenly planets; *sa-bhā-gaṇam* — along with all the celestial bodies; *trai-lokyam* — the three worlds; *āsīt* — became; *saha* — along with; *digbhiḥ*—all the directions; *āplutam* — flooded; *saḥ*—he; *ekaḥ* —alone; *eva* — indeed; *urvaritaḥ*—remaining; *mahā-muniḥ*—the great sage; *babhrāma* — wandered about; *vikṣipya* — scattering; *jaṭāḥ*—his matted locks; *jaḍa* — a dumb person; *andha* — a blind person; *vat* — like.

TRANSLATION

The water inundated the earth, outer space, heaven and the celestial region. Indeed, the entire expanse of the universe was flooded in all directions, and out of all its inhabitants only Mārkaṇḍeya remained. His matted hair scattered, the great sage wandered about alone in the water as if dumb and blind.

TEXT 16

क्षुत्तृट्परीतो मकरैस्तिमिंगिलैर्
उपद्रुतो वीचिनभस्वताहतः ।
तमस्यपारे पतितो भ्रमन् दिशो
न वेद खं गां च परिश्रमेषितः ॥ १६ ॥

kṣut-tṛṭ-parīto makarais timiṅgilair
upadruto vīci-nabhasvatāhataḥ
tamasy apāre patito bhraman diśo
na veda khaṁ gāṁ ca pariśrameṣitaḥ

kṣut — by hunger; *tṛṭ*—and thirst; *parītaḥ*—enveloped; *makaraiḥ*—by the *makaras,* a species of monster crocodile; *timiṅgilaiḥ*—and by the *timiṅgila,* a variety of huge fish that eats whales; *upadrutaḥ*—harassed; *vīci* — by the waves; *nabhasvatā* — and the wind; *āhataḥ*—tormented; *tamasi* — in the darkness; *apāre* — which was unlimited; *patitaḥ*—having fallen; *bhraman* — wandering; *diśaḥ*—the directions; *na veda* — did not recognize; *kham* — the sky; *gām* — the earth; *ca* — and; *pariśrama-iṣitaḥ*—overcome by exhaustion.

TRANSLATION

Tormented by hunger and thirst, attacked by monstrous makaras and timiṅgila fish and battered by the wind and waves, he moved aimlessly through the infinite darkness into which he had fallen. As he grew increasingly exhausted, he lost all sense of direction and could not tell the sky from the earth.

TEXTS 17–18

क्वचिन्मग्नो महावर्ते तरलैस्ताडितः क्वचित् ।
यादोभिर्भक्ष्यते क्वापि स्वयमन्योन्यघातिभिः ॥ १७ ॥
क्वचिच्छोकं क्वचिन्मोहं क्वचिद्दुःखं सुखं भयम् ।
क्वचिन्मृत्युमवाप्नोति व्याध्यादिभिरुतार्दितः ॥ १८ ॥

kracin magno mahāvarte
taralais tāḍitaḥ kvacit
yādobhir bhakṣyate kvāpi
svayam anyonya-ghātibhiḥ

kvacic chokaṁ kvacin mohaṁ
kvacid duḥkhaṁ sukhaṁ bhayam
kvacin mṛtyum avāpnoti
vyādhy-ādibhir utārditaḥ

kvacit — sometimes; *magnaḥ*—drowning; *mahā-āvarte* — in a great whirlpool; *taralaiḥ*—by the waves; *tāḍitaḥ*—beaten; *kvacit* — sometimes; *yādobhiḥ*—by the aquatic monsters; *bhakṣyate* — he was threatened with being eaten; *kva api* — sometimes; *svayam* — himself; *anyonya* — each other; *ghātibhiḥ*—attacking; *kvacit* — sometimes; *śokam* — depression;

kvacit — sometimes; *moham* — bewilderment; *kvacit* — sometimes; *duḥkham* — misery; *sukham* — happiness; *bhayam* — fear; *kvacit* — sometimes; *mṛtyum* — death; *avāpnoti* — he experienced; *vyādhi* — by disease; *ādibhiḥ*—and other pains; *uta* — also; *arditaḥ*—distressed.

TRANSLATION

At times he was engulfed by the great whirlpools, sometimes he was beaten by the mighty waves, and at other times the aquatic monsters threatened to devour him as they attacked one another. Sometimes he felt lamentation, bewilderment, misery, happiness or fear, and at other times he experienced such terrible illness and pain that he felt himself dying.

TEXT 19

अयुतायुतवर्षाणां सहस्राणि शतानि च ।
व्यतीयुर्भ्रमतस्तस्मिन् विष्णुमायावृतात्मनः ॥ १९ ॥

ayutāyuta-varṣāṇāṁ
sahasrāṇi śatāni ca
vyatīyur bhramatas tasmin
viṣṇu-māyāvṛtātmanaḥ

ayuta — tens of thousands; *ayuta* — by tens of thousands; *varṣāṇām* — of years; *sahasrāṇi* — thousands; *śatāni* — hundreds; *ca* — and; *vyatīyuḥ*— passed by; *bhramataḥ*—as he wandered; *tasmin* — in that; *viṣṇu-māyā* — by the illusory energy of Lord Viṣṇu; *āvṛta* — covered; *ātmanaḥ*—his mind.

TRANSLATION

Countless millions of years passed as Mārkaṇḍeya wandered about in that deluge, his mind bewildered by the illusory energy of Lord Viṣṇu, the Supreme Personality of Godhead.

TEXT 20

स कदाचिद् भ्रमंस्तस्मिन् पृथिव्याः ककुदि द्विजः ।
न्यग्रोधपोतं ददृशे फलपल्लवशोभितम् ॥ २० ॥

sa kadācid bhramaṁs tasmin
pṛthivyāḥ kakudi dvijaḥ
nyāgrodha-potaṁ dadṛśe
phala-pallava-śobhitam

saḥ—he; *kadācit* — on one occasion; *bhraman* — while wandering; *tasmin* — in that water; *pṛthivyāḥ*—of earth; *kakudi* — upon a raised place; *dvijaḥ*—the *brāhmaṇa; nyāgrodha-potam* — a young banyan tree; *dadṛśe* — saw; *phala* — with fruits; *pallava* — and blossoms; *śobhitam* — decorated.

TRANSLATION

Once, while wandering in the water, the brāhmaṇa Mārkaṇḍeya discovered a small island, upon which stood a young banyan tree bearing blossoms and fruits.

TEXT 21

प्रागुत्तरस्यां शाखायां तस्यापि ददृशे शिशुम् ।
शयानं पर्णपुटके ग्रसन्तं प्रभया तमः ॥ २१ ॥

prāg-uttarasyāṁ śākhāyāṁ
tasyāpi dadṛśe śiśum
śayānaṁ parṇa-puṭake
grasantaṁ prabhayā tamaḥ

prāk-uttarasyām — toward the northeast; *śākhāyām* — upon a branch; *tasya* — of that tree; *api* — indeed; *dadṛśe* — he saw; *śiśum* — an infant boy; *śayānam* — lying; *parṇa-puṭake* — within the concavity of a leaf; *grasantam* — swallowing; *prabhayā* — with His effulgence; *tamaḥ*—the darkness.

TRANSLATION

Upon a branch of the northeast portion of that tree he saw an infant boy lying within a leaf. The child's effulgence was swallowing up the darkness.

TEXTS 22–25

महामरकतश्यामं श्रीमद्वदनपंकजम् ।
कम्बुग्रीवं महोरस्कं सुनासं सुन्दरभ्रुवम् ॥ २२ ॥
श्वासैजदलकाभातं कम्बुश्रीकर्णदाडिमम् ।
विद्रुमाधरभासेषच्छोणायितसुधास्मितम् ॥ २३ ॥
पद्मगर्भारुणापांगं हृद्यहासावलोकनम् ।
श्वासैजद्वलिसंविग्ननिम्ननाभिदलोदरम् ॥ २४ ॥

चार्वंगुलिभ्यां पाणिभ्यामुन्नीय चरणाम्बुजम् ।
मुखे निधाय विप्रेन्द्रो धयन्तं वीक्ष्य विस्मितः ॥ २५ ॥

mahā-marakata-śyāmaṁ
śrīmad-vadana-paṅkajam
kambu-grīvaṁ mahoraskaṁ
su-nasaṁ sundara-bhruvam

śvāsaijad-alakābhātaṁ
kambu-śrī-karṇa-dāḍimam
vidrumādhara-bhāseṣac-
choṇāyita-sudhā-smitam

padma-garbhāruṇāpāṅgaṁ
hṛdya-hāsāvalokanam
śvāsaijad-vali-saṁvigna-
nimna-nābhi-dalodaram

cārv-aṅgulibhyāṁ pāṇibhyām
unnīya caraṇāmbujam
mukhe nidhāya viprendro
dhayantaṁ vīkṣya vismitaḥ

mahā-marakata — like a great emerald; *śyāmam* — dark blue; *śrīmat* — beautiful; *vadana-paṅkajam* — whose lotus face; *kambu* — like a conchshell; *grīvam* — whose throat; *mahā* — broad; *uraskam* — whose chest; *su-nasam* — having a beautiful nose; *sundara-bhruvam* — having beautiful eyebrows; *śvāsa* — by His breath; *ejat* — trembling; *alaka* — with the hair; *ābhātam* — splendid; *kambu* — like a conchshell; *śrī* — beautiful; *karṇa* — His ears; *dāḍimam* — resembling pomegranate flowers; *vidruma* — like coral; *adhara* — of His lips; *bhāsā* — by the effulgence; *īṣat* — slightly; *śoṇāyita* — reddened; *sudhā* — nectarean; *smitam* — His smile; *padma-garbha* — like the whorl of a lotus; *aruṇa* — reddish; *apāṅgam* — the corners of His eyes; *hṛdya* — charming; *hāsa* — with a smile; *avalokanam* — His countenance; *śvāsa* — by His breath; *ejat* — made to move; *vali* — by the lines; *saṁvigna* — contorted; *nimna* — deep; *nābhi* — with His navel; *dala* — like a leaf; *udaram* — whose abdomen; *cāru* — attractive; *aṅgulibhyām* — having fingers; *pāṇibhyām* — by His two hands; *unnīya* — picking up; *caraṇa-ambujam* — His lotus foot;

mukhe — in His mouth; *nidhāya* — placing; *vipra-indraḥ*—the best of *brāhmaṇas,* Mārkaṇḍeya; *dhayantam* — drinking; *vīkṣya* — seeing; *vismitaḥ*— was amazed.

TRANSLATION

The infant's dark-blue complexion was the color of a flawless emerald, His lotus face shone with a wealth of beauty, and His throat bore marks like the lines on a conchshell. He had a broad chest, a finely shaped nose, beautiful eyebrows, and lovely ears that resembled pomegranate flowers and that had inner folds like a conchshell's spirals. The corners of His eyes were reddish like the whorl of a lotus, and the effulgence of His corallike lips slightly reddened the nectarean, enchanting smile on His face. As He breathed, His splendid hair trembled and His deep navel became distorted by the moving folds of skin on His abdomen, which resembled a banyan leaf. The exalted brāhmaṇa watched with amazement as the infant took hold of one of His lotus feet with His graceful fingers, placed a toe within His mouth and began to suck.

PURPORT

The young child was the Supreme Personality of Godhead. According to Śrīla Viśvanātha Cakravartī Ṭhākura, Lord Kṛṣṇa wondered, "So many devotees are hankering for the nectar of My lotus feet. Therefore let Me personally experience that nectar." Thus the Lord, playing like an ordinary baby, began to suck on His toes.

TEXT 26

तद्दर्शनाद् वीतपरिश्रमो मुदा
प्रोत्फुल्लहृत्पद्मविलोचनाम्बुजः ।
प्रहृष्टरोमाद्भुतभावशंकितः
प्रष्टुं पुरस्तं प्रससार बालकम् ॥ २६ ॥

tad-darśanād vīta-pariśramo mudā
protphulla-hṛt-padma-vilocanāmbujaḥ
prahṛṣṭa-romādbhuta-bhāva-śaṅkitaḥ
praṣṭuṁ puras taṁ prasasāra bālakam

tat-darśanāt — by seeing the child; *vīta* — dispelled; *pariśramaḥ*—his weariness; *mudā* — out of pleasure; *protphulla* — expanded wide; *hṛt-padma*

— the lotus of his heart; *vilocana-ambujaḥ* — and his lotus eyes; *prahṛṣṭa* — standing on end; *romā* — the hairs on his body; *adbhuta-bhāva* — about the identity of this wonderful form; *śaṅkitaḥ* — confused; *praṣṭum* — in order to inquire; *puraḥ* — in front; *tam* — of Him; *prasasāra* — he approached; *bālakam* — the child.

TRANSLATION

As Mārkaṇḍeya beheld the child, all his weariness vanished. Indeed, so great was his pleasure that the lotus of his heart, along with his lotus eyes, fully blossomed and the hairs on his body stood on end. Confused as to the identity of the wonderful infant, the sage approached Him.

PURPORT

Mārkaṇḍeya wanted to ask the child about His identity and therefore approached Him.

TEXT 27

तावच्छिशोर्वै श्वसितेन भार्गवः
सोऽन्तः शरीरं मशको यथाविशत् ।
तत्राप्यदो न्यस्तमचष्ट कृत्स्नशो
यथा पुरामुह्यदतीव विस्मितः ॥ २७ ॥

tāvac chiśor vai śvasitena bhārgavaḥ
so 'ntaḥ śarīraṁ maśako yathāviśat
tatrāpy ado nyastam acaṣṭa kṛtsnaśo
yathā purāmuhyad atīva vismitaḥ

tāvat — at that very moment; *śiśoḥ* — of the infant; *vai* — indeed; *śvasitena* — with the breathing; *bhārgavaḥ* — the descendant of Bhṛgu; *saḥ* — he; *antaḥ śarīram* — within the body; *maśakaḥ* — a mosquito; *yathā* — just like; *aviśat* — entered; *tatra* — therein; *api* — indeed; *adaḥ* — this universe; *nyastam* — placed; *acaṣṭa* — he saw; *kṛtsnaśaḥ* — entire; *yathā* — as; *purā* — previously; *amuhyat* — he became bewildered; *atīva* — extremely; *vismitaḥ* — surprised.

TRANSLATION

Just then the child inhaled, drawing Mārkaṇḍeya within His body like a mosquito. There the sage found the entire universe arrayed as it had

been before its dissolution. Seeing this, Mārkaṇḍeya was most astonished and perplexed.

TEXTS 28–29

खं रोदसी भागणानद्रिसागरान्
द्वीपान् सवर्षान् ककुभः सुरासुरान् ।
वनानि देशान् सरितः पुराकरान्
खेटान् व्रजानाश्रमवर्णवृत्तयः ॥ २८ ॥
महान्ति भूतान्यथ भौतिकान्यसौ
कालं च नानायुगकल्पकल्पनम् ।
यत् किञ्चिदन्यद् व्यवहारकारणं
ददर्श विश्वं सदिवावभासितम् ॥ २९ ॥

khaṁ rodasī bhā-gaṇān adri-sāgarān
dvīpān sa-varṣān kakubhaḥ surāsurān
vanāni deśān saritaḥ purākarān
kheṭān vrajān āśrama-varṇa-vṛttayaḥ

mahānti bhūtāny atha bhautikāny asau
kālaṁ ca nānā-yuga-kalpa-kalpanam
yat kiñcid anyad vyavahāra-kāraṇaṁ
dadarśa viśvaṁ sad ivāvabhāsitam

kham — the sky; *rodasī* — the heavens and earth; *bhā-gaṇān* — all the stars; *adri* — the mountains; *sāgarān* — and oceans; *dvīpān* — the great islands; *sa-varṣān* — along with the continents; *kakubhaḥ* — the directions; *sura-asurān* — the saintly devotees and the demons; *vanāni* — the forests; *deśān* — the various countries; *saritaḥ* — the rivers; *pura* — the cities; *ākarān* — and the mines; *kheṭān* — the agricultural villages; *vrajān* — the cow pastures; *āśrama-varṇa* — of the various spiritual and occupational divisions of society; *vṛttayaḥ* — the engagements; *mahānti bhūtāni* — the basic elements of nature; *atha* — and; *bhautikāni* — all their gross manifestations; *asau* — he; *kālam* — time; *ca* — also; *nānā-yuga-kalpa* — of the different millennia and the days of Brahmā; *kalpanam* — the regulating agent; *yat kiñcit* — whatever; *anyat* — other; *vyavahāra-kāraṇam* — object intended for use in material life; *dadarśa* — he saw; *viśvam* — the universe; *sat* — real; *iva* — as if; *avabhāsitam* — manifest.

TRANSLATION

The sage saw the entire universe: the sky, heavens and earth, the stars, mountains, oceans, great islands and continents, the expanses in every direction, the saintly and demoniac living beings, the forests, countries, rivers, cities and mines, the agricultural villages and cow pastures, and the occupational and spiritual activities of the various social divisions. He also saw the basic elements of creation along with all their by-products, as well as time itself, which regulates the progression of countless ages within the days of Brahmā. In addition, he saw everything else created for use in material life. All this he saw manifested before him as if it were real.

TEXT 30

हिमालयं पुष्पवहां च तां नदीं
निजाश्रमं यत्र ऋषी अपश्यत ।
विश्वं विपश्यञ्छ्‌वसिताच्छिशोर्वै
बहिर्निरस्तो न्यपतल्लयाब्धौ ॥ ३० ॥

himālayaṁ puṣpavahāṁ ca tāṁ nadīṁ
nijāśramaṁ yatra ṛṣī apaśyata
viśvaṁ vipaśyañ chvasitāc chiśor vai
bahir nirasto nyapatal layābdhau

himālayam — the Himālaya Mountains; *puṣpa-vahām* — Puṣpabhadrā; *ca* — and; *tām* — that; *nadīm* — river; *nija-āśramam* — his own hermitage; *yatra* — where; *ṛṣī* — the two sages, Nara-Nārāyaṇa; *apaśyata* — he saw; *viśvam* — the universe; *vipaśyan* — while observing; *śvasitāt* — by the breath; *śiśoḥ* — of the infant; *vai* — indeed; *bahiḥ* — outside; *nirastaḥ* — expelled; *nyapatat* — he fell; *laya-abdhau* — into the ocean of dissolution.

TRANSLATION

He saw before him the Himālaya Mountains, the Puṣpabhadrā River, and his own hermitage, where he had had the audience of the sages Nara-Nārāyaṇa. Then, as Mārkaṇḍeya beheld the entire universe, the infant exhaled, expelling the sage from His body and casting him back into the ocean of dissolution.

TEXTS 31–32

तस्मिन् पृथिव्याः ककुदि प्ररूढं
वटं च तत्पर्णपुटे शयानम् ।
तोकं च तत्प्रेमसुधास्मितेन
निरीक्षितोऽपांगनिरीक्षणेन ॥ ३१ ॥
अथ तं बालकं वीक्ष्य नेत्राभ्यां धिष्ठितं हृदि ।
अभ्ययादतिसक्लिष्टः परिष्वक्तुमधोक्षजम् ॥ ३२ ॥

tasmin pṛthivyāḥ kakudi prarūḍhaṁ
vaṭaṁ ca tat-parṇa-puṭe śayānam
tokaṁ ca tat-prema-sudhā-smitena
nirīkṣito 'pāṅga-nirīkṣaṇena

atha taṁ bālakaṁ vīkṣya
netrābhyāṁ dhiṣṭhitaṁ hṛdi
abhyayād ati-saṅkliṣṭaḥ
pariṣvaktum adhokṣajam

tasmin — in that water; *pṛthivyāḥ* — of land; *kakudi* — on the raised place; *prarūḍham* — growing up; *vaṭam* — the banyan tree; *ca* — and; *tat* — of it; *parṇa-puṭe* — within the slight depression of the leaf; *śayānam* — lying; *tokam* — the child; *ca* — and; *tat* — for himself; *prema* — of love; *sudhā* — like nectar; *smitena* — with a smile; *nirīkṣitaḥ* — being looked upon; *apāṅga* — of the corner of His eyes; *nirīkṣaṇena* — by the glance; *atha* — then; *tam* — that; *bālakam* — infant; *vīkṣya* — looking upon; *netrābhyām* — by his eyes; *dhiṣṭhitam* — placed; *hṛdi* — within his heart; *abhyayāt* — ran forward; *ati-saṅkliṣṭaḥ* — greatly agitated; *pariṣvaktum* — to embrace; *adhokṣajam* — the transcendental Supreme Lord.

TRANSLATION

In that vast sea he again saw the banyan tree growing on the tiny island and the infant boy lying within the leaf. The child glanced at him from the corner of His eyes with a smile imbued with the nectar of love, and Mārkaṇḍeya took Him into his heart through his eyes. Greatly agitated, the sage ran to embrace the transcendental Personality of Godhead.

TEXT 33

तावत् स भगवान् साक्षाद् योगाधीशो गुहाशयः ।
अन्तर्दध ऋषेः सद्यो यथेहानीशनिर्मिता ॥ ३३ ॥

tāvat sa bhagavān sākṣād
yogādhīśo guhā-śayaḥ
antardadha ṛṣeḥ sadyo
yathehānīśa-nirmitā

tāvat — just then; *saḥ*—He; *bhagavān* — the Personality of Godhead; *sākṣāt* — directly; *yoga-adhīśaḥ*—the supreme master of *yoga; guhā-śayaḥ* —who is hidden within the heart of all living beings; *antardadhe* — disappeared; *ṛṣeḥ*—in front of the sage; *sadyaḥ*—suddenly; *yathā* — in the same way as; *īhā* — the object of endeavor; *anīśa* — by an incompetent person; *nirmitā* — created.

TRANSLATION

At that moment the Supreme Personality of Godhead, who is the original master of all mysticism and who is hidden within everyone's heart, became invisible to the sage, just as the achievements of an incompetent person can suddenly vanish.

TEXT 34

तमन्वथ वटो ब्रह्मन् सलिलं लोकसम्प्लवः ।
तिरोधायि क्षणादस्य स्वाश्रमे पूर्ववत् स्थितः ॥ ३४ ॥

tam anv atha vaṭo brahman
salilaṁ loka-samplavaḥ
tirodhāyi kṣaṇād asya
svāśrame pūrva-vat sthitaḥ

tam — Him; *anu* — following; *atha* — then; *vaṭaḥ*—the banyan tree; *brahman* — O *brāhmaṇa,* Śaunaka; *salilam* — the water; *loka-samplavaḥ*— the annihilation of the universe; *tirodhāyi* — they disappeared; *kṣaṇāt* — immediately; *asya* — in front of him; *sva-āśrame* — in his own hermitage; *pūrva-vat* — as previously; *sthitaḥ*— he was present.

TRANSLATION

After the Lord disappeared, O brāhmaṇa, the banyan tree, the great water and the dissolution of the universe all vanished as well, and in an instant Mārkaṇḍeya found himself back in his own hermitage, just as before.

Thus end the purports of the humble servants of His Divine Grace A.C. Bhaktivedanta Swami Prabhupāda to the Twelfth Canto, Ninth Chapter, of the Śrīmad-Bhāgavatam, *entitled "Mārkaṇḍeya Ṛṣi Sees the Illusory Potency of the Lord."*

CHAPTER TEN

Lord Śiva and Umā Glorify Mārkaṇḍeya Ṛṣi

In this chapter Śrī Sūta Gosvāmī describes how Mārkaṇḍeya Ṛṣi received benedictions from Lord Śiva.

Once, as Lord Śiva was traveling in the sky with his wife, Pārvatī, he came across Śrī Mārkaṇḍeya merged in meditative trance. At the request of Pārvatī, Lord Śiva presented himself before the sage to grant him the result of his austerities. Coming out of his trance, Śrī Mārkaṇḍeya saw Lord Śiva, the spiritual master of the three worlds, together with Pārvatī, and he worshiped them by offering them obeisances, words of greeting and a sitting place.

Then Lord Śiva praised the saintly devotees of the Personality of Godhead and requested Śrī Mārkaṇḍeya to choose whatever benediction he desired. Mārkaṇḍeya begged for unflinching devotion to the Supreme Lord Śrī Hari, to the devotees of the Supreme Lord and to Lord Śiva himself. Satisfied with Mārkaṇḍeya's devotion, Lord Śiva awarded him the boons of renown, freedom from old age and death until the time of universal dissolution, knowledge of all three phases of time, renunciation, realized knowledge and the position of a teacher of the *Purāṇas.*

Those who chant and hear the story of Mārkaṇḍeya Ṛṣi will attain liberation from material life, which is based on the accumulated desires generated from fruitive work.

TEXT 1

सूत उवाच
स एवमनुभूयेदं नारायणविनिर्मितम् ।
वैभवं योगमायायास्तमेव शरणं ययौ ॥ १ ॥

sūta uvāca
sa evam anubhūyedaṁ
nārāyaṇa-vinirmitam
vaibhavaṁ yoga-māyāyās
tam eva śaraṇaṁ yayau

sūtaḥ uvāca — Sūta Gosvāmī said; *saḥ*—he, Mārkaṇḍeya; *evam* — in this way; *anubhūya* — experiencing; *idam* — this; *nārāyaṇa-vinirmitam* — manufactured by the Supreme Personality of Godhead, Nārāyaṇa; *vaibhavam* — the opulent exhibition; *yoga-māyāyāḥ*—of His internal mystic energy; *tam* — to Him; *eva* — indeed; *śaraṇam* — for shelter; *yayau* — he went.

TRANSLATION

Sūta Gosvāmī said: The Supreme Lord Nārāyaṇa had arranged this opulent display of His bewildering potency. Mārkaṇḍeya Ṛṣi, having experienced it, took shelter of the Lord.

TEXT 2

श्रीमार्कण्डेय उवाच
प्रपन्नोऽस्म्यङ्घ्रिमूलं ते प्रपन्नाभयदं हरे ।
यन्माययापि विबुधा मुह्यन्ति ज्ञानकाशया ॥ २ ॥

śrī-mārkaṇḍeya uvāca
prapanno'smy aṅghri-mūlaṁ te
prapannābhaya-daṁ hare
yan-māyayāpi vibudhā
muhyanti jñāna-kāśayā

śrī-mārkaṇḍeyaḥ uvāca — Śrī Mārkaṇḍeya said; *prapannaḥ*—surrendered; *asmi* — I am; *aṅghri-mūlam* — to the soles of the lotus feet; *te* — Your; *prapanna* — of those who surrender; *abhaya-dam* — the giver of fearlessness; *hare* — O Lord Hari; *yat-māyayā* — by whose illusory potency; *api* — even; *vibudhāḥ*—intelligent demigods; *muhyanti* — become bewildered; *jñāna-kāśayā* — which falsely appears as knowledge.

TRANSLATION

Śrī Mārkaṇḍeya said: O Lord Hari, I take shelter of the soles of Your lotus feet, which bestow fearlessness upon all who surrender to them. Even the great demigods are bewildered by Your illusory energy, which appears to them in the guise of knowledge.

PURPORT

Conditioned souls are attracted to material sense gratification, and thus they meticulously study the workings of nature. Although they appear to be advancing in scientific knowledge, they become increasingly entangled in their false identification with the material body and therefore increasingly merge into ignorance.

TEXT 3

सूत उवाच
तमेवं निभृतात्मानं वृषेण दिवि पर्यटन् ।
रुद्राण्या भगवान् रुद्रो ददर्श स्वगणैर्वृतः ॥ ३ ॥

sūta uvāca
tam evaṁ nibhṛtātmānaṁ
vṛṣeṇa divi paryaṭan
rudrāṇyā bhagavān rudro
dadarśa sva-gaṇair vṛtaḥ

sūtaḥ uvāca — Sūta Gosvāmī said; *tam* — him, Mārkaṇḍeya Ṛṣi; *evam* — thus; *nibhṛta-ātmānam* — his mind completely absorbed in trance; *vṛṣeṇa* — on his bull; *divi* — in the sky; *paryaṭan* — traveling; *rudrāṇyā* — accompanied by his consort, Rudrāṇī (Umā); *bhagavān* — the powerful lord; *rudraḥ*—Śiva; *dadarśa* — saw; *sva-gaṇaiḥ*—by his entourage; *vṛtaḥ*—surrounded.

TRANSLATION

Sūta Gosvāmī said: Lord Rudra, traveling in the sky on his bull and accompanied by his consort, Rudrāṇī, as well as his personal associates, observed Mārkaṇḍeya in trance.

TEXT 4

अथोमा तमृषिं वीक्ष्य गिरिशं समभाषत ।
पश्येमं भगवन् विप्रं निभृतात्मेन्द्रियाशयम् ॥ ४ ॥

athomā tam ṛṣiṁ vīkṣya
giriśaṁ samabhāṣata
paśyemaṁ bhagavan vipraṁ
nibhṛtātmendriyāśayam

atha — then; *umā* — Umā; *tam* — that; *ṛṣim* — sage; *vīkṣya* — seeing; *giriśam* — to Lord Śiva; *samabhāṣata* — spoke; *paśya* — just see; *imam* — this; *bhagavan* — my lord; *vipram* — learned *brāhmaṇa; nibhṛta* — motionless; *ātma-indriya-āśayam* — his body, senses and mind.

TRANSLATION

Goddess Umā, seeing the sage, addressed Lord Giriśa: My lord, just see this learned brāhmaṇa, his body, mind and senses motionless in trance.

TEXT 5

निभृतोदझषव्रातो वातापाये यथार्णवः ।
कुर्वस्य तपसः साक्षात् संसिद्धिं सिद्धिदो भवान् ॥ ५ ॥

nibhṛtoda-jhaṣa-vrāto
vātāpāye yathārṇavaḥ
kurv asya tapasaḥ sākṣāt
saṁsiddhiṁ siddhi-do bhavān

nibhṛta — stationary; *uda* — water; *jhaṣa-vrātaḥ*—and schools of fish; *vāta* — of the wind; *apāye* — upon the ceasing; *yathā* — just as; *arṇavaḥ*— the ocean; *kuru* — please make; *asya* — his; *tapasaḥ*—of the austerities; *sākṣāt* — manifest; *saṁsiddhim* — perfection; *siddhi-daḥ*—the bestower of perfection; *bhavān* — you.

TRANSLATION

He is as calm as the waters of the ocean when the wind has ceased and the fish remain still. Therefore, my lord, since you bestow perfection on the performers of austerity, please award this sage the perfection that is obviously due him.

TEXT 6

श्रीभगवानुवाच
नैवेच्छत्याशिषः क्वापि ब्रह्मर्षिर्मोक्षमप्युत ।
भक्तिं परां भगवति लब्धवान् पुरुषेऽव्यये ॥ ६ ॥

śrī-bhagavān uvāca
naivecchaty āśiṣaḥ kvāpi
brahmarṣir mokṣam apy uta
bhaktiṁ parāṁ bhagavati
labdhavān puruṣe'vyaye

śrī-bhagavān uvāca — the powerful lord said; *na* — not; *eva* — indeed; *icchati* — desires; *āśiṣaḥ*—benedictions; *kva api* — in any realm; *brahma-*

ṛṣiḥ—the saintly *brāhmaṇa; mokṣam* — liberation; *api uta* — even; *bhaktim* — devotional service; *parām* — transcendental; *bhagavati* — for the Supreme Lord; *labdhavān* — he has achieved; *puruṣe* — for the Personality of Godhead; *avyaye* — who is inexhaustible

TRANSLATION

Lord Śiva replied: Surely this saintly brāhmaṇa does not desire any benediction, not even liberation itself, for he has attained pure devotional service unto the inexhaustible Personality of Godhead.

PURPORT

The words *naivecchaty āśiṣaḥ kvāpi* indicate that Mārkaṇḍeya Ṛṣi was uninterested in any reward available on any planet within the universe. Nor did he want liberation, for he had achieved the Supreme Lord Himself.

TEXT 7

अथापि संवदिष्यामो भवान्येतेन साधुना ।
अयं हि परमो लाभो नृणां साधुसमागमः ॥ ७ ॥

athāpi saṁvadiṣyāmo
bhavāny etena sādhunā
ayaṁ hi paramo lābho
nṛṇāṁ sādhu-samāgamaḥ

atha api — nevertheless; *saṁvadiṣyāmaḥ*—we shall converse; *bhavāni* — my dear Bhavānī; *etena* — with this; *sādhunā* — pure devotee; *ayam* — this; *hi* — indeed; *paramaḥ*—the best; *lābhaḥ*—gain; *nṛṇām* — for men; *sādhu-samāgamaḥ*—the association of saintly devotees.

TRANSLATION

Still, my dear Bhavānī, let us talk with this saintly personality. After all, association with saintly devotees is man's highest achievement.

TEXT 8

सूत उवाच
इत्युक्त्वा तमुपेयाय भगवान् स सतां गतिः ।
ईशानः सर्वविद्यानामीश्वरः सर्वदेहिनाम् ॥ ८ ॥

sūta uvāca
ity uktvā tam upeyāya
bhagavān sa satāṁ gatiḥ
īśānaḥ sarva-vidyānām
īśvaraḥ sarva-dehinām

sūtaḥ uvāca — Sūta Gosvāmī said; *iti* — thus; *uktvā* — having said; *tam* — to the sage; *upeyāya* — going; *bhagavān* — the exalted demigod; *saḥ* — he; *satām* — of the pure souls; *gatiḥ* — the shelter; *īśānaḥ* — the master; *sarva-vidyānām* — of all branches of knowledge; *īśvaraḥ* — the controller; *sarva-dehinām* — of all embodied living beings.

TRANSLATION

Sūta Gosvāmī said: Having spoken thus, Lord Śaṅkara — the shelter of pure souls, master of all spiritual sciences and controller of all embodied living beings — approached the sage.

TEXT 9

तयोरागमनं साक्षादीशयोर्जगदात्मनोः ।
न वेद रुद्धधीवृत्तिरात्मानं विश्वमेव च ॥ ९ ॥

tayor āgamanaṁ sākṣād
īśayor jagad-ātmanoḥ
na veda ruddha-dhī-vṛttir
ātmānaṁ viśvam eva ca

tayoḥ — of the two of them; *āgamanam* — the arrival; *sākṣāt* — in person; *īśayoḥ* — of the powerful personalities; *jagat-ātmanoḥ* — the controllers of the universe; *na veda* — he did not notice; *ruddha* — checked; *dhī-vṛttiḥ* — the functioning of his mind; *ātmānam* — himself; *viśvam* — the external universe; *eva* — indeed; *ca* — also.

TRANSLATION

Because Mārkaṇḍeya's material mind had stopped functioning, the sage failed to notice that Lord Śiva and his wife, the controllers of the universe, had personally come to see him. Mārkaṇḍeya was so absorbed in meditation that he was unaware of either himself or the external world.

TEXT 10

भगवांस्तदभिज्ञाय गिरिशो योगमायया ।
आविशत्तद्गुहाकाशं वायुश्छिद्रमिवेश्वरः ॥ १० ॥

bhagavāṁs tad abhijñāya
giriśo yoga-māyayā
āviśat tad-guhākāśaṁ
vāyuś chidram iveśvaraḥ

bhagavān — the great personality; *tat* — that; *abhijñāya* — understanding; *giriśaḥ* — Lord Giriśa; *yoga-māyayā* — by his mystic power; *āviśat* — entered; *tat* — of Mārkaṇḍeya; *guhā-ākāśam* — the hidden sky of the heart; *vāyuḥ* — the air; *chidram* — a hole; *iva* — as if; *īśvaraḥ* — the lord.

TRANSLATION

Understanding the situation very well, the powerful Lord Śiva employed his mystic power to enter within the sky of Mārkaṇḍeya's heart, just as the wind passes through an opening.

TEXTS 11–13

आत्मन्यपि शिवं प्राप्तं तडित्पिंगजटाधरम् ।
त्र्यक्षं दशभुजं प्रांशुमुद्यन्तमिव भास्करम् ॥ ११ ॥
व्याघ्रचर्माम्बरं शूलधनुरिष्वसिचर्मभिः ।
अक्षमालाडमरुककपालं परशुं सह ॥ १२ ॥
बिभ्राणं सहसा भातं विचक्ष्य हृदि विस्मितः ।
किमिदं कुत एवेति समाधेर्विरतो मुनिः ॥ १३ ॥

ātmany api śivaṁ prāptaṁ
taḍit-piṅga-jaṭā-dharam
try-akṣaṁ daśa-bhujaṁ prāṁśum
udyantam iva bhāskaram

vyāghra-carmāmbaraṁ śūla-
dhanur-iṣv-asi-carmabhiḥ
akṣa-mālā-ḍamaruka-
kapālaṁ paraśuṁ saha

bibhrāṇaṁ sahasā bhātaṁ
vicakṣya hṛdi vismitaḥ
kim idaṁ kuta eveti
samādher virato muniḥ

ātmani — within himself; *api* — also; *śivam* — Lord Śiva; *prāptam* — arrived; *taḍit* — like lightning; *piṅga* — yellowish; *jaṭā* — locks of hair; *dharam* — carrying; *tri-akṣam* — with three eyes; *daśa-bhujam* — and ten arms; *prāṁśum* — very tall; *udyantam* — rising; *iva* — as; *bhāskaram* — the sun; *vyāghra* — of a tiger; *carma* — the fur; *ambaram* — as his garment; *śūla* — with his trident; *dhanuḥ*—bow; *iṣu* — arrows; *asi* — sword; *carmabhiḥ*— and shield; *akṣa-mālā* — his prayer beads; *ḍamaruka* — small drum; *kapālam* — and skull; *paraśum* — ax; *saha* — together with; *bibhrāṇam* — exhibiting; *sahasā* — suddenly; *bhātam* — manifest; *vicakṣya* — seeing; *hṛdi* — in his heart; *vismitaḥ*—surprised; *kim* — what; *idam* — this; *kutaḥ*—from where; *eva* — indeed; *iti* — thus; *samādheḥ*—from his trance; *virataḥ*—desisted; *muniḥ*—the sage.

TRANSLATION

Śrī Mārkaṇḍeya saw Lord Śiva suddenly appear within his heart. Lord Śiva's golden hair resembled lightning, and he had three eyes, ten arms and a tall body that shone like the rising sun. He wore a tiger skin, and he carried a trident, a bow, arrows, a sword and a shield, along with prayer beads, a ḍamaru drum, a skull and an ax. Astonished, the sage came out of his trance and thought, "Who is this, and where has he come from?"

TEXT 14

नेत्रे उन्मील्य ददृशे सगणं सोमयागतम् ।
रुद्रं त्रिलोकैकगुरुं ननाम शिरसा मुनिः ॥ १४॥

netre unmīlya dadṛśe
sa-gaṇaṁ somayāgatam
rudraṁ tri-lokaika-guruṁ
nanāma śirasā muniḥ

netre — his eyes; *unmīlya* — opening; *dadṛśe* — he saw; *sa-gaṇam* — with his associates; *sa-umayā* — and with Umā; *āgatam* — having arrived; *rudram* — Lord Rudra; *tri-loka* — of the three worlds; *eka-gurum* — the one spiritual master; *nanāma* — he offered his obeisances; *śirasā* — with his head; *muniḥ*—the sage.

TRANSLATION

Opening his eyes, the sage saw Lord Rudra, the spiritual master of the three worlds, together with Umā and Rudra's followers. Mārkaṇḍeya then offered his respectful obeisances by bowing his head.

PURPORT

When Mārkaṇḍeya Ṛṣi saw Lord Śiva and Umā within his heart, he immediately became aware of them and thus also of his own individual self. During his trance, on the other hand, he had simply been absorbed in awareness of the Supreme Lord and had thus forgotten himself as the conscious perceiver.

TEXT 15

तस्मै सपर्यां व्यदधात् सगणाय सहोमया ।
स्वागतासनपाद्यार्घ्यगन्धस्रग्धूपदीपकैः ॥ १५ ॥

tasmai saparyāṁ vyadadhāt
sa-gaṇāya sahomayā
svāgatāsana-pādyārghya-
gandha-srag-dhūpa-dīpakaiḥ

tasmai — to him; *saparyām* — worship; *vyadadhāt* — he offered; *sa-gaṇāya* — together with his associates; *saha umayā* — together with Umā; *su-āgata* — by words of greeting; *āsana* — offering of sitting places; *pādya* — water for bathing the feet; *arghya* — fragrant drinking water; *gandha* — perfumed oil; *srak* — garlands; *dhūpa* — incense; *dīpakaiḥ*—and lamps.

TRANSLATION

Mārkaṇḍeya worshiped Lord Śiva, along with Umā and Śiva's associates, by offering them words of welcome, sitting places, water for washing their feet, scented drinking water, fragrant oils, flower garlands and ārati lamps.

TEXT 16

आह त्वात्मानुभावेन पूर्णकामस्य ते विभो ।
करवाम किमीशान येनेदं निर्वृतं जगत् ॥ १६ ॥

āha tv ātmānubhāvena
pūrṇa-kāmasya te vibho
karavāma kim īśāna
yenedaṁ nirvṛtaṁ jagat

āha — Mārkaṇḍeya said; *tu* — indeed; *ātma-anubhāvena* — by your own experience of ecstasy; *pūrṇa-kāmasya* — who is satisfied in all respects; *te* — for you; *vibho* — O mighty one; *karavāma* — I can do; *kim* — what; *īśāna* — O lord; *yena* — by whom; *idam* — this; *nirvṛtam* — is made peaceful; *jagat* — the entire world.

TRANSLATION

Mārkaṇḍeya said: O mighty lord, what can I possibly do for you, who are fully satisfied by your own ecstasy? Indeed, by your mercy you satisfy this entire world.

TEXT 17

नमः शिवाय शान्ताय सत्त्वाय प्रमृडाय च ।
रजोजुषेऽथ घोराय नमस्तुभ्यं तमोजुषे ॥ १७ ॥

namaḥ śivāya śāntāya
sattvāya pramṛḍāya ca
rajo-juṣe 'tha ghorāya
namas tubhyaṁ tamo-juṣe

namaḥ — obeisances; *śivāya* — to the all-auspicious; *śāntāya* — peaceful; *sattvāya* — the personification of material goodness; *pramṛḍāya* — the giver of pleasure; *ca* — and; *rajaḥ-juṣe* — to him who is in contact with the mode of passion; *atha* — also; *ghorāya* — terrible; *namaḥ* — obeisances; *tubhyam* — to you; *tamaḥ-juṣe* — who associates with the mode of ignorance.

TRANSLATION

Again and again I offer my obeisances unto you, O all-auspicious transcendental personality. As the lord of goodness you give pleasure, in contact with the mode of passion you appear most fearful, and you also associate with the mode of ignorance.

TEXT 18

सूत उवाच
एवं स्तुतः स भगवानादिदेवः सतां गतिः ।
परितुष्टः प्रसन्नात्मा प्रहसंस्तमभाषत ॥ १८ ॥

sūta uvāca
evaṁ stutaḥ sa bhagavān
ādi-devaḥ satāṁ gatiḥ
parituṣṭaḥ prasannātmā
prahasaṁs tam abhāṣata

sūtaḥ uvāca — Sūta Gosvāmī said; *evam* — in these words; *stutaḥ* — praised; *saḥ* — he; *bhagavān* — the powerful Lord Śiva; *ādi-devaḥ* — the foremost of demigods; *satām* — of the saintly devotees; *gatiḥ* — the shelter; *parituṣṭaḥ* — perfectly satisfied; *prasanna-ātmā* — happy in his mind; *prahasan* — smiling; *tam* — to Mārkaṇḍeya; *abhāṣata* — spoke.

TRANSLATION

Sūta Gosvāmī said: Lord Śiva, the foremost demigod and the shelter of the saintly devotees, was satisfied by Mārkaṇḍeya's praise. Pleased, he smiled and addressed the sage.

TEXT 19

श्रीभगवानुवाच
वरं वृणीष्व नः कामं वरदेशा वयं त्रयः ।
अमोघं दर्शनं येषां मर्त्यो यद् विन्दतेऽमृतम् ॥ १९ ॥

śrī-bhagavān uvāca
varaṁ vṛṇīṣva naḥ kāmaṁ
vara-deśā vayaṁ trayaḥ
amoghaṁ darśanaṁ yeṣāṁ
martyo yad vindate 'mṛtam

śrī-bhagavān uvāca — Lord Śiva said; *varam* — a benediction; *vṛṇīṣva* — please choose; *naḥ* — from us; *kāmam* — as desired; *vara-da* — of all givers of benedictions; *īśāḥ* — the controlling lords; *vayam* — we; *trayaḥ* — three (Brahmā, Viṣṇu and Maheśvara); *amogham* — never in vain; *darśanam* —

the seeing; *yeṣām* — of whom; *martyaḥ*—a mortal being; *yat* — by which; *vindate* — achieves; *amṛtam* — immortality.

TRANSLATION

Lord Śiva said: Please ask me for some benediction, since among all givers of benedictions, we three — Brahmā, Viṣṇu and I — are the best. Seeing us never goes in vain, because simply by seeing us a mortal achieves immortality.

TEXTS 20–21

ब्राह्मणाः साधवः शान्ता निःसंगा भूतवत्सलाः ।
एकान्तभक्ता अस्मासु निर्वैराः समदर्शिनः ॥ २० ॥
सलोका लोकपालास्तान् वन्दन्त्यर्चन्त्युपासते ।
अहं च भगवान् ब्रह्मा स्वयं च हरिरीश्वरः ॥ २१ ॥

brāhmaṇāḥ sādhavaḥ śāntā
niḥsaṅgā bhūta-vatsalāḥ
ekānta-bhaktā asmāsu
nirvairāḥ sama-darśinaḥ

sa-lokā loka-pālās tān
vandanty arcanty upāsate
ahaṁ ca bhagavān brahmā
svayaṁ ca harir īśvaraḥ

brāhmaṇāḥ— *brāhmaṇas; sādhavaḥ*—saintly in behavior; *śāntāḥ*—peaceful and free of envy and other bad qualities; *niḥsaṅgāḥ*—free of material association; *bhūta-vatsalāḥ*—compassionate to all living beings; *eka-anta-bhaktāḥ*—unalloyed devotees; *asmāsu* — of ourselves (Brahmā, Lord Śrī Hari and Śiva); *nirvairāḥ*—never hateful; *sama-darśinaḥ*—seeing equally; *sa-lokāḥ*—with the inhabitants of all the worlds; *loka-pālāḥ*—the rulers of the various planets; *tān* — those *brāhmaṇas; vandanti* — glorify; *arcanti* — worship; *upāsate* — assist; *aham* — I; *ca* — also; *bhagavān* — the great lord; *brahmā* — Brahmā; *svayam* — Himself; *ca* — also; *hariḥ*—Lord Hari; *īśvaraḥ* —the Supreme Personality of Godhead.

TRANSLATION

The inhabitants and ruling demigods of all planets, along with Lord Brahmā, the Supreme Lord Hari and I, glorify, worship and assist those

brāhmaṇas who are saintly, always peaceful, free of material attachment, compassionate to all living beings, purely devoted to us, devoid of hatred and endowed with equal vision.

TEXT 22

न ते मय्यच्युतेऽजे च भिदामण्वपि चक्षते ।
नात्मनश्च जनस्यापि तद्युष्मान् वयमीमहि ॥ २२ ॥

na te mayy acyute 'je ca
bhidām aṇv api cakṣate
nātmanaś ca janasyāpi
tad yuṣmān vayam īmahi

na — do not; *te* — they; *mayi* — in me; *acyute* — in Lord Viṣṇu; *aje* — in Lord Brahmā; *ca* — and; *bhidām* — difference; *aṇu* — slight; *api* — even; *cakṣate* — see; *na* — not; *ātmanaḥ* — of themselves; *ca* — and; *janasya* — of other people; *api* — also; *tat* — therefore; *yuṣmān* — yourselves; *vayam* — we; *īmahi* — worship.

TRANSLATION

These devotees do not differentiate between Lord Viṣṇu, Lord Brahmā and me, nor do they differentiate between themselves and other living beings. Therefore, because you are this kind of saintly devotee, we worship you.

PURPORT

Lord Brahmā and Lord Śiva are, respectively, manifestations of the creating and annihilating potencies of the Personality of Godhead, Viṣṇu. Thus unity exists among these three ruling deities of the material world. One should not, on the basis of the modes of nature, find material duality within the ruling potency of the Supreme Lord, although that potency is manifested in three divisions as Brahmā, Viṣṇu and Śiva.

TEXT 23

न ह्यम्मयानि तीर्थानि न देवाश्चेतनोज्झिताः ।
ते पुनन्त्युरुकालेन यूयं दर्शनमात्रतः ॥ २३ ॥

na hy am-mayāni tīrthāni
na devāś cetanojjhitāḥ

te punanty uru-kālena
yūyaṁ darśana-mātrataḥ

na — not; *hi* — indeed; *ap-mayāni* — consisting of sacred water; *tīrthāni* — holy places; *na* — not; *devāḥ* — deity forms of demigods; *cetana-ujjhitāḥ* — devoid of life; *te* — they; *punanti* — purify; *uru-kālena* — after a long time; *yūyam* — yourselves; *darśana-mātrataḥ* — simply by being seen.

TRANSLATION

Mere bodies of water do not constitute holy places, nor are lifeless statues of the demigods actual worshipable deities. Because external vision fails to appreciate the higher essence of the holy rivers and the demigods, these purify only after a considerable time. But devotees like you purify immediately, just by being seen.

TEXT 24

ब्राह्मणेभ्यो नमस्यामो येऽस्मद्रूपं त्रयीमयम् ।
बिभ्रत्यात्मसमाधानतपःस्वाध्यायसंयमैः ॥ २४ ॥

brāhmaṇebhyo namasyāmo
ye'smad-rūpaṁ trayī-mayam
bibhraty ātma-samādhāna-
tapaḥ-svādhyāya-saṁyamaiḥ

brāhmaṇebhyaḥ — to the *brāhmaṇas; namasyāmaḥ* — we offer our respects; *ye* — who; *asmat-rūpam* — the form of ourselves (Śiva, Brahmā and Viṣṇu); *trayī-mayam* — represented by the three *Vedas; bibhrati* — carry; *ātma-samādhāna* — by meditative trance focused on the Self; *tapaḥ* — by austerities; *svādhyāya* — by study; *saṁyamaiḥ* — and by following regulative principles.

TRANSLATION

By meditating upon the Supreme Soul, performing austerities, engaging in Vedic study and following regulative principles, the brāhmaṇas sustain within themselves the three Vedas, which are nondifferent from Lord Viṣṇu, Lord Brahmā and me. Therefore I offer my obeisances unto the brāhmaṇas.

PURPORT

A pure devotee of the Supreme Lord is considered the most elevated of *brāhmaṇas,* since all spiritual endeavor culminates in the loving service of God.

TEXT 25

श्रवणाद्दर्शनाद् वापि महापातकिनोऽपि वः ।
शुध्येरन्नन्त्यजाश्चापि किमु सम्भाषणादिभिः ॥ २५ ॥

śravaṇād darśanād vāpi
mahā-pātakino'pi vaḥ
śudhyerann antya-jāś cāpi
kim u sambhāṣaṇādibhiḥ

śravaṇāt — by hearing about; *darśanāt* — by seeing; *vā* — or; *api* — also; *mahā-pātakinaḥ*— those who commit the worst kinds of sins; *api* — even; *vaḥ*—you; *śudhyeran* — they become purified; *antya-jāḥ*— outcastes; *ca* — and; *api* — even; *kim u* — what to speak of; *sambhāṣaṇa-ādibhiḥ*— by directly speaking with, and so on.

TRANSLATION

Even the worst sinners and social outcastes are purified just by hearing about or seeing personalities like you. Imagine, then, how purified they become by directly speaking with you.

TEXT 26

सूत उवाच
इति चन्द्रललामस्य धर्मगुह्योपबृंहितम् ।
वचोऽमृतायनमृषिर्नातृप्यत् कर्णयोः पिबन् ॥ २६ ॥

sūta uvāca
iti candra-lalāmasya
dharma-guhyopabṛṁhitam
vaco'mṛtāyanam ṛṣir
nātṛpyat karṇayoḥ piban

sūtaḥ uvāca — Sūta Gosvāmī said; *iti* — thus; *candra-lalāmasya* — of Lord Śiva, who is decorated with the moon; *dharma-guhya* — with the secret essence of religion; *upabṛṁhitam* — filled; *vacaḥ*—the words; *amṛta-ayanam* — the reservoir of nectar; *ṛṣiḥ*—the sage; *na atṛpyat* — did not feel satiated; *karṇayoḥ*—with his ears; *piban* — drinking.

TRANSLATION

Sūta Gosvāmī said: Drinking with his ears Lord Śiva's nectarean words, full of the confidential essence of religion, Mārkaṇḍeya Ṛṣi could not be satiated.

PURPORT

Mārkaṇḍeya Ṛṣi was not eager to hear himself praised by Lord Śiva, but he appreciated Lord Śiva's deep realization of religious principles and therefore desired to hear more.

TEXT 27

स चिरं मायया विष्णोर्भ्रामितः कर्शितो भृशम् ।
शिववागमृतध्वस्तक्लेशपुञ्जस्तमब्रवीत् ॥२७॥

sa ciraṁ māyayā viṣṇor
bhrāmitaḥ karśito bhṛśam
śiva-vāg-amṛta-dhvasta-
kleśa-puñjas tam abravīt

saḥ—he; *ciram* — for a long time; *māyayā* — by the illusory energy; *viṣṇoḥ*—of the Supreme Personality of Godhead, Viṣṇu; *bhrāmitaḥ*—made to wander; *karśitaḥ*—exhausted; *bhṛśam* — extremely; *śiva* — of Lord Śiva; *vāk-amṛta* — by the words of nectar; *dhvasta* — destroyed; *kleśa-puñjaḥ*— his heaps of suffering; *tam* — to him; *abravīt* — spoke.

TRANSLATION

Mārkaṇḍeya, having been forced by Lord Viṣṇu's illusory energy to wander about for a long time in the water of dissolution, had become extremely exhausted. But Lord Śiva's words of nectar vanquished his accumulated suffering. Thus he addressed Lord Śiva.

PURPORT

Mārkaṇḍeya Ṛṣi had desired to see Lord Viṣṇu's illusory energy and had suffered extensive miseries. But now, in the person of Śiva, Lord Viṣṇu again appeared before the sage and relieved all his suffering by imparting blissful spiritual instructions.

TEXT 28

श्रीमार्कण्डेय उवाच
अहो ईश्वरलीलेयं दुर्विभाव्या शरीरिणाम् ।
यन्नमन्तीशितव्यानि स्तुवन्ति जगदीश्वराः ॥ २८ ॥

śrī-mārkaṇḍeya uvāca
aho īśvara-līleyaṁ
durvibhāvyā śarīriṇām
yan namantīśitavyāni
stuvanti jagad-īśvarāḥ

śrī-mārkaṇḍeyaḥ uvāca — Śrī Mārkaṇḍeya said; *aho* — ah; *īśvara* — of the great lords; *līlā* — the pastime; *iyam* — this; *durvibhāvyā* — inconceivable; *śarīriṇām* — for embodied souls; *yat* — since; *namanti* — they offer obeisances; *īśitavyāni* — to those who are controlled by them; *stuvanti* — they praise; *jagat-īśvarāḥ* — the rulers of the universe.

TRANSLATION

Śrī Mārkaṇḍeya said: It is indeed most difficult for embodied souls to understand the pastimes of the universal controllers, for such lords bow down to and offer praise to the very living beings they rule.

PURPORT

In the material world, conditioned souls strive to lord it over one another. Therefore they cannot understand the pastimes of the actual lords of the universe. Such bona fide lords have a wonderfully magnanimous mentality and thus sometimes bow down to the most qualified and saintly among their own subjects.

TEXT 29

धर्मं ग्राहयितुं प्रायः प्रवक्तारश्च देहिनाम् ।
आचरन्त्यनुमोदन्ते क्रियमाणं स्तुवन्ति च ॥ २९ ॥

dharmaṁ grāhayituṁ prāyaḥ
pravaktāraś ca dehinām

ācaranty anumodante
kriyamāṇaṁ stuvanti ca

dharmam — religion; *grāhayitum* — to cause the acceptance of; *prāyaḥ* — for the most part; *pravaktāraḥ*— the authorized speakers; *ca* — and; *dehinām* — for ordinary embodied souls; *ācaranti* — they act; *anumodante* — they encourage; *kriyamāṇam* — one who is executing; *stuvanti* — they praise; *ca* — also.

TRANSLATION

Generally it is to induce embodied souls to accept religious principles that the authorized teachers of religion exhibit ideal behavior while encouraging and praising the proper behavior of others.

TEXT 30

नैतावता भगवतः स्वमायामयवृत्तिभिः ।
न दुष्येतानुभावस्तैर्मायिनः कुहकं यथा ॥ ३० ॥

naitāvatā bhagavataḥ
sva-māyā-maya-vṛttibhiḥ
na duṣyetānubhāvas tair
māyinaḥ kuhakaṁ yathā

na — not; *etāvatā* — by such (a show of humility); *bhagavataḥ*— of the Personality of Godhead; *sva-māyā* — of His own illusory energy; *maya* — consisting of; *vṛttibhiḥ*— by the activities; *na duṣyeta* — is not spoiled; *anubhāvaḥ* — the power; *taiḥ*— by them; *māyinaḥ*— of a magician; *kuhakam* — the tricks; *yathā* — just as.

TRANSLATION

This apparent humility is simply a show of mercy. Such behavior of the Supreme Lord and His personal associates, which the Lord effects by His own bewildering potency, does not spoil His power any more than a magician's powers are diminished by his exhibition of tricks.

TEXTS 31–32

सृष्ट्वेदं मनसा विश्वमात्मनानुप्रविश्य यः ।
गुणैः कुर्वद्भिराभाति कर्तेव स्वप्नदृग् यथा ॥ ३१ ॥

तस्मै नमो भगवते त्रिगुणाय गुणात्मने।
केवलायाद्वितीयाय गुरवे ब्रह्ममूर्तये ॥ ३२ ॥

sṛṣṭvedaṁ manasā viśvam
ātmanānupraviśya yaḥ
guṇaiḥ kurvadbhir ābhāti
karteva svapna-dṛg yathā

tasmai namo bhagavate
tri-guṇāya guṇātmane
kevalāyādvitīyāya
gurave brahma-mūrtaye

sṛṣṭvā — creating; *idam* — this; *manasā* — by His mind, simply by His desire; *viśvam* — the universe; *ātmanā* — as the Supersoul; *anupraviśya* — subsequently entering; *yaḥ*—who; *guṇaiḥ*—by the modes of nature; *kurvadbhiḥ* —which are acting; *ābhāti* — appears; *kartā iva* — as if the doer; *svapna-dṛk* — a person who is seeing a dream; *yathā* — as; *tasmai* — unto Him; *namaḥ* —obeisances; *bhagavate* — unto the Supreme Personality of Godhead; *tri-guṇāya* — who possesses the three modes of nature; *guṇa-ātmane* — who is the ultimate controller of the modes of nature; *kevalāya* — to the pure; *advitīyāya* — who has no equal; *gurave* — the supreme spiritual master; *brahma-mūrtaye* — the personal form of the Absolute Truth.

TRANSLATION

I offer my obeisances to that Supreme Personality of Godhead, who has created this entire universe simply by His desire and then entered into it as the Supersoul. By making the modes of nature act, He seems to be the direct creator of this world, just as a dreamer seems to be acting within his dream. He is the owner and ultimate controller of the three modes of nature, yet He remains alone and pure, without any equal. He is the supreme spiritual master of all, the original personal form of the Absolute Truth.

PURPORT

The Supreme Lord releases His material potencies, and by their interaction creation takes place. The Lord remains aloof, as the supreme transcendental entity. Still, because the entire creation unfolds according to His design and will, His controlling hand is perceived within all things. People thus imagine that God is the direct builder of this world, although He remains aloof, creating through the manipulation of His multifarious potencies.

TEXT 33

कं वृणे नु परं भूमन् वरं त्वद्वरदर्शनात् ।
यद्दर्शनात् पूर्णकामः सत्यकामः पुमान् भवेत् ॥ ३३ ॥

kaṁ vṛṇe nu paraṁ bhūman
varaṁ tvad vara-darśanāt
yad-darśanāt pūrṇa-kāmaḥ
satya-kāmaḥ pumān bhavet

kam — what; *vṛṇe* — shall I choose; *nu* — indeed; *param* — other; *bhūman* — O all-pervading lord; *varam* — benediction; *tvat* — from you; *vara-darśanāt* — the sight of whom is itself the highest benediction; *yat* — of whom; *darśanāt* — from the seeing; *pūrṇa-kāmaḥ* — full in all desires; *satya-kāmaḥ* — able to achieve anything desired; *pumān* — a person; *bhavet* — becomes.

TRANSLATION

O all-pervading lord, since I have received the benediction of seeing you, what other benediction can I ask for? Simply by seeing you, a person fulfills all his desires and can achieve anything imaginable.

TEXT 34

वरमेकं वृणेऽथापि पूर्णात् कामाभिवर्षणात् ।
भगवत्यच्युतां भक्तिं तत्परेषु तथा त्वयि ॥ ३४ ॥

varam ekaṁ vṛṇe 'thāpi
pūrṇāt kāmābhivarṣaṇāt
bhagavaty acyutāṁ bhaktiṁ
tat-pareṣu tathā tvayi

varam — benediction; *ekam* — one; *vṛṇe* — I request; *atha api* — nevertheless; *pūrṇāt* — from him who is completely full; *kāma-abhivarṣaṇāt* — who showers down the fulfillment of desires; *bhagavati* — for the Supreme Personality of Godhead; *acyutām* — infallible; *bhaktim* — devotional service;

tat-pareṣu — for those who are dedicated to Him; *tathā* — and also; *tvayi* — for yourself.

TRANSLATION

But I do request one benediction from you, who are full of all perfection and able to shower down the fulfillment of all desires. I ask to have unfailing devotion for the Supreme Personality of Godhead and for His dedicated devotees, especially you.

PURPORT

The words *tat-pareṣu tathā tvayi* clearly indicate that Lord Śiva is a devotee of the Supreme Lord, not the Supreme Lord Himself. Because the representative of God is offered the same protocol as God Himself, Mārkaṇḍeya Ṛṣi addressed Lord Śiva as "lord" in previous verses. But now it is clearly revealed that, as stated throughout Vedic literature, Lord Śiva is an eternal servant of God and not God Himself.

Desire manifests itself within the mind and heart according to the subtle laws governing consciousness. Pure desire to engage in the loving service of the Lord brings one to the most exalted platform of consciousness, and such a perfect understanding of life is available only by the special mercy of the Lord's devotees.

TEXT 35

सूत उवाच
इत्यर्चितोऽभिष्टुतश्च मुनिना सूक्तया गिरा ।
तमाह भगवाञ्छर्वः शर्वया चाभिनन्दितः ॥ ३५ ॥

sūta uvāca
ity arcito 'bhiṣṭutaś ca
muninā sūktayā girā
tam āha bhagavāñ charvaḥ
śarvayā cābhinanditaḥ

sūtaḥ uvāca — Sūta Gosvāmī said; *iti* — in these words; *arcitaḥ* — worshiped; *abhiṣṭutaḥ* — glorified; *ca* — and; *muninā* — by the sage; *su-uktayā* — well-spoken; *girā* — with words; *tam* — to him; *āha* — spoke; *bhagavān śarvaḥ* — Lord Śiva; *śarvayā* — by his consort, Śarvā; *ca* — and; *abhinanditaḥ* — encouraged.

TRANSLATION

Sūta Gosvāmī said: Thus worshiped and glorified by the eloquent statements of the sage Mārkaṇḍeya, Lord Śarva [Śiva], encouraged by his consort, replied to him as follows.

TEXT 36

कामो महर्षे सर्वोऽयं भक्तिमांस्त्वमधोक्षजे ।
आकल्पान्ताद्यशः पुण्यमजरामरता तथा ॥ ३६ ॥

kāmo maharṣe sarvo 'yaṁ
bhaktimāṁs tvam adhokṣaje
ā-kalpāntād yaśaḥ puṇyam
ajarāmaratā tathā

kāmaḥ—desire; *mahā-ṛṣe*—O great sage; *sarvaḥ*—all; *ayam*—this; *bhakti-mān*—full of devotion; *tvam*—you; *adhokṣaje*—for the transcendental Personality of Godhead; *ā-kalpa-antāt*—up until the end of the day of Brahmā; *yaśaḥ*—fame; *puṇyam*—pious; *ajara-amaratā*—freedom from old age and death; *tathā*—also.

TRANSLATION

O great sage, because you are devoted to Lord Adhokṣaja, all your desires will be fulfilled. Until the very end of this creation cycle, you will enjoy pious fame and freedom from old age and death.

TEXT 37

ज्ञानं त्रैकालिकं ब्रह्मन् विज्ञानं च विरक्तिमत् ।
ब्रह्मवर्चस्विनो भूयात् पुराणाचार्यतास्तु ते ॥ ३७ ॥

jñānaṁ trai-kālikaṁ brahman
vijñānaṁ ca viraktimat
brahma-varcasvino bhūyāt
purāṇācāryatāstu te

jñānam—knowledge; *trai-kālikam*—of all three phases of time (past, present and future); *brahman*—O *brāhmaṇa; vijñānam*—transcendental realization; *ca*—also; *virakti-mat*—including renunciation; *brahma-varcasv-*

inaḥ — of him who is endowed with brahminical potency; *bhūyāt* — let there be; *purāṇa-ācāryatā* — the status of being a teacher of the *Purāṇas; astu* — may there be; *te* — of you.

TRANSLATION

O brāhmaṇa, may you have perfect knowledge of past, present and future, along with transcendental realization of the Supreme, enriched by renunciation. You have the brilliance of an ideal brāhmaṇa, and thus may you achieve the post of spiritual master of the Purāṇas.

TEXT 38

सूत उवाच
एवं वरान् स मुनये दत्त्वागात् त्र्यक्ष ईश्वरः ।
देव्यै तत्कर्म कथयन्ननुभूतं पुरामुना ॥ ३८ ॥

sūta uvāca
evaṁ varān sa munaye
dattvāgāt try-akṣa īśvaraḥ
devyai tat-karma kathayann
anubhūtaṁ purāmunā

sūtaḥ uvāca — Sūta Gosvāmī said; *evam* — in this way; *varān* — benedictions; *saḥ* — he; *munaye* — to the sage; *dattvā* — giving; *agāt* — went; *tri-akṣaḥ* — he who has three eyes; *īśvaraḥ* — Lord Śiva; *devyai* — to Goddess Pārvatī; *tat-karma* — the activities of Mārkaṇḍeya; *kathayan* — recounting; *anubhūtam* — what was experienced; *purā* — before; *amunā* — by him, Mārkaṇḍeya.

TRANSLATION

Sūta Gosvāmī said: Having thus granted Mārkaṇḍeya Ṛṣi benedictions, Lord Śiva went on his way, continuing to describe to Goddess Devī the accomplishments of the sage and the direct exhibition of the Lord's illusory power that he had experienced.

TEXT 39

सोऽप्यवाप्तमहायोगमहिमा भार्गवोत्तमः ।
विचरत्यधुनाप्यद्धा हरावेकान्ततां गतः ॥ ३९ ॥

so 'py avāpta-mahā-yoga-
mahimā bhārgavottamaḥ
vicaraty adhunāpy addhā
harāv ekāntatāṁ gataḥ

saḥ—he, Mārkaṇḍeya; *api* — indeed; *avāpta* — having achieved; *mahā-yoga* — of the topmost perfection of *yoga; mahimā* — the glories; *bhārgava-uttamaḥ*—the best descendant of Bhṛgu; *vicarati*—is traveling about; *adhunā api*—even today; *addhā*—directly; *harau*—for Lord Hari; *eka-antatām*—the platform of exclusive devotion; *gataḥ*—having attained.

TRANSLATION

Mārkaṇḍeya Ṛṣi, the best of the descendants of Bhṛgu, is glorious because of his achievement of perfection in mystic yoga. Even today he travels about this world, fully absorbed in unalloyed devotion for the Supreme Personality of Godhead.

TEXT 40

अनुवर्णितमेतत्ते मार्कण्डेयस्य धीमतः ।
अनुभूतं भगवतो मायावैभवमद्भुतम् ॥ ४० ॥

anuvarṇitam etat te
mārkaṇḍeyasya dhīmataḥ
anubhūtaṁ bhagavato
māyā-vaibhavam adbhutam

anuvarṇitam — described; *etat* — this; *te* — to you; *mārkaṇḍeyasya* — by Mārkaṇḍeya; *dhī-mataḥ*—the intelligent; *anubhūtam* — experienced; *bhagavataḥ*—of the Personality of Godhead; *māyā-vaibhavam* — the opulence of the illusory energy; *adbhutam* — amazing.

TRANSLATION

I have thus narrated to you the activities of the highly intelligent sage Mārkaṇḍeya, especially how he experienced the amazing power of the Supreme Lord's illusory energy.

TEXT 41

एतत् केचिदविद्वांसो मायासंसृतिरात्मनः ।
अनाद्यावर्तितं नृणां कादाचित्कं प्रचक्षते ॥ ४१ ॥

etat kecid avidvāṁso
māyā-saṁsṛtir ātmanaḥ
anādy-āvartitaṁ nṛṇāṁ
kādācitkaṁ pracakṣate

etat — this; *kecit* — some persons; *avidvāṁsaḥ* — who are not learned; *māyā-saṁsṛtiḥ* — the illusory creation; *ātmanaḥ* — of the Supreme Soul; *anādi* — from time immemorial; *āvartitam* — repeating; *nṛṇām* — of conditioned living beings; *kādācitkam* — unprecedented; *pracakṣate* — they say.

TRANSLATION

Although this event was unique and unprecedented, some unintelligent persons compare it to the cycle of illusory material existence the Supreme Lord has created for the conditioned souls — an endless cycle that has been continuing since time immemorial.

PURPORT

Mārkaṇḍeya's being drawn into the Lord's body by His inhalation and expelled again by His exhalation should not be considered a symbolic description of the perennial cycles of material creation and annihilation. This portion of the *Śrīmad-Bhāgavatam* describes a real, historical event experienced by a great devotee of the Lord, and those trying to relegate this story to mere symbolic allegory are here declared to be unintelligent fools.

TEXT 42

य एवमेतद् भृगुवर्य वर्णितं
रथांगपाणेरनुभावभावितम् ।
संश्रावयेत् संशृणुयादु तावुभौ
तयोर्न कर्माशयसंसृतिर्भवेत् ॥ ४२ ॥

ya evam etad bhṛgu-varya varṇitaṁ
rathāṅga-pāṇer anubhāva-bhāvitam

saṁśrāvayet saṁśṛṇuyād u tāv ubhau
tayor na karmāśaya-saṁsṛtir bhavet

yaḥ—who; *evam* — thus; *etat* — this; *bhṛgu-varya* — O best of the descendants of Bhṛgu (Śaunaka); *varṇitam* — described; *ratha-aṅga-pāṇeḥ*— of Lord Śrī Hari, who carries a chariot wheel in His hand; *anubhāva* — with the potency; *bhāvitam* — infused; *saṁśrāvayet* — causes anyone to hear; *saṁśṛṇuyāt* — himself hears; *u* — or; *tau* — they; *ubhau* — both; *tayoḥ*—of them; *na* — not; *karma-āśaya* — based on the mentality of fruitive work; *saṁsṛtiḥ*—the cycle of material life; *bhavet* — there is.

TRANSLATION

O best of the Bhṛgus, this account concerning Mārkaṇḍeya Ṛṣi conveys the transcendental potency of the Supreme Lord. Anyone who properly narrates or hears it will never again undergo material existence, which is based on the desire to perform fruitive activities.

Thus end the purports of the humble servants of His Divine Grace A.C. Bhaktivedanta Swami Prabhupāda to the Twelfth Canto, Tenth Chapter, of the Śrīmad-Bhāgavatam, *entitled "Lord Śiva and Umā Glorify Mārkaṇḍeya Ṛṣi."*

CHAPTER ELEVEN

Summary Description of the Mahāpuruṣa

In the context of worship, this chapter describes the Mahāpuruṣa and the various expansions of the sun in each month. Śrī Sūta first tells Śaunaka Ṛṣi about the material objects through which one can understand the major limbs, the secondary limbs, the weapons and the garments of Lord Śrī Hari. Then he outlines the process of practical service by which a mortal soul can attain immortality. When Śaunaka shows further interest in learning about the expansion of Lord Hari in the form of the sun god, Sūta replies that Lord Śrī Hari — the indwelling controller of the universe and its original creator — manifests Himself in the form of the demigod of the sun. Sages describe this sun god in many features according to his different material designations. To sustain the world, the Personality of Godhead manifests His potency of time as the sun and travels throughout the twelve months, beginning with Caitra, along with twelve sets of personal associates. One who remembers the opulences of the Personality of Godhead Śrī Hari in His form as the sun will become free of his sinful reactions.

TEXT 1

श्रीशौनक उवाच

अथेममर्थं पृच्छामो भवन्तं बहुवित्तमम् ।
समस्ततन्त्रराद्धान्ते भवान् भागवत तत्त्ववित् ॥ १ ॥

śrī-śaunaka uvāca
athemam arthaṁ pṛcchāmo
bhavantaṁ bahu-vittamam
samasta-tantra-rāddhānte
bhavān bhāgavata tattva-vit

śrī-śaunakaḥ uvāca — Śrī Śaunaka said; *atha* — now; *imam* — this; *artham* — matter; *pṛcchāmaḥ* — we are inquiring about; *bhavantam* — from you; *bahu-vit-tamam* — the possessor of the broadest knowledge; *samasta* — of all; *tantra* — the scriptures prescribing practical methods of worship; *rāddha-ante* — in the definitive conclusions; *bhavān* — you; *bhāgavata* — O great devotee of the Supreme Lord; *tattva-vit* — the knower of the essential facts.

TRANSLATION

Śrī Śaunaka said: O Sūta, you are the best of learned men and a great devotee of the Supreme Lord. Therefore we now inquire from you about the definitive conclusion of all tantra scriptures.

TEXTS 2–3

तान्त्रिकाः परिचर्यायां केवलस्य श्रियः पतेः ।
अंगोपांगायुधाकल्पं कल्पयन्ति यथा च यैः ॥ २ ॥
तन्नो वर्णय भद्रं ते क्रियायोगं बुभुत्सताम् ।
येन क्रियानैपुणेन मर्त्यो यायादमर्त्यताम् ॥ ३ ॥

tāntrikāḥ paricaryāyāṁ
kevalasya śriyaḥ pateḥ
aṅgopāṅgāyudhākalpaṁ
kalpayanti yathā ca yaiḥ

tan no varṇaya bhadraṁ te
kriyā-yogaṁ bubhutsatām
yena kriyā-naipuṇena
martyo yāyād amartyatām

tāntrikāḥ — the followers of the methods of the tantric literatures; *paricaryāyām* — in regulated worship; *kevalasya* — who is pure spirit; *śriyaḥ* — of the goddess of fortune; *pateḥ* — of the master; *aṅga* — His limbs, such as His feet; *upāṅga* — His secondary limbs, such as associates like Garuḍa; *āyudha* — His weapons, such as the Sudarśana disc; *ākalpam* — and His ornaments, such as the Kaustubha gem; *kalpayanti* — they conceive of; *yathā* — how; *ca* — and; *yaiḥ* — by which (material representations); *tat* — that; *naḥ* — to us; *varṇaya* — please describe; *bhadram* — all-auspiciousness; *te* — unto you; *kriyā-yogam* — the practical method of cultivation; *bubhutsatām* — who are eager to learn; *yena* — by which; *kriyā* — in the systematic practice; *naipuṇena* — expertise; *martyaḥ* — a mortal being; *yāyāt* — may attain; *amartyatām* — immortality.

TRANSLATION

All good fortune to you! Please explain to us, who are very eager to learn, the process of kriyā-yoga practiced through regulated worship of the transcendental Lord, the husband of the goddess of fortune. Please also explain how the Lord's devotees conceive of His limbs, associates, weapons and ornaments in terms of particular material representations. By expertly worshiping the Supreme Lord, a mortal can attain immortality.

TEXT 4

सूत उवाच
नमस्कृत्य गुरून् वक्ष्ये विभूतीर्वैष्णवीरपि ।
याः प्रोक्ता वेदतन्त्राभ्यामाचार्यैः पद्मजादिभिः ॥ ४ ॥

sūta uvāca
namaskṛtya gurūn vakṣye
vibhūtīr vaiṣṇavīr api
yāḥ proktā veda-tantrābhyām
ācāryaiḥ padmajādibhiḥ

sūtaḥ uvāca — Sūta Gosvāmī said; *namaskṛtya* — offering obeisances; *gurūn* — to the spiritual masters; *vakṣye* — I shall speak; *vibhūtīḥ* — the opulences; *vaiṣṇavīḥ* — belonging to Lord Viṣṇu; *api* — indeed; *yāḥ* — which; *proktāḥ* — are described; *veda-tantrābhyām* — by the *Vedas* and the *tantras;* *ācāryaiḥ* — by standard authorities; *padmaja-ādibhiḥ* — beginning with Lord Brahmā.

TRANSLATION

Sūta Gosvāmī said: Offering obeisances to my spiritual masters, I shall repeat to you the description of the opulences of Lord Viṣṇu given in the Vedas and tantras by great authorities, beginning from lotus-born Brahmā.

TEXT 5

मायाद्यैर्नवभिस्तत्त्वैः स विकारमयो विराट् ।
निर्मितो दृश्यते यत्र सचित्के भुवनत्रयम् ॥ ५ ॥

māyādyair navabhis tattvaiḥ
sa vikāra-mayo virāṭ

nirmito dṛśyate yatra
sa-citke bhuvana-trayam

māyā-ādyaiḥ—beginning with the unmanifest stage of nature; *navabhiḥ*—with the nine; *tattvaiḥ*—elements; *saḥ*—that; *vikāra-mayaḥ*—also comprising the transformations (of the eleven senses and the five gross elements); *virāṭ*—the universal form of the Lord; *nirmitaḥ*—constructed; *dṛśyate* — are seen; *yatra* — in which; *sa-citke* — being conscious; *bhuvana-trayam* — the three planetary systems.

TRANSLATION

The universal form [virāṭ] of the Personality of Godhead includes the nine basic elements of creation, starting with the unmanifest nature, and their subsequent transformations. Once this universal form is instilled with consciousness, the three planetary systems become visible within it.

PURPORT

The nine basic elements of creation are *prakṛti, sūtra, mahat-tattva,* false ego, and the five subtle perceptions. The transformations are the eleven senses and the five gross material elements.

TEXTS 6–8

एतद् वै पौरुषं रूपं भूः पादौ द्यौः शिरो नभः ।
नाभिः सूर्योऽक्षिणी नासे वायुः कर्णौ दिशः प्रभोः ॥ ६ ॥
प्रजापतिः प्रजननम् अपानो मृत्युरीशितुः ।
तद्बाहवो लोकपाला मनश्चन्द्रो भ्रुवौ यमः ॥ ७ ॥
लज्जोत्तरोऽधरो लोभो दन्ता ज्योत्स्ना स्मयो भ्रमः ।
रोमाणि भूरुहा भूम्नो मेघाः पुरुषमूर्धजाः ॥ ८ ॥

etad vai pauruṣaṁ rūpaṁ
bhūḥ pādau dyauḥ śiro nabhaḥ
nābhiḥ sūryo 'kṣiṇī nāse
vāyuḥ karṇau diśaḥ prabhoḥ

prajāpatiḥ prajananam
apāno mṛtyur īśituḥ

tad-bāhavo loka-pālā
manaś candro bhruvau yamaḥ

lajjottaro 'dharo lobho
dantā jyotsnā smayo bhramaḥ
romāṇi bhūruhā bhūmno
meghāḥ puruṣa-mūrdhajāḥ

etat—this; *vai*—indeed; *pauruṣam*—of the Virāṭ-puruṣa; *rūpam*—the form; *bhūḥ*—the earth; *pādau*—His feet; *dyauḥ*—heaven; *śiraḥ*—His head; *nabhaḥ*—the sky; *nābhiḥ*—His navel; *sūryaḥ*—the sun; *akṣiṇī*—His eyes; *nāse*—His nostrils; *vāyuḥ*—the air; *karṇau*—His ears; *diśaḥ*—the directions; *prabhoḥ*—of the Supreme Lord; *prajā-patiḥ*—the demigod of procreation; *prajananam*—His genitals; *apānaḥ*—His anus; *mṛtyuḥ*—death; *īśituḥ*—of the absolute controller; *tat-bāhavaḥ*—His many arms; *loka-pālāḥ*—the presiding demigods of the various planets; *manaḥ*—His mind; *candraḥ*—the moon; *bhruvau*—His eyebrows; *yamaḥ*—the god of death; *lajjā*—shame; *uttaraḥ*—His upper lip; *adharaḥ*—His lower lip; *lobhaḥ*—greed; *dantāḥ*—His teeth; *jyotsnā*—the light of the moon; *smayaḥ*—His smile; *bhramaḥ*—delusion; *romāṇi*—the hairs of the body; *bhū-ruhāḥ*—the trees; *bhūmnaḥ*—of the almighty Lord; *meghāḥ*—the clouds; *puruṣa*—of the Virāṭ-puruṣa; *mūrdha-jāḥ*—the hairs upon the head.

TRANSLATION

This is the representation of the Supreme Lord as the universal person, in which the earth is His feet, the sky His navel, the sun His eyes, the wind His nostrils, the demigod of procreation His genitals, death His anus and the moon His mind. The heavenly planets are His head, the directions His ears, and the demigods protecting the various planets His many arms. The god of death is His eyebrows, shame His lower lip, greed His upper lip, delusion His smile, and moonshine His teeth, while the trees are the almighty Puruṣa's bodily hairs, and the clouds the hair on His head.

PURPORT

Various aspects of material creation, such as the earth, the sun and the trees, are sustained by various limbs of the universal body of the Lord. Thus they are considered nondifferent from Him, as described in this verse, which is meant for meditation.

TEXT 9

यावानयं वै पुरुषो यावत्या संस्थया मितः ।
तावानसावपि महापुरुषो लोकसंस्थया ॥ ९ ॥

yāvān ayaṁ vai puruṣo
yāvatyā saṁsthayā mitaḥ
tāvān asāv api mahā-
puruṣo loka-saṁsthayā

yāvān — to which extent; *ayam* — this; *vai* — indeed; *puruṣaḥ* — ordinary individual person; *yāvatyā* — extending to which dimensions; *saṁsthayā* — by the position of his limbs; *mitaḥ* — measured; *tāvān* — to that extent; *asau* — He; *api* — also; *mahā-puruṣaḥ* — the transcendental personality; *loka-saṁsthayā* — according to the positions of the planetary systems.

TRANSLATION

Just as one can determine the dimensions of an ordinary person of this world by measuring his various limbs, one can determine the dimensions of the Mahāpuruṣa by measuring the arrangement of the planetary systems within His universal form.

TEXT 10

कौस्तुभव्यपदेशेन स्वात्मज्योतिर्बिभर्त्यजः ।
तत्प्रभा व्यापिनी साक्षात् श्रीवत्समुरसा विभुः ॥ १० ॥

kaustubha-vyapadeśena
svātma-jyotir bibharty ajaḥ
tat-prabhā vyāpinī sākṣāt
śrīvatsam urasā vibhuḥ

kaustubha-vyapadeśena — represented by the Kaustubha gem; *sva-ātma* — of the pure *jīva* soul; *jyotiḥ* — the spiritual light; *bibharti* — carries; *ajaḥ* — the unborn Lord; *tat-prabhā* — the effulgence of this (Kaustubha); *vyāpinī* — expansive; *sākṣāt* — directly; *śrīvatsam* — of the Śrīvatsa mark; *urasā* — upon His chest; *vibhuḥ* — the almighty.

TRANSLATION

Upon His chest the almighty, unborn Personality of Godhead bears the Kaustubha gem, which represents the pure spirit soul, along with the Śrīvatsa mark, which is the direct manifestation of this gem's expansive effulgence.

TEXTS 11–12

स्वमायां वनमालाख्यां नानागुणमयीं दधत् ।
वासश्छन्दोमयं पीतं ब्रह्मसूत्रं त्रिवृत् स्वरम् ॥ ११ ॥
बिभर्ति सांख्यं योगं च देवो मकरकुण्डले ।
मौलिं पदं पारमेष्ठ्यं सर्वलोकाभयंकरम् ॥ १२ ॥

sva-māyāṁ vana-mālākhyāṁ
nānā-guṇa-mayīṁ dadhat
vāsaś chando-mayaṁ pītaṁ
brahma-sūtraṁ tri-vṛt svaram

bibharti sāṅkhyaṁ yogaṁ ca
devo makara-kuṇḍale
mauliṁ padaṁ pārameṣṭhyaṁ
sarva-lokābhayaṅ-karam

sva-māyām — His own material energy; *vana-mālā-ākhyām* — represented as His flower garland; *nānā-guṇa* — various combinations of the modes of nature; *mayīm* — composed of; *dadhat* — wearing; *vāsaḥ* — His garment; *chandaḥ-mayam* — consisting of the Vedic meters; *pītam* — yellow; *brahma-sūtram* — His sacred thread; *tri-vṛt* — threefold; *svaram* — the sacred sound *oṁkāra; bibharti* — He carries; *sāṅkhyam* — the process of Sāṅkhya; *yogam* — the process of *yoga; ca* — and; *devaḥ* — the Lord; *makara-kuṇḍale* — His shark-shaped earrings; *maulim* — His crown; *padam* — the position; *pārameṣṭhyam* — supreme (of Lord Brahmā); *sarva-loka* — to all the worlds; *abhayam* — fearlessness; *karam* — which gives.

TRANSLATION

His flower garland is His material energy, comprising various combinations of the modes of nature. His yellow garment is the Vedic meters, and His sacred thread the syllable oṁ composed of three sounds. In the form of His two shark-shaped earrings, the Lord carries the processes

of Sāṅkhya and yoga, and His crown, bestowing fearlessness on the inhabitants of all the worlds, is the supreme position of Brahmaloka.

TEXT 13

अव्याकृतमनन्ताख्यमासनं यदधिष्ठितः ।
धर्मज्ञानादिभिर्युक्तं सत्त्वं पद्ममिहोच्यते ॥ १३ ॥

avyākṛtam anantākhyam
āsanaṁ yad-adhiṣṭhitaḥ
dharma-jñānādibhir yuktaṁ
sattvaṁ padmam ihocyate

avyākṛtam — the unmanifest phase of material creation; *ananta-ākhyam* — known as Lord Ananta; *āsanam* — His personal seat; *yat-adhiṣṭhitaḥ*— upon which He is sitting; *dharma-jñāna-ādibhiḥ*—together with religion, knowledge and so on; *yuktam* — conjoined; *sattvam* — in the mode of goodness; *padmam* — His lotus; *iha* — thereupon; *ucyate* — is said.

TRANSLATION

Ananta, the Lord's sitting place, is the unmanifest phase of material nature, and the Lord's lotus throne is the mode of goodness, endowed with religion and knowledge.

TEXTS 14–15

ओजःसहोबलयुतं मुख्यतत्त्वं गदां दधत् ।
अपां तत्त्वं दरवरं तेजस्तत्त्वं सुदर्शनम् ॥ १४ ॥
नभोनिभं नभस्तत्त्वमसिं चर्म तमोमयम् ।
कालरूपं धनुः शार्ङ्गं तथा कर्ममयेषुधिम् ॥ १५ ॥

ojaḥ-saho-bala-yutaṁ
mukhya-tattvaṁ gadāṁ dadhat
apāṁ tattvaṁ dara-varaṁ
tejas-tattvaṁ sudarśanam

nabho-nibhaṁ nabhas-tattvam
asiṁ carma tamo-mayam

kāla-rūpaṁ dhanuḥ śārṅgaṁ
tathā karma-mayeṣudhim

ojaḥ-sahaḥ-bala — with the power of the senses, the power of the mind and the power of the body; *yutam* — conjoined; *mukhya-tattvam* — the principle element, air, which is the vital force within the material body; *gadām* — His club; *dadhat* — carrying; *apām* — of water; *tattvam* — the element; *dara* — His conchshell; *varam* — excellent; *tejaḥ-tattvam* — the element fire; *sudarśanam* — His Sudarśana disc; *nabhaḥ-nibham* — just like the sky; *nabhaḥ-tattvam* — the element ether; *asim* — His sword; *carma* — His shield; *tamaḥ-mayam* — composed of the mode of ignorance; *kāla-rūpam* — appearing as time; *dhanuḥ*— His bow; *śārṅgam* — named Śārṅga; *tathā* — and; *karma-maya* — representing the active senses; *iṣu-dhim* — the quiver holding His arrows.

TRANSLATION

The club the Lord carries is the chief element, prāṇa, incorporating the potencies of sensory, mental and physical strength. His excellent conchshell is the element water, His Sudarśana disc the element fire, and His sword, pure as the sky, the element ether. His shield embodies the mode of ignorance, His bow, named Śārṅga, time, and His arrow-filled quiver the working sensory organs.

TEXT 16

इन्द्रियाणि शरानाहुराकूतीरस्य स्यन्दनम् ।
तन्मात्राण्यस्याभिव्यक्तिं मुद्रयार्थक्रियात्मताम् ॥ १६ ॥

indriyāṇi śarān āhur
ākūtīr asya syandanam
tan-mātrāṇy asyābhivyaktiṁ
mudrayārtha-kriyātmatām

indriyāṇi — the senses; *śarān* — His arrows; *āhuḥ*— they say; *ākūtīḥ*— (the mind with its) active functions; *asya* — of Him; *syandanam* — the chariot; *tat-mātrāṇi* — the objects of perception; *asya* — His; *abhivyaktim* — external appearance; *mudrayā* — by the gestures of His hands (symbolizing the giving of benedictions, the offering of fearlessness, and so on); *artha-kriyā-ātmatām* — the essence of purposeful activity.

TRANSLATION

His arrows are said to be the senses, and His chariot is the active, forceful mind. His external appearance is the subtle objects of perception, and the gestures of His hands are the essence of all purposeful activity.

PURPORT

All activity is ultimately aimed at the supreme perfection of life, and this perfection is awarded by the merciful hands of the Lord. The gestures of the Lord remove all fear from the heart of a devotee and elevate him to the Lord's own association in the spiritual sky.

TEXT 17

मण्डलं देवयजनं दीक्षा संस्कार आत्मनः ।
परिचर्या भगवत आत्मनो दुरितक्षयः ॥ १७ ॥

maṇḍalaṁ deva-yajanaṁ
dīkṣā saṁskāra ātmanaḥ
paricaryā bhagavata
ātmano durita-kṣayaḥ

maṇḍalam — the sun globe; *deva-yajanam* — the place where the Supreme Lord is worshiped; *dīkṣā* — spiritual initiation; *saṁskāraḥ* — the process of purification; *ātmanaḥ* — for the spirit soul; *paricaryā* — devotional service; *bhagavataḥ* — of the Personality of Godhead; *ātmanaḥ* — for the *jīva* soul; *durita* — of sinful reactions; *kṣayaḥ* — the destruction.

TRANSLATION

The sun globe is the place where the Supreme Lord is worshiped, spiritual initiation is the means of purification for the spirit soul, and rendering devotional service to the Personality of Godhead is the process for eradicating all one's sinful reactions.

PURPORT

One should meditate on the fiery sun globe as a place where God is worshiped. Lord Kṛṣṇa is the reservoir of all effulgence, and thus it is fitting that He be properly worshiped on the glowing sun.

TEXT 18

भगवान् भगशब्दार्थं लीलाकमलमुद्वहन् ।
धर्मं यशश्च भगवांश्चामरव्यजनेऽभजत् ॥ १८ ॥

bhagavān bhaga-śabdārthaṁ
līlā-kamalam udvahan
dharmaṁ yaśaś ca bhagavāṁś
cāmara-vyajane'bhajat

bhagavān — the Personality of Godhead; *bhaga-śabda* — of the word *bhaga; artham* — the meaning (namely, "opulence"); *līlā-kamalam* — His pastime lotus; *udvahan* — carrying; *dharmam* — religion; *yaśaḥ*—fame; *ca* — and; *bhagavān* — the Personality of Godhead; *cāmara-vyajane* — the pair of yak-tail fans; *abhajat* — has accepted.

TRANSLATION

Playfully carrying a lotus, which represents the various opulences designated by the word bhaga, the Supreme Lord accepts service from a pair of cāmara fans, which are religion and fame.

TEXT 19

आतपत्रं तु वैकुण्ठं द्विजा धामाकुतोभयम् ।
त्रिवृद् वेदः सुपर्णाख्यो यज्ञं वहति पूरुषम् ॥ १९ ॥

ātapatraṁ tu vaikuṇṭhaṁ
dvijā dhāmākuto-bhayam
tri-vṛd vedaḥ suparṇākhyo
yajñaṁ vahati pūruṣam

ātapatram — His umbrella; *tu* — and; *vaikuṇṭham* — His spiritual abode, Vaikuṇṭha; *dvijāḥ*—O *brāhmaṇas; dhāma* — His personal abode, the spiritual world; *akutaḥ-bhayam* — free from fear; *tri-vṛt* — threefold; *vedaḥ*—the *Veda; suparṇa-ākhyaḥ*—named Suparṇa, or Garuḍa; *yajñam* — sacrifice personified; *vahati* — carried; *pūruṣam* — the Supreme Personality of Godhead.

TRANSLATION

O brāhmaṇas, the Lord's umbrella is His spiritual abode, Vaikuṇṭha, where there is no fear, and Garuḍa, who carries the Lord of sacrifice, is the threefold Veda.

TEXT 20

अनपायिनी भगवती श्रीः साक्षादात्मनो हरेः ।
विष्वक्सेनस्तन्त्रमूर्तिर्विदितः पार्षदाधिपः ।
नन्दादयोऽष्टौ द्वाःस्थाश्च तेऽणिमाद्या हरेर्गुणाः ॥ २० ॥

anapāyinī bhagavatī
śrīḥ sākṣād ātmano hareḥ
viṣvaksenas tantra-mūrtir
viditaḥ pārṣadādhipaḥ
nandādayo 'ṣṭau dvāḥ-sthāś ca
te 'ṇimādyā harer guṇāḥ

anapāyinī—inseparable; *bhagavatī*—the goddess of fortune; *śrīḥ*—Śrī; *sākṣāt* — directly; *ātmanaḥ*—of the internal nature; *hareḥ*—of Lord Hari; *viṣvaksenaḥ*—Viṣvaksena; *tantra-mūrtiḥ*—as the personification of the *tantra* scriptures; *viditaḥ*—is known; *pārṣada-adhipaḥ*—the chief of His personal associates; *nanda-ādayaḥ*—Nanda and the others; *aṣṭau* — the eight; *dvāḥ-sthāḥ*—doorkeepers; *ca* — and; *te* — they; *aṇimā-ādyāḥ*— *aṇimā* and the other mystic perfections; *hareḥ*—of the Supreme Lord; *guṇāḥ*—the qualities.

TRANSLATION

The goddess of fortune, Śrī, who never leaves the Lord's side, appears with Him in this world as the representation of His internal potency. Viṣvaksena, the chief among His personal associates, is known to be the personification of the Pañcarātra and other tantras. And the Lord's eight doorkeepers, headed by Nanda, are His mystic perfections, beginning with aṇimā.

PURPORT

According to Śrīla Jīva Gosvāmī, the goddess of fortune is the original source of all material opulence. Material nature is directly controlled by the

Lord's inferior energy, Mahā-māyā, whereas the goddess of fortune is His internal, superior energy. Still, the opulence of the Lord's inferior nature has its source in the supreme spiritual opulence of the goddess of fortune. As stated in *Śrī Hayaśīrṣa Pañcarātra:*

paramātmā harir devas
tac-chaktiḥ śrīr ihoditā
śrīr devī prakṛtiḥ proktā
keśavaḥ puruṣaḥ smṛtaḥ
na viṣṇunā vinā devī
na hariḥ padmajāṁ vinā

"The Supreme Soul is Lord Hari, and His potency is known in this world as Śrī. Goddess Śrī is known as *prakṛti,* and the Supreme Lord Keśava is known as the *puruṣa.* The divine goddess is never present without Him, nor does He ever appear without her."

Also, *Śrī Viṣṇu Purāṇa* (1.8.15) states:

nityaiva sā jagan-mātā
viṣṇoḥ śrīr anapāyinī
yathā sarva-gato viṣṇus
tathaiveyaṁ dvijottamāḥ

"She is the eternal mother of the universe, the goddess of fortune of Lord Viṣṇu, and she is never separated from Him. In the same way that Lord Viṣṇu is present everywhere, so is she, O best of *brāhmaṇas."*

Also in *Viṣṇu Purāṇa* (1.9.140):

evaṁ yathā jagat-svāmī
deva-devo janārdanaḥ
avatāraṁ karoty eva
tathā śrīs tat-sahāyinī

"Thus, in the same way that the Lord of the universe, the God of gods, Janārdana, descends to this world, so His consort, the goddess of fortune, does also."

The pure spiritual status of the goddess of fortune is described in the *Skanda Purāṇa:*

aparaṁ tv akṣaraṁ yā sā
prakṛtir jaḍa-rūpikā

śrīḥ parā prakṛtiḥ proktā
cetanā viṣṇu-saṁśrayā

taṁ akṣaraṁ paraṁ prāhuḥ
parataḥ param akṣaram
harir evākhila-guṇo'py
akṣara-trayam īritam

"The inferior infallible entity is that nature who manifests as the material world. The goddess of fortune, on the other hand, is known as the superior nature. She is pure consciousness and is under the direct shelter of Lord Viṣṇu. While she is said to be the superior infallible entity, that infallible entity who is greater than the greatest is Lord Hari Himself, the original possessor of all transcendental qualities. In this way, three distinct infallible entities are described."

Thus, although the inferior energy of the Lord is infallible in her function, her power to manifest temporary illusory opulences exists by the grace of the internal energy, the goddess of fortune, who is the personal consort of the Supreme Lord.

The *Padma Purāṇa* (256.9–21) lists eighteen doorkeepers of the Lord: Nanda, Sunanda, Jaya, Vijaya, Caṇḍa, Pracaṇḍa, Bhadra, Subhadra, Dhātā, Vidhātā, Kumuda, Kumudākṣa, Pundarīkṣa, Vāmana, Śaṅkukarṇa, Sarvanetra, Sumukha and Supratiṣṭhita.

TEXT 21

वासुदेवः संकर्षणः प्रद्युम्नः पुरुषः स्वयम् ।
अनिरुद्ध इति ब्रह्मन्मूर्तिव्यूहोऽभिधीयते ॥ २१ ॥

vāsudevaḥ saṅkarṣaṇaḥ
pradyumnaḥ puruṣaḥ svayam
aniruddha iti brahman
mūrti-vyūho 'bhidhīyate

vāsudevaḥ saṅkarṣaṇaḥ pradyumnaḥ—Vāsudeva, Saṅkarṣaṇa and Pradyumna; *puruṣaḥ*—the Supreme Personality of Godhead; *svayam*—Himself; *aniruddhaḥ*—Aniruddha; *iti*—thus; *brahman*—O *brāhmaṇa,* Śaunaka; *mūrti-vyūhaḥ*—the expansion of personal forms; *abhidhīyate*—is designated.

TRANSLATION

Vāsudeva, Saṅkarṣaṇa, Pradyumna and Aniruddha are the names of the direct personal expansions of the Supreme Godhead, O brāhmaṇa Śaunaka.

TEXT 22

स विश्वस्तैजसः प्राज्ञस्तुरीय इति वृत्तिभिः ।
अर्थेन्द्रियाशयज्ञानैर्भगवान् परिभाव्यते ॥ २२ ॥

sa viśvas taijasaḥ prājñas
turīya iti vṛttibhiḥ
arthendriyāśaya-jñānair
bhagavān paribhāvyate

saḥ—He; *viśvaḥ taijasaḥ prājñaḥ*—the manifestations of waking consciousness, sleep and deep sleep; *turīyaḥ*—the fourth, transcendental stage; *iti*—thus termed; *vṛttibhiḥ*—by the functions; *artha*—by the external objects of perception; *indriya*—the mind; *āśaya*—covered consciousness; *jñānaiḥ*—and spiritual knowledge; *bhagavān*—the Personality of Godhead; *paribhāvyate*—is conceived of.

TRANSLATION

One can conceive of the Supreme Personality of Godhead in terms of awakened consciousness, sleep and deep sleep—which function respectively through external objects, the mind and material intelligence—and also in terms of the fourth, transcendental level of consciousness, which is characterized by pure knowledge.

TEXT 23

अंगोपांगायुधाकल्पैर्भगवांस्तच्चतुष्टयम् ।
बिभर्ति स्म चतुर्मूर्तिर्भगवान् हरिरीश्वरः ॥ २३ ॥

aṅgopāṅgāyudhākalpair
bhagavāṁs tac catuṣṭayam
bibharti sma catur-mūrtir
bhagavān harir īśvaraḥ

aṅga — with His major limbs; *upāṅga* — minor limbs; *āyudha* — weapons; *ākalpaiḥ* — and ornaments; *bhagavān* — the Personality of Godhead; *tat catuṣṭayam* — these four manifestations (of *viśva, taijasa, prājña* and *turīya*); *bibharti* — maintains; *sma* — indeed; *catuḥ-mūrtiḥ* — in His four personal features (Vāsudeva, Saṅkarṣaṇa, Pradyumna and Aniruddha); *bhagavān* — the Lord; *hariḥ* — Hari; *īśvaraḥ* — the supreme controller.

TRANSLATION

The Supreme Personality of Godhead, Lord Hari, thus appears in four personal expansions, each exhibiting major limbs, minor limbs, weapons and ornaments. Through these distinct features, the Lord maintains the four phases of existence.

PURPORT

The Lord's spiritual body, weapons, ornaments and associates are all pure transcendental existence, identical with Him.

TEXT 24

द्विजऋषभ स एष ब्रह्मयोनिः स्वयंदृक्
स्वमहिमपरिपूर्णो मायया च स्वयैतत् ।
सृजति हरति पातीत्याख्ययानावृताक्षो
विवृत इव निरुक्तस्तत्परैरात्मलभ्यः ॥ २४ ॥

dvija-ṛṣabha sa eṣa brahma-yoniḥ svayaṁ-dṛk
sva-mahima-paripūrṇo māyayā ca svayaitat
sṛjati harati pātīty ākhyayānāvṛtākṣo
vivṛta iva niruktas tat-parair ātma-labhyaḥ

dvija-ṛṣabha — O best of the *brāhmaṇas; saḥ eṣaḥ* — He alone; *brahma-yoniḥ* — the source of the *Vedas; svayam-dṛk* — who is self-illuminating; *sva-mahima* — in His own glory; *paripūrṇaḥ* — perfectly complete; *māyayā* — by the material energy; *ca* — and; *svayā* — His own; *etat* — this universe; *sṛjati* — He creates; *harati* — He withdraws; *pāti* — He maintains; *iti ākhyayā* — conceived of as such; *anāvṛta* — uncovered; *akṣaḥ* — His transcendental awareness; *vivṛtaḥ* — materially divided; *iva* — as if; *niruktaḥ* — described; *tat-paraiḥ* — by those who are devoted to Him; *ātma* — as their very Soul; *labhyaḥ* — realizable.

TRANSLATION

O best of brāhmaṇas, He alone is the self-luminous, original source of the Vedas, perfect and complete in His own glory. By His material energy He creates, destroys and maintains this entire universe. Because He is the performer of various material functions, He is sometimes described as materially divided, yet He always remains transcendentally situated in pure knowledge. Those who are dedicated to Him in devotion can realize Him to be their true Soul.

PURPORT

Śrīla Viśvanātha Cakravartī Ṭhākura recommends that we become humble by practicing the following meditation: "The earth, which is always visible to me, is the expansion of the lotus feet of my Lord, who is always to be meditated upon. All moving and nonmoving living beings have taken shelter of the earth and are thus sheltered at the lotus feet of my Lord. For this reason I should respect every living being and not envy anyone. In fact, all living entities constitute the Kaustubha gem on My Lord's chest. Therefore I should never envy or deride any living entity." By practicing this meditation one can achieve success in life.

TEXT 25

श्रीकृष्ण कृष्णसख वृष्ण्यृषभावनिध्रुग्
राजन्यवंशदहनानपवर्गवीर्य ।
गोविन्द गोपवनिताव्रजभृत्यगीत-
तीर्थश्रवः श्रवणमंगल पाहि भृत्यान् ॥ २५ ॥

śrī-kṛṣṇa kṛṣṇa-sakha vṛṣṇy-ṛṣabhāvani-dhrug-
rājanya-vaṁśa-dahanānapavarga-vīrya
govinda gopa-vanitā-vraja-bhṛtya-gīta
tīrtha-śravaḥ śravaṇa-maṅgala pāhi bhṛtyān

śrī-kṛṣṇa — O Śrī Kṛṣṇa; *kṛṣṇa-sakha* — O friend of Arjuna; *vṛṣṇi* — of the descendants of Vṛṣṇi; *ṛṣabha* — O chief; *avani* — on the earth; *dhruk* — rebellious; *rājanya-vaṁśa* — of the dynasties of kings; *dahana* — O annihilator; *anapavarga* — without deterioration; *vīrya* — whose prowess; *govinda* — O proprietor of Goloka-dhāma; *gopa* — of the cowherd men; *vanitā* — and the cowherd women; *vraja* — by the multitude; *bhṛtya* — and by their servants;

gīta — sung; *tīrtha* — pious, as the most holy place of pilgrimage; *śravaḥ*— whose glories; *śravaṇa* — just to hear about whom; *maṅgala* — auspicious; *pāhi* — please protect; *bhṛtyān* — Your servants.

TRANSLATION

O Kṛṣṇa, O friend of Arjuna, O chief among the descendants of Vṛṣṇi, You are the destroyer of those political parties that are disturbing elements on this earth. Your prowess never deteriorates. You are the proprietor of the transcendental abode, and Your most sacred glories, which are sung by Vṛndāvana's cowherd men and women and their servants, bestow all auspiciousness just by being heard. O Lord, please protect Your devotees.

TEXT 26

य इदं कल्य उत्थाय महापुरुषलक्षणम् ।
तच्चित्तः प्रयतो जप्त्वा ब्रह्म वेद गुहाशयम् ॥ २६ ॥

ya idaṁ kalya utthāya
mahā-puruṣa-lakṣaṇam
tac-cittaḥ prayato japtvā
brahma veda guhāśayam

yaḥ—anyone who; *idam* — this; *kalye* — at dawn; *utthāya* — rising; *mahā-puruṣa-lakṣaṇam* — the characteristics of the Supreme Personality in His universal form; *tat-cittaḥ*—with mind absorbed in Him; *prayataḥ*—purified; *japtvā* — chanting to oneself; *brahma* — the Absolute Truth; *veda* — he comes to know; *guhā-śayam* — situated within the heart.

TRANSLATION

Anyone who rises early in the morning and, with a purified mind fixed upon the Mahāpuruṣa, quietly chants this description of His characteristics will realize Him as the Supreme Absolute Truth residing within the heart.

TEXTS 27–28

श्रीशौनक उवाच

शुको यदाह भगवान् विष्णुराताय शृण्वते ।
सौरो गणो मासि मासि नाना वसति सप्तकः ॥ २७ ॥

तेषां नामानि कर्माणि नियुक्तानामधीश्वरैः ।
ब्रूहि नः श्रद्दधानानां व्यूहं सूर्यात्मनो हरेः ॥ २८ ॥

śrī-śaunaka uvāca
śuko yad āha bhagavān
viṣṇu-rātāya śṛṇvate
sauro gaṇo māsi māsi
nānā vasati saptakaḥ

teṣāṁ nāmāni karmāṇi
niyuktānām adhīśvaraiḥ
brūhi naḥ śraddadhānānāṁ
vyūhaṁ sūryātmano hareḥ

śrī-śaunakaḥ uvāca—Śrī Śaunaka said; *śukaḥ*—Śukadeva Gosvāmī; *yat*—which; *āha*—described; *bhagavān*—the great sage; *viṣṇu-rātāya*—to King Parīkṣit; *śṛṇvate*—who was listening; *sauraḥ*—of the sun god; *gaṇaḥ*—the associates; *māsi māsi*—in each month; *nānā*—various; *vasati*—who reside; *saptakaḥ*—the group of seven; *teṣām*—of them; *nāmāni*—the names; *karmāṇi*—the activities; *niyuktānām*—who are engaged; *adhīśvaraiḥ*—by the various features of the sun-god, who are their controllers; *brūhi*—please speak; *naḥ*—to us; *śraddadhānānām*—who are faithful; *vyūham*—the personal expansions; *sūrya-ātmanaḥ*—in His personal expansion as the sun god; *hareḥ*—of the Supreme Personality of Godhead, Lord Hari.

TRANSLATION

Śrī Śaunaka said: Please describe to us, who have great faith in your words, the different sets of seven personal features and associates the sun-god exhibits during each month, along with their names and activities. The associates of the sun-god, who serve their lord, are personal expansions of the Supreme Personality of Godhead Hari in His feature as the presiding deity of the sun.

PURPORT

After hearing an account of the exalted conversation between Śukadeva Gosvāmī and Mahārāja Parīkṣit, Śaunaka now inquires about the sun as the expansion of the Supreme Lord. Although the sun is the king of all planets, Śrī

Śaunaka is specifically interested in this effulgent globe as the expansion of Śrī Hari, the Supreme Personality of Godhead.

The personalities related with the sun are of seven categories. In the course of the sun's orbit there are twelve months, and in each month a different sun god and a different set of his six associates preside. In each of the twelve months beginning from Vaiśākha there are different names for the sun-god himself, the sage, the Yakṣa, the Gandharva, the Apsarā, the Rākṣasa and the Nāga, making a total of seven categories.

TEXT 29

सूत उवाच
अनाद्यविद्यया विष्णोरात्मनः सर्वदेहिनाम् ।
निर्मितो लोकतन्त्रोऽयं लोकेषु परिवर्तते ॥ २९ ॥

sūta uvāca
anādy-avidyayā viṣṇor
ātmanaḥ sarva-dehinām
nirmito loka-tantro'yaṁ
lokeṣu parivartate

sūtaḥ uvāca — Sūta Gosvāmī said; *anādi* — beginningless; *avidyayā* — by the illusory energy; *viṣṇoḥ*—of Lord Viṣṇu; *ātmanaḥ*—who is the Supreme Soul; *sarva-dehinām* — of all embodied living beings; *nirmitaḥ*—produced; *loka-tantraḥ*—the regulator of the planets; *ayam* — this; *lokeṣu* — among the planets; *parivartate* — travels.

TRANSLATION

Sūta Gosvāmī said: The sun travels among all the planets and thus regulates their movements. It has been created by Lord Viṣṇu, the Supreme Soul of all embodied beings, through His beginningless material energy.

TEXT 30

एक एव हि लोकानां सूर्य आत्मादिकृद्धरिः ।
सर्ववेदक्रियामूलमृषिभिर्बहुधोदितः ॥ ३० ॥

eka eva hi lokānāṁ
sūrya ātmādi-kṛd dhariḥ

sarva-veda-kriyā-mūlam
ṛṣibhir bahudhoditaḥ

ekaḥ—one; *eva* — only; *hi* — indeed; *lokānām* — of the worlds; *sūryaḥ* —the sun; *ātmā* — their soul; *ādi-kṛt* — the original creator; *hariḥ*—the Personality of Godhead, Hari; *sarva-veda* — in all the *Vedas; kriyā* — of the ritualistic activities; *mūlam* — the basis; *ṛṣibhiḥ*—by the sages; *bahudhā* — variously; *uditaḥ*—designated.

TRANSLATION

The sun-god, being nondifferent from Lord Hari, is the one soul of all the worlds and their original creator. He is the source of all the ritualistic activities prescribed in the Vedas and has been given many names by the Vedic sages.

TEXT 31

कालो देशः क्रिया कर्ता करणं कार्यमागमः ।
द्रव्यं फलमिति ब्रह्मन्नवधोक्तोऽजया हरिः ॥ ३१ ॥

kālo deśaḥ kriyā kartā
karaṇaṁ kāryam āgamaḥ
dravyaṁ phalam iti brahman
navadhokto 'jayā hariḥ

kālaḥ—time; *deśaḥ*—place; *kriyā* — endeavor; *kartā* — performer; *karaṇam* — instrument; *kāryam* — specific ritual; *āgamaḥ*—scripture; *dravyam* — paraphernalia; *phalam* — result; *iti* — thus; *brahman* — O *brāhmaṇa,* Śaunaka; *navadhā* — in nine phases; *uktaḥ*—described; *ajayā* — in terms of the material energy; *hariḥ*—Lord Hari.

TRANSLATION

Being the source of the material energy, the Personality of Godhead Lord Hari in His expansion as the sun-god is described in nine aspects, O Śaunaka: the time, the place, the endeaor, the performer, the instrument, the specific ritual, the scripture, the paraphernalia of worship and the result to be achieved.

TEXT 32

मध्वादिषु द्वादशसु भगवान् कालरूपधृक् ।
लोकतन्त्राय चरति पृथग् द्वादशभिर्गणैः ॥ ३२ ॥

madhv-ādiṣu dvādaśasu
bhagavān kāla-rūpa-dhṛk
loka-tantrāya carati
pṛthag dvādaśabhir gaṇaiḥ

madhu-ādiṣu — beginning with Madhu; *dvādaśasu* — in the twelve (months); *bhagavān* — the Supreme Lord; *kāla-rūpa* — the form of time; *dhṛk* — assuming; *loka-tantrāya* — to regulate planetary motion; *carati* — travels; *pṛthak* — separately; *dvādaśabhiḥ*—with twelve; *gaṇaiḥ*—sets of associates.

TRANSLATION

The Supreme Personality of Godhead, manifesting His potency of time as the sun god, travels about in each of the twelve months, beginning with Madhu, to regulate planetary motion within the universe. Traveling with the sun god in each of the twelve months is a different set of six associates.

TEXT 33

धाता कृतस्थली हेतिर्वासुकी रथकृन्मुने ।
पुलस्त्यस्तुम्बुरुरिति मधुमासं नयन्त्यमी ॥ ३३ ॥

dhātā kṛtasthalī hetir
vāsukī rathakṛn mune
pulastyas tumburur iti
madhu-māsaṁ nayanty amī

dhātā kṛtasthalī hetiḥ—Dhātā, Kṛtasthalī and Heti; *vāsukiḥ rathakṛt* — Vāsuki and Rathakṛt; *mune* — O sage; *pulastyaḥ tumburuḥ*—Pulastya and Tumburu; *iti* — thus; *madhu-māsam* — the month of Madhu (Caitra, at the time of the spring equinox); *nayanti* — lead forth; *amī*—these.

TRANSLATION

My dear sage, Dhātā as the sun god, Kṛtasthalī as the Apsarā, Heti as the Rākṣasa, Vāsuki as the Nāga, Rathakṛt as the Yakṣa,

Pulastya as the sage and Tumburu as the Gandharva rule the month of Madhu.

TEXT 34

अर्यमा पुलहोऽथौजाः प्रहेतिः पुञ्जिकस्थली ।
नारदः कच्छनीरश्च नयन्त्येते स्म माधवम् ॥ ३४ ॥

aryamā pulaho 'thaujāḥ
prahetiḥ puñjikasthalī
nāradaḥ kacchanīraś ca
nayanty ete sma mādhavam

aryamā pulahaḥ athaujāḥ—Aryamā, Pulaha and Athaujā; *prahetiḥ puñjikasthalī*—Praheti and Puñjikasthalī; *nāradaḥ kacchanīraḥ*—Nārada and Kacchanīra; *ca* — also; *nayanti* — rule; *ete* — these; *sma* — indeed; *mādhavam* — the month of Mādhava (Vaiśākha).

TRANSLATION

Aryamā as the sun-god, Pulaha as the sage, Athaujā as the Yakṣa, Praheti as the Rākṣasa, Puñjikasthalī as the Apsarā, Nārada as the Gandharva and Kacchanīra as the Nāga rule the month of Mādhava.

TEXT 35

मित्रोऽत्रिः पौरुषेयोऽथ तक्षको मेनका हहाः ।
रथस्वन इति ह्येते शुक्रमासं नयन्त्यमी ॥ ३५ ॥

mitro 'triḥ pauruṣeyo 'tha
takṣako menakā hahāḥ
rathasvana iti hy ete
śukra-māsaṁ nayanty amī

mitraḥ atriḥ pauruṣeyaḥ—Mitra, Atri and Pauruṣeya; *atha* — as well; *takṣakaḥ menakā hahāḥ*—Takṣaka, Menakā and Hāhā; *rathasvanaḥ*—Rathasvana; *iti* — thus; *hi* — indeed; *ete* — these; *śukra-māsam* — the month of Śukra (Jyaiṣṭha); *nayanti* — rule; *amī*—these.

TRANSLATION

Mitra as the sun-god, Atri as the sage, Pauruṣeya as the Rākṣasa,

Takṣaka as the Nāga, Menakā as the Apsarā, Hāhā as the Gandharva and Rathasvana as the Yakṣa rule the month of Śukra.

TEXT 36

वसिष्ठो वरुणो रम्भा सहजन्यस्तथा हुहूः ।
शुक्रश्चित्रस्वनश्चैव शुचिमासं नयन्त्यमी ॥ ३६ ॥

vasiṣṭho varuṇo rambhā
sahajanyas tathā huhūḥ
śukraś citrasvanaś caiva
śuci-māsaṁ nayanty amī

vasiṣṭhaḥ varuṇaḥ rambhā — Vasiṣṭha, Varuṇa and Rambhā; *sahajanyaḥ* — Sahajanya; *tathā* — also; *huhūḥ* — Hūhū; *śukraḥ citrasvanaḥ* — Śukra and Citrasvana; *ca eva* — as well; *śuci-māsam* — the month of Śuci (Āṣāḍha); *nayanti* — rule; *amī* — these.

TRANSLATION

Vasiṣṭha as the sage, Varuṇa as the sun-god, Rambhā as the Apsarā, Sahajanya as the Rākṣasa, Hūhū as the Gandharva, Śukra as the Nāga and Citrasvana as the Yakṣa rule the month of Śuci.

TEXT 37

इन्द्रो विश्वावसुः श्रोता एलापत्रस्तथागिंराः ।
प्रम्लोचा राक्षसो वर्यो नभोमासं नयन्त्यमी ॥ ३७ ॥

indro viśvāvasuḥ śrotā
elāpatras tathāṅgirāḥ
pramlocā rākṣaso varyo
nabho-māsaṁ nayanty amī

indraḥ viśvāvasuḥ śrotāḥ — Indra, Viśvāvasu and Śrotā; *elāpatraḥ* — Elāpatra; *tathā* — and; *aṅgirāḥ* — Aṅgirā; *pramlocā* — Pramlocā; *rākṣasaḥ varyaḥ* — the Rākṣasa named Varya; *nabhaḥ-māsam* — the month of Nabhas (Śrāvaṇa); *nayanti* — rule; *amī* — these.

TRANSLATION

Indra as the sun-god, Viśvāvasu as the Gandharva, Śrotā as the Yakṣa, Elāpatra as the Nāga, Aṅgirā as the sage, Pramlocā as the Apsarā and Varya as the Rākṣasa rule the month of Nabhas.

TEXT 38

विवस्वानुग्रसेनश्च व्याघ्र आसारणो भृगुः ।
अनुम्लोचा शंखपालो नभस्याख्यं नयन्त्यमी ॥ ३८ ॥

vivasvān ugrasenaś ca
vyāghra āsāraṇo bhṛguḥ
anumlocā śaṅkhapālo
nabhasyākhyaṁ nayanty amī

vivasvān ugrasenaḥ—Vivasvān and Ugrasena; *ca*—also; *vyāghraḥ āsāraṇaḥ bhṛguḥ*—Vyāghra, Āsāraṇa and Bhṛgu; *anumlocā śaṅkhapālaḥ*—Anumlocā and Śaṅkhapāla; *nabhasya-ākhyam*—the month named Nabhasya (Bhādra); *nayanti*—rule; *amī*—these.

TRANSLATION

Vivasvān as the sun-god, Ugrasena as the Gandharva, Vyāghra as the Rākṣasa, Āsāraṇa as the Yakṣa, Bhṛgu as the sage, Anumlocā as the Apsarā and Śaṅkhapāla as the Nāga rule the month of Nabhasya.

TEXT 39

पूषा धनञ्जयो वातः सुषेणः सुरुचिस्तथा ।
घृताची गौतमश्चेति तपोमासं नयन्त्यमी ॥ ३९ ॥

pūṣā dhanañjayo vātaḥ
suṣeṇaḥ surucis tathā
ghṛtācī gautamaś ceti
tapo-māsaṁ nayanty amī

pūṣā dhanañjayaḥ vātaḥ—Pūṣā, Dhanañjaya and Vāta; *suṣeṇaḥ suruciḥ*—Suṣeṇa and Suruci; *tathā*—also; *ghṛtācī gautamaḥ*—Ghṛtācī and Gautama; *ca*—as well; *iti*—thus; *tapaḥ-māsam*—the month of Tapas (Māgha); *nayanti*—rule; *amī*—these.

TRANSLATION

Pūṣā as the sun-god, Dhanañjaya as the Nāga, Vāta as the Rākṣasa, Suṣeṇa as the Gandharva, Suruci as the Yakṣa, Ghṛtācī as the Apsarā and Gautama as the sage rule the month of Tapas.

TEXT 40

ऋतुर्वर्चा भरद्वाजः पर्जन्यः सेनजित्तथा ।
विश्व ऐरावतश्चैव तपस्याख्यं नयन्त्यमी ॥ ४० ॥

ṛtur varcā bharadvājaḥ
parjanyaḥ senajit tathā
viśva airāvataś caiva
tapasyākhyaṁ nayanty amī

ṛtuḥ varcā bharadvājaḥ— Ṛtu, Varcā and Bharadvāja; *parjanyaḥ senajit* — Parjanya and Senajit; *tathā* — also; *viśvaḥ airāvataḥ*— Viśva and Airāvata; *ca eva* — also; *tapasya-ākhyam* — the month known as Tapasya (Phālguna); *nayanti* — rule; *amī*— these.

TRANSLATION

Ṛtu as the Yakṣa, Varcā as the Rākṣasa, Bharadvāja as the sage, Parjanya as the sun god, Senajit as the Apsarā, Viśva as the Gandharva and Airāvata as the Nāga rule the month known as Tapasya.

TEXT 41

अथांशुः कश्यपस्तार्क्ष्य ऋतसेनस्तथोर्वशी ।
विद्युच्छत्रुर्महाशंखः सहोमासं नयन्त्यमी ॥ ४१ ॥

athāṁśuḥ kaśyapas tārkṣya
ṛtasenas tathorvaśī
vidyucchatrur mahāśaṅkhaḥ
saho-māsaṁ nayanty amī

atha — then; *aṁśuḥ kaśyapaḥ tārkṣyaḥ*— Aṁśu, Kaśyapa and Tārkṣya; *ṛtasenaḥ*— Ṛtasena; *tathā* — and; *urvaśī*— Urvaśī; *vidyucchatruḥ mahāśaṅkhaḥ*— Vidyucchatru and Mahāśaṅkha; *sahaḥ-māsam* — the month of Sahas (Mārgaśīrṣa); *nayanti* — rule; *amī*— these.

TRANSLATION

Aṁśu as the sun-god, Kaśyapa as the sage, Tārkṣya as the Yakṣa, Ṛtasena as the Gandharva, Urvaśī as the Apsarā, Vidyucchatru as the Rākṣasa and Mahāśaṅkha as the Nāga rule the month of Sahas.

TEXT 42

भगः स्फूर्जोऽरिष्टनेमिरूर्ण आयुश्च पञ्चमः ।
कर्कोटकः पूर्वचित्तिः पुष्यमासं नयन्त्यमी ॥ ४२ ॥

bhagaḥ sphūrjo 'riṣṭanemir
ūrṇa āyuś ca pañcamaḥ
karkoṭakaḥ pūrvacittiḥ
puṣya-māsaṁ nayanty amī

bhagaḥ sphūrjaḥ ariṣṭanemiḥ—Bhaga, Sphūrja and Ariṣṭanemi; *ūrṇaḥ*—Ūrṇa; *āyuḥ*—Āyur; *ca* — and; *pañcamaḥ*—the fifth associate; *karkoṭakaḥ pūrvacittiḥ*—Karkoṭaka and Pūrvacitti; *puṣya-māsam* — the month of Puṣya; *nayanti* — rule; *amī*—these.

TRANSLATION

Bhaga as the sun-god, Sphūrja as the Rākṣasa, Ariṣṭanemi as the Gandharva, Ūrṇa as the Yakṣa, Āyur as the sage, Karkoṭaka as the Nāga and Pūrvacitti as the Apsarā rule the month of Puṣya.

TEXT 43

त्वष्टा ऋचीकतनयः कम्बलश्च तिलोत्तमा ।
ब्रह्मापेतोऽथ शतजिद्धृतराष्ट्र इषम्भराः ॥ ४३ ॥

tvaṣṭā ṛcīka-tanayaḥ
kambalaś ca tilottamā
brahmāpeto 'tha satajid
dhṛtarāṣṭra iṣam-bharāḥ

tvaṣṭā — Tvaṣṭā; *ṛcīka-tanayaḥ*—the son of Ṛcīka (Jamadagni); *kambalaḥ* —Kambala; *ca* — and; *tilottamā* — Tilottamā; *brahmāpetaḥ*—Brahmāpeta; *atha* — and; *śatajit* — Śatajit; *dhṛtarāṣṭraḥ*—Dhṛtarāṣṭra; *iṣam-bharāḥ*—the maintainers of the month Iṣa (Āśvina).

TRANSLATION

Tvaṣṭā as the sun-god; Jamadagni, the son of Ṛcīka, as the sage; Kambalāśva as the Nāga; Tilottamā as the Apsarā; Brahmāpeta as the Rākṣasa; Śatajit as the Yakṣa; and Dhṛtarāṣṭra as the Gandharva maintain the month of Iṣa.

TEXT 44

विष्णुरश्वतरो रम्भा सूर्यवर्चाश्च सत्यजित् ।
विश्वामित्रो मखापेत ऊर्जमासं नयन्त्यमी ॥ ४४ ॥

viṣṇur aśvataro rambhā
sūryavarcāś ca satyajit
viśvāmitro makhāpeta
ūrja-māsaṁ nayanty amī

viṣṇuḥ aśvataraḥ rambhā — Viṣṇu, Aśvatara and Rambhā; *sūryavarcāḥ* — Sūryavarcā; *ca* — and; *satyajit* — Satyajit; *viśvāmitraḥ makhāpetaḥ* — Viśvāmitra and Makhāpeta; *ūrja-māsam* — the month of Ūrja (Kārttika); *nayanti* — rule; *amī* — these.

TRANSLATION

Viṣṇu as the sun-god, Aśvatara as the Nāga, Rambhā as the Apsarā, Sūryavarcā as the Gandharva, Satyajit as the Yakṣa, Viśvāmitra as the sage and Makhāpeta as the Rākṣasa rule the month of Ūrja.

PURPORT

All these sun-gods and their associates are mentioned in divisions in the *Kūrma Purāṇa,* as follows:

dhātāryamā ca mitraś ca
varuṇaś cendra eva ca
vivasvān atha pūṣā ca
parjanyaś cāṁśur eva ca

bhagas tvaṣṭā ca viṣṇuś ca
ādityā dvādaśa smṛtāḥ
pulastyaḥ pulahaś cātrir
vasiṣṭo'thāṅgirā bhṛguḥ

gautamo 'tha bharadvājaḥ
kaśyapaḥ kratur eva ca
jamadagniḥ kauśikaś ca
munayo brahma-vādināḥ

rathakṛc cāpy athojāś ca
grāmaṇīḥ surucis tathā
ratha-citrasvanaḥ śrotā
aruṇaḥ senajit tathā
tārkṣya ariṣṭanemiś ca
ṛtajit satyajit tathā

atha hetiḥ prahetiś ca
pauruṣeyo vadhas tathā
varyo vyāghras tathāpaś ca
vāyur vidyud divākaraḥ

brahmāpetaś ca vipendrā
yajñāpetaś ca rākṣakāḥ
vāsukiḥ kacchanīraś ca
takṣakaḥ śukra eva ca

elāpatraḥ śaṅkhapālas
tathairāvata-saṁjñitaḥ
dhanañjayo mahāpadmas
tathā karkoṭako dvijāḥ

kambalo 'śvataraś caiva
vahanty enaṁ yathā-kramam
tumburur nārado hāhā
hūhūr viśvāvasus tathā

ugraseno vasurucir
viśvavasur athāparaḥ
citrasenas tathorṇāyur
dhṛtarāṣṭro dvijottamāḥ

sūryavarcā dvādaśaite
gandharvā gāyatāṁ varāḥ
kṛtasthaly apsaro-varyā
tathānyā puñjikasthalī

menakā sahajanyā ca
pramlocā ca dvijottamāḥ
anumlocā ghṛtācī ca
viśvācī corvaśī tathā

anyā ca pūrvacittiḥ syād
anyā caiva tilottamā
rambhā ceti dvija-śreṣṭhās
tathaivāpsarasaḥ smṛtāḥ

TEXT 45

एता भगवतो विष्णोरादित्यस्य विभूतयः ।
स्मरतां सन्ध्ययोर्नृणां हरन्त्यंहो दिने दिने ॥ ४५ ॥

etā bhagavato viṣṇor
ādityasya vibhūtayaḥ
smaratāṁ sandhyayor nṝṇāṁ
haranty aṁho dine dine

etāḥ—these; *bhagavataḥ*—of the Personality of Godhead; *viṣṇoḥ*—Lord Viṣṇu; *ādityasya* — of the sun-god; *vibhūtayaḥ*—the opulences; *smaratām* — for those who remember; *sandhyayoḥ*—at the junctures of the day; *nṝṇām* — for such men; *haranti* — they take away; *aṁhaḥ*—sinful reactions; *dine dine* — day after day.

TRANSLATION

All these personalities are the opulent expansions of the Supreme Personality of Godhead, Viṣṇu, in the form of the sun-god. These deities take away all the sinful reactions of those who remember them each day at dawn and sunset.

TEXT 46

द्वादशस्वपि मासेषु देवोऽसौ षड्भिरस्य वै ।
चरन् समन्तात्तनुते परत्रेह च सन्मतिम् ॥ ४६ ॥

dvādaśasv api māseṣu
devo 'sau ṣaḍbhir asya vai
caran samantāt tanute
paratreha ca san-matim

dvādaśasu — in each of the twelve; *api* — indeed; *māseṣu* — months; *devaḥ*—the lord; *asau* — this; *ṣaḍbhiḥ*—with his six types of associates; *asya* — for the population of this universe; *vai* — certainly; *caran* — traveling; *samantāt* — in all directions; *tanute* — spreads; *paratra* — in the next life; *iha* — in this life; *ca* — and; *sat-matim* — pure consciousness.

TRANSLATION

Thus, throughout the twelve months, the lord of the sun travels in all directions with his six types of associates, disseminating among the inhabitants of this universe purity of consciousness for both this life and the next.

TEXTS 47–48

सामर्ग्यजुर्भिस्तल्लिंगैरृषयः संस्तुवन्त्यमुम् ।
गन्धर्वास्तं प्रगायन्ति नृत्यन्त्यप्सरसोऽग्रतः ॥ ४७ ॥
उन्नह्यन्ति रथं नागा ग्रामण्यो रथयोजकाः ।
चोदयन्ति रथं पृष्ठे नैरृता बलशालिनः ॥ ४८ ॥

sāmarg-yajurbhis tal-liṅgair
ṛṣayaḥ saṁstuvanty amum
gandharvās taṁ pragāyanti
nṛtyanty apsaraso 'grataḥ

unnahyanti rathaṁ nāgā
grāmaṇyo ratha-yojakāḥ
codayanti rathaṁ pṛṣṭhe
nairṛtā bala-śālinaḥ

sāma-ṛk-yajurbhiḥ—with the hymns of the *Sāma, Ṛg* and *Yajur Vedas; tat-liṅgaiḥ*—which reveal the sun; *ṛṣayaḥ*—the sages; *saṁstuvanti* — glorify; *amum* — him; *gandharvāḥ*—the Gandharvas; *tam* — about him; *pragāyanti* — sing loudly; *nṛtyanti* — dance; *apsarasaḥ*—the Apsarās; *agrataḥ*—in front; *unnahyanti* — bind up; *ratham* — the chariot; *nāgāḥ*—the Nāgas; *grāmaṇyaḥ*—the Yakṣas; *ratha-yojakāḥ*—those who harness the horses to the chariot; *codayanti* — drive; *ratham* — the chariot; *pṛṣṭhe* — from the rear; *nairṛtāḥ*—the Rākṣasas; *bala-śālinaḥ*—strong.

TRANSLATION

While the sages glorify the sun-god with the hymns of the Sāma, Ṛg and Yajur Vedas, which reveal his identity, the Gandharvas also sing his praises and the Apsarās dance before his chariot. The Nāgas arrange the chariot ropes and the Yakṣas harness the horses to the chariot, while the powerful Rākṣasas push from behind.

TEXT 49

वालखिल्याः सहस्राणि षष्टिर्ब्रह्मर्षयोऽमलाः ।
पुरतोऽभिमुखं यान्ति स्तुवन्ति स्तुतिभिर्विभुम् ॥४९॥

vālakhilyāḥ sahasrāṇi
ṣaṣṭir brahmarṣayo 'malāḥ
purato 'bhimukhaṁ yānti
stuvanti stutibhir vibhum

vālakhilyāḥ—the Vālakhilyas; *sahasrāṇi* — thousands; *ṣaṣṭiḥ*—sixty; *brahma-ṛṣayaḥ*—great sages among the *brāhmaṇas; amalāḥ*—pure; *purataḥ*—in front; *abhimukham* — facing the chariot; *yānti* — they go; *stuvanti* — they offer praise; *stutibhiḥ*—with Vedic prayers; *vibhum* — to the almighty lord.

TRANSLATION

Facing the chariot, the sixty thousand brāhmaṇa sages known as Vālakhilyas travel in front and offer prayers to the almighty sun god with Vedic mantras.

TEXT 50

एवं ह्यनादिनिधनो भगवान् हरिरीश्वरः ।
कल्पे कल्पे स्वमात्मानं व्यूह्य लोकानवत्यजः ॥५०॥

evaṁ hy anādi-nidhano
bhagavān harir īśvaraḥ
kalpe kalpe svam ātmānaṁ
vyūhya lokān avaty ajaḥ

evam — thus; *hi* — indeed; *anādi* — without beginning; *nidhanaḥ*—or end; *bhagavān* — the Personality of Godhead; *hariḥ*—Lord Hari; *īśvaraḥ*—the supreme controller; *kalpe kalpe* — in each day of Brahmā; *svam ātmānam* — Himself; *vyūhya* — expanding into various forms; *lokān* — the worlds; *avati* — protects; *ajaḥ*—the unborn Lord.

TRANSLATION

For the protection of all the worlds, the Supreme Personality of Godhead Hari, who is unborn and without beginning or end, thus expands Himself during each day of Brahmā into these specific categories of His personal representations.

Thus end the purports of the humble servants of His Divine Grace A.C. Bhaktivedanta Swami Prabhupāda to the Twelfth Canto, Eleventh Chapter, of the Śrīmad-Bhāgavatam, *entitled "Summary Description of the Mahāpuruṣa."*

CHAPTER TWELVE

The Topics of Śrīmad-Bhāgavatam Summarized

In this chapter, Śrī Sūta Gosvāmī summarizes the subjects discussed in *Śrīmad-Bhāgavatam.*

The Supreme Lord, Śrī Hari, personally removes all the distress of a person who hears about His glories. Whatever words glorify the innumerable transcendental qualities of the Personality of Godhead are truthful, auspicious and conducive to piety, whereas all other words are impure. Discussions of topics concerning the Supreme Lord bestow ecstasy, which remains constantly new, but persons who are like crows become absorbed in unessential topics, those unrelated to the Personality of Godhead.

By chanting and hearing the countless names of Lord Śrī Hari, which describe His glorious qualities, all human beings can be relieved of their sins. Neither knowledge devoid of devotion for Lord Viṣṇu nor fruitive work not offered to Him have any real beauty. By constant remembrance of Lord Kṛṣṇa, on the other hand, all one's inauspicious desires are destroyed, one's mind is purified, and one attains devotion for Lord Śrī Hari along with knowledge filled with realization and detachment.

Sūta Gosvāmī then states that previously, in the assembly of Mahārāja Parīkṣit, he heard from the mouth of Śrī Śukadeva the glories of Śrī Kṛṣṇa, which annihilate all sinful reactions, and that now he has related these glories to the sages at Naimiṣāraṇya. By hearing *Śrīmad-Bhāgavatam*, the spirit soul is purified and obtains salvation from all sins and all kinds of fear. Through the study of this scripture, one achieves the same result as that achieved by one who studies all the Vedas, and one also achieves the fulfillment of all desires. By studying with a controlled mind this essential compilation of all the *Purāṇas*, one will reach the supreme abode of the Personality of Godhead. Every verse of this scripture, *Śrīmad-Bhāgavatam*, contains the narrations of Lord Śrī Hari, who has innumerable personal forms.

Finally, Śrī Sūta offers obeisances to the unborn and unlimited Supreme Soul, Śrī Kṛṣṇa, as well as to Śrī Śukadeva, the son of Vyāsa, who is capable of destroying the sins of all living beings.

TEXT 1

सूत उवाच
नमो धर्माय महते नमः कृष्णाय वेधसे ।
ब्रह्मणेभ्यो नमस्कृत्य धर्मान् वक्ष्ये सनातनान् ॥ १ ॥

sūta uvāca
namo dharmāya mahate
namaḥ kṛṣṇāya vedhase
brahmaṇebhyo namaskṛtya
dharmān vakṣye sanātanān

sūtaḥ uvāca — Sūta Gosvāmī said; *namaḥ*—obeisances; *dharmāya* — to the principle of religion; *mahate* — greatest; *namaḥ*—obeisances; *kṛṣṇāya* — to Lord Kṛṣṇa; *vedhase* — the creator; *brahmaṇebhyaḥ*—to the *brāhmaṇas; namaskṛtya* — offering my obeisances; *dharmān* — the principles of religion; *vakṣye* — I shall speak; *sanātanān* — eternal.

TRANSLATION

Sūta Gosvāmī said: Offering my obeisances to the supreme religious principle, devotional service; to Lord Kṛṣṇa, the supreme creator; and to all the brāhmaṇas, I shall now describe the eternal principles of religion.

PURPORT

In this Twelfth Chapter of the Twelfth Canto, Sūta Gosvāmī will summarize all the topics of *Śrīmad-Bhāgavatam,* beginning from the First Canto.

TEXT 2

एतद्वः कथितं विप्रा विष्णोश्चरितमद्भुतम् ।
भवद्भिर्यदहं पृष्टो नराणां पुरुषोचितम् ॥ २ ॥

etad vaḥ kathitaṁ viprā
viṣṇoś caritam adbhutam
bhavadbhir yad ahaṁ pṛṣṭo
narāṇāṁ puruṣocitam

etat — these; *vaḥ*—to you; *kathitam* — narrated; *viprāḥ*—O sages; *viṣṇoḥ*—of Lord Viṣṇu; *caritam* — the pastimes; *adbhutam* — wonderful;

bhavadbhiḥ—by your good selves; *yat* — which; *aham* — I; *pṛṣṭaḥ*—was asked about; *narāṇām* — among men; *puruṣa* — for an actual human being; *ucitam* — suitable.

TRANSLATION

O great sages, I have narrated to you the wonderful pastimes of Lord Viṣṇu, as you inquired about them from me. Hearing such narrations is the suitable engagement for a person who is actually a human being.

PURPORT

The words *narāṇāṁ puruṣocitam* indicate that men and women who actually come to the standard of human life hear and chant the glories of the Supreme Lord, whereas uncivilized persons may not be interested in the science of God.

TEXT 3

अत्र संकीर्तितः साक्षात्सर्वपापहरो हरिः ।
नारायणो हृषीकेशो भगवान् सात्वतां पतिः ॥ ३ ॥

atra saṅkīrtitaḥ sākṣāt
sarva-pāpa-haro hariḥ
nārāyaṇo hṛṣīkeśo
bhagavān sātvatāṁ patiḥ

atra — here, in the *Śrīmad-Bhāgavatam; saṅkīrtitaḥ*—is fully glorified; *sākṣāt* — directly; *sarva-pāpa* — of all sins; *haraḥ*—the remover; *hariḥ*—the Personality of Godhead, Lord Hari; *nārāyaṇaḥ*—Nārāyaṇa; *hṛṣīkeśaḥ*—Hṛṣīkeśa, the Lord of the senses; *bhagavān* — the Supreme Personality; *sātvatām* — of the Yadus; *patiḥ*—the master.

TRANSLATION

This literature fully glorifies the Supreme Personality of Godhead Hari, who removes all His devotees' sinful reactions. The Lord is glorified as Nārāyaṇa, Hṛṣīkeśa and the Lord of the Sātvatas.

PURPORT

Lord Kṛṣṇa's many holy names indicate His extraordinary transcendental qualities. The name *Hari* indicates that the Lord removes all sins from the heart of His devotee. *Nārāyaṇa* indicates that the Lord sustains the existence of all other beings. *Hṛṣīkeśa* indicates that Lord Kṛṣṇa is the ultimate controller of the senses of all living beings. The word *bhagavān* indicates that Lord Kṛṣṇa is the all-attractive Supreme Being. And the words *sātvatāṁ patiḥ* indicate that the Lord is naturally the master of saintly and religious people, especially the members of the exalted Yadu family.

TEXT 4

अत्र ब्रह्म परं गुह्यं जगतः प्रभवाप्ययम् ।
ज्ञानं च तदुपाख्यानं प्रोक्तं विज्ञानसंयुतम् ॥ ४ ॥

atra brahma paraṁ guhyaṁ
jagataḥ prabhavāpyayam
jñānaṁ ca tad-upākhyānaṁ
proktaṁ vijñāna-saṁyutam

atra — here; *brahma* — the Absolute Truth; *param* — supreme; *guhyam* — confidential; *jagataḥ* — of this universe; *prabhava* — the creation; *apyayam* — and annihilation; *jñānam* — knowledge; *ca* — and; *tat-upākhyānam* — the means of cultivating it; *proktam* — are spoken; *vijñāna* — transcendental realization; *saṁyutam* — including.

TRANSLATION

This literature describes the mystery of the Supreme Absolute Truth, the source of the creation and annihilation of this universe. Also presented are divine knowledge of Him together with the process of its cultivation, and the transcendental realization one achieves.

TEXT 5

भक्तियोगः समाख्यातो वैराग्यं च तदाश्रयम् ।
पारीक्षितमुपाख्यानं नारदाख्यानमेव च ॥ ५ ॥

bhakti-yogaḥ samākhyāto
vairāgyaṁ ca tad-āśrayam
pārīkṣitam upākhyānaṁ
nāradākhyānam eva ca

bhakti-yogaḥ—the process of devotional service; *samākhyātaḥ*—is thoroughly enunciated; *vairāgyam* — renunciation; *ca* — and; *tat-āśrayam* — which is subsidiary to it; *pārīkṣitam* — of Mahārāja Parīkṣit; *upākhyānam* — the history; *nārada* — of Nārada; *ākhyānam* — the history; *eva* — indeed; *ca* — also.

TRANSLATION

The following topics are also narrated: the process of devotional service together with its subsidiary feature of renunciation, and the histories of Mahārāja Parīkṣit and the sage Nārada.

TEXT 6

प्रायोपवेशो राजर्षेर्विप्रशापात् परीक्षितः ।
शुकस्य ब्रह्मर्षभस्य संवादश्च परीक्षितः ॥ ६ ॥

prāyopaveśo rājarṣer
vipra-śāpāt parīkṣitaḥ
śukasya brahmarṣabhasya
saṁvādaś ca parīkṣitaḥ

prāya-upaveśaḥ—the fast until death; *rāja-ṛṣeḥ*—of the sage among kings; *vipra-śāpāt* — because of the curse of the *brāhmaṇa's* son; *parīkṣitaḥ* —of King Parīkṣit; *śukasya* — of Śukadeva; *brahma-ṛṣabhasya* — the best of *brāhmaṇas; saṁvādaḥ*—the conversation; *ca* — and; *parīkṣitaḥ*— with Parīkṣit.

TRANSLATION

Also described are saintly King Parīkṣit's sitting down to fast until death in response to the curse of a brāhmaṇa's son, and the conversations between Parīkṣit and Śukadeva Gosvāmī, who is the best of all brāhmaṇas.

TEXT 7

योगधारणयोत्क्रान्तिः संवादो नारदाजयोः ।
अवतारानुगीतं च सर्गः प्राधानिकोऽग्रतः ॥ ७ ॥

yoga-dhāraṇayotkrāntiḥ
saṁvādo nāradājayoḥ

avatārānugītaṁ ca
sargaḥ prādhāniko 'grataḥ

yoga-dhāraṇayā — by fixed meditation in *yoga; utkrāntiḥ*—the attainment of liberation at the time of passing away; *saṁvādaḥ*—the conversation; *nārada-ajayoḥ*—between Nārada and Brahmā; *avatāra-anugītam* — the listing of the incarnations of the Supreme Lord; *ca* — and; *sargaḥ*—the process of creation; *prādhānikaḥ*—from the unmanifest material nature; *agrataḥ*—in progressive order.

TRANSLATION

The Bhāgavatam explains how one can attain liberation at the time of death by practicing fixed meditation in yoga. It also contains a discussion between Nārada and Brahmā, an enumeration of the incarnations of the Supreme Personality of Godhead, and a description of how the universe was created in progressive sequence, beginning from the unmanifest stage of material nature.

PURPORT

Śrīla Viśvanātha Cakravartī Ṭhākura explains that it would be difficult to give a complete list of the numerous accounts and topics contained in the *Śrīmad-Bhāgavatam.* Therefore it is understood that Sūta Gosvāmī is merely summarizing the topics. We should not consider the topics he fails to mention here less important or superfluous, since every letter and word of *Śrīmad-Bhāgavatam* is absolute, Kṛṣṇa conscious sound vibration.

TEXT 8

विदुरोद्धवसंवादः क्षत्तृमैत्रेययोस्ततः ।
पुराणसंहिताप्रश्नो महापुरुषसंस्थितिः ॥ ८ ॥

viduroddhava-saṁvādaḥ
kṣattṛ-maitreyayos tataḥ
purāṇa-saṁhitā-praśno
mahā-puruṣa-saṁsthitiḥ

vidura-uddhava — between Vidura and Uddhava; *saṁvādaḥ*—the discussion; *kṣattṛ-maitreyayoḥ*—between Vidura and Maitreya; *tataḥ*—then; *purāṇa-saṁhitā* — concerning this Purāṇic compilation; *praśnaḥ*—inquiries;

mahā-puruṣa — within the Supreme Personality of Godhead; *saṁsthitiḥ*— the winding up of creation.

TRANSLATION

This scripture also relates the discussions Vidura had with Uddhava and with Maitreya, inquiries about the subject matter of this Purāṇa, and the winding up of creation within the body of the Supreme Lord at the time of annihilation.

TEXT 9

ततः प्राकृतिकः सर्गः सप्त वैकृतिकाश्च ये।
ततो ब्रह्माण्डसम्भूतिर्वैराजः पुरुषो यतः ॥ ९ ॥

tataḥ prākṛtikaḥ sargaḥ
sapta vaikṛtikāś ca ye
tato brahmāṇḍa-sambhūtir
vairājaḥ puruṣo yataḥ

tataḥ—then; *prākṛtikaḥ*—from material nature; *sargaḥ*—the creation; *sapta* — the seven; *vaikṛtikāḥ*—stages of creation derived by transformation; *ca* — and; *ye* — which; *tataḥ*—then; *brahma-aṇḍa* — of the universal egg; *sambhūtiḥ*—the construction; *vairājaḥ puruṣaḥ*—the universal form of the Lord; *yataḥ*—from which.

TRANSLATION

The creation effected by the agitation of the modes of material nature, the seven stages of evolution by elemental transformation, and the construction of the universal egg, from which arises the universal form of the Supreme Lord — all these are thoroughly described.

TEXT 10

कालस्य स्थूलसूक्ष्मस्य गतिः पद्मसमुद्भवः।
भुव उद्धरणेऽम्भोधेर्हिरण्याक्षवधो यथा ॥ १० ॥

kālasya sthūla-sūkṣmasya
gatiḥ padma-samudbhavaḥ
bhuva uddharaṇe 'mbhodher
hiraṇyākṣa-vadho yathā

kālasya — of time; *sthūla-sūkṣmasya* — gross and subtle; *gatiḥ*—the movement; *padma* — of the lotus; *samudbhavaḥ*—the generation; *bhuvaḥ* —of the earth; *uddharaṇe* — in connection with the deliverance; *ambhodheḥ* —from the ocean; *hiraṇyākṣa-vadhaḥ*—the killing of the demon Hiraṇyākṣa; *yathā* — as it occurred.

TRANSLATION

Other topics include the subtle and gross movements of time, the generation of the lotus from the navel of Garbhodakaśāyī Viṣṇu, and the killing of the demon Hiraṇyākṣa when the earth was delivered from the Garbhodaka Ocean.

TEXT 11

ऊर्ध्वतिर्यगवाक्सर्गो रुद्रसर्गस्तथैव च ।
अर्धनारीश्वरस्याथ यतः स्वायम्भुवो मनुः ॥ ११ ॥

ūrdhva-tiryag-avāk-sargo
rudra-sargas tathaiva ca
ardha-nārīśvarasyātha
yataḥ svāyambhuvo manuḥ

ūrdhva — of the higher species, the demigods; *tiryak* — of the animals; *avāk* — and of lower species; *sargaḥ*—the creation; *rudra* — of Lord Śiva; *sargaḥ*—the creation; *tathā* — and; *eva* — indeed; *ca* — also; *ardha-nārī*— as a half man, half woman; *īśvarasya* — of the lord; *atha* — then; *yataḥ*— from whom; *svāyambhuvaḥ manuḥ*—Svāyambhuva Manu.

TRANSLATION

The Bhāgavatam also describes the creation of demigods, animals and demoniac species of life; the birth of Lord Rudra; and the appearance of Svāyambhuva Manu from the half-man, half-woman Īśvara.

TEXT 12

शतरूपा च या स्त्रीणामाद्या प्रकृतिरुत्तमा ।
सन्तानो धर्मपत्नीनां कर्दमस्य प्रजापतेः ॥ १२ ॥

śatarūpā ca yā strīṇām
ādyā prakṛtir uttamā

santāno dharma-patnīnāṁ
kardamasya prajāpateḥ

śatarūpā — Śatarūpā; *ca* — and; *yā* — who; *strīṇām* — of women; *ādyā* — the first; *prakṛtiḥ* — the consort; *uttamā* — best; *santānaḥ* — the progeny; *dharma-patnīnām* — of the pious wives; *kardamasya* — of the sage Kardama; *prajāpateḥ* — the progenitor.

TRANSLATION

Also related are the appearance of the first woman, Śatarūpā, who was the excellent consort of Manu, and the offspring of the pious wives of Prajāpati Kardama.

TEXT 13

अवतारो भगवतः कपिलस्य महात्मनः ।
देवहूत्याश्च संवादः कपिलेन च धीमता ॥ १३ ॥

avatāro bhagavataḥ
kapilasya mahātmanaḥ
devahūtyāś ca saṁvādaḥ
kapilena ca dhīmatā

avatāraḥ — the descent; *bhagavataḥ* — of the Supreme Personality of Godhead; *kapilasya* — Lord Kapila; *mahā-ātmanaḥ* — the Supreme Soul; *devahūtyāḥ* — of Devahūti; *ca* — and; *saṁvādaḥ* — the conversation; *kapilena* — with Lord Kapila; *ca* — and; *dhī-matā* — the intelligent.

TRANSLATION

The Bhāgavatam describes the incarnation of the Supreme Personality of Godhead as the exalted sage Kapila and records the conversation between that greatly learned soul and His mother, Devahūti.

TEXTS 14–15

नवब्रह्मसमुत्पत्तिर्दक्षयज्ञविनाशनम् ।
ध्रुवस्य चरितं पश्चात्पृथोः प्राचीनबर्हिषः ॥ १४ ॥
नारदस्य च संवादस्ततः प्रैयव्रतं द्विजाः ।
नाभेस्ततोऽनु चरितमृषभस्य भरतस्य च ॥ १५ ॥

nava-brahma-samutpattir
dakṣa-yajña-vināśanam
dhruvasya caritaṁ paścāt
pṛthoḥ prācīnabarhiṣaḥ

nāradasya ca saṁvādas
tataḥ praiyavrataṁ dvijāḥ
nābhes tato 'nucaritam
ṛṣabhasya bharatasya ca

nava-brahma — of the nine *brāhmaṇas* (the sons of Lord Brahmā, headed by Marīci); *samutpattiḥ* — the descendants; *dakṣa-yajña* — of the sacrifice performed by Dakṣa; *vināśanam* — the destruction; *dhruvasya* — of Dhruva Mahārāja; *caritam* — the history; *paścāt* — then; *pṛthoḥ* — of King Pṛthu; *prācīnabarhiṣaḥ* — of Prācīnabarhi; *nāradasya* — with Nārada Muni; *ca* — and; *saṁvādaḥ* — his conversation; *tataḥ* — then; *praiyavratam* — the story of Mahārāja Priyavrata; *dvijāḥ* — O *brāhmaṇas; nābheḥ* — of Nābhi; *tataḥ* — then; *anucaritam* — the life story; *ṛṣabhasya* — of Lord Ṛṣabha; *bharatasya* — of Bharata Mahārāja; *ca* — and.

TRANSLATION

Also described are the progeny of the nine great brāhmaṇas, the destruction of Dakṣa's sacrifice, and the history of Dhruva Mahārāja, followed by the histories of King Pṛthu and King Prācīnabarhi, the discussion between Prācīnabarhi and Nārada, and the life of Mahārāja Priyavrata. Then, O brāhmaṇas, the Bhāgavatam tells of the character and activities of King Nābhi, Lord Ṛṣabha and King Bharata.

TEXT 16

द्वीपवर्षसमुद्राणां गिरिनद्युपवर्णनम् ।
ज्योतिश्चक्रस्य संस्थानं पातालनरकस्थितिः ॥ १६ ॥

dvīpa-varṣa-samudrāṇāṁ
giri-nady-upavarṇanam
jyotiś-cakrasya saṁsthānaṁ
pātāla-naraka-sthitiḥ

dvīpa-varṣa-samudrāṇām — of the continents, great islands and oceans; *giri-nadī* — of the mountains and rivers; *upavarṇanam* — the detailed description; *jyotiḥ-cakrasya* — of the celestial sphere; *saṁsthānam* — the arrangement; *pātāla* — of the subterranean regions; *naraka* — and of hell; *sthitiḥ* — the situation.

TRANSLATION

The Bhāgavatam gives an elaborate description of the earth's continents, regions, oceans, mountains and rivers. Also described are the arrangement of the celestial sphere and the conditions found in the subterranean regions and in hell.

TEXT 17

दक्षजन्म प्रचेतोभ्यस्तत्पुत्रीणां च सन्ततिः ।
यतो देवासुरनरास्तिर्यङ्नगखगादयः ॥ १७ ॥

dakṣa-janma pracetobhyas
tat-putrīṇāṁ ca santatiḥ
yato devāsura-narās
tiryaṅ-naga-khagādayaḥ

dakṣa-janma — the birth of Dakṣa; *pracetobhyaḥ* — from the Pracetās; *tat-putrīṇām* — of his daughters; *ca* — and; *santatiḥ* — the progeny; *yataḥ* — from which; *deva-asura-narāḥ* — the demigods, demons and human beings; *tiryak-naga-khaga-ādayaḥ* — the animals, serpents, birds and other species.

TRANSLATION

The rebirth of Prajāpati Dakṣa as the son of the Pracetās, and the progeny of Dakṣa's daughters, who initiated the races of demigods, demons, human beings, animals, serpents, birds and so on — all this is described.

TEXT 18

त्वाष्ट्रस्य जन्म निधनं पुत्रयोश्च दितेर्द्विजाः ।
दैत्येश्वरस्य चरितं प्रह्लादस्य महात्मनः ॥ १८ ॥

tvāṣṭrasya janma-nidhanaṁ
putrayoś ca diter dvijāḥ
daityeśvarasya caritaṁ
prahrādasya mahātmanaḥ

tvāṣṭrasya — of the son of Tvaṣṭā (Vṛtra); *janma-nidhanam* — the birth and death; *putrayoḥ*—of the two sons, Hiraṇyākṣa and Hiraṇyakaśipu; *ca* — and; *diteḥ*—of Diti; *dvijāḥ*—O *brāhmaṇas; daitya-īśvarasya* — of the greatest of the Daityas; *caritam* — the history; *prahrādasya* — of Prahlāda; *mahā-ātmanaḥ*—the great soul.

TRANSLATION

O brāhmaṇas, also recounted are the births and deaths of Vṛtrāsura and of Diti's sons Hiraṇyākṣa and Hiraṇyakaśipu, as well as the history of the greatest of Diti's descendants, the exalted soul Prahlāda.

TEXT 19

मन्वन्तरानुकथनं गजेन्द्रस्य विमोक्षणम् ।
मन्वन्तरावताराश्च विष्णोर्हयशिरादयः ॥ १९ ॥

manv-antarānukathanaṁ
gajendrasya vimokṣaṇam
manvantarāvatārāś ca
viṣṇor hayaśirādayaḥ

manu-antara — of reigns of the various Manus; *anukathanam* — the detailed description; *gaja-indrasya* — of the king of the elephants; *vimokṣaṇam* — the liberation; *manuantara-avatārāḥ*—the particular incarnations of the Supreme Personality of Godhead in each *manvantara; ca* — and; *viṣṇoḥ*—of Lord Viṣṇu; *hayaśirā-ādayaḥ*—such as Lord Hayaśīrṣā.

TRANSLATION

The reign of each Manu, the liberation of Gajendra, and the special incarnations of Lord Viṣṇu in each manvantara, such as Lord Hayaśīrṣā, are described as well.

TEXT 20

कौर्मं मात्स्यं नारसिंहं वामनं च जगत्पतेः ।
क्षीरोदमथनं तद्वदमृतार्थे दिवौकसाम् ॥ २० ॥

kaurmaṁ mātsyaṁ nārasiṁhaṁ
vāmanaṁ ca jagat-pateḥ

kṣīroda-mathanaṁ tadvad
amṛtārthe divaukasām

kaurmam — the incarnation as a tortoise; *mātsyam* — as a fish; *nārasiṁham* — as a man-lion; *vāmanam* — as a dwarf; *ca* — and; *jagat-pateḥ* — of the Lord of the universe; *kṣīra-uda* — of the Ocean of Milk; *mathanam* — the churning; *tadvat* — thus; *amṛta-arthe* — for the sake of nectar; *diva-okasām* — on the part of the inhabitants of heaven.

TRANSLATION

The Bhāgavatam also tells of the appearances of the Lord of the universe as Kūrma, Matsya, Narasiṁha and Vāmana, and of the demigods' churning of the Milk Ocean to obtain nectar.

TEXT 21

देवासुरमहायुद्धं राजवंशानुकीर्तनम् ।
इक्ष्वाकुजन्म तद्वंशः सुद्युम्नस्य महात्मनः ॥ २१ ॥

devāsura-mahā-yuddhaṁ
rāja-vaṁśānukīrtanam
ikṣvāku-janma tad-vaṁśaḥ
sudyumnasya mahātmanaḥ

deva-asura — of the demigods and demons; *mahā-yuddham* — the great war; *rāja-vaṁśa* — of the dynasties of kings; *anukīrtanam* — the reciting in sequence; *ikṣvāku-janma* — the birth of Ikṣvāku; *tat-vaṁśaḥ* — his dynasty; *sudyamnasya* — (and the dynasty) of Sudyumna; *mahā-ātmanaḥ* — the great soul.

TRANSLATION

An account of the great battle fought between the demigods and the demons, a systematic description of the dynasties of various kings, and narrations concerning Ikṣvāku's birth, his dynasty and the dynasty of the pious Sudyumna — all are presented within this literature.

TEXT 22

इलोपाख्यानमत्रोक्तं तारोपाख्यानमेव च ।
सूर्यवंशानुकथनं शशादाद्या नृगादयः ॥ २२ ॥

ilopākhyānam atroktaṁ
tāropākhyānam eva ca
sūrya-vaṁśānukathanaṁ
śaśādādyā nṛgādayaḥ

ilā-upākhyānam — the history of Ilā; *atra* — herein; *uktam* — is spoken; *tārā-upākhyānam* — the history of Tārā; *eva* — indeed; *ca* — also; *sūrya-vaṁśa* — of the dynasty of the sun god; *anukathanam* — the narration; *śaśāda-ādyāḥ* — Śaśāda and others; *nṛga-ādayaḥ* — Nṛga and others.

TRANSLATION

Also related are the histories of Ilā and Tārā, and the description of the descendants of the sun god, including such kings as Śaśāda and Nṛga.

TEXT 23

सौकन्यं चाथ शर्यातेः ककुत्स्थस्य च धीमतः ।
खट्वांगस्य च मान्धातुः सौभरेः सगरस्य च ॥ २३ ॥

saukanyaṁ cātha śaryāteḥ
kakutsthasya ca dhīmataḥ
khaṭvāṅgasya ca māndhātuḥ
saubhareḥ sagarasya ca

saukanyam — the story of Sukanyā; *ca* — and; *atha* — then; *śaryāteḥ* — that of Śaryāti; *kakutsthasya* — of Kakutstha; *ca* — and; *dhī-mataḥ* — who was an intelligent king; *khaṭvāṅgasya* — of Khaṭvāṅga; *ca* — and; *māndhātuḥ* — of Māndhātā; *saubhareḥ* — of Saubhari; *sagarasya* — of Sagara; *ca* — and.

TRANSLATION

The histories of Sukanyā, Śaryāti, the intelligent Kakutstha, Khaṭvāṅga, Māndhātā, Saubhari and Sagara are narrated.

TEXT 24

रामस्य कोशलेन्द्रस्य चरितं किल्बिषापहम् ।
निमेरंगपरित्यागो जनकानां च सम्भवः ॥ २४ ॥

rāmasya kośalendrasya
caritaṁ kilbiṣāpaham

nimer aṅga-parityāgo
janakānāṁ ca sambhavaḥ

rāmasya — of Lord Rāmacandra; *kośala-indrasya* — the King of Kośala; *caritam* — the pastimes; *kilbiṣa-apaham* — which drive away all sins; *nimeḥ* — of King Nimi; *aṅga-parityāgaḥ* — the giving up of his body; *janakānām* — of the descendants of Janaka; *ca* — and; *sambhavaḥ* — the appearance.

TRANSLATION

The Bhāgavatam narrates the sanctifying pastimes of Lord Rāmacandra, the King of Kośala, and also explains how King Nimi abandoned his material body. The appearance of the descendants of King Janaka is also mentioned.

TEXTS 25–26

रामस्य भार्गवेन्द्रस्य निःक्षत्रीकरणं भुवः ।
ऐलस्य सोमवंशस्य ययातेर्नहुषस्य च ॥ २५ ॥
दौष्मन्तेर्भरतस्यापि शान्तनोस्तत्सुतस्य च ।
ययातेर्ज्येष्ठपुत्रस्य यदोर्वंशोऽनुकीर्तितः ॥ २६ ॥

rāmasya bhārgavendrasya
niḥkṣatrī-karaṇaṁ bhuvaḥ
ailasya soma-vaṁśasya
yayāter nahuṣasya ca

dauṣmanter bharatasyāpi
śāntanos tat-sutasya ca
yayāter jyeṣṭha-putrasya
yador vaṁśo 'nukīrtitaḥ

rāmasya — by Lord Paraśurāma; *bhārgava-indrasya* — the greatest of the descendants of Bhṛgu Muni; *niḥkṣatrī-karaṇam* — the elimination of all the *kṣatriyas; bhuvaḥ* — of the earth; *ailasya* — of Mahārāja Aila; *soma-vaṁśasya* — of the dynasty of the moon god; *yayāteḥ* — of Yayāti; *nahuṣasya* — of Nahuṣa; *ca* — and; *dauṣmanteḥ* — of the son of Duṣmanta; *bharatasya* — Bharata; *api* — also; *śāntanoḥ* — of King Śāntanu; *tat* — his; *sutasya* — of the son, Bhīṣma; *ca* — and; *yayāteḥ* — of Yayāti; *jyeṣṭha-putrasya* — of the eldest son; *yadoḥ* — Yadu; *vaṁśaḥ* — the dynasty; *anu-kīrtitaḥ* — is glorified.

TRANSLATION

The Śrīmad-Bhāgavatam describes how Lord Paraśurāma, the greatest descendant of Bhṛgu, annihilated all the kṣatriyas on the face of the earth. It further recounts the lives of glorious kings who appeared in the dynasty of the moon-god — kings such as Aila, Yayāti, Nahuṣa, Duṣmanta's son Bharata, Śāntanu and Śāntanu's son Bhīṣma. Also described is the great dynasty founded by King Yadu, the eldest son of Yayāti.

TEXT 27

यत्रावतीर्णो भगवान् कृष्णाख्यो जगदीश्वरः ।
वसुदेवगृहे जन्म ततो वृद्धिश्च गोकुले ॥ २७ ॥

yatrāvatīrṇo bhagavān
kṛṣṇākhyo jagad-īśvaraḥ
vasudeva-gṛhe janma
tato vṛddhiś ca gokule

yatra — in which dynasty; *avatīrṇaḥ* — descended; *bhagavān* — the Supreme Personality of Godhead; *kṛṣṇa-ākhyaḥ* — known as Kṛṣṇa; *jagat-īśvaraḥ* — the Lord of the universe; *vasudeva-gṛhe* — in the home of Vasudeva; *janma* — His birth; *tataḥ* — subsequently; *vṛddhiḥ* — His growing up; *ca* — and; *gokule* — in Gokula.

TRANSLATION

How Śrī Kṛṣṇa, the Supreme Personality of Godhead and Lord of the universe, descended into this Yadu dynasty, how He took birth in the home of Vasudeva, and how He then grew up in Gokula — all this is described in detail.

TEXTS 28–29

तस्य कर्माण्यपाराणि कीर्तितान्यसुरद्विषः ।
पूतनासुपयःपानं शकटोच्चाटनं शिशोः ॥ २८ ॥
तृणावर्तस्य निष्पेषस्तथैव बकवत्सयोः ।
अघासुरवधो धात्रा वत्सपालावगूहनम् ॥ २९ ॥

tasya karmāṇy apārāṇi
kīrtitāny asura-dviṣaḥ

pūtanāsu-payaḥ-pānaṁ
śakaṭoccāṭanaṁ śiśoḥ

tṛṇāvartasya niṣpeṣas
tathaiva baka-vatsayoḥ
aghāsura-vadho dhātrā
vatsa-pālāvagūhanam

tasya — His; *karmāṇi* — activities; *apārāṇi* — innumerable; *kīrtitāni* — are glorified; *asura-dviṣaḥ*—of the enemy of the demons; *pūtanā* — of the witch Pūtanā; *asu* — along with her life air; *payaḥ*—of the milk; *pānam* — the drinking; *śakaṭa* — of the cart; *uccāṭanam* — the breaking; *śiśoḥ*—by the child; *tṛṇāvartasya* — of Tṛṇāvarta; *niṣpeṣaḥ*—the trampling; *tathā* — and; *eva* — indeed; *baka-vatsayoḥ*—of the demons named Baka and Vatsa; *agha-asura* — of the demon Agha; *vadhaḥ*—the killing; *dhātrā* — by Lord Brahmā; *vatsa-pāla* — of the calves and cowherd boys; *avagūhanam* — the hiding away.

TRANSLATION

Also glorified are the innumerable pastimes of Śrī Kṛṣṇa, the enemy of the demons, including His childhood pastimes of sucking out Pūtanā's life air along with her breast milk, breaking the cart, trampling down Tṛṇāvarta, killing Bakāsura, Vatsāsura and Aghāsura, and the pastimes He enacted when Lord Brahmā hid His calves and cowherd boyfriends in a cave.

TEXT 30

धेनुकस्य सहभ्रातुः प्रलम्बस्य च सङ्क्षयः ।
गोपानां च परित्राणं दावाग्नेः परिसर्पतः ॥ ३० ॥

dhenukasya saha-bhrātuḥ
pralambasya ca saṅkṣayaḥ
gopānāṁ ca paritrāṇaṁ
dāvāgneḥ parisarpataḥ

dhenukasya — of Dhenuka; *saha-bhrātuḥ*—along with his companions; *pralambasya* — of Pralamba; *ca* — and; *saṅkṣayaḥ*—the destruction; *gopānām* — of the cowherd boys; *ca* — and; *paritrāṇam* — the saving; *dāva-agneḥ*—from the forest fire; *parisarpataḥ*—which was encircling.

TRANSLATION

The Śrīmad-Bhāgavatam tells how Lord Kṛṣṇa and Lord Balarāma killed the demon Dhenukāsura and his companions, how Lord Balarāma destroyed Pralambāsura, and also how Kṛṣṇa saved the cowherd boys from a raging forest fire that had encircled them.

TEXTS 31–33

दमनं कालियस्याहेर्महाहेर्नन्दमोक्षणम् ।
व्रतचर्या तु कन्यानां यत्र तुष्टोऽच्युतो व्रतैः ॥ ३१ ॥
प्रसादो यज्ञपत्नीभ्यो विप्राणां चानुतापनम् ।
गोवर्धनोद्धारणं च शक्रस्य सुरभेरथ ॥ ३२ ॥
यज्ञाभिषेकः कृष्णस्य स्त्रीभिः क्रीडा च रात्रिषु ।
शंखचूडस्य दुर्बुद्धेर्वधोऽरिष्टस्य केशिनः ॥ ३३ ॥

damanaṁ kāliyasyāher
mahāher nanda-mokṣaṇam
vrata-caryā tu kanyānāṁ
yatra tuṣṭo 'cyuto vrataiḥ

prasādo yajña-patnībhyo
viprāṇāṁ cānutāpanam
govardhanoddhāraṇaṁ ca
śakrasya surabher atha

yajñabhiṣekaḥ kṛṣṇasya
strībhiḥ krīḍā ca rātriṣu
śaṅkhacūḍasya durbuddher
vadho 'riṣṭasya keśinaḥ

damanam — the subduing; *kāliyasya* — of Kāliya; *aheḥ*—the snake; *mahā-aheḥ*—from the great serpent; *nanda-mokṣaṇam* — the rescue of Mahārāja Nanda; *vrata-caryā* — the execution of austere vows; *tu* — and; *kanyānām* — of the *gopīs; yatra* — by which; *tuṣṭaḥ*—became satisfied; *acyutaḥ*—Lord Kṛṣṇa; *vrataiḥ*—with their vows; *prasādaḥ*—the mercy; *yajña-patnībhyaḥ*—to the wives of the *brāhmaṇas* performing Vedic sacrifices; *viprāṇām* — of the *brāhmaṇa* husbands; *ca* — and; *anutāpanam* — the experience of remorse; *govardhana-uddhāraṇam* — the lifting of Govardhana Hill; *ca* — and; *śakrasya* — by Indra; *surabheḥ*—along with the Surabhi cow; *atha* — then; *yajña-abhiṣekaḥ*—the worship and ritual bathing; *kṛṣṇasya* — of Lord Kṛṣṇa; *strībhiḥ*—together with the women; *krīḍā* — the sporting; *ca* — and; *rātriṣu* — in the nights; *śaṅkhacūḍasya* — of the demon Śaṅkhacūḍa; *durbuddheḥ*—who was foolish; *vadhaḥ*—the killing; *ariṣṭasya* — of Ariṣṭa; *keśinaḥ*—of Keśī.

TRANSLATION

The chastisement of the serpent Kāliya; the rescue of Nanda Mahārāja from a great snake; the severe vows performed by the young gopīs, who thus satisfied Lord Kṛṣṇa; the mercy He showed the wives of the Vedic brāhmaṇas, who felt remorse; the lifting of Govardhana Hill followed by the worship and bathing ceremony performed by Indra and the Surabhi cow; Lord Kṛṣṇa's nocturnal pastimes with the cowherd girls; and the killing of the foolish demons Śaṅkhacūḍa, Ariṣṭa and Keśī—all these pastimes are elaborately recounted.

TEXT 34

अक्रूरागमनं पश्चात्प्रस्थानं रामकृष्णयोः ।
व्रजस्त्रीणां विलापश्च मथुरालोकनं ततः ॥ ३४ ॥

akrūrāgamanaṁ paścāt
prasthānaṁ rāma-kṛṣṇayoḥ
vraja-strīṇāṁ vilāpaś ca
mathurālokanaṁ tataḥ

akrūra — of Akrūra; *āgamanam* — the coming; *paścāt* — after that; *prasthānam* — the departure; *rāma-kṛṣṇayoḥ*—of Lord Balarāma and Lord Kṛṣṇa; *vraja-strīṇām* — of the women of Vṛndāvana; *vilāpaḥ*—the lamentation; *ca* — and; *mathurā-ālokanam* — the seeing of Mathurā; *tataḥ*—then.

TRANSLATION

The Bhāgavatam describes the arrival of Akrūra, the subsequent departure of Kṛṣṇa and Balarāma, the lamentation of the gopīs and the touring of Mathurā.

TEXT 35

गजमुष्टिकचाणूरकंसादीनां तथा वधः ।
मृतस्यानयनं सूनोः पुनः सान्दीपनेर्गुरोः ॥ ३५ ॥

gaja-muṣṭika-cāṇūra-
kaṁsādīnāṁ tathā vadhaḥ
mṛtasyānayanaṁ sūnoḥ
punaḥ sāndīpaner guroḥ

gaja — of the elephant Kuvalayāpīḍa; *muṣṭika-cāṇūra* — of the wrestlers Muṣṭika and Cāṇūra; *kaṁsa* — of Kaṁsa; *ādīnām* — and of others; *tathā* — also; *vadhaḥ*—the killing; *mṛtasya* — who had died; *ānayanam* — the bringing back; *sūnoḥ*—of the son; *punaḥ*—again; *sāndīpaneḥ*—of Sāndīpani; *guroḥ*—their spiritual master.

TRANSLATION

Also narrated are how Kṛṣṇa and Balarāma killed the elephant Kuvalayāpīḍa, the wrestlers Muṣṭika and Cāṇūra, and Kaṁsa and other demons, as well as how Kṛṣṇa brought back the dead son of His spiritual master, Sāndīpani Muni.

TEXT 36

मथुरायां निवसता यदुचक्रस्य यत्प्रियम् ।
कृतमुद्धवरामाभ्यां युतेन हरिणा द्विजाः ॥ ३६ ॥

mathurāyāṁ nivasatā
yadu-cakrasya yat priyam
kṛtam uddhava-rāmābhyāṁ
yutena hariṇā dvijāḥ

mathurāyām — in Mathurā; *nivasatā* — by Him who was residing; *yadu-cakrasya* — for the circle of Yadus; *yat* — which; *priyam* — gratifying; *kṛtam* — was done; *uddhava-rāmābhyām* — with Uddhava and Balarāma; *yutena* — joined; *hariṇā* — by Lord Hari; *dvijāḥ*— O *brāhmaṇas.*

TRANSLATION

Then, O brāhmaṇas, this scripture recounts how Lord Hari, while residing in Mathurā in the company of Uddhava and Balarāma, performed pastimes for the satisfaction of the Yadu dynasty.

TEXT 37

जरासन्धसमानीतसैन्यस्य बहुशो वधः ।
घातनं यवनेन्द्रस्य कुशस्थल्या निवेशनम् ॥ ३७ ॥

jarāsandha-samānīta-
sainyasya bahuśo vadhaḥ
ghātanaṁ yavanendrasya
kuśasthalyā niveśanam

jarāsandha — bv King Jarāsandha; *samānīta* — assembled; *sainyasya* — of the army; *bahuśaḥ* — many times; *vadhaḥ* — the annihilation; *ghātanam* — the killing; *yavana-indrasya* — of the king of the barbarians; *kuśasthalyāḥ* — of Dvārakā; *niveśanam* — the founding.

TRANSLATION

Also described are the annihilation of each of the many armies brought by Jarāsandha, the killing of the barbarian king Kālayavana and the establishment of Dvārakā City.

TEXT 38

आदानं पारिजातस्य सुधर्मायाः सुरालयात् ।
रुक्मिण्या हरणं युद्धे प्रमथ्य द्विषतो हरेः ॥ ३८ ॥

ādānaṁ pārijātasya
sudharmāyāḥ surālayāt
rukmiṇyā haraṇaṁ yuddhe
pramathya dviṣato hareḥ

ādānam — the receiving; *pārijātasya* — of the *pārijāta* tree; *sudharmāyāḥ* — of the Sudharmā assembly hall; *sura-ālayāt* — from the abode of the demigods; *rukmiṇyāḥ* — of Rukmiṇī; *haraṇam* — the kidnapping; *yuddhe* — in battle; *pramathya* — defeating; *dviṣataḥ* — His rivals; *hareḥ* — by Lord Hari.

TRANSLATION

This work also describes how Lord Kṛṣṇa brought from heaven the pārijāta tree and the Sudharmā assembly hall, and how He kidnapped Rukmiṇī by defeating all His rivals in battle.

TEXT 39

हरस्य जृम्भणं युद्धे बाणस्य भुजकृन्तनम् ।
प्राग्ज्योतिषपतिं हत्वा कन्यानां हरणं च यत् ॥ ३९ ॥

harasya jṛmbhaṇaṁ yuddhe
bāṇasya bhuja-kṛntanam
prāgjyotiṣa-patiṁ hatvā
kanyānāṁ haraṇaṁ ca yat

harasya — of Lord Śiva; *jṛmbhaṇam* — the forced yawning; *yuddhe* — in battle; *bāṇasya* — of Bāṇa; *bhuja* — of the arms; *kṛntanam* — the cutting,; *prāgjyotiṣa-patim* — the master of the city Prāgjyotiṣa; *hatvā* — killing; *kanyānām* — of the unmarried virgins; *haraṇam* — the removal; *ca* — and; *yat* — which.

TRANSLATION

Also narrated are how Lord Kṛṣṇa, in the battle with Bāṇāsura, defeated Lord Śiva by making him yawn, how the Lord cut off Bāṇāsura's arms, and how He killed the master of Prāgjyotiṣapura and then rescued the young princesses held captive in that city.

TEXTS 40–41

चैद्यपौण्ड्रकशाल्वानां दन्तवक्रस्य दुर्मतेः ।
शम्बरो द्विविदः पीठो मुरः पञ्चजनादयः ॥ ४० ॥
माहात्म्यं च वधस्तेषां वाराणस्याश्च दाहनम् ।
भारावतरणं भूमेर्निमित्तीकृत्य पाण्डवान् ॥ ४१ ॥

caidya-pauṇḍraka-śālvānāṁ
dantavakrasya durmateḥ
śambaro dvividaḥ pīṭho
muraḥ pañcajanādayaḥ

māhātmyaṁ ca vadhas teṣāṁ
vārāṇasyāś ca dāhanam
bhārāvataraṇaṁ bhūmer
nimittī-kṛtya pāṇḍavān

caidya — of the King of Cedi, Śiśupāla; *pauṇḍraka* — of Pauṇḍraka; *śālvānām* — and of Śālva; *dantavakrasya* — of Dantavakra; *durmateḥ*—the foolish; *śambaraḥ dvividaḥ pīṭhaḥ*—the demons Śambara, Dvivida and Pīṭha; *muraḥ pañcajana-ādayaḥ*—Mura, Pañcajana and others; *māhātmyam* — the prowess; *ca* — and; *vadhaḥ* — the death; *teṣām* — of these; *vārāṇasyāḥ*— of the holy city of Benares; *ca* — and; *dāhanam* — the burning; *bhāra* — of the burden; *avataraṇam* — the reduction; *bhūmeḥ*—of the earth; *nimittī-kṛtya* — making the apparent cause; *pāṇḍavān* — the sons of Pāṇḍu.

TRANSLATION

There are descriptions of the powers and the deaths of the King of Cedi, Pauṇḍraka, Śālva, the foolish Dantavakra, Śambara, Dvivida, Pīṭha, Mura, Pañcajana and other demons, along with a description of how Vārāṇasī was burned to the ground. The Bhāgavatam also recounts how Lord Kṛṣṇa relieved the earth's burden by engaging the Pāṇḍavas in the Battle of Kurukṣetra.

TEXTS 42–43

विप्रशापापदेशेन संहारः स्वकुलस्य च ।
उद्धवस्य च संवादो वसुदेवस्य चाद्भुतः ॥ ४२ ॥
यत्रात्मविद्या ह्यखिला प्रोक्ता धर्मविनिर्णयः ।
ततो मर्त्यपरित्याग आत्मयोगानुभावतः ॥ ४३ ॥

vipra-śāpāpadeśena
saṁhāraḥ sva-kulasya ca
uddhavasya ca saṁvādo
vasudevasya cādbhutaḥ

yatrātma-vidyā hy akhilā
proktā dharma-vinirṇayaḥ
tato martya-parityāga
ātma-yogānubhāvataḥ

vipra-śāpa — of the curse by the *brāhmaṇas; apadeśena* — on the pretext; *saṁhāraḥ* — the withdrawal; *sva-kulasya* — of His own family; *ca* — and; *uddhavasya* — with Uddhava; *ca* — and; *saṁvādaḥ* — the discussion; *vasudevasya* — of Vasudeva (with Nārada); *ca* — and; *adbhutaḥ* — wonderful; *yatra* — in which; *ātma-vidyā* — the science of the self; *hi* — indeed; *akhilā* — completely; *proktā* — was spoken; *dharma-vinirṇayaḥ* — the ascertainment of the principles of religion; *tataḥ* — then; *martya* — of the mortal world; *parityāgaḥ* — the giving up; *ātma-yoga* — of His personal mystic power; *anubhāvataḥ* — on the strength.

TRANSLATION

How the Lord withdrew His own dynasty on the pretext of the brāhmaṇas' curse; Vasudeva's conversation with Nārada; the extraordinary conversation between Uddhava and Kṛṣṇa, which reveals the science of the self in complete detail and elucidates the religious principles of human society; and then how Lord Kṛṣṇa gave up this mortal world by His own mystic power — the Bhāgavatam narrates all these events.

TEXT 44

युगलक्षणवृत्तिश्च कलौ नृणामुपप्लवः ।
चतुर्विधश्च प्रलय उत्पत्तिस्त्रिविधा तथा ॥ ४४ ॥

yuga-lakṣaṇa-vṛttiś ca
kalau nṛṇām upaplavaḥ
catur-vidhaś ca pralaya
utpattis tri-vidhā tathā

yuga — of the different ages; *lakṣaṇa* — the characteristics; *vṛttiḥ* — and the corresponding activities; *ca* — also; *kalau* — in the present age of Kali; *nṛṇām* — of men; *upaplavaḥ* — the total disturbance; *catuḥ-vidhaḥ* — fourfold; *ca* — and; *pralayaḥ* — the process of annihilation; *utpattiḥ* — creation; *tri-vidhā* — of three kinds; *tathā* — and.

TRANSLATION

This work also describes people's characteristics and behavior in the different ages, the chaos men experience in the age of Kali, the four kinds of annihilation and the three kinds of creation.

TEXT 45

देहत्यागश्च राजर्षेर्विष्णुरातस्य धीमतः ।
शाखाप्रणयनमृषेर्मार्कण्डेयस्य सत्कथा ।
महापुरुषविन्यासः सूर्यस्य जगदात्मनः ॥ ४५ ॥

deha-tyāgaś ca rājarṣer
viṣṇu-rātasya dhīmataḥ
śākhā-praṇayanam ṛṣer
mārkaṇḍeyasya sat-kathā
mahā-puruṣa-vinyāsaḥ
sūryasya jagad-ātmanaḥ

deha-tyāgaḥ—the relinquishing of his body; *ca* — and; *rāja-ṛṣeḥ*—by the saintly king; *viṣṇu-rātasya* — Parīkṣit; *dhī-mataḥ*—the intelligent; *śākhā* — of the branches of the *Vedas; praṇayanam* — the dissemination; *ṛṣeḥ*—from the great sage Vyāsadeva; *mārkaṇḍeyasya* — of Mārkaṇḍeya Ṛṣi; *sat-kathā* — the pious narration; *mahā-puruṣa* — of the universal form of the Lord; *vinyāsaḥ*—the detailed arrangement; *sūryasya* — of the sun; *jagat-ātmanaḥ* —who is the soul of the universe.

TRANSLATION

There are also an account of the passing away of the wise and saintly King Viṣṇurāta [Parīkṣit], an explanation of how Śrīla Vyāsadeva disseminated the branches of the Vedas, a pious narration concerning Mārkaṇḍeya Ṛṣi, and a description of the detailed arrangement of the Lord's universal form and His form as the sun, the soul of the universe.

TEXT 46

इति चोक्तं द्विजश्रेष्ठा यत्पृष्टोऽहमिहास्मि वः ।
लीलावतारकर्माणि कीर्तितानीह सर्वशः ॥ ४६ ॥

iti coktaṁ dvija-śreṣṭhā
yat pṛṣṭo 'ham ihāsmi vaḥ
līlāvatāra-karmāṇi
kīrtitānīha sarvaśaḥ

iti — thus; *ca* — and; *uktam* — spoken; *dvija-śreṣṭhāḥ*—O best of the *brāhmaṇas; yat* — what; *pṛṣṭaḥ*—inquired; *aham* — I; *iha* — here; *asmi* —

have been; *vaḥ*—by you; *līlā-avatāra* — of the divine descents of the Supreme Lord for His own enjoyment; *karmāṇi* — the activities; *kīrtitāni* — have been glorified; *iha* — in this scripture; *sarvaśaḥ*—completely.

TRANSLATION

Thus, O best of the brāhmaṇas, I have explained herein what you have inquired from me. This literature has glorified in full detail the activities of the Lord's pastime incarnations.

TEXT 47

पतितः स्खलितश्चार्तः क्षुत्त्वा वा विवशो गृणन्।
हरये नम इत्युच्चैर्मुच्यते सर्वपातकात् ॥ ४७ ॥

patitaḥ skhalitaś cārtaḥ
kṣuttvā vā vivaśo gṛṇan
haraye nama ity uccair
mucyate sarva-pātakāt

patitaḥ—falling; *skhalitaḥ*—tripping; *ca* — and; *ārtaḥ*—feeling pain; *kṣuttvā* — sneezing; *vā* — or; *vivaśaḥ*—involuntarily; *gṛṇan* — chanting; *haraye namaḥ*—"obeisances to Lord Hari"; *iti* — thus; *uccaiḥ*—loudly; *mucyate* — one is freed; *sarva-pātakāt* — from all sinful reactions.

TRANSLATION

If when falling, slipping, feeling pain or sneezing one involuntarily cries out in a loud voice, "Obeisances to Lord Hari!" one will be automatically freed from all his sinful reactions.

PURPORT

Śrīla Bhaktisiddhānta Sarasvatī Ṭhākura explains that Lord Śrī Caitanya is always loudly chanting the song *haraye namaḥ kṛṣṇa* in the courtyard of Śrīvāsa Ṭhākura and that this same Lord Caitanya will free us from our materialistic enjoying propensity if we also loudly chant the glories of the Supreme Lord Hari.

TEXT 48

संकीर्त्यमानो भगवाननन्तः
श्रुतानुभावो व्यसनं हि पुंसाम् ।

प्रविश्य चित्तं विधुनोत्यशेषं
यथा तमोऽर्कोऽभ्रमिवातिवातः ॥ ४८ ॥

saṅkīrtyamāno bhagavān anantaḥ
śrutānubhāvo vyasanaṁ hi puṁsām
praviśya cittaṁ vidhunoty aśeṣaṁ
yathā tamo'rko'bhram ivāti-vātaḥ

saṅkīrtyamānaḥ—being properly chanted about; *bhagavān*—the Supreme Personality of Godhead; *anantaḥ*—the unlimited; *śruta*—being heard about; *anubhāvaḥ*—His potency; *vyasanam*—the misery; *hi*—indeed; *puṁsām*—of persons; *praviśya*—enter; *cittam*—the heart; *vidhunoti*—cleans away; *aśeṣam*—entirely; *yathā*—just as; *tamaḥ*—darkness; *arkaḥ*—the sun; *abhram*—clouds; *iva*—as; *ati-vātaḥ*—a strong wind.

TRANSLATION

When people properly glorify the Supreme Personality of Godhead or simply hear about His power, the Lord personally enters their hearts and cleanses away every trace of misfortune, just as the sun removes the darkness or as a powerful wind drives away the clouds.

PURPORT

One may not be satisfied by the example of the sun removing the darkness, since sometimes the darkness in a cave is not removed by the sun. Therefore the example is given of a strong wind that drives away a cover of clouds. It is thus emphatically stated here that the Supreme Lord will remove from the heart of His devotee the darkness of material illusion.

TEXT 49

मृषा गिरस्ता ह्यसतीरसत्कथा
न कथ्यते यद् भगवानधोक्षजः ।
तदेव सत्यं तदुहैव मंगलं
तदेव पुण्यं भगवद्गुणोदयम् ॥ ४९ ॥

mṛṣā giras tā hy asatīr asat-kathā
na kathyate yad bhagavān adhokṣajaḥ

tad eva satyaṁ tad u haiva maṅgalaṁ
tad eva puṇyaṁ bhagavad-guṇodayam

mṛṣāḥ—false; *giraḥ*—words; *tāḥ*—they; *hi*— indeed; *asatīḥ*—untrue; *asat-kathāḥ*—useless discussions of that which is not eternal; *na kathyate*— is not discussed; *yat*— wherein; *bhagavān*— the Personality of Godhead; *adhokṣajaḥ*—the transcendental Lord; *tat*— that; *eva*— alone; *satyam*— true; *tat*— that; *u ha*— indeed; *eva*— alone; *maṅgalam*— auspicious; *tat*— that; *eva*— alone; *puṇyam*— pious; *bhagavat-guṇa*— the qualities of the Supreme Personality; *udayam*— which manifests.

TRANSLATION

Words that do not describe the transcendental Personality of Godhead but instead deal with temporary matters are simply false and useless. Only those words that manifest the transcendental qualities of the Supreme Lord are actually truthful, auspicious and pious.

PURPORT

Sooner or later, all material literature and discussion must fail the test of time. On the other hand, the transcendental descriptions of the Supreme Lord can free us from the bondage of illusion and restore us to our eternal status as loving servants of the Lord. Although men who are like animals may criticize the glorification of the Absolute Truth, those who are civilized should go on vigorously propagating the transcendental glories of the Lord.

TEXT 50

तदेव रम्यं रुचिरं नवं नवं
तदेव शश्वन्मनसो महोत्सवम् ।
तदेव शोकार्णवशोषणं नृणां
यदुत्तमःश्लोकयशोऽनुगीयते ॥५०॥

tad eva ramyaṁ ruciraṁ navaṁ navaṁ
tad eva śaśvan manaso mahotsavam
tad eva śokārṇava-śoṣaṇaṁ nṛṇāṁ
yad uttamaḥśloka-yaśo 'nugīyate

tat— that; *eva*— indeed; *ramyam*— attractive; *ruciram*— palatable; *navam navam*— newer and newer; *tat*— that; *eva*— indeed; *śaśvat*— constantly; *manasaḥ*—for the mind; *mahā-utsavam* — a great festival; *tat* — that; *eva* — indeed; *śoka-arṇava* — the ocean of misery; *śoṣaṇam* — that which dries; *nṛṇām* — for all persons; *yat* — in which; *uttamaḥśloka* — of the all-famous Supreme Personality of Godhead; *yaśaḥ*—the glories; *anugīyate* — are sung.

TRANSLATION

Those words describing the glories of the all-famous Personality of Godhead are attractive, relishable and ever fresh. Indeed, such words are a perpetual festival for the mind, and they dry up the ocean of misery.

TEXT 51

न यद्वचश्चित्रपदं हरेर्यशो
जगत्पवित्रं प्रगृणीत कर्हिचित् ।
तद् ध्वाङ्‌क्षतीर्थं न तु हंससेवितं
यत्राच्युतस्तत्र हि साधवोऽमलाः ॥ ५१ ॥

na yad vacaś citra-padaṁ harer yaśo
jagat-pavitraṁ pragṛṇīta karhicit
tad dhvāṅkṣa-tīrthaṁ na tu haṁsa-sevitaṁ
yatrācyutas tatra hi sādhavo 'malāḥ

na — not; *yat* — which; *vacaḥ*—vocabulary; *citra-padam* — decorative words; *hareḥ*—of the Lord; *yaśaḥ*—the glories; *jagat* — the universe; *pavitram* — sanctifying; *pragṛṇīta* — describe; *karhicit* — ever; *tat* — that; *dhvāṅkṣa* — of the crows; *tīrtham* — a place of pilgrimage; *na* — not; *tu* — on the other hand; *haṁsa* — by saintly persons situated in knowledge; *sevitam* — served; *yatra* — in which; *acyutaḥ*—Lord Acyuta (is described); *tatra* — there; *hi* — alone; *sādhavaḥ*—the saints; *amalāḥ*—who are pure.

TRANSLATION

Those words that do not describe the glories of the Lord, who alone can sanctify the atmosphere of the whole universe, are considered to be like unto a place of pilgrimage for crows, and are never resorted to by those situated in transcendental knowledge. The pure and saintly devotees take interest only in topics glorifying the infallible Supreme Lord.

TEXT 52

तद्वाग्विसर्गो जनताघसम्प्लवो
यस्मिन् प्रतिश्लोकमबद्धवत्यपि ।
नामान्यनन्तस्य यशोऽङ्कितानि यत्
शृण्वन्ति गायन्ति गृणन्ति साधवः ॥ ५२ ॥

tad vāg-visargo janatāgha-samplavo
yasmin prati-ślokam abaddhavaty api
nāmāny anantasya yaśo 'ṅkitāni yat
śṛṇvanti gāyanti gṛṇanti sādhavaḥ

tat — that; *vāk* — vocabulary; *visargaḥ*—creation; *janatā* — of the people in general; *agha* — of the sins; *samplavaḥ*—a revolution; *yasmin* — in which; *prati-ślokam* — each and every stanza; *abaddhavati* — is irregularly composed; *api* — although; *nāmāni* — the transcendental names, etc; *anantasya* — of the unlimited Lord; *yaśaḥ*—the glories; *aṅkitāni* — depicted; *yat* — which; *śṛṇvanti* — do hear; *gāyanti* — do sing; *gṛṇanti* — do accept; *sādhavaḥ*—the purified men who are honest.

TRANSLATION

On the other hand, that literature which is full of descriptions of the transcendental glories of the name, fame, forms, pastimes and so on of the unlimited Supreme Lord is a different creation, full of transcendental words directed toward bringing about a revolution in the impious lives of this world's misdirected civilization. Such transcendental literatures, even though imperfectly composed, are heard, sung and accepted by purified men who are thoroughly honest.

TEXT 53

नैष्कर्म्यमप्यच्युतभाववर्जितं
न शोभते ज्ञानमलं निरञ्जनम् ।
कुतः पुनः शश्वदभद्रमीश्वरे
न ह्यर्पितं कर्म यदप्यनुत्तमम् ॥ ५३ ॥

naiṣkarmyam apy acyuta-bhāva-varjitaṁ
na śobhate jñānam alaṁ nirañjanam

kutaḥ punaḥ śaśvad abhadram īśvare
na hy arpitaṁ karma yad apy anuttamam

naiṣkarmyam — self-realization, being freed from the reactions of fruitive work; *api* — although; *acyuta* — of the infallible Lord; *bhāva* — conception; *varjitam* — devoid of; *na* — does not; *śobhate* — look well; *jñānam* — transcendental knowledge; *alam* — actually; *nirañjanam* — free from designations; *kutaḥ*—where is; *punaḥ*—again; *śaśvat* — always; *abhadram* — uncongenial; *īśvare* — unto the Lord; *na* — not; *hi* — indeed; *arpitam* — offered; *karma* — fruitive work; *yat* — which is; *api* — even; *anuttamam* — unsurpassed.

TRANSLATION

Knowledge of self-realization, even though free from all material affinity, does not look well if devoid of a conception of the Infallible [God]. What, then, is the use of even the most properly performed fruitive activities, which are naturally painful from the very beginning and transient by nature, if they are not utilized for the devotional service of the Lord?

PURPORT

This and the previous two verses are found in a slightly different form in the First Canto of *Śrīmad-Bhāgavatam* (1.5.10–12). The translations are based on Śrīla Prabhupāda's.

TEXT 54

यशःश्रियामेव परिश्रमः परो
वर्णाश्रमाचारतपःश्रुतादिषु ।
अविस्मृतिः श्रीधरपादपद्मयोर्
गुणानुवादश्रवणादरादिभिः ॥ ५४ ॥

yaśaḥ-śriyām eva pariśramaḥ paro
varṇāśramācāra-tapaḥ-śrutādiṣu
avismṛtiḥ śrīdhara-pāda-padmayor
guṇānuvāda-śravaṇādarādibhiḥ

yaśaḥ—in fame; *śriyām* — and opulence; *eva* — only; *pariśramaḥ*—the labor; *paraḥ*—great; *varṇa-āśrama-ācāra* — by one's execution of duties in the *varṇāśrama* system; *tapaḥ* — austerities; *śruta* — hearing of sacred scripture; *ādiṣu* — and so on; *avismṛtiḥ* — remembrance; *śrīdhara* — of the maintainer of the goddess of fortune; *pāda-padmayoḥ* — of the lotus feet; *guṇa-anuvāda* — of the chanting of the qualities; *śravaṇa* — by hearing; *ādara* — respecting; *ādibhiḥ* — and so on.

TRANSLATION

The great endeavor one undergoes in executing the ordinary social and religious duties of the varṇāśrama system, in performing austerities, and in hearing from the Vedas culminates only in the achievement of mundane fame and opulence. But by respecting and attentively hearing the recitation of the transcendental qualities of the Supreme Lord, the husband of the goddess of fortune, one can remember His lotus feet.

TEXT 55

अविस्मृतिः कृष्णपदारविन्दयोः
क्षिणोत्यभद्राणि च शं तनोति ।
सत्त्वस्य शुद्धिं परमात्मभक्तिं
ज्ञानं च विज्ञानविरागयुक्तम् ॥ ५५ ॥

avismṛtiḥ kṛṣṇa-padāravindayoḥ
kṣiṇoty abhadrāṇi ca śaṁ tanoti
sattvasya śuddhiṁ paramātma-bhaktiṁ
jñānaṁ ca vijñāna-virāga-yuktam

avismṛtiḥ — remembrance; *kṛṣṇa-pada-aravindayoḥ* — of Lord Kṛṣṇa's lotus feet; *kṣiṇoti* — destroys; *abhadrāṇi* — everything inauspicious; *ca* — and; *śam* — good fortune; *tanoti* — expands; *sattvasya* — of the heart; *śuddhim* — the purification; *parama-ātma* — for the Supreme Soul; *bhaktim* — devotion; *jñānam* — knowledge; *ca* — and; *vijñāna* — with direct realization; *virāga* — and detachment; *yuktam* — endowed.

TRANSLATION

Remembrance of Lord Kṛṣṇa's lotus feet destroys everything inauspicious and awards the greatest good fortune. It purifies the heart and bestows devotion for the Supreme Soul, along with knowledge enriched with realization and renunciation.

TEXT 56

यूयं द्विजाग्र्या बत भूरिभागा
यच्छश्वदात्मन्यखिलात्मभूतम् ।
नारायणं देवमदेवमीशम्
अजस्रभावा भजताविवेश्य ॥ ५६ ॥

yūyaṁ dvijāgryā bata bhūri-bhāgā
yac chaśvad ātmany akhilātma-bhūtam
nārāyaṇaṁ devam adevam īśam
ajasra-bhāvā bhajatāviveśya

yūyam — all of you; *dvija-agryāḥ* — O most eminent of *brāhmaṇas; bata* — indeed; *bhūri-bhāgāḥ* — extremely fortunate; *yat* — because; *śaśvat* — constantly; *ātmani* — in your hearts; *akhila* — of all; *ātma-bhūtam* — who is the ultimate Soul; *nārāyaṇam* — Lord Nārāyaṇa; *devam* — the Personality of Godhead; *adevam* — beyond whom there is no other god; *īśam* — the supreme controller; *ajasra* — without interruption; *bhāvāḥ* — having love; *bhajata* — you should worship; *āviveśya* — placing Him.

TRANSLATION

O most eminent of brāhmaṇas, you are all indeed extremely fortunate, since you have already placed within your hearts Lord Śrī Nārāyaṇa — the Personality of Godhead, the supreme controller and the ultimate Soul of all existence — beyond whom there is no other god. You have undeviating love for Him, and thus I request you to worship Him.

TEXT 57

अहं च संस्मारित आत्मतत्त्वं
श्रुतं पुरा मे परमर्षिवक्त्रात् ।
प्रायोपवेशे नृपतेः परीक्षितः
सदस्यृषीणां महतां च शृण्वताम् ॥ ५७ ॥

ahaṁ ca saṁsmārita ātma-tattvaṁ
śrutaṁ purā me paramarṣi-vaktrāt
prāyopaveśe nṛpateḥ parīkṣitaḥ
sadasy ṛṣīṇāṁ mahatāṁ ca śṛṇvatām

aham — I; *ca* — also; *saṁsmāritaḥ* — have been made to remember; *ātma-tattvam* — the science of the Supersoul; *śrutam* — heard; *purā* — previously; *me* — by me; *parama-ṛṣi* — of the greatest of sages, Śukadeva; *vaktrāt* — from the mouth; *prāya-upaveśe* — during the fast to death; *nṛpateḥ* — of the king; *parīkṣitaḥ* — Parīkṣit; *sadasi* — in the assembly; *ṛṣīṇām* — of sages; *mahatām* — great; *ca* — and; *śṛṇvatām* — while they were listening.

TRANSLATION

I also have now been fully reminded of the science of God, which I previously heard from the mouth of the great sage Śukadeva Gosvāmī. I was present in the assembly of great sages who heard him speak to King Parīkṣit as the monarch sat fasting until death.

TEXT 58

एतद्वः कथितं विप्राः कथनीयोरुकर्मणः ।
माहात्म्यं वासुदेवस्य सर्वाशुभविनाशनम् ॥ ५८ ॥

etad vaḥ kathitaṁ viprāḥ
kathanīyoru-karmaṇaḥ
māhātmyaṁ vāsudevasya
sarvāśubha-vināśanam

etat — this; *vaḥ* — to you; *kathitam* — narrated; *viprāḥ* — O *brāhmaṇas;* *kathanīya* — of Him who is most worthy of being described; *uru-karmaṇaḥ* — and whose activities are very great; *māhātmyam* — the glories; *vāsudevasya* — of Lord Vāsudeva; *sarva-aśubha* — all inauspiciousness; *vināśanam* — which completely destroys.

TRANSLATION

O brāhmaṇas, I have thus described to you the glories of the Supreme Lord Vāsudeva, whose extraordinary activities are most worthy of glorification. This narration destroys all that is inauspicious.

TEXT 59

य एतत् श्रावयेन्नित्यं यामक्षणमनन्यधीः ।
श्लोकमेकं तदर्धं वा पादं पादार्धमेव वा ।
श्रद्धावान् योऽनुशृणुयात् पुनात्यात्मानमेव सः ॥ ५९ ॥

ya etat śrāvayen nityaṁ
yāma-kṣaṇam ananya-dhīḥ
ślokam ekaṁ tad-ardhaṁ vā
pādaṁ pādārdham eva vā
śraddhāvān yo 'nuśṛṇuyāt
punāty ātmānam eva saḥ

yaḥ—who; *etat* — this; *śrāvayet* — makes others hear; *nityam* — always; *yāma-kṣaṇam* — every hour and every minute; *ananya-dhīḥ*—with undeviated attention; *ślokam* — verse; *ekam* — one; *tat-ardham* — half of that; *vā* — or; *pādam* — a single line; *pāda-ardham* — half a line; *eva* — indeed; *vā* — or; *śraddhā-vān* — with faith; *yaḥ*—who; *anuśṛṇuyāt* — hears from the proper source; *punāti* — purifies; *ātmānam* — his very self; *eva* — indeed; *saḥ*—he.

TRANSLATION

One who with undeviating attention constantly recites this literature at every moment of every hour, as well as one who faithfully hears even one verse or half a verse or a single line or even half a line, certainly purifies his very self.

TEXT 60

द्वादश्यामेकादश्यां वा शृण्वन्नायुष्यवान् भवेत् ।
पठत्यनश्नन् प्रयतस्पूतो भवति पातकात् ॥ ६० ॥

dvādaśyām ekādaśyāṁ vā
śṛṇvann āyuṣyavān bhavet
paṭhaty anaśnan prayataḥ
pūto bhavati pātakāt

dvādaśyām — on the twelfth day of either fortnight of the month; *ekādaśyām* — on the auspicious eleventh day; *vā* — or; *śṛṇvan* — hearing; *āyuṣya-vān* — possessed of long life; *bhavet* — one becomes; *paṭhati* — if one recites; *anaśnan* — while refraining from eating; *prayataḥ*—with careful attention; *pūtaḥ*—purified; *bhavati* — one becomes; *pātakāt* — from sinful reactions.

TRANSLATION

One who hears this Bhāgavatam on the Ekādaśī or Dvādaśī day is assured of long life, and one who recites it with careful attention while fasting is purified of all sinful reactions.

TEXT 61

पुष्करे मथुरायां च द्वारवत्यां यतात्मवान् ।
उपोष्य संहितामेतां पठित्वा मुच्यते भयात् ॥ ६१ ॥

puṣkare mathurāyāṁ ca
dvāravatyāṁ yatātmavān
upoṣya saṁhitām etāṁ
paṭhitvā mucyate bhayāt

puṣkare — at the holy place Puṣkara; *mathurāyām* — at Mathurā; *ca* — and; *dvāravatyām* — at Dvārakā; *yata-ātma-vān* — self-controlled; *upoṣya* — fasting; *saṁhitām* — literature; *etām* — this; *paṭhitvā* — reciting; *mucyate* — one becomes freed; *bhayāt* — from fear.

TRANSLATION

One who controls his mind, fasts at the holy places Puṣkara, Mathurā or Dvārakā, and studies this scripture will be freed from all fear.

TEXT 62

देवता मुनयः सिद्धाः पितरो मनवो नृपाः ।
यच्छन्ति कामान् गृणतः शृण्वतो यस्य कीर्तनात् ॥ ६२ ॥

devatā munayaḥ siddhāḥ
pitaro manavo nṛpāḥ
yacchanti kāmān gṛṇataḥ
śṛṇvato yasya kīrtanāt

devatāḥ—the demigods; *munayaḥ*—the sages; *siddhāḥ*—the perfected *yogīs; pitaraḥ*—the forefathers; *manavaḥ*—the progenitors of mankind; *nṛpāḥ*—the kings of the earth; *yacchanti* — bestow; *kāmān* — desires; *gṛṇataḥ*—to one who is chanting; *śṛṇvataḥ*—or who is hearing; *yasya* — of which; *kīrtanāt* — because of the glorification.

TRANSLATION

Upon the person who glorifies this Purāṇa by chanting or hearing it, the demigods, sages, Siddhas, Pitās, Manus and kings of the earth bestow all desirable things.

TEXT 63

ऋचो यजूंषि सामानि द्विजोऽधीत्यानुविन्दते ।
मधुकुल्या घृतकुल्याः पयःकुल्याश्च तत्फलम् ॥ ६३ ॥

ṛco yajūṁṣi sāmāni
dvijo 'dhītyānuvindate
madhu-kulyā ghṛta-kulyāḥ
payaḥ-kulyāś ca tat phalam

ṛcaḥ—the *mantras* of the *Ṛg Veda; yajūṁṣi*—those of the *Yajur Veda; sāmāni*—and those of the *Sāma Veda; dvijaḥ*—a *brāhmaṇa; adhītya*—studying; *anuvindate*—obtains; *madhu-kulyāḥ*—rivers of honey; *ghṛta-kulyāḥ*—rivers of ghee; *payaḥ-kulyāḥ*—rivers of milk; *ca*—and; *tat*—that; *phalam*—fruit.

TRANSLATION

By studying this Bhāgavatam, a brāhmaṇa can enjoy the same rivers of honey, ghee and milk he enjoys by studying the hymns of the Ṛg, Yajur and Sāma Vedas.

TEXT 64

पुराणसंहितामेतामधीत्य प्रयतो द्विजः ।
प्रोक्तं भगवता यत्तु तत्पदं परमं व्रजेत् ॥ ६४ ॥

purāṇa-saṁhitām etām
adhītya prayato dvijaḥ
proktaṁ bhagavatā yat tu
tat padaṁ paramaṁ vrajet

purāṇa-saṁhitām—essential compilation of all the *Purāṇas; etām*—this; *adhītya*—studying; *prayataḥ*—carefully; *dvijaḥ*—a *brāhmaṇa; proktam*—described; *bhagavatā*—by the Personality of Godhead; *yat*—which;

tu — indeed; *tat* — that; *padam* — position; *paramam* — supreme; *vrajet* — he attains.

TRANSLATION

A brāhmaṇa who diligently reads this essential compilation of all the Purāṇas will go to the supreme destination, which the Supreme Lord Himself has herein described.

TEXT 65

विप्रोऽधीत्याप्नुयात्प्रज्ञां राजन्योदधिमेखलाम् ।
वैश्यो निधिपतित्वं च शूद्रः शुध्येत पातकात् ॥ ६५ ॥

vipro 'dhītyāpnuyāt prajñāṁ
rājanyodadhi-mekhalām
vaiśyo nidhi-patitvaṁ ca
śūdraḥ śudhyeta pātakāt

vipraḥ — a *brāhmaṇa; adhītya* — studying; *āpnuyāt* — achieves; *prajñām* — intelligence in devotional service; *rājanya* — a king; *udadhi-mekhalām* — (the earth) bounded by the seas; *vaiśyaḥ* — a businessman; *nidhi* — of treasures; *patitvam* — lordship; *ca* — and; *śūdraḥ* — a worker; *śudhyeta* — becomes purified; *pātakāt* — from sinful reactions.

TRANSLATION

A brāhmaṇa who studies the Śrīmad-Bhāgavatam achieves firm intelligence in devotional service, a king who studies it gains sovereignty over the earth, a vaiśya acquires great treasure and a śūdra is freed from sinful reactions.

TEXT 66

कलिमलसंहतिकालनोऽखिलेशो
हरिरितरत्र न गीयते ह्यभीक्ष्णम् ।
इह तु पुनर्भगवानशेषमूर्तिः
परिपठितोऽनुपदं कथाप्रसंगैः ॥ ६६ ॥

kali-mala-saṁhati-kālano 'khileśo
harir itaratra na gīyate hy abhīkṣṇam

iha tu punar bhagavān aśeṣa-mūrtiḥ
paripaṭhito 'nu-padaṁ kathā-prasaṅgaiḥ

kali — of the age of quarrel; *mala-saṁhati* — of all the contamination; *kālanaḥ*—the annihilator; *akhila-īśaḥ*—the supreme controller of all beings; *hariḥ*—Lord Hari; *itaratra* — elsewhere; *na gīyate* — is not described; *hi* — indeed; *abhīkṣṇam* — constantly; *iha* — here; *tu* — however; *punaḥ*—on the other hand; *bhagavān* — the Personality of Godhead; *aśeṣa-mūrtiḥ*—who expands in unlimited personal forms; *paripaṭhitaḥ*—is openly described in narration; *anu-padam* — in each and every verse; *kathā-prasaṅgaiḥ*—on the pretext of stories.

TRANSLATION

Lord Hari, the supreme controller of all beings, annihilates the accumulated sins of the Kali age, yet other literatures do not constantly glorify Him. But that Supreme Personality of Godhead, appearing in His innumerable personal expansions, is abundantly and constantly described throughout the various narrations of this Śrīmad-Bhāgavatam.

TEXT 67

तमहमजमनन्तमात्मतत्त्वं
जगदुदयस्थितिसंयमात्मशक्तिम् ।
द्युपतिभिरजशक्रशंकराद्यैर्
दुरवसितस्तवमच्युतं नतोऽस्मि ॥ ६७ ॥

tam aham ajam anantam ātma-tattvaṁ
jagad-udaya-sthiti-saṁyamātma-śaktim
dyu-patibhir aja-śakra-śaṅkarādyair
duravasita-stavam acyutaṁ nato'smi

tam — to Him; *aham* — I; *ajam* — to the unborn; *anantam* — the unlimited; *ātma-tattvam* — the original Supersoul; *jagat* — of the material universe; *udaya* — the creation; *sthiti* — maintenance; *saṁyama* — and destruction; *ātma-śaktim* — by whose personal energies; *dyu-patibhiḥ*—by the masters of heaven; *aja-śakra-śaṅkara-ādyaiḥ*—headed by Brahmā, Indra and Śiva; *duravasita* — incomprehensible; *stavam* — whose praises; *acyutam* — to the infallible Supreme Lord; *nataḥ*—bowed down; *asmi* — I am.

TRANSLATION

I bow down to that unborn and infinite Supreme Soul, whose personal energies effect the creation, maintenance and destruction of the material universe. Even Brahmā, Indra, Śaṅkara and the other lords of the heavenly planets cannot fathom the glories of that infallible Personality of Godhead.

TEXT 68

उपचितनवशक्तिभिः स्व आत्मन्य्
उपरचितस्थिरजंगमालयाय ।
भगवत उपलब्धिमात्रधाम्ने
सुरऋषभाय नमः सनातनाय ॥ ६८ ॥

upacita-nava-śaktibhiḥ sva ātmany
uparacita-sthira-jaṅgamālayāya
bhagavata upalabdhi-mātra-dhāmne
sura-ṛṣabhāya namaḥ sanātanāya

upacita — fully developed; *nava-śaktibhiḥ* — by His nine energies (*prakṛti, puruṣa, mahat,* false ego and the five subtle forms of perception); *sve ātmani* — within Himself; *uparacita* — arranged in proximity; *sthira jaṅgama* — of both the nonmoving and the moving living beings; *ālayāya* — the abode; *bhagavate* — to the Supreme Personality of Godhead; *upalabhdhi-mātra* — pure consciousness; *dhāmne* — whose manifestation; *sura* — of deities; *ṛṣabhāya* — the chief; *namaḥ* — my obeisances; *sanātanāya* — to the eternal Lord.

TRANSLATION

I offer my obeisances to the Supreme Personality of Godhead, who is the eternal Lord and the leader of all other deities, who by evolving His nine material energies has arranged within Himself the abode of all moving and nonmoving creatures, and who is always situated in pure, transcendental consciousness.

TEXT 69

स्वसुखनिभृतचेतास्तद्व्युदस्तान्यभावो-
ऽप्यजितरुचिरलीलाकृष्टसारस्तदीयम् ।

व्यतनुत कृपया यस्तत्त्वदीपं पुराणं
तमखिलवृजिनघ्नं व्याससूनुं नतोऽस्मि ॥६९॥

sva-sukha-nibhṛta-cetās tad-vyudastānya-bhāvo
'py ajita-rucira-līlākṛṣṭa-sāras tadīyam
vyatanuta kṛpayā yas tattva-dīpaṁ purāṇaṁ
tam akhila-vṛjina-ghnaṁ vyāsa-sūnuṁ nato'smi

sva-sukha — in the happiness of the self; *nibhṛta* — solitary; *cetāḥ* — whose consciousness; *tat* — because of that; *vyudasta* — given up; *anya-bhāvaḥ* — any other type of consciousness; *api* — although; *ajita* — of Śrī Kṛṣṇa, the unconquerable Lord; *rucira* — pleasing; *līlā* — by the pastimes; *ākṛṣṭa* — attracted; *sāraḥ* — whose heart; *tadīyam* — consisting of the activities of the Lord; *vyatanuta* — spread, manifested; *kṛpayā* — mercifully; *yaḥ* — who; *tattva-dīpam* — the bright light of the Absolute Truth; *purāṇam* — the *Purāṇa* (*Śrīmad-Bhāgavatam*); *tam* — unto Him; *akhila-vṛjina-ghnam* — defeating everything inauspicious; *vyāsa-sūnum* — son of Vyāsadeva; *nataḥ asmi* — I offer my obeisances.

TRANSLATION

Let me offer my respectful obeisances unto my spiritual master, the son of Vyāsadeva, Śukadeva Gosvāmī. It is he who defeats all inauspicious things within this universe. Although in the beginning he was absorbed in the happiness of Brahman realization and was living in a secluded place, giving up all other types of consciousness, he became attracted by the pleasing, most melodious pastimes of Lord Śrī Kṛṣṇa. He therefore mercifully spoke this supreme Purāṇa, Śrīmad-Bhāgavatam, which is the bright light of the Absolute Truth and which describes the activities of the Lord.

PURPORT

Without offering respectful obeisances to Śukadeva Gosvāmī and other great *ācāryas* in his line, one cannot possibly gain the privilege of entering into the deep transcendental meaning of *Śrīmad-Bhāgavatam.*

Thus end the purports of the humble servants of His Divine Grace A.C. Bhaktivedanta Swami Prabhupāda to the Twelfth Canto, Twelfth Chapter, of the Śrīmad-Bhāgavatam, *entitled "The Topics of Śrīmad-Bhāgavatam Summarized."*

CHAPTER THIRTEEN

The Glories of Śrīmad-Bhāgavatam

In this final chapter Śrī Sūta Gosvāmī describes the length of each of the *Purāṇas,* along with the subject matter of *Śrīmad-Bhāgavatam,* its purpose, how to give it as a gift, the glories of such gift-giving and the glories of chanting and hearing it.

The total corpus of the *Purāṇas* includes four hundred thousand verses, eighteen thousand of which constitute *Śrīmad-Bhāgavatam.* The Supreme Personality of Godhead, Nārāyaṇa, instructed Brahmā in this *Śrīmad-Bhāgavatam,* whose narrations produce detachment from matter and which contains the essence of all the *Vedānta.* One who gives the *Śrīmad-Bhāgavata Purāṇa* as a gift will attain the highest destination. Among all the *Purāṇas, Śrīmad-Bhāgavatam* is the best, and it is the most dear thing to the Vaiṣṇavas. It reveals that spotless, supreme knowledge accessible to the *paramahaṁsas,* and it also reveals the process by which one can become free from the reactions of material work — a process enriched with knowledge, renunciation and devotion.

Having thus glorified the *Bhāgavatam,* Sūta Gosvāmī meditates upon Lord Śrī Nārāyaṇa as the original Absolute Truth, who is perfectly pure, free from all contamination, devoid of sorrow and immortal. Then he offers obeisances to the greatest *yogī,* Śrī Śukadeva, who is nondifferent from the Absolute Truth. Finally, praying with true devotion, Sūta Gosvāmī offers respects to the Supreme Personality of Godhead, Lord Śrī Hari, who takes away all misery.

TEXT 1

सूत उवाच

यं ब्रह्मा वरुणेन्द्ररुद्रमरुतः स्तुन्वन्ति दिव्यैः स्तवैर्
वेदैः सांगपदक्रमोपनिषदैर्गायन्ति यं सामगाः ।
ध्यानावस्थिततद्गतेन मनसा पश्यन्ति यं योगिनो
यस्यान्तं न विदुः सुरासुरगणा देवाय तस्मै नमः ॥ १ ॥

sūta uvāca
yaṁ brahmā varuṇendra-rudra-marutaḥ stunvanti divyaiḥ stavair
vedaiḥ sāṅga-pada-kramopaniṣadair gāyanti yaṁ sāma-gāḥ
dhyānāvasthita-tad-gatena manasā paśyanti yaṁ yogino
yasyāntaṁ na viduḥ surāsura-gaṇā devāya tasmai namaḥ

sūtaḥ uvāca — Sūta Gosvāmī said; *yam* — whom; *brahmā* — Lord Brahmā; *varuṇa-indra-rudra-marutaḥ* — as well as Varuṇa, Indra, Rudra and the Maruts; *stunvanti* — praise; *divyaiḥ* — with transcendental; *stavaiḥ* — prayers; *vedaiḥ* — with the *Vedas; sa* — along with; *aṅga* — the corollary branches; *pada-krama* — the special sequential arrangement of *mantras; upaniṣadaiḥ* — and the *Upaniṣads; gāyanti* — they sing about; *yam* — whom; *sāma-gāḥ* — the singers of the *Sāma Veda; dhyāna* — in meditative trance; *avasthita* — situated; *tat-gatena* — which is fixed upon Him; *manasā* — within the mind; *paśyanti* — they see; *yam* — whom; *yoginaḥ* — the mystic *yogīs; yasya* — whose; *antam* — end; *na viduḥ* — they do not know; *sura-asura-gaṇāḥ* — all the demigods and demons; *devāya* — to the Supreme Personality of Godhead; *tasmai* — to Him; *namaḥ* — obeisances.

TRANSLATION

Sūta Gosvāmī said: Unto that personality whom Brahmā, Varuṇa, Indra, Rudra and the Maruts praise by chanting transcendental hymns and reciting the Vedas with all their corollaries, pada-kramas and Upaniṣads, to whom the chanters of the Sāma Veda always sing, whom the perfected yogīs see within their minds after fixing themselves in trance and absorbing themselves within Him, and whose limit can never be found by any demigod or demon — unto that Supreme Personality of Godhead I offer my humble obeisances.

TEXT 2

पृष्ठे भ्राम्यदमन्दमन्दरगिरिग्रावाग्रकण्डूयनान्
निद्रालोः कमठाकृतेर्भगवतः श्वासानिलाः पान्तु वः ।
यत्संस्कारकलानुवर्तनवशाद् वेलानिभेनाम्भसां
यातायातमतन्द्रितं जलनिधेर्नाद्यापि विश्राम्यति ॥ २ ॥

pṛṣṭhe bhrāmyad amanda-mandara-giri-grāvāgra-kaṇḍūyanān
nidrāloḥ kamaṭhākṛter bhagavataḥ śvāsānilāḥ pāntu vaḥ

yat-saṁskāra-kalānuvartana-vaśād velā-nibhenāmbhasāṁ
yātāyātam atandritaṁ jala-nidher nādyāpi viśrāmyati

pṛṣṭhe — upon His back; *bhrāmyat* — rotating; *amanda* — most heavy; *mandara-giri* — of Mandara Mountain; *grāva-agra* — by the edges of the stones; *kaṇḍūyanāt* — by the scratching; *nidrāloḥ*—who became sleepy; *kamaṭha-ākṛteḥ*—in the form of a tortoise; *bhagavataḥ*—of the Supreme Personality of Godhead; *śvāsa* — coming from the breathing; *anilāḥ*—the winds; *pāntu* — may they protect; *vaḥ*—all of you; *yat* — of which; *saṁskāra* — of the remnants; *kalā* — the traces; *anuvartana-vaśāt* — as the effect of following; *velā-nibhena* — by that which resembles the flow; *ambhasām* — of the water; *yāta-āyātam* — the coming and going; *atandritam* — ceaseless; *jala-nidheḥ*—of the ocean; *na* — does not; *adya api* — even today; *viśrāmy-ati* — stop.

TRANSLATION

When the Supreme Personality of Godhead appeared as Lord Kūrma, a tortoise, His back was scratched by the sharp-edged stones lying on massive, whirling Mount Mandara, and this scratching made the Lord sleepy. May you all be protected by the winds caused by the Lord's breathing in this sleepy condition. Ever since that time, even up to the present day, the ocean tides have imitated the Lord's inhalation and exhalation by piously coming in and going out.

PURPORT

At times we alleviate an itching sensation by blowing upon it. Similarly, Śrīla Bhaktisiddhānta Sarasvatī Ṭhākura explains, the breathing of the Supreme Personality of Godhead can alleviate the itching sensation within the minds of mental speculators, as well as the itching of the material senses of conditioned souls engaged in sense gratification. Thus by meditating on the windy breath of Lord Kūrma — the tortoise incarnation — all categories of conditioned souls can be relieved of the deficiencies of material existence and come to the liberated, spiritual platform. One must simply allow the pastimes of Lord Kūrma to blow within one's heart like a favorable breeze; then one will surely find spiritual peace.

TEXT 3

पुराणसंख्यासम्भूतिमस्य वाच्यप्रयोजने ।
दानं दानस्य माहात्म्यं पाठादेश्च निबोधत ॥ ३ ॥

purāṇa-saṅkhyā-sambhūtim
asya vācya-prayojane
dānaṁ dānasya māhātmyaṁ
pāṭhādeś ca nibodhata

purāṇa — of the *Purāṇas; saṅkhyā* — of the counting (of verses); *sambhūtim* — the summation; *asya* — of this *Bhāgavatam; vācya* — the subject matter; *prayojane* — and the purpose; *dānam* — the method of giving as a gift; *dānasya* — of such gift-giving; *māhātmyam* — the glories; *pāṭha-ādeḥ* — of teaching and so on; *ca* — and; *nibodhata* — please hear.

TRANSLATION

Now please hear a summation of the verse length of each of the Purāṇas. Then hear of the prime subject and purpose of this Bhāgavata Purāṇa, the proper method of giving it as a gift, the glories of such gift-giving, and finally the glories of hearing and chanting this literature.

PURPORT

Śrīmad-Bhāgavatam is the best of all *Purāṇas.* Śrīla Viśvanātha Cakravartī Ṭhākura explains that the other *Purāṇas* will now be mentioned just as the assistants of a king are mentioned in connection with his glorification.

TEXTS 4–9

ब्राह्मं दश सहस्राणि पाद्मं पञ्चोनषष्टि च ।
श्रीवैष्णवं त्रयोविंशच्चतुर्विंशति शैवकम् ॥४॥
दशाष्टौ श्रीभागवतं नारदं पञ्चविंशति ।
मार्कण्डं नव वाह्नं च दशपञ्च चतुःशतम् ॥५॥
चतुर्दश भविष्यं स्यात्तथा पञ्चशतानि च ।
दशाष्टौ ब्रह्मवैवर्तं लैंगमेकादशैव तु ॥ ६ ॥
चतुर्विंशति वाराहमेकाशीतिसहस्रकम् ।
स्कान्दं शतं तथा चैकं वामनं दश कीर्तितम् ॥७॥

कौर्मं सप्तदशाख्यातं मात्स्यं तत्तु चतुर्दश ।
एकोनविंशत्सौपर्णं ब्रह्माण्डं द्वादशैव तु ॥ ८ ॥
एवं पुराणसन्दोहश्चतुर्लक्ष उदाहृतः ।
तत्राष्टदशसाहस्रं श्रीभागवतमिष्यते ॥ ९ ॥

brāhmaṁ daśa sahasrāṇi
pādmaṁ pañcona-ṣaṣṭi ca
śrī-vaiṣṇavaṁ trayo-viṁśac
catur-viṁśati śaivakam

daśāṣṭau śrī-bhāgavataṁ
nāradaṁ pañca-viṁśati
mārkaṇḍaṁ nava vāhnaṁ ca
daśa-pañca catuḥ-śatam

catur-daśa bhaviṣyaṁ syāt
tathā pañca-śatāni ca
daśāṣṭau brahma-vaivartaṁ
laiṅgam ekādaśaiva tu

catur-viṁśati vārāham
ekāśīti-sahasrakam
skāndaṁ śataṁ tathā caikaṁ
vāmanaṁ daśa kīrtitam

kaurmaṁ sapta-daśākhyātaṁ
mātsyaṁ tat tu catur-daśa
ekona-viṁśat sauparṇaṁ
brahmāṇḍaṁ dvādaśaiva tu

evaṁ purāṇa-sandohaś
catur-lakṣa udāhṛtaḥ
tatrāṣṭadaśa-sāhasraṁ
śrī-bhāgavatam iṣyate

brāhmam — the *Brahma Purāṇa; daśa* — ten; *sahasrāṇi* — thousands; *pādmam* — the *Padma Purāṇa; pañca-ūna-ṣaṣṭi* — five less than sixty; *ca* — and; *śrī-vaiṣṇavam* — the *Viṣṇu Purāṇa; trayaḥ-viṁśat* — twenty-three; *catuḥ-viṁśati* — twenty-four; *śaivakam* — the *Śiva Purāṇa; daśa-aṣṭau* — eighteen; *śrī-bhāgavatam* — *Śrīmad-Bhāgavatam; nāradam* — the *Nārada*

Purāṇa; pañca-viṁśati — twenty-five; *mārkaṇḍam* — the *Mārkaṇḍeya Purāṇa; nava* — nine; *vāhnam* — the *Agni Purāṇa;* ca — and; *daśa-pañca-catuḥ-śatam* — fifteen thousand four hundred; *catuḥ-daśa* — fourteen; *bhaviṣyam* — the *Bhaviṣya Purāṇa; syāt* — consists of; *tathā* — plus; *pañca-śatāni* — five hundred (verses); ca — and; *daśa-aṣṭau* — eighteen; *brahma-vaivartam* — the *Brahma-vaivarta Purāṇa; laiṅgam* — the *Liṅga Purāṇa; ekādaśa* — eleven; eva — indeed; tu — and; *catuḥ-viṁśati* — twenty-four; *vārāham* — the *Varāha Purāṇa; ekāśīti-sahasrakam* — eighty-one thousand; *skāndam* — the *Skanda Purāṇa; śatam* — hundred; *tathā* — plus; *ca* — and; *ekam* — one; *vāmanam* — the *Vāmana Purāṇa; daśa* — ten; *kīrtitam* — is described; *kaurmam* — the *Kūrma Purāṇa; sapta-daśa* — seventeen; *ākhyā-tam* — is said; *mātsyam* — the *Matsya Purāṇa; tat* — that; *tu* — and; *catuḥ-daśa* — fourteen; *eka-ūna-viṁśat* — nineteen; *sauparṇam* — the *Garuḍa Purāṇa; brahmāṇḍam* — the *Brahmāṇḍa Purāṇa; dvādaśa* — twelve; *eva* — indeed; *tu* — and; *evam* — in this way; *Purāṇa* — of the *Purāṇas; sandohaḥ* — the sum; *catuḥ-lakṣaḥ* — four hundred thousand; *udāhṛtaḥ* — is described; tatra — therein; *aṣṭa-daśa-sāhasram* — eighteen thousand; *śrī-bhāgavatam* — *Śrīmad-Bhāgavatam; iṣyate* — is said.

TRANSLATION

The Brahmā Purāṇa consists of ten thousand verses, the Padma Purāṇa of fifty-five thousand, Śrī Viṣṇu Purāṇa of twenty-three thousand, the Śiva Purāṇa of twenty-four thousand and Śrīmad-Bhāgavatam of eighteen thousand. The Nārada Purāṇa has twenty-five thousand verses, the Mārkaṇḍeya Purāṇa nine thousand, the Agni Purāṇa fifteen thousand four hundred, the Bhaviṣya Purāṇa fourteen thousand five hundred, the Brahma-vaivarta Purāṇa eighteen thousand and the Liṅga Purāṇa eleven thousand. The Varāha Purāṇa contains twenty-four thousand verses, the Skanda Purāṇa eighty-one thousand one hundred, the Vāmana Purāṇa ten thousand, the Kūrma Purāṇa seventeen thousand, the Matsya Purāṇa fourteen thousand, the Garuḍa Purāṇa nineteen thousand and the Brahmāṇḍa Purāṇa twelve thousand. Thus the total number of verses in all the Purāṇas is four hundred thousand. Eighteen thousand of these, once again, belong to the beautiful Bhāgavatam.

PURPORT

Śrīla Jīva Gosvāmī has quoted from the *Matsya Purāṇa* as follows:

aṣṭādaśa purāṇāni
kṛtvā satyavatī-sutaḥ
bhāratākhyānam akhilaṁ
cakre tad-upabṛṁhitam

lakṣaṇaikena tat proktaṁ
vedārtha-paribṛṁhitam
vālmīkināpi yat proktaṁ
rāmopakhyānam uttamam

brahmaṇābhihitaṁ tac ca
śata-koṭi-pravistarāt
āhṛtya nāradenaiva
vālmīkāya punaḥ punaḥ

vālmīkinā ca lokeṣu
dharma-kāmārtha-sādhanam
evaṁ sa-pādāḥ pañcaite
lakṣās teṣu prakīṛtitāḥ

"After compiling the eighteen *Purāṇas,* Vyāsadeva, the son of Satyavatī, composed the entire *Mahābhārata,* which contains the essence of all the *Purāṇas.* It consists of over one hundred thousand verses and is filled with all the ideas of the *Vedas.* There is also the account of the pastimes of Lord Rāmacandra, spoken by Vālmīki — an account originally related by Lord Brahmā in one billion verses. That *Rāmāyaṇa* was later summarized by Nārada and related to Vālmīki, who further presented it to mankind so that human beings could attain the goals of religiosity, sense gratification and economic development. The total number of verses in all the *Purāṇas* and *itihāsas* (histories) is thus known in human society to amount to 525,000."

Śrīla Viśvanātha Cakravartī Ṭhākura points out that in the First Canto, Third Chapter, of this work, after Sūta Gosvāmī lists the incarnations of Godhead, he adds the special phrase *kṛṣṇas tu bhagavān svayam:* "But Kṛṣṇa is the original Personality of Godhead." Similarly, after mentioning all of the *Purāṇas,* Śrī Suta Gosvāmī again mentions the *Śrīmad-Bhāgavatam* to emphasize that it is the chief of all Purāṇic literatures.

TEXT 10

इदं भगवता पूर्वं ब्रह्मणे नाभिपंकजे ।
स्थिताय भवभीताय कारुण्यात्सम्प्रकाशितम् ॥ १० ॥

idaṁ bhagavatā pūrvaṁ
brahmaṇe nābhi-paṅkaje
sthitāya bhava-bhītāya
kāruṇyāt samprakāśitam

idam — this; *bhagavatā* — by the Supreme Personality of Godhead; *pūrvam* — first; *brahmaṇe* — to Brahmā; *nābhi-paṅkaje* — upon the lotus growing from the navel; *sthitāya* — who was situated; *bhava* — of material existence; *bhītāya* — who was fearful; *kāruṇyāt* — out of mercy; *samprakāśitam* — was fully revealed.

TRANSLATION

It was to Lord Brahmā that the Supreme Personality of Godhead first revealed the Śrīmad-Bhāgavatam in full. At the time, Brahmā, frightened by material existence, was sitting on the lotus flower that had grown from the Lord's navel.

PURPORT

Lord Kṛṣṇa enlightened Brahmā with the knowledge of *Śrīmad-Bhāgavatam* before the creation of this universe, as indicated here by the word *pūrvam.* Also, the first verse of the *Bhāgavatam* states, *tene brahma hṛdā ya ādi-kavaye:* "Lord Kṛṣṇa expanded perfect knowledge into the heart of Lord Brahmā." Because conditioned souls can experience only temporary objects, which are created, maintained and destroyed, they cannot readily understand that *Śrīmad-Bhāgavatam* is an eternal, transcendental literature nondifferent from the Absolute Truth.

As stated in the *Muṇḍaka Upaniṣad* (1.1.1):

brahmā devānāṁ prathamaḥ sambabhūva
viśvasya kartā bhuvanasya goptā
sa brahma-vidyāṁ sarva-vidyā-pratiṣṭhām
atharvāya jyeṣṭha-putrāya prāha

"Among all the demigods, Brahmā was the first to take birth. He is the creator of this universe and also its protector. To his eldest son, Atharvā, He instructed the spiritual science of the self, which is the basis of all other branches of knowledge." Despite his exalted position, however, Brahmā still fears the influence of the Lord's illusory potency. Thus this energy seems virtually insurmountable. But Lord Caitanya is so kind that during His missionary activities in eastern and southern India, He freely distributed Kṛṣṇa consciousness to everyone, urging them to become teachers of *Bhagavad-gītā.* Lord Caitanya, who is Kṛṣṇa Himself, encouraged the people by saying, "By My order just become a teacher of Lord Kṛṣṇa's message and save this country. I assure you that the waves of *māyā* will never stop your progress." (*Cc. Madhya* 7.128)

If we give up all sinful activities and engage constantly in the *saṅkīrtana* movement of Caitanya Mahāprabhu, victory is assured in our personal lives and also in our missionary efforts.

TEXTS 11–12

आदिमध्यावसानेषु वैराग्याख्यानसंयुतम् ।
हरिलीलाकथाव्रातामृतानन्दितसत्सुरम् ॥ ११ ॥
सर्ववेदान्तसारं यद् ब्रह्मात्मैकत्वलक्षणम् ।
वस्त्वद्वितीयं तन्निष्ठं कैवल्यैकप्रयोजनम् ॥ १२ ॥

ādi-madhyāvasāneṣu
vairāgyākhyāna-saṁyutam
hari-līlā-kathā-vrātā-
mṛtānandita-sat-suram

sarva-vedānta-sāraṁ yad
brahmātmaikatva-lakṣaṇam
vastv advitīyaṁ tan-niṣṭhaṁ
kaivalyaika-prayojanam

ādi — in the beginning; *madhya* — the middle; *avasāneṣu* — and the end; *vairāgya* — concerning renunciation of material things; *ākhyāna* — with narrations; *saṁyutam* — full; *hari-līlā* — of the pastimes of Lord Hari; *kathā-vrāta* — of the many discussions; *amṛta* — by the nectar; *ānandita* — in which are made ecstatic; *sat-suram* — the saintly devotees and demigods; *sarva-vedānta* — of all the *Vedānta* ; *sāram* — the essence; *yat* — which; *brahma* — the Absolute Truth; *ātma-ekatva* — in terms of nondifference from the spirit soul; *lakṣaṇam* — characterized; *vastu* — the reality; *advitīyam* — one without a second; *tat-niṣṭham* — having that as its prime subject matter;

kaivalya — exclusive devotional service; *eka* — the only; *prayojanam* — ultimate goal.

TRANSLATION

From beginning to end, the Śrīmad-Bhāgavatam is full of narrations that encourage renunciation of material life, as well as nectarean accounts of Lord Hari's transcendental pastimes, which give ecstasy to the saintly devotees and demigods. This Bhāgavatam is the essence of all Vedānta philosophy because its subject matter is the Absolute Truth, which, while nondifferent from the spirit soul, is the ultimate reality, one without a second. The goal of this literature is exclusive devotional service unto that Supreme Truth.

PURPORT

Vairāgya, renunciation, means giving up everything that has no relation with the Absolute Truth. Saintly devotees and demigods are enthused by the nectar of the Lord's spiritual pastimes, which are the essence of all Vedic knowledge. Vedic knowledge elaborately negates the ultimate reality of material things by emphasizing their temporary, fleeting existence. The ultimate goal is *vastu,* the factual substance, which is *advitīyam,* one without a second. That unique Absolute Truth is a transcendental person far beyond the mundane categories and characteristics of personality found in our pale material world. Thus the ultimate goal of *Śrīmad-Bhāgavatam* is to train the sincere reader in love of Godhead. Lord Kṛṣṇa is supremely lovable because of His eternal, transcendental qualities. The beauty of this world is a dim reflection of the unlimited beauty of the Lord. Without compromise, *Śrīmad-Bhāgavatam* persistently declares the glories of the Absolute Truth and is therefore the supreme spiritual literature, awarding a full taste of the nectar of love of Kṛṣṇa in full Kṛṣṇa consciousness.

TEXT 13

प्रौष्ठपद्यां पौर्णमास्यां हेमसिंहसमन्वितम् ।
ददाति यो भागवतं स याति परमां गतिम् ॥ १३ ॥

prauṣṭhapadyāṁ paurṇamāsyāṁ
hema-siṁha-samanvitam
dadāti yo bhāgavataṁ
sa yāti paramāṁ gatim

prauṣṭhapadyām — in the month of Bhādra; *paurṇamāsyām* — on the full-moon day; *hema-siṁha* — upon a golden throne; *samanvitam* — seated; *dadāti* — gives as a gift; *yaḥ*—who; *bhāgavatam* — *Śrīmad-Bhāgavatam; saḥ* — he; *yāti* — goes; *paramām* — to the supreme; *gatim* — destination.

TRANSLATION

If on the full moon day of the month of Bhādra one places Śrīmad-Bhāgavatam on a golden throne and gives it as a gift, he will attain the supreme transcendental destination.

PURPORT

One should place *Śrīmad-Bhāgavatam* on a golden throne because it is the king of all literature. On the full-moon day of the month of Bhādra, the sun, which is compared to this king of literatures, is present in the constellation Leo and looks as if raised up on a royal throne. (According to astrology, the sun is said to be exalted in the sign of Leo). Thus one may unreservedly worship *Śrīmad-Bhāgavatam,* the supreme divine scripture.

TEXT 14

राजन्ते तावदन्यानि पुराणानि सतां गणे ।
यावद् भागवतं नैव श्रूयतेऽमृतसागरम् ॥ १४ ॥

rājante tāvad anyāni
purāṇāni satāṁ gaṇe
yāvad bhāgavataṁ naiva
śrūyate 'mṛta-sāgaram

rājante — they shine forth; *tāvat* — that long; *anyāni* — the other; *purāṇāni* — *Purāṇas*; *satām* — of saintly persons; *gaṇe* — in the assembly; *yāvat* — as long as; *bhāgavatam* — *Śrīmad-Bhāgavatam; na* — not; *eva* — indeed; *śrūyate* — is heard; *amṛta-sāgaram* — the great ocean of nectar.

TRANSLATION

All other Purāṇic scriptures shine forth in the assembly of saintly devotees only as long as that great ocean of nectar, Śrīmad-Bhāgavatam, is not heard.

PURPORT

Other Vedic literatures and other scriptures of the world remain prominent until the *Śrīmad-Bhāgavatam* is duly heard and understood. *Śrīmad-Bhāgavatam* is the ocean of nectar and the supreme literature. By faithful hearing, recitation and distribution of *Śrīmad-Bhāgavatam,* the world will be sanctified and other, inferior literatures will fade to minor status.

TEXT 15

सर्ववेदान्तसारं हि श्रीभागवतमिष्यते ।
तद्रसामृततृप्तस्य नान्यत्र स्याद् रतिः क्वचित् ॥ १५ ॥

sarva-vedānta-sāraṁ hi
śrī-bhāgavatam iṣyate
tad-rasāmṛta-tṛptasya
nānyatra syād ratiḥ kvacit

sarva-vedānta — of all *Vedānta* philosophy; *sāram* — the essence; *hi* — indeed; *śrī-bhāgavatam* — *Śrīmad-Bhāgavatam; iṣyate* — is said to be; *tat* — of it; *rasa-amṛta* — by the nectarean taste; *tṛptasya* — for one who is satisfied; *na* — not; *anyatra* — elsewhere; *syāt* — there is; *ratiḥ* — attraction; *kvacit* — ever.

TRANSLATION

Śrīmad-Bhāgavatam is declared to be the essence of all Vedānta philosophy. One who has felt satisfaction from its nectarean mellow will never be attracted to any other literature.

TEXT 16

निम्नगानां यथा गंगा देवानामच्युतो यथा ।
वैष्णवानां यथा शम्भुः पुराणानामिदं तथा ॥ १६ ॥

nimna-gānāṁ yathā gaṅgā
devānām acyuto yathā
vaiṣṇavānāṁ yathā śambhuḥ
purāṇānām idam tathā

nimna-gānām — of rivers flowing down to the sea; *yathā* — as; *gaṅgā* — the Ganges; *devānām* — of all deities; *acyutaḥ* — the infallible Supreme Personality of Godhead; *yathā* — as; *vaiṣṇavānām* — of devotees of Lord Viṣṇu; *yathā* — as; *śambhuḥ*—Śiva; *purāṇānām* — of *Purāṇas; idam* — this; *tathā* — similarly.

TRANSLATION

Just as the Gaṅgā is the greatest of all rivers, Lord Acyuta the supreme among deities and Lord Śambhu [Śiva] the greatest of Vaiṣṇavas, so Śrīmad-Bhāgavatam is the greatest of all Purāṇas.

TEXT 17

क्षेत्राणां चैव सर्वेषां यथा काशी ह्यनुत्तमा ।
तथा पुराणव्रातानां श्रीमद्भागवतं द्विजाः ॥ १७ ॥

kṣetrāṇāṁ caiva sarveṣāṁ
yathā kāśī hy anuttamā
tathā purāṇa-vrātānāṁ
śrīmad-bhāgavataṁ dvijāḥ

kṣetrāṇām — of holy places; *ca* — and; *eva* — indeed; *sarveṣām* — of all; *yathā* — as; *kāśī*—Benares; *hi* — indeed; *anuttamā* — unexcelled; *tathā* — thus; *purāṇa-vrātānām* — of all the *Purāṇas; śrīmat-bhāgavatam* — *Śrīmad-Bhāgavatam; dvijāḥ*—O *brāhmaṇas.*

TRANSLATION

O brāhmaṇas, in the same way that the city of Kāśī is unexcelled among holy places, Śrīmad-Bhāgavatam is supreme among all the Purāṇas.

TEXT 18

श्रीमद्भागवतं पुराणममलं यद्वैष्णवानां प्रियं
यस्मिन् पारमहंस्यमेकममलं ज्ञानं परं गीयते ।
तत्र ज्ञानविरागभक्तिसहितं नैष्कर्म्यमाविष्कृतं
तच्छृण्वन् सुपठन् विचारणपरो भक्त्या विमुच्येन्नरः ॥ १८ ॥

śrīmad-bhāgavataṁ purāṇam amalaṁ yad vaiṣṇavānāṁ priyaṁ
yasmin pāramahaṁsyam ekam amalaṁ jñānaṁ paraṁ gīyate
tatra jñāna-virāga-bhakti-sahitaṁ naiṣkarmyam āviṣkṛtaṁ
tac chṛṇvan su-paṭhan vicāraṇa-paro bhaktyā vimucyen naraḥ

śrīmat-bhāgavatam — *Śrīmad-Bhāgavatam; purāṇam* — the *Purāṇa; amalam* — perfectly pure; *yat* — which; *vaiṣṇavānām* — to the Vaiṣṇavas; *priyam* — most dear; *yasmin* — in which; *pāramahaṁsyam* — attainable by the topmost devotees; *ekam* — exclusive; *amalam* — perfectly pure; *jñānam* — knowledge; *param* — supreme; *gīyate* — is sung; *tatra* — there; *jñāna-virāga-bhakti-sahitam* — together with knowledge, renunciation and devotion; *naiṣkarmyam* — freedom from all material work; *āviṣkṛtam* — is revealed; *tat* — that; *śṛṇvan* — hearing; *su-paṭhan* — properly chanting; *vicāraṇa-paraḥ* — who is serious about understanding; *bhaktyā* — with devotion; *vimucyet* — becomes totally liberated; *naraḥ* — a person.

TRANSLATION

Śrīmad-Bhāgavatam is the spotless Purāṇa. It is most dear to the Vaiṣṇavas because it describes the pure and supreme knowledge of the paramahaṁsas. This Bhāgavatam reveals the means for becoming free from all material work, together with the processes of transcendental knowledge, renunciation and devotion. Anyone who seriously tries to understand Śrīmad-Bhāgavatam, who properly hears and chants it with devotion, becomes completely liberated.

PURPORT

Because *Śrīmad-Bhāgavatam* is completely free of contamination by the modes of nature, it is endowed with extraordinary spiritual beauty and is therefore dear to the pure devotees of the Lord. The word *pāramahaṁsyam* indicates that even completely liberated souls are eager to hear and narrate *Śrīmad-Bhāgavatam.* Those who are trying to be liberated should faithfully serve this literature by hearing and reciting it with faith and devotion.

TEXT 19

कस्मै येन विभासितोऽयमतुलो ज्ञानप्रदीपः पुरा
तद्रूपेण च नारदाय मुनये कृष्णाय तद्रूपिणा ।
योगीन्द्राय तदात्मनाथ भगवद्राताय कारुण्यतस्
तच्छुद्धं विमलं विशोकममृतं सत्यं परं धीमहि ॥ १९ ॥

kasmai yena vibhāsito 'yam atulo jñāna-pradīpaḥ purā
tad-rūpeṇa ca nāradāya munaye kṛṣṇāya tad-rūpiṇā
yogīndrāya tad-ātmanātha bhagavad-rātāya kāruṇyatas
tac chuddhaṁ vimalaṁ viśokam amṛtaṁ satyaṁ paraṁ dhīmahi

kasmai — unto Brahmā; *yena* — by whom; *vibhāsitaḥ*—thoroughly revealed; *ayam* — this; *atulaḥ*—incomparable; *jñāna* — of transcendental knowledge; *pradīpaḥ*—the torchlight; *purā* — long ago; *tat-rūpeṇa* — in the form of Brahmā; *ca* — and; *nāradāya* — to Nārada; *munaye* — the great sage; *kṛṣṇāya* — to Kṛṣṇa-dvaipāyana Vyāsa; *tat-rūpiṇā* — in the form of Nārada; *yogi-indrāya* — to the best of *yogīs,* Śukadeva; *tat-ātmanā* — as Nārada; *atha* — then; *bhagavat-rātāya* — to Parīkṣit Mahārāja; *kāruṇyataḥ*—out of mercy; *tat* — that; *śuddham* — pure; *vimalam* — uncontaminated; *viśokam* — free from misery; *amṛtam* — immortal; *satyam* — upon the truth; *param* — supreme; *dhīmahi* — I meditate.

TRANSLATION

I meditate upon that pure and spotless Supreme Absolute Truth, who is free from suffering and death and who in the beginning personally revealed this incomparable torchlight of knowledge to Brahmā. Brahmā then spoke it to the sage Nārada, who narrated it to Kṛṣṇa-dvaipāyana Vyāsa. Śrīla Vyāsa revealed this Bhāgavatam to the greatest of sages, Śukadeva Gosvāmī, and Śukadeva mercifully spoke it to Mahārāja Parīkṣit.

PURPORT

The first verse of *Śrīmad-Bhāgavatam* states, *satyaṁ paraṁ dhīmahi*—"I meditate upon the Supreme Truth"—and now at the conclusion of this magnificent transcendental literature, the same auspicious sounds are vibrated. The words *tad-rūpeṇa, tad-rūpiṇā* and *tad-ātmanā* in this verse clearly indicate that Lord Kṛṣṇa Himself originally spoke *Śrīmad-Bhāgavatam* to Brahmā and then continued to speak this literature through the agency of Nārada Muni, Dvaipāyana Vyāsa, Śukadeva Gosvāmī and other great sages. In other words, whenever saintly devotees vibrate *Śrīmad-Bhāgavatam,* it is to be understood that Lord Kṛṣṇa Himself is speaking the Absolute Truth through the agency of His pure representatives. Anyone who submissively hears this literature from the Lord's bona fide devotees transcends his conditioned state and becomes qualified to meditate upon the Absolute Truth and serve Him.

TEXT 20

नमस्तस्मै भगवते वासुदेवाय साक्षिणे ।
य इदं कृपया कस्मै व्याचचक्षे मुमुक्षवे ॥ २० ॥

namas tasmai bhagavate
vāsudevāya sākṣiṇe
ya idaṁ kṛpayā kasmai
vyācacakṣe mumukṣave

namaḥ—obeisances; *tasmai*—to Him; *bhagavate*—the Supreme Personality of Godhead; *vāsudevāya*—Lord Vāsudeva; *sākṣiṇe*—the supreme witness; *yaḥ*—who; *idam*—this; *kṛpayā*—out of mercy; *kasmai*—to Brahmā; *vyācacakṣe*—explained; *mumukṣave*—who was desiring liberation.

TRANSLATION

We offer our obeisances to the Supreme Personality of Godhead, Lord Vāsudeva, the all-pervading witness, who mercifully explained this science to Brahmā when he anxiously desired salvation.

TEXT 21

योगीन्द्राय नमस्तस्मै शुकाय ब्रह्मरूपिणे ।
संसारसर्पदष्टं यो विष्णुरातममूमुचत् ॥ २१ ॥

yogīndrāya namas tasmai
śukāya brahma-rūpiṇe
saṁsāra-sarpa-daṣṭaṁ yo
viṣṇu-rātam amūmucat

yogi-indrāya—to the king of mystics; *namaḥ*—obeisances; *tasmai*—to him; *śukaya*—Śukadeva Gosvāmī; *brahma-rūpiṇe*—who is a personal manifestation of the Absolute Truth; *saṁsāra-sarpa*—by the snake of material existence; *daṣṭam*—bitten; *yaḥ*—who; *viṣṇu-rātam*—Parīkṣit Mahārāja; *amūmucat*—freed.

TRANSLATION

I offer my humble obeisances to Śrī Śukadeva Gosvāmī, the best of mystic sages and a personal manifestation of the Absolute Truth. He saved Mahārāja Parīkṣit, who was bitten by the snake of material existence.

PURPORT

Sūta Gosvāmī now offers obeisances to his own spiritual master, Śukadeva Gosvāmī. Śrīla Viśvanātha Cakravartī Ṭhākura clarifies that just as Arjuna was placed into material confusion so that *Bhagavad-gītā* might be spoken, so King Parīkṣit, a pure, liberated devotee of the Lord, was cursed to die so that *Śrīmad-Bhāgavatam* might be spoken. Actually, King Parīkṣit is *viṣṇu-rāta,* eternally under the protection of the Lord. Śukadeva Gosvāmī liberated the king from his so-called illusion to exhibit the merciful nature of a pure devotee and the enlightening effect of his association.

TEXT 22

भवे भवे यथा भक्तिः पादयोस्तव जायते ।
तथा कुरुष्व देवेश नाथस्त्वं नो यतः प्रभो ॥ २२ ॥

bhave bhave yathā bhaktiḥ
pādayos tava jāyate
tathā kuruṣva deveśa
nāthas tvaṁ no yataḥ prabho

bhave bhave — in life after life; *yathā* — so that; *bhaktiḥ* — devotional service; *pādayoḥ* — at the lotus feet; *tava* — of You; *jāyate* — arises; *tathā* — so; *kuruṣva* — please do; *deva-īśa* — O Lord of lords; *nāthaḥ* — the master; *tvam* — You; *naḥ* — our; *yataḥ* — because; *prabho* — O Lord.

TRANSLATION

O Lord of lords, O master, please grant us pure devotional service at Your lotus feet, life after life.

TEXT 23

नामसंकीर्तनं यस्य सर्वपापप्रणाशनम् ।
प्रणामो दुःखशमनस्तं नमामि हरिं परम् ॥ २३ ॥

nāma-saṅkīrtanaṁ yasya
sarva-pāpa praṇāśanam
praṇāmo duḥkha-śamanas
taṁ namāmi hariṁ param

nāma-saṅkīrtanam — the congregational chanting of the holy name; *yasya* — of whom; *sarva-pāpa* — all sins; *praṇāśanam* — which destroys; *praṇāmaḥ* — the bowing down; *duḥkha* — misery; *śamanaḥ* — which subdues; *tam* — to Him; *namāmi* — I offer my obeisances; *harim* — to Lord Hari; *param* — the Supreme.

TRANSLATION

I offer my respectful obeisances unto the Supreme Lord, Hari, the congregational chanting of whose holy names destroys all sinful reactions, and the offering of obeisances unto whom relieves all material suffering.

Thus end the purports of the humble servants of His Divine Grace A.C. Bhaktivedanta Swami Prabhupāda to the Twelfth Canto, Thirteenth Chapter, of the Śrīmad-Bhāgavatam, *entitled "The Glories of Śrīmad-Bhāgavatam."*

The Twelfth Canto was completed at Gainesville, Florida, on Sunday, July 18, 1982.

END OF THE TWELFTH CANTO

CONCLUSION

We offer our most respectful obeisances at the lotus feet of His Divine Grace Oṁ Viṣṇupāda Paramahaṁsa Parivrājakācārya Aṣṭottara-śata Śrī Śrīmad Bhaktivedanta Swami Prabhupāda and, by his mercy, to the Six Gosvāmīs of Vṛndāvana, to Lord Caitanya and His eternal associates, to Śrī Śrī Rādhā-Kṛṣṇa and to the supreme transcendental literature, *Śrīmad-Bhāgavatam.* By the causeless mercy of Śrīla Prabhupāda we have been able to approach the lotus feet of Śrīla Bhaktisiddhānta Sarasvatī Ṭhākura, Śrīla Jīva Gosvāmī, Śrīla Viśvanātha Cakravartī Ṭhākura, Śrīla Śrīdhara Svāmī, and other great Vaiṣṇava *ācāryas,* and by carefully studying their liberated commentaries we have humbly tried to complete the *Śrīmad-Bhāgavatam.* We are the insignificant servants of our spiritual master, Śrīla Prabhupāda, and by his mercy we have been allowed to serve him through the presentation of *Śrīmad-Bhāgavatam.*

Appendixes

His Divine Grace
A. C. Bhaktivedanta Swami Prabhupāda

His Divine Grace A.C. Bhaktivedanta Swami Prabhupāda appeared in this world in 1896 in Calcutta, India. He first met his spiritual master, Śrīla Bhaktisiddhānta Sarasvatī Gosvāmī, in Calcutta in 1922. Śrīla Bhaktisiddhānta Sarasvatī, a prominent religious scholar and the founder of sixty-four Gauḍīya Maṭhas (Vedic institutes) in India, liked this educated young man and convinced him to dedicate his life to teaching Vedic knowledge. Śrīla Prabhupāda became his student and, in 1933, his formally initiated disciple.

At their first meeting, Śrīla Bhaktisiddhānta Sarasvatī requested Śrīla Prabhupāda to broadcast Vedic knowledge in English. In the years that followed, Śrīla Prabhupāda wrote a commentary on the *Bhagavad-gītā,* assisted the Gauḍīya Maṭha in its work, and, in 1944, started *Back to Godhead,* an English fortnightly magazine. Single-handedly, Śrīla Prabhupāda edited it, typed the manuscripts, checked the galley proofs, and even distributed the individual copies. The magazine is now being continued by his disciples all over the world.

In 1950 Śrīla Prabhupāda retired from married life, adopting the *vānaprastha* (retired) order to devote more time to his studies and writing. He traveled to the holy city of Vṛndāvana, where he lived in humble circumstances in the historic temple of Rādhā-Dāmodara. There he engaged for several years in deep study and writing. He accepted the renounced order of life (*sannyāsa*) in 1959. At Rādhā-Dāmodara, Śrīla Prabhupāda began work on his life's masterpiece: a multivolume commentated translation of the eighteen-thousand-verse *Śrīmad-Bhāgavatam* (*Bhāgavata Purāṇa*). He also wrote *Easy Journey to Other Planets.*

After publishing three volumes of the *Bhāgavatam,* Śrīla Prabhupāda came to the United States, in September 1965, to fulfill the mission of his spiritual master. Subsequently, His Divine Grace wrote more than sixty volumes of authoritative commentated translations and summary studies of the philosophical and religious classics of India.

When he first arrived by freighter in New York City, Śrīla Prabhupāda was practically penniless. It was after almost a year of great difficulty that he established the International Society for Krishna Consciousness in July of 1966. Before he passed away on November 14, 1977, he had guided the Society and seen it grow to a worldwide confederation of more than one hundred *ashrams,* schools, temples, institutes, and farm communities.

In 1972 His Divine Grace introduced the Vedic system of primary and secondary education in the West by founding the *gurukula* school in Dallas, Texas. Since then his disciples have established similar schools throughout the United States and the rest of the world.

Śrīla Prabhupāda also inspired the construction of several large international cultural centers in India. The center at Śrīdhāma Māyāpur is the site for a planned spiritual city, an ambitious project for which construction will extend over many years to come. In Vṛndāvana are the magnificent Kṛṣṇa-Balarāma Temple and International Guesthouse, *gurukula* school, and Śrīla Prabhupāda Memorial and Museum. There is also a major cultural and educational center in Mumbai. There are beautiful temples in Delhi, Bangalore, Ahmedabad and Vadodara besides many other centers throughout India.

Śrīla Prabhupāda's most significant contribution, however, is his books. Highly respected by scholars for their authority, depth, and clarity, they are used as textbooks in numerous college courses. His writings have been translated into over fifty languages. The Bhaktivedanta Book Trust, established in 1972 exclusively to publish the works of His Divine Grace, has thus become the world's largest publisher of books in the field of Indian religion and philosophy.

In just twelve years, despite his advanced age, Śrīla Prabhupāda circled the globe fourteen times on lecture tours that took him to six continents. In spite of such a vigorous schedule, Śrīla Prabhupāda continued to write prolifically. His writings constitute a veritable library of Vedic philosophy, religion, literature, and culture.

References

The purports of *Śrīmad-Bhāgavatam* are all confirmed by standard Vedic authorities. The following authentic scriptures are cited in this volume. For specific page references, consult the general index.

Bhagavad-gītā

Bṛhan-nāradīya Purāṇa

Cāturmāsya-māhātmya

Hayaśīrṣa Pañcarātra

Matsya Purāṇa

Muṇḍaka Upaniṣad

Padma Purāṇa

Ṛg Veda

Sāma Veda

Skanda Purāṇa

Śrīmad-Bhāgavatam

Vedānta-sūtra

Viṣṇu Purāṇa

Yajur Veda

Glossary

A

Ācārya—a spiritual master who teaches by his own example, and who sets the proper religious example for all human beings.

Acyuta—a name for the Supreme Personality of Godhead, who can never fall down from His position.

Apsarā—a heavenly courtesan. The most beautiful women in the heavenly planets, who are expert at dancing.

Ārati— a ceremony in which one greets and worships the Lord in His form of a Deity by offerings such as incense, a flame, water, a fine cloth, a fragrant flower, a peacock-feather, and yak-tail whisk, accompanied by ringing of a bell and chanting of *mantras*.

Arghya—a ceremonial offering, in a conch shell, of water and other auspicious items.

Āśrama—a spiritual order of life. The four *āśramas* are *brahmacārī* or student life, *gṛhastha* or married life, *vānaprastha* or retired life, and *sannyāsa* or the renounced order of life; the home of the spiritual master, a place where spiritual practices are executed.

Atharva Veda—one of the four *Vedas*, the original revealed scriptures spoken by the Lord Himself, consisting primarily of formulas and chants designed to counteract the effects of disease and calamity.

Avatāra—literally "one who descends." A partially or fully empowered incarnation of Lord Kṛṣṇa who descends from the spiritual sky to the material universe with a particular mission described in scriptures. Lord Kṛṣṇa is the original Personality of Godhead from whom all *avatāras* originate. There are two broad categories of *avatāras*. Some, like Śrī Kṛṣṇa, Śrī Rāma and Śrī Nṛsiṁha, are Viṣṇu-tattva, i.e. direct forms of God Himself, the source of all power. Others are ordinary souls (*jīva-tattva*) who are called *śaktyāveśa avatāras*, and are empowered by the Lord to execute a certain purpose.

B

Balarāma (Baladeva)—the first plenary expansion of the Supreme Personality of Godhead, Lord Kṛṣṇa. He appeared as the son of Rohiṇī and elder brother of Lord Kṛṣṇa. Also known as Balabhadra or Baladeva, He is worshipped in Pūri along wih His younger brother Kṛṣṇa and sister Subhadra.

Bhagavad-gītā—a seven-hundred verse record of a conversation between Lord Kṛṣṇa and His disciple, Arjuna, from the *Bhīṣma Parva* of the *Mahābhārata* of Vedavyāsa. The conversation took place between two armies minutes before the start of an immense fratricidal battle. Kṛṣṇa teaches the science of the Absolute Truth and the importance of devotional service to the despondent Arjuna, and it contains the essence of all Vedic wisdom. Śrīla Prabhupāda's annotated English translation is called *Bhagavad-gītā As It Is;* This most essential text of spiritual knowledge, The Song of the Lord, contains Kṛṣṇa's instructions to Arjuna at Kurukṣetra. It is found in the *Mahābhārata*. The *Mahābhārata* is classified as *smṛti-śāstra*, a supplement of the *śruti-śāstra*. *Śruti*, the core Vedic literature, includes the four Vedas (*Ṛg, Sāma, Yajur* and *Atharva*) and the *Upaniṣads*. *Śruti* advances the understanding of the absolute. *Bhagavad-gītā* is also known as *Gītopaniṣad*, or a *śruti* text spoken by the Supreme Personality of Godhead Himself. Therefore, Śrīla Prabhupāda wrote in a letter, the *Gītā* should be taken as *śruti*. But they take it as smṛti because it is part of the *smṛti* (*Mahābhārata*). In one sense it is both *śruti* and *smṛti*. In only 700 verses, the *Bhagavad-gītā* summarizes all Vedic knowledge about the soul, God, *sanātana-dharma*, sacrifice, *yoga*, *karma*, reincarnation, the modes of material nature, *Vedānta* and pure devotion.

Bhīṣmadeva—the grandfather of the Pāṇḍavas, and the most powerful and venerable warrior on the Battlefield of Kurukṣetra. The noble general respected as the "grandfather" of the Kuru dynasty, is recognized as one of the twelve *mahājanas*, authorities on devotional service to the Lord. He was given a boon of being able to leave his body any time he pleased, consequently he decided to leave while laying on a bed of arrows on the battlefield in full view of Lord Śrī Kṛṣṇa.

Bhūr—the lower material planets.

Bhuvar—the middle material planets.

Brahmā—the first created living being and secondary creator of the material universe. Directed by Lord Viṣṇu, he creates all life forms in the universes. He also rules the mode of passion. Twelve of his hours equal 4,320,000,000 earth-years, and his life span is more than 311 trillion of our years. The first living being in the universe, Brahmā was born, not of a womb, but the lotus that grows from Lord Viṣṇu's navel. He is the forefather and guru of the demigods, the giver of the Vedas, and the director of the *vaikṛta* or secondary phase of cosmic creation by which all species of plants, animals, human beings and demigods come into existence.

Brahmacarya—celibate student life, the first order of Vedic spiritual life; the vow of strict abstinence from sex indulgence.

Brāhmaṇa—a member of the intellectual, priestly class; a person wise in Vedic knowledge, fixed in goodness and knowledge of Brahman, the Absolute Truth; one of the four orders of Vedic society. Their occupation consists of learning and teaching Vedic literature, learning and teaching Deity worship, and receiving and giving charity.

Bṛhan-nāradīya Purāṇa—one of the eighteen *Purāṇas* or Vedic histories.

Bṛhaspati—the spiritual master of King Indra and chief priest of the demigods.

C

Cāṇakya Paṇḍita—the *brāhmaṇa* advisor to King Candragupta responsible for checking Alexander the Great's invasion of India. His book *Cāṇakya-nīti-śāstra* is renowned for its aphorisms on politics and morality.

Candragupta—a king of the Maurya dynasty in India. His armies repelled Alexander the Great's advance into India.

Cedirāja—the king of Cedi; also known as Śiśupāla. Lord Kṛṣṇa killed him because of his blasphemy.

D

Daityas—demons; a race of demons descending from Diti.

Dharma—religious principles; one's natural occupation; the quality of rendering service, which is the essential, eternal quality of the soul, regarded as inseparable from it. The Sanskrit term *dharma* is variously translated as duty, virtue, morality, righteousness, or religion, but no single English word conveys the actual import of *dharma*. Dharma ultimately means to surrender to the Supreme Lord, as Lord Kṛṣṇa commands Arjuna in the *Gīta*.

Dhenukāsura—a mystic demon who took the form of a donkey, and was killed by Kṛṣṇa.

Dhṛtarāṣṭra—the father of the Kauravas. He was born of the union of Vyāsadeva and Ambikā. He was born blind because Ambikā closed her eyes during conception, out of fear of the sage. He was reputed to have the strength of ten thousand elephants. He was the uncle of the Pāṇḍavas whose attempt to usurp their kingdom for the sake of his own sons resulted in the Kurukṣetra war. *Bhagavad-gītā* was related to Dhṛtarāṣṭra by his secretary as it was being spoken on the Battlefield of Kurukṣetra.

Dhruva Mahārāja—a great devotee who at the age of five performed severe austerities and realized the Supreme Personality of Godhead. He received an entire planet, the Pole Star or Dhruvaloka from the Supreme Lord Viṣṇu.

Diti—a wife of Kaśyapa Muni, and the mother of the demons Hiraṇyākṣa and Hiraṇyakaśipu.

Droṇācārya—the martial preceptor of the Pāṇḍavas and the Kauravas. The military teacher of Arjuna and the other Pāṇḍavas and the commander-in-chief of the Kurus, who was obliged to fight the Pāṇḍavas on the Battlefield of Kurukṣetra. He was the son of the great sage Bharadvāja. He wife was Kāpī, and his son was Aśvatthāmā. He was killed by Dhṛṣṭadyumna during the Kurukṣetra war.

Dvāpara-yuga—the third age of the cycle of a *mahā-yuga*. It lasts more than 864,000 years.

Dvārakā—the island kingdom of Lord Kṛṣṇa, lying off India's west coast, near Gujarat, where He performed pastimes five thousand years ago. The capital city of the Yadus. Lord Kṛṣṇa had this city built to protect the Yadus from the attacks by the demons. When Lord Kṛṣṇa left this world, the ocean enveloped the whole city.

G

Gajendra—the king of the elephants. He was saved from a crocodile by Lord Viṣṇu and awarded liberation.

Gandharvas—the celestial demigod dancers, singers, and musicians of the heavenly planets.

Gaṅgā—the famous and holy Ganges river of India, which runs throughout the entire universe. She originates from the spiritual world, and descended when Lord Vāmanadeva kicked a hole in the top of the universe. One is recommended to bathe in the Ganges for purification. She married Mahārāja Śantanu and begot the famous devotee and warrior, Bhīṣmadeva.

Garbhodaka Ocean—the body of water that fills the bottom half of each material universe.

Garuḍa—Lord Viṣṇu's eternal carrier, a great devotee, and the son of Aditi and Kaśyapa who takes the form of an eagle. He is often found atop a pole facing the entrance of Viṣṇu temples. The emblem of Garuḍa is always on the chariot of Lord Kṛṣṇa.

Gopīs—the cowherd girls of Vraja, who are generally the counterparts of Śrī Kṛṣṇa's *hlādini-śākti*, Śrīmatī Rādhārāṇī, and His most surrendered and confidential devotees. They assist Her as maidservants in her conjugal pastimes with the Supreme Personality of Godhead.

Gosvāmī—a person who has his senses under full control: the title of a *sannyāsi*, a person in the renounced order of life.

Govardhana—a large hill dear to Lord Kṛṣṇa and His devotees. Kṛṣṇa held it up for seven days to protect His devotees in Vṛndāvana from a devastating storm sent by Indra.

Guru—spiritual master; one of the three spiritual authorities for a Vaiṣṇava. Literally, this term means heavy. The spiritual master is heavy with knowledge.

H

Hare Kṛṣṇa mantra—a sixteen-word prayer composed of the names Hare, Kṛṣṇa, and Rāma: Hare Kṛṣṇa, Hare Kṛṣṇa, Kṛṣṇa Kṛṣṇa, Hare Hare, Hare

Rāma, Hare Rāma, Rāma Rāma, Hare Hare. Hare is an address to Harā, another name for His eternal consort, Śrīmatī Rādhārāṇī. Kṛṣṇa, "the all-attractive one," and Rāma, "the all-pleasing one," are names of God. The chanting of this *mantra* is the most recommended means for spiritual progress in this age of Kali, as it cleanses the mind of all impurities, and helps to understand one's true identity as an eternal spiritual being. Lord Caitanya personally designated it as the *mahā-mantra* and practically demonstrated the effects of the chanting.

Hari—the Supreme Lord, who removes all obstacles to spiritual progress; Lord Viṣṇu.

Hari-kīrtana—the chanting of the names of Lord Hari (Kṛṣṇa)

Hayagriva (Hayaśīrṣā)—the horse-headed incarnation of Lord Kṛṣṇa who returned the stolen *Vedas* to Brahmā and spoke the *Vedas* to him.

Hiraṇyakaśipu—a powerful demon and great atheist who tormented his son Prahlāda Mahārāja, a great devotee, and was killed by Lord Nṛsiṁhadeva, the half man-half lion form of Lord Viṣṇu.

Hiraṇyākṣa—the demoniac son of Kaśyapa, younger brother of Hiraṇyakaśipu who was killed by Lord Varāha.

I

Indra—the chief demigod of heaven, presiding deity of rain, and the father of Arjuna. He is the son of Aditi.

J

Janamejaya—the son of King Parīkṣit.

Jīva Gosvāmī—one of the Six Gosvāmīs of Vṛndāvana and the nephew of Rupa and Sanātana Gosvāmīs. He grew up absorbed in the worship of Kṛṣṇa and Balarāma. Lord Caitanya instructed him in a dream to proceed to Navadvīpa, and there he toured that sacred place in the association of Śrī Nityānanda Prabhu. He became a disciple of Rūpa Gosvāmī and wrote eighteen major works on Vaiṣṇava philosophy, comprising more than 400,000 verses. He is considered by many philosophers and Sanskrit scholars to be the greatest scholar who ever lived.

K

Kāliya—the many-hooded serpent chastised by Lord Kṛṣṇa for poisoning a section of the Yamunā River.

Kali-yuga—the present age, the Age of Kalī, the Age of Quarrel and Hypocrisy. The fourth and last age in the cycle of a *mahā-yuga*. It began 5,000 years ago, and lasts for a total of 432,000 years. It is characterized by irreligious practice and stringent material miseries.

Kalki—the incarnation of Lord Viṣṇu, who comes on a white horse at the end of *Kali-yuga* to annihilate all the demons and atheists.

Kapila—an incarnation of Kṛṣṇa who appeared in *Satya-yuga* as the son of Devahūti and Kardama Muni and expounded the devotional *Sāṅkhya* philosophy, the analysis of matter and spirit, as a means of cultivating devotional service to the Lord. (There is also an atheist philosopher named Kapila, but he is not an incarnation of the Lord.)

Karma—1. material action performed according to scriptural regulations; 2. action pertaining to the development of the material body; 3. any material action which will incur a subsequent reaction and 4. the material reaction one incurs due to fruitive activities. The soul receives due reaction to work by taking his next birth in a lower species, or the human species, or a higher species. Or the soul may be liberated from birth and death altogether. All this depends upon whether the *karma* performed within this lifetime is ignorant, passionate, good or transcendental.

Keśava—the Supreme Lord, Kṛṣṇa, who has fine, long black hair.

Keśī—a demon who attacked the inhabitants of Vṛndāvana in the form of a wild horse but was killed by Lord Kṛṣṇa.

Khaṭvāṅga—a saintly king who is famous for attaining unalloyed Kṛṣṇa consciousness just moments before his death.

Kṛṣṇa—the original, two-armed form of the Supreme Lord who is the origin of all incarnations and expansions.

Kṛṣṇa Dvaipāyana—another name of Śrīla Vyāsadeva.

Kṣatriya—second of the four social orders of the *varṇāśrama* system; a warrior who is inclined to fight and lead others; the administrative or protective occupation.

Kūrma—the Supreme Lord's incarnation as a tortoise.

Kurus—all of the descendants of King Kuru, but specifically the 100 sons of Dhṛtarāṣṭra. The Pāṇḍavas were also descendants of King Kuru, but Dhṛtarāṣṭra wished to exclude them from the family tradition; enemies of the Pāṇḍavas.

M

Magadha—a province of ancient India; also the capital city of King Jarāsandha.

Mahābhārata—An important and famous *itihāsa* (historical) scripture belonging to the *smṛti* section of the Vedic scriptures; an ancient, epic history of Bhārata or India composed in 100,000 verses by Kṛṣṇa Dvaipāyana Vyāsadeva, the literary incarnation of Godhead. The essence of all Vedic philosophy, the *Bhagavad-gītā*, is a part of this great work. *Mahābhārata* is a history of the earth from its creation to the great Kurukṣetra war fought between the Kuru and Pāṇḍava factions of the Kaurava dynasty, which took place about five thousand years ago.

Mahat-tattva—the original, undifferentiated form of the total material energy, from which the material world is manifested when the three modes of material nature are activated by the glance of Mahā-Viṣṇu.

Mantra—a transcendental sound or Vedic hymn, a prayer or chant; a pure sound vibration when repeated over and over delivers the mind from its material inclinations and illusion. The Vedic scriptures are composed of many thousands of *mantras.*

Manu—son of Brahmā who is the original father and lawgiver of the human race; a generic name for any of the fourteen universal rulers also known as *Manvantara-avataras* who appear in each day of Lord Brahmā. Their names are (1) Svāyambhuva; (2) Svārociṣa; (3) Uttama; (4) Tāmasa; (5) Raivata; (6) Cākṣusa; (7) Vaivasvata; (8) Sāvarṇi; (9) Dakṣa-sāvarṇi; (10) Brahma-sāvarṇi; (11) Dharma-sāvarṇi; (12) Rudra-sāvarṇi; (13) Deva-sāvarni; (14) Indra-sāvarṇi

Mathurā—Lord Kṛṣṇa's abode, and birth place, surrounding Vṛndāvana. Lord Krsṇa displayed many of His pastimes here after leaving Vṛndāvana. At the end of Lord Kṛṣṇa's manifest *līlā*, Vajranābha, His grandson, was put in charge of this sacred city.

Matsya—the fish incarnation of the Supreme Lord.

Māyā—Māyāvāda philosophy. Māyāvāda in Sanskrit means doctrine of illusion. In India, the philosophies of the Buddha and of Śaṅkarācārya are called Māyāvāda. The second grew out of the first. The fundamental principles accepted by both are the following: (1) name, form, individuality, thoughts, desires and words arise from *māyā* or illusion, not God; (2) *māyā* cannot be rationally explained, since the very idea that anything needs explaining is itself *māyā*; (3) the individual self or soul is not eternal, because upon liberation it ceases to exist; (4) like *māyā*, the state of liberation is beyond all explanation. The main difference between the two is that Śaṅkarācārya's Māyāvāda asserts that beyond *māyā* is an eternal impersonal monistic reality, Brahman, the nature of which is the self. Buddhism, however, aims at extinction (*nirodha*) as the final goal. Of the two, Śaṅkarācārya's Māyāvāda is more dangerous, as it apparently derives its authority from the *Vedas*. Much word-jugglery is employed to defend the Vedic origins of Śaṅkarācārya's Māyāvāda. But ultimately Māyāvādīs dispense with Vedic authority by concluding that the Supreme cannot be known through *śabda*, that the name of Kṛṣṇa is a material vibration, that the form of Kṛṣṇa is illusion, and so on. The Śaṅkarites agree with the Buddhists that *nāma-rūpa* (name and form) must always be *māyā*. Therefore Vaiṣṇavas reject both kinds of Māyāvāda as atheism. Buddhists generally do not deny that they are atheists, whereas the Śaṅkarite Māyāvādīs claim to be theists. But actually they are monists and pantheists. Their claim to theism is refuted by their belief that the Supreme Self is overcome by *māyā* and becomes the bound soul. Śaṅkarācārya's Māyāvāda is similar in significant ways to the Western doctrine of solipsism. Like solipsism, it arrives at a philosophical dead end. The questions that remain unanswered are: If my consciousness is the only reality, why can't I change the universe at will, simply by thought? And if my own self is the only reality, why am I dependent for my life, learning and happiness upon a world full of living entities that refuse to acknowledge this reality?

Māyā—illusion; an energy of Krṣna's which deludes the living entity into forgetfulness of the Supreme Lord. That which is not, unreality, deception, forgetfulness, material illusion. Under illusion a man thinks he can be happy in this temporary material world. The nature of the material world is that the more a man tries to exploit the material situation, the more he is bound by *māyā's* complexities; This is a Sanskrit term of many meanings. It may mean energy; *yoga-māyā* is the spiritual energy sustaining the transcendental manifestation of the spiritual Vaikuṇṭha world, while the reflection, *mahā-māyā*, is the energy of the material world. The Lord's twofold *māyā* bewilders the jīva, hence *māyā* also means bewilderment or illusion. Transcendental bewilderment is in love, by which the devotee sees God as his master, friend, dependent or amorous beloved. The material bewilderment of the living entity begins with his attraction to the glare of the brahmajyoti. That attraction leads to his entanglement in the modes of material nature. According to Bhaktisiddhānta Sarasvatī Ṭhākura, *māyā* also means that which can be measured. This is the feature of Lord Kṛṣṇa's *prakṛti* that captures the minds of scientific materialists. The Vaiṣṇava and Māyāvāda explanations of *māyā* are not the same.

Mleccha—uncivilized humans, outside the Vedic system of society, who are generally meat-eaters, and whose consciousness is lower than a *śūdra*.

N

Nābhi—the saintly king who was the father of Lord Ṛṣabhadeva.

Nāgas—a race of serpents.

Nanda—one of the chief personal servants of Lord Nārāyaṇa in His spiritual abode, Vaikuṇṭha.

Nārada Muni—a pure devotee of the Lord, one of the sons of Lord Brahmā, who travels throughout the universes in his eternal body, glorifying devotional service while delivering the science of *bhakti*. He is the spiritual master of Vyāsadeva and of many other great devotees. A great sage among the demigods and one of the foremost authorities on *viṣṇu-bhakti*. Among Nārada's other prominent disciples are Prahlāda, Dhruva, Citraketu (Vṛtrāsura), and the Haryaśvas.

Narasiṁha, Lord (Nṛsiṁhadeva)—the half-man, half-lion incarnation of Lord Kṛṣṇa, who killed the demon Hiranyakasipu and saved His devotee, Prahlada Mahārāja.

Nārāyaṇa—the majestic four-armed expansion of the Supreme Personality of Godhead who is the resting place of all living entities, and presides over the Vaikuṇṭha planets.

Nṛga—a king who was cursed to become a snake because of a slight discrepancy in his service to *brāhmaṇas*. He was delivered by Lord Kṛṣṇa.

O

Oṁkāra—oṁ, the root of Vedic knowledge; known as the *mahā-vākya*, the supreme sound; the transcendental syllable which represents Kṛṣṇa, and which is vibrated by transcendentalists for attainment of the Supreme while undertaking sacrifices, charities and penances; it denotes the Personality of Godhead as the root of the creation, maintenance and destruction of the cosmic manifestation.

P

Padma Purāṇa—one of the eighteen *Purāṇas*, or Vedic historical scriptures. It consists of conversations between Lord Śiva and his wife, Pārvati.

Pañcarātra—Vedic literatures such as *Nārada-pañcarātra* which describe the process of Deity worship.

Pāṇḍavas—the five pious ksatriya brothers Yudhiṣṭhira, Bhīma, Arjuna, Nakula, and Sahadeva. They were intimate friends and associates of Lord Kṛṣṇa who inherited the leadership of the world upon their victory over the Kauravas in the Battle of Kurukṣetra.

Parīkṣit Mahārāja—the son of Abhimanyu and grandson of Arjuna. When the Pāṇḍavas retired from kingly life, he was crowned king of the entire world. He was later cursed to die by an immature *brāhmaṇa* boy and heard *Śrīmad-Bhāgavatam* from Śukadeva Gosvāmī, and thus attained perfection.

Pauṇḍraka—an enemy of Lord Kṛṣṇa who attempted to imitate Him.

Pracetās—the ten sons of King Prācīnabarhi. They achieved perfection by worshiping Lord Viṣṇu.

Prācīnabarhi (Barhiṣat/Barhiṣmān)—a king who, while being entangled in fruitive activities, received instructions on devotional service from Nārada Muni.

Pradhāna—the total material energy in its unmanifest state; the unmanifest (*avyakta*) material nature.

Prahlāda Maharāja—a great devotee of Lord Kṛṣṇa who was persecuted by his atheistic father, Hiraṇyakaśipu, but was always protected by the Lord and ultimately saved by the Lord in the form of Nṛsiṁhadeva; one of the foremost authorities on *bhakti-yoga*.

Prakṛti—material nature, the energy of the Supreme (literally that which is predominated); the female principle enjoyed by the male *puruṣa*. There are two *prakrtis*—*apara-prakṛti* or the material nature, and *para-prakrti* or the spiritual nature (living entities)—which are both predominated over by the Supreme Personality of Godhead; one of the five *tattvas* or Vedic ontological truths.

Priyavrata—the son of Svāyambhuva Manu and brother of Uttānapāda who once ruled the universe.

Pṛthu Mahārāja—an empowered incarnation of Lord Kṛṣṇa who set an example of an ideal ruler.

Purāṇas— Literally, very old; the eighteen major and eighteen minor ancient Vedic literatures compiled about five thousand years ago in India by Śrīla Vyāsadeva that are histories of this and other planets; literatures supplementary to the *Vedas*, discussing such topics as the creation of the universe, incarnations of the Supreme Lord and demigods, and the history of dynasties of saintly kings. The eighteen principal *Purāṇas* discuss ten primary subject matters: (1) the primary creation, (2) the secondary creation, (3) the planetary systems, (4) protection and maintenance by the *avatāras*, (5) the Manus. (6) dynasties of great kings, (7) noble character and activities of great kings, (8) dissolution of the universe and liberation of the living entity, (9) the *jīva* (the spirit soul), (10) the Supreme Lord.

Pūtanā—a witch who was sent by Kaṁsa to appear in the form of a beautiful woman to kill baby Kṛṣṇa, but who was killed by Him and granted liberation.

R

Rākṣasa—a class of *asura* or ungodly people. The *rākṣasas* are always opposed to God's will. Generally, they are man-eaters and have grotesque forms.

Rāmacandra— the incarnation of the Supreme Personality of Godhead as the perfect king, and the killer of the ten-headed demon king Rāvaṇa. Rāma was exiled to the forest on the order of His father, Mahārāja Daśaratha.

His wife Sītā was kidnapped by Rāvaṇa, but by employing a huge army of monkeys, who were the powerful and intelligent offspring of demigods, He regained his wife in battle, and eventually His ancestral kingdom too. This history is recorded in the great epic *Rāmāyaṇa* written by the sage Vālmīki.

Rāvaṇa—a powerful ten-headed demon king of Laṅkā who wanted to build a staircase to heaven but was killed by Kṛṣṇa in His incarnation as Lord Rāmacandra. The pastime is described in the epic poem *Rāmāyaṇa*, by the sage Vālmīki.

Ṛg Veda—one of the four *Vedas*, the original scriptures spoken by the Lord Himself.

Ṛṣabhadeva—an incarnation of the Supreme Lord as a devotee king who, after instructing his sons in spiritual life, renounced His kingdom for a life of austerity.

Rudras— the expansions of Lord Śiva who rule over the material mode of ignorance. *See:* Śiva

Rukmiṇī—Lord Kṛṣṇa's principal queen in Dvārakā; the chief of Lord Kṛṣṇa's wives.

S

Sama—control of the mind.

Sāma Veda—one of the four original *Vedas*. It consists of musical settings of the sacrificial hymns. The *Sāma Veda* is rich with beautiful songs played by the various demigods.

Saṁhitās—supplementary Vedic literatures expressing the conclusions of self-realized authorities.

Saṅkarṣaṇa—one of the four original expansions of Lord Kṛṣṇa in the spiritual world; also, another name of Balarāma.

Sāṅkhya—analytical discrimination between spirit and matter and the path of devotional service as described by Lord Kapila, the son of Devahūti.

Saṅkīrtana—congregational or public glorification of the Supreme Lord Kṛṣṇa through chanting of His holy names, and glorification of His fame and pastimes.

Sannyāsa—the renounced order, the fourth stage of Vedic spiritual life in the Vedic system of *varṇāsrama-dharma*, which is free from family relationships, and in which all activities are completely dedicated to Kṛṣṇa. It is the order of ascetics who travel and constantly preach the message of Godhead for the benefit of all. It is usually accepted at age fifty, after a man has fulfilled his household responsibilities.

Satya-yuga—the first and best of the four cyclic ages of a *mahā-yuga* in the progression of universal time. *Satya-yuga* is characterized by virtue, wisdom and religion. It is known as the golden age, when people lived as long as one hundred thousand years. It lasts 1,728,000 years.

Saubhari Muni—a powerful mystic who accidentally fell down to sex attraction.

Śiva—Also known as Hara, Mahādeva, Maheśvara, Āśutoṣa (one who is easily pleased), Giriśa (lord of the mountains) and Gopīśvara, he is the *guṇa-avatāra* who is the superintendent of the mode of ignorance (*tamoguṇa*) and who takes charge of destroying the universe at the time of annihilation. He is also considered the greatest Vaiṣṇava, or devotee, of Lord Kṛṣṇa. He is confused by some with the Supreme Lord.

Skanda Purāṇa—one of the eighteen *Purāṇas*, or Vedic historical scriptures. It extensively describes *Kali-yuga*.

Śrīdhara Svāmī—the author of the earliest extant Vaiṣṇava commentaries on *Bhagavad-gītā* and *Śrīmad-Bhāgavatam*. A spiritual master in the line of Śri Viśṇusvāmi, he taught pure Vaiṣṇava philosophy. He was a devotee of Lord Nṛsiṁhadeva, and his works were highly regarded by Lord Caitanya, especially his *Śrīmad-Bhāgavatam* gloss, *Bhāvārtha-dīpikā*. Lord Caitanya commented that anyone who wanted to write a commentary on *Śrīmad-Bhāgavatam* must follow the commentary of Śrīdhara Svāmī.

Śūdra—a member of the fourth social order, laborer class, in the traditional Vedic social system. They render service to the three higher classes, namely the *brāhmaṇas*, the *kṣatriyas*, and the *vaiśyas*.

Śukadeva Gosvāmī—the exalted devotee, son of Śrīla Vyāsadeva, who recited the *Śrīmad-Bhāgavatam* to King Parīkṣit during the last seven days of the King's life.

Supersoul—Paramātmā, the localized aspect of Viṣṇu; expansion of the Supreme Lord known as Kṣīrodakaśāyī Viṣṇu, who expands into the heart of every living entity and every atom within the universe, pervading the entire material nature. His spiritual form is four-armed and the size of a thumb. From Him come the living entity's knowledge, remembrance and forgetfulness. The Supersoul is the witness and the one who sanctions all *karma*.

Sūtra—the intermediate manifestation of the *mahat-tattva*, when it is predominated by the mode of passion; an aphorism expressing essential knowledge in minimum words; a book of such aphorisms.

Svāmī—*See:* Goswami

Svar—the upper material planets.

Svāyambhuva Manu—the Manu who appears first in Brahmā's day and who was the grandfather of Dhruva Mahārāja.

T

Takṣaka—the king of the snakes who killed Mahārāja Parīkṣit.

Tārā—the wife of Bṛhaspati. She was kidnapped by the moon-god.

Tilaka—sacred clay markings placed on the forehead and other parts of the body to designate one as a follower of Viṣṇu, Rāma, Śiva etc.

Tretā-yuga—the second in the cycle of the four ages of the universe or *mahā-yuga*. It lasts 1,296,000 years. Lord Rāmacandra appeared in this age.

Tṛṇāvarta—a whirlwind-shaped demon who was sent by Kaṁsa to kill Kṛṣṇa, but whom Kṛṣṇa killed instead.

U

Uddhava—a learned disciple of Bṛhaspati and confidential friend of Lord Kṛṣṇa in Dvārakā. He visited the residents of Vṛndāvana to console them in their grief due to Kṛṣṇa's absence. Lord Kṛṣṇa imparted transcendental knowledge comprising knowledge of the mystic *yoga* system, the mystic yogic perfections, the philosophy of *sānkhya*, the modes of nature and pure devotional service.

V

Vaiśya—member of the mercantile and agricultural class in the Vedic *varṇāśrama* system; the third Vedic social order.

Vaivasvata Manu—the current Manu, the seventh of the fourteen Manus in a day of Brahmā.

Vāmanadeva—the Supreme Lord's incarnation as a dwarf *brāhmaṇa* to reclaim the heavenly kingdom, which the king of the demons Bali Mahārāja had conquered. Bali Mahārāja surrendered all his possessions to Lord Vāmanadeva, and became celebrated as one of the *mahājanas*, or great spiritual authorities.

Varṇāśrama-dharma—the system of four social and four spiritual orders of Vedic society, based on the individual's psycho-physical qualities and tendencies toward particular types of work.

Vāsudeva—the Supreme Lord Kṛṣṇa who is the son of Vasudeva, and proprietor of everything, material and spiritual.

Vatsāsura—a demon who came to Vṛndāvana in the form of a calf to kill Kṛṣṇa, but who was instead killed by Him.

Vedānta-sūtra—also known as *Brahma-sūtra*, it is Śrīla Vyāsadeva's conclusive summary of Vedic philosophical knowledge, written in brief codes. All apparent contradictory statements of the vast literature of the *Vedas* are resolved in this work. There are four divisions: (1) reconciliation of all scriptures (2) the consistent reconciliation of apparently conflicting hymns (3) the means or process of attaining the goal (spiritual realization) and (4) the object (or desired fruit) achieved by the spiritual process. The codes of the *Vedānta-sūtra* are very terse, and without a fuller explanation or commentary, their meaning is difficult to grasp. In India all the five main schools of Vedānta have explained the *sūtras* through their respecfive *bhāṣyas* (commentaries). The natural commentary on the *Vedānta-sūtra* is the *Śrīmad-Bhāgavatam*.

Vedas—the original *Veda* was divided into four by Śrīla Vyāsadeva. The four original Vedic scriptures, *Saṁhitās* (*Ṛg, Sāma, Atharva* and *Yajur*) and the 108 *Upaniṣads*, *Mahābhārata*, *Vedānta-sūtra*, etc. The system of eternal wisdom compiled by Śrīla Vyāsadeva, the literary incarnation of the Supreme Lord, for the gradual upliftment of all mankind from the state of bondage to the state of liberation. The word *veda* literally means "knowledge", and thus in a wider sense it refers to the whole body of Indian Sanskrit religious literature that is in harmony with the philosophical conclusions found in the original four Vedic *Saṁhitās* and *Upaniṣads.* The message of the transcendental realm that has come down to this phenomenal world through the medium of sound is known as the *Veda.* Being the very words of Godhead Himself, the *Vedas* have existed from eternity. Lord Kṛṣṇa originally revealed the *Vedas* to Brahmā, the first soul to appear in the realm of physical nature, and by him they were subsequently made available to other souls through the channel of spiritual disciplic succession; *Veda, Vedas,* Vedic knowledge. The Sanskrit root of the word *Veda* is *vid*, knowledge. This root is widespread even in modern Western language: e.g. *video* (from the Latin word to see) and idea (Gr. *ida*). The term Vedic refers to the teachings of the Vedic literatures. From these literatures we learn that this universe, along with countless others, was produced from the breath of Mahā-Viṣṇu some 155,250,000,000,000 years ago. The Lord's divine breath simultaneously transmitted all the knowledge mankind requires to meet his material needs and revive his dormant God consciousness. This knowledge is called *Veda.* Caturmukha (four-faced) Brahmā, the first created being within this universe, received *Veda* from Viṣṇu. Brahmā, acting as an obedient servant of the Supreme Lord, populated the planetary systems with all species of life. He spoke four *Vedas,* one from each of his mouths, to guide human beings in their spiritual and material progress. The *Vedas* are thus traced to the very beginning of the cosmos. Some of the most basic Vedic teachings are: (1) every living creature is an eternal soul covered by a material body; (2) as long as the souls are bewildered by *māyā* (the illusion of identifying the self with the body) they must reincarnate from body to body, life after life; (3) to accept a material body means to suffer the four-fold pangs of birth, old age, disease and death; (4) depending upon the quality of work (*karma*) in the human form, a soul may take its next birth in a subhuman species, or the human species, or a superhuman species, or it may be freed from birth and death altogether; (5) *karma* dedicated in sacrifice to Viṣṇu as directed by Vedic injunctions elevates and liberates the soul.

Vidura—the son fathered by Vyāsadeva in the maidservant of Ambalikā; the half brother of Dhṛtarāṣṭra. He was an incarnation of Yamarāja, and an uncle of the Pāṇḍavas. A great devotee of Kṛṣṇa, he inquired and heard from Maitreya Muni transcecendantal knowledge. He was cursed to become a *śūdra* by Māṇḍavya Muni. He was constantly trying to restrain Dhṛtarāṣṭra from ill-treating the Pāṇḍavas, and finally when Dhṛtarāṣṭra lost everything, Vidura was able to deliver his brother to the path of self-realization.

Viṣṇu—literally, the all-pervading God; the Supreme Personality of Godhead in His four-armed expansion in Vaikuṇṭha. A plenary expansion of the original Supreme Personality of Godhead, Śrī Kṛṣṇa, He supervises the maintenance of the created universe, and enters into the material universe before creation. He is worshiped by all the demigods and sages, and described throughout the *Vedas* as the summum bonum of all knowledge.

Viṣṇu Purāṇa—one of the eighteen *Purāṇas*, or Vedic historical scriptures.

Viśvanātha Cakravartī Ṭhākura—a great *ācārya* in the Caitanya school of Vaiṣṇavism, and the most prominent *ācārya* after Narottama dāsa Ṭhākura. He wrote twenty-four books on the science of *bhakti*, including commentaries on *Śrīmad-Bhāgavatam* and *Bhagavad-gītā*. He established the Gokulānanda Temple in Vṛndāvana. In his final years he lived at Rādhā-kuṇḍa.

Vṛndāvana—Kṛṣṇa's eternal abode, where He fully manifests His quality of sweetness; the village on this earth in which He enacted His childhood pastimes five thousand years ago; the topmost transcendental abode of the Supreme Lord. It is His personal spiritual abode descended to the earthly plane. It is situated on the western bank of the river Yamunā.

Vyāsadeva—the literary incarnation of God, and the greatest philosopher of ancient times. The son of Parāśara Muni and Satyavatī devī, he rendered the *Vedas* into written texts some 5000 years ago. He divided the *Veda* into four parts, the Ṛg, *Yajur*, *Sāma* and *Atharva Veda*, and also compiled the supplementary Vedic literature such as the eighteen *Purāṇas*, *Vedānta-sūtra*, and the *Mahābhārata*. He played a very important part in guiding the Pāṇḍavas during crucial times. He gave the vision of the battle of Kurukṣetra to Sañjaya so that he could relate it to Dhṛtarāṣṭra. He is still living in this world; he is also known as Vedavyāsa, Bādarāyaṇa and Dvaipāyana Vyāsa.

Y

Yadu (Yādava) dynasty—the dynasty in which Lord Kṛṣṇa appeared.

Yakṣas—ghostly followers of the demigod Kuvera, the treasurer of the demigods. They were born from the feet of Lord Brahmā.

Yoga— Literally, connection; the discipline of self-realization. a spiritual discipline meant for linking one's consciousness with the Supreme Lord, Kṛṣṇa; one of the six systems of Vedic philosophy, taught by Patañjali. Through the process of *bhakti-yoga*, the consciousness of the individual soul connects with its source, Kṛṣṇa.

Yogī—a transcendentalist who practices one of the many authorized forms of *yoga* or processes of spiritual purification; one who practices the eight-fold mystic *yoga* process to gain mystic *siddhis yoga* process or Paramātmā realization.

Sanskrit Pronunciation Guide

Throughout the centuries, the Sanskrit language has been written in a variety of alphabets. The mode of writing most widely used throughout India, however, is called *devanāgarī*, which means, literally, the writing used in "the cities of the demigods." The *devanāgarī* alphabet consists of forty-eight characters: thirteen vowels and thirty-five consonants. Ancient Sanskrit grammarians arranged this alphabet according to practical linguistic principles, and this order has been accepted by all Western scholars. The system of transliteration used in this book conforms to a system that scholars have accepted to indicate the pronunciation of each Sanskrit sound.

Vowels

अ a आ ā इ i ई ī उ u ऊ ū ऋ ṛ ॠ ṝ ऌ ḷ

ए e ऐ ai ओ o औ **au**

Consonants

Gutturals:	क ka	ख kha	ग ga	घ gha	ङ ṅa
Palatals:	च ca	छ cha	ज ja	झ jha	ञ ña
Cerebrals:	ट ṭa	ठ ṭha	ड ḍa	ढ ḍha	ण ṇa
Dentals:	त ta	थ tha	द da	ध dha	न na
Labials:	प pa	फ pha	ब ba	भ bha	म ma
Semivowels:	य ya	र ra	ल la	व va	
Sibilants:	श śa	ष ṣa	स sa		
Aspirate :	ह ha	Anusvāra : ं ṁ	Visarga : ः ḥ		

Numerals

० –0 १–1 २–2 ३–3 ४–4 ५–5 ६–6 ७–7 ८–8 ९–9

The vowels are written as follows after a consonant:

ा ā ि i ी ī ु u ू ū ृ ṛ ॄ ṝ े e ै ai ो o ौ au

For example : क ka का kā कि ki की kī कु ku कू kū
कृ kṛ कॄ kṝ के ke कै kai को ko कौ kau

Generally two or more consonants in conjunction are written together in a special form, as for example: क्ष **kṣa** त्र **tra**

The vowel "a" is implied after a consonant with no vowel symbol.

The symbol virāma (्) indicates that there is no final vowel: क्

The vowels are pronounced as follows:.

a	—	as in b**u**t	o	—	as in **go**
ā	—	as in f**a**r but held twice as long as **a**	ṛ	—	as in **ri**m
ai	—	as in **ai**sle	ṝ	—	as in **ree**d but held twice as long as **ṛ**
au	—	as in h**ow**	u	—	as in p**u**sh
e	—	as in th**ey**	ū	—	as in r**u**le but held twice as long as **u**
i	—	as in p**i**n			
ī	—	as in pique but held twice as long as **i**			
ḷ	—	as in **lree**			

The consonants are pronounced as follows:

Gutturals
(pronounced from the throat)

k	—	as in **k**ite
kh	—	as in Ec**kh**art
g	—	as in **g**ive
gh	—	as in di**g-h**ard
ṅ	—	as in si**ng**

Labials
(pronounced with the lips)

p	—	as in **p**ine
ph	—	as in u**p-h**ill
b	—	as in **b**ird
bh	—	as in ru**b-h**ard
m	—	as in **m**other

Cerebrals
(pronounced with the tip of the tongue against the roof of the mouth)

ṭ	—	as in **t**ub
ṭh	—	as in ligh**t-h**eart
ḍ	—	as in **d**ove
ḍh	—	as in re**d-h**ot
ṇ	—	as in si**ng**

Palatals
(pronounced with the middle of the tongue against the palate)

c	—	as in **ch**air
ch	—	as in staun**ch-h**eart
j	—	as in **j**oy
jh	—	as in he**dgeh**og
ñ	—	as in ca**ny**on

Dentals
(pronounced like the cerebrals but with the tongue against the teeth)

t	—	as in **t**ub
th	—	as in ligh**t-h**eart
d	—	as in **d**ove
dh	—	as in re**d-h**ot
n	—	as in **n**ut

Semivowels

y	—	as in **y**es
r	—	as in **r**un
l	—	as in **l**ight
v	—	as in **v**ine, except when preceded in the same syllable by a consonant, then like in s**w**an

Aspirate

h	—	as in **h**ome

Sibilants

ś	—	as in the German word *sprechen*
ṣ	—	as in **sh**ine
s	—	as in **s**un

Anusvāra

ṁ	—	a resonant nasal sound as in the French word *bon*

Visarga

ḥ	—	a final **h**-sound: **aḥ** is pronounced like **aha**; **iḥ** like **ihi**.

There is no strong accentuation of syllables in Sanskrit, or pausing between words in a line, only a flowing of short and long syllables (the long twice as long as the short). A long syllable is one whose vowel is long (**ā, ai, au, e , ī, o, ṝ, ū**) or whose short vowel is followed by more than one consonant (including **ḥ** and **ṁ**). Aspirated consonants (consonants followed by an **h**) count as single consonants.

Index of Sanskrit Verses

This index constitutes a complete listing of the first and third lines of each of the Sanskrit poetry verses of this volume of *Śrīmad-Bhāgavatam*, arranged in English alphabetical order. The first column gives the Sanskrit transliteration; the second, the chapter-verse reference. Apostrophes are alphabetized as a's.

A

L

M

P

R

S

U

V

Y

Index of Verses Quoted

This index lists the verses quoted in the purports of this volume of *Śrīmad-Bhāgavatam*. Numerals in boldface type refer to the first or third lines of verses quoted in full; numerals in roman type refer to partially quoted verses.

General Index

The references to the translations and purports of the verses of *Śrīmad-Bhāgavatam* are presented in the following format: "xx.yy (para n)", where 'xx' is the chapter number, 'yy' is the verse number (text number) and 'n' is the paragraph number in the purport. Numerals in the boldface type indicate the translations and those in regular type indicate the purports. Numerals in the mixed type indicate both translation and purports. While counting the paragraphs in the purports, please remember that, the new paragraph begins (in the purport) only where the first word is indented.

A

Ābhīra dynasty, 1.27, 1.29–31
Ābhīra province, **1.36**
Abortion, 2.1 (para 6)
Absolute Truth
  compared to fire, **4.24–25**
  compared to sun, **4.32**, **4.33**
  duality absent in, **4.30**
  false ego &, **4.32**
  form of
    unlimited, 3.43 (para 7)
    See also: Kṛṣṇa, Lord
  as free from suffering & death, **13.19**
  as intelligence's basis, **4.23**, **4.24–25**
  knowledge about, as requisite for truthfulness, 2.1 (para 4)
  knowledge about, fear defeated via, **6.4–5**
  material world not, 3.43 (para 1)
  as objects of senses' basis, **4.23**
  oṁkāra representation of, **6.38–39**
  perceptions of, various, **4.31**
  personality of, 13.11–12
  pervasiveness of, **7.19–20**
  phases of, three, **6.38–39**
  presentation of, factual, 4.31
  search for, tendency for, 3.43 (para 2)
  as sense objects' basis, **4.23**
  senses &, **4.23**, **4.24–25**
  soul expansion of, **4.32**
  three phases of, **6.38–39**
  as ultimate reality, **13.11–12**
  See also: Kṛṣṇa; Supreme Lord
Acyuta, Lord. *See:* Kṛṣṇa; Supreme Lord
Adhokṣaja, Lord. *See:* Kṛṣṇa; Supreme Lord
Adultery, 3.42 (para 3)
Age(s) of world
Age(s) of world (*continued*)
  as cyclical, **2.39**, **4.2–3**
  Dvāpara. *See:* Dvāpara-yuga
  Kali. *See:* Kali-yuga
  kalpa's measurement &, **4.2–3**
  present. *See:* Kali-yuga
  Satya. *See:* Satya-yuga
  sub-ages in, 3.26
  Tretā. *See:* Tretā-yuga
  See also: specific ages (yugas)
Aghāsura, **12.28–29**
Agnimitra, King, **1.15–17**
Agnimitra, sage, **6.54–56**
Agnosticism, 2.1 (para 5)
  See also: Atheism
Aila, King, **12.25–26**
Airāvata, **11.39–40**
Air, qualities of, 4.14
Ajātaśatru, King, **1.5**
Ajaya, King, **1.5**, **1.6–8**
Akṛtavraṇa, **7.5–6**, **7.7–8**
Akrūra, **12.34–35**
A, letter, **6.40–42**
Alphabet, Vedic, **6.40–42**, **6.43**
Aṁśu as sun, **11.41–42**
Analogies
  bottles & bodies, 2.3 (para 5)
  breaking pot & death, **5.5–6**
  bubbles of foam & body, **3.2**
  calm water & Mārkaṇḍeya, **10.5**
  clay & Lord, 7.20
  cloth & universe, **4.27–28**
  cloud & false ego, **4.32**, **4.33**
  clouds & universe, **4.26**
  darkness & material intelligence, 4.25
  darkness & misfortune, **12.48**
  dreamer & Lord, **10.31–32**
  father & spiritual master, 6.63

C

K

N

Q

R

S

on elements, material, 4.14
on modes of nature, 3.26
on Parīkṣit's spiritual status, 5.13
on Purañjaya's reign, 1.41 (para 1)
See also: Śrīmad-Bhāgavatam quoted
Śrīmad-Bhāgavatam quoted
on devotional service
on Kṛṣṇa enlightening Brahmā, 13.10 (para 1)
on Parīkṣit's request to Śukadeva, 5.2 (para 1)
on *Purāṇa's* subject matter, 7.9–10 (para 1–2)
on strength (physical) in Kali-yuga, **2.1**, 2.1 (para 7)
on Supreme Lord & philosophers, 6.30–31 (para 2)
See also: Śrīmad-Bhāgavatam cited
Śrīvāsa Ṭhākura, 12.47
Śrotā, **11. 37–38**
Students
cleanliness &, 3.33 (para 1)
See also: Brahmacārīs
Subhadra, 11.20 (para 6)
Subterranean regions, **12.16**
Subtle body, **5.5–6**, **5.7–8**, 7.21
Śuci, month of, **11.36**
Sudharmā assembly hall, **12.38**
Śūdras
as Kali-yuga's population, **3.24–25**
as rulers, **1.6–8**, **1.37–38**
Sudyumna, **12.21**
Suffering
Absolute Truth free of, **13.19**
freedom from, via obeisances to Kṛṣṇa, **13.23**
Suicide, 3.42 (para 2)
Sujyeṣṭha, King, 1.14, **1.15–17**
Śukadeva Gosvāmī
Śukadeva Gosvāmī (*continued*)
compared with Kṛṣṇa, 5.2 (para 2)
departure of, from bank of Ganges, **6.7–8**
impersonalists hearing from, 6.1
obeisances to, by Sūta Gosvāmī, **13.21**
obeisances to, importance of, **12.69**
Parīkṣit instructed by. *See: specific subject matter*
Parīkṣit saved by, **13.21**
as Parīkṣit's spiritual master, 2.44, 3.49, 4.6, 5.2 (para 2)
pastimes of Kṛṣṇa attract, **12.69**
prediction regarding, **4.43**
quoted. *See: specific subject matter*
Sūta disciple of, 13.21
Vyāsadeva speaks *Bhāgavatam* to, **4.42**, **13.19**
as Vyāsadeva's son, **6.1**, **6.7–8**, **12.69**
Sukarmā, **6.76–77**
Śukra, **11.36**
Śukra, month of, **11.34–35**
Sumālya, King, **1.10**
Sumantu
Atharva Veda entrusted to, **6.52–53**
as son of Jaimini, **6.75**
Sutvān son of, **6.75**
Sumantu Ṛṣi, **7.1**, 7.1
Sumukha, 11.20 (para 6)
Sun
annihilation aided by, **4.8–9**
as cloud's source, **4.32**
as creation of Lord, **11.29–30**
dynasty descendent from, 1.1–2 (para 1)
Earth maintained by, **6.67**
as expansion of Lord, **11.27–28**
god of. *See:* Sun god
in Leo constellation, 13.13
movements of, calculations according to, 6.70
planets regulated by, **11.32–33**
position of, at Satya-yuga's beginning, **2.24–25**
as representative of Kṛṣṇa, 6.70
as soul of universe, **12.45–46**
worship to Lord on, **11.17**
Śunaka, **1.1–2**, **7.2–3**
Sunanda, 11.20 (para 6)
Sunanda, King, **1.21–27**
Śuṅga dynasty, **1.15–17**
Sun god(s)
associates of, **11.32–44**
as chief of demigods, **6.68**
descendants of, as topics of *Bhāgavatam,* **12.22**
Sun god(s) (*continued*)
description of, in nine aspects, **11.31**
as expansions of Lord, **6.67**, 6.67, **11.29–30**, **11.45–46**
glorification of, **11.47–48**
horse form assumed by, **6.73–74**
list of various, **11.32–44**
as nondifferent from Lord, **11.29–30**
prayers to, by Vālakhilya *brāhmaṇas,* **11.47–48**
sinful reactions ended via remembering, **11.45–46**
as source of ritualistic activities, **11.29–30**
travels of, purpose of, **11.32–33**, **11.45–46**
worship to, **6.65–72**

V

W

Y